THIS PEOPLE'S NAVY

THIS
PEOPLE'S NAVY

The Making of American Sea Power

Kenneth J. Hagan

THE FREE PRESS
New York   London   Toronto   Sydney   Tokyo   Singapore

The Free Press
A Division of Simon & Schuster Inc.
1230 Avenue of the Americas
New York, N.Y. 10020

First Free Press Paperback Edition 1992

Printed in the United States of America

printing number
3 4 5 6 7 8 9 10

Library of Congress Cataloging-in-Publication Data

Hagan, Kenneth J.
    This people's Navy: the making of American sea power/Kenneth
J. Hagan.
        p.   cm.
    Includes bibliographical references and index.
    ISBN 0-02-913471-4
    1. United States—History, Naval.   2. United States. Navy—
History.   I. Title.
E182.HI6   1991
359'.00973—dc20   90-44722
                                                                CIP

TO
CHARLES SOUTTER CAMPBELL
Mentor
AND
CHARLES CONRAD CAMPBELL
Critic

Contents

Acknowledgments

T_{HIS} book evolved during my teaching of American naval history at the U.S. Naval Academy for the last seventeen years and while I was counseling officer-instructors in the Naval R.O.T.C. program on how to teach the subject at fifty-plus universities and colleges across the land. My greatest debt therefore is to the midshipmen and naval officers who have more or less willingly endured my lectures, discussions, and questions. I hasten to add that nothing herein necessarily represents their views or the opinions of anyone else in any way connected with the United States Navy. The interpretations offered in this work are mine alone.

The members of the history department at the Naval Academy who helped in special ways were Thomas Brennan, Elaine Maurer, and Max Shaw. Dean Karl Lamb made a crucial decision permitting the completion of the book, and John Cummings of Nimitz Library provided me with a study carrel for seven years. Lieutenant Commander Don Thomas Sine was present at the inception, for which I am especially grateful. Joyce Seltzer of The Free Press was present throughout the writing, and her abiding confidence was a great inspiration. Among the others who encouraged me were Louis Mortimer, Thomas Paterson, Michal McMahon, and the late Patricia Berg.

My most devoted academic readers were Michael T. Corgan, Lincoln Paine, and Sari Hornstein. Patti Patterson read proof and spotted many errors that the word processing "spell checker" missed. Jane Price and Maureen Ward helped me find time to respond to last-minute inquiries from New York. Patty Maddocks and Sigrid Trumpy made a joy of the search for illustrations.

Charles Soutter Campbell, my doctoral advisor at Claremont Graduate School, was generous enough to approve my dissertation on naval history two decades ago. At the other end of the temporal spectrum, Charles Conrad Campbell has made the repeated reading and editing of the present work a labor of love for the last two years. Whatever merits this book may have are the result of his merciless but beneficent interrogations of the author.

My family once again endured my preoccupation with matters that most people find only marginally interesting. For their tolerance, I thank my parents, James and Mary Hagan; my wife, Vera; my children, Douglas, Meiling, and Kevin; my son-in-law, Matthew Curtis; and the recently arrived but allegedly as yet unspoiled Joshua James Curtis.

Introduction

W<small>HEN</small> John Paul Jones pleaded for a fast-sailing ship because he intended "to go in harm's way," he set the tone for the first hundred years of American naval history. The navy in the age of sail and in the early years of steam was built around fast ships skippered by bold captains, officered by ambitious lieutenants, and manned by individualistic seamen. The navy in the era of the sailing frigate was designed to hit and run, to attack enemy merchant vessels and small warships and flee if faced with a stronger naval opponent. This strategy, which the French call *guerre de course*, reached its apogee in the transitional years between sail and steam, when Captain Raphael Semmes set a world-class standard for commerce raiding as skipper of the famed Confederate raider *Alabama*.

By the end of the nineteenth century the technology of warships was changing remarkably, as was the geopolitical balance of Europe. Battleships with enormously destructive guns and heavy belts of armor seemed to make all other ships obsolete, and Germany challenged Britain for the supremacy of the Atlantic that the Royal Navy had commanded since the Battle of Trafalgar (1805). American naval observers sensed the magnitude of the changes and sought a new philosophy of sea power. They welcomed the theories of Captain Alfred Thayer Mahan, whose books, beginning with *The Influence of Sea Power upon History, 1660–1783* in 1890, shattered commerce raiding and commerce protection as the backbone of American naval strategy. Mahan and his disciples advocated a peculiarly British strategy centered on very large warships designed to fight fleet engagements against concentrations of similar enemy fleets, a strategy the French call *guerre d'escadre*.

Since the age of Mahan, the U.S. Navy has hewn to a doctrine of challenging all rivals for command of the sea. One mode of encounter has been massive fleet operations, most notably those in the

Pacific during World War II, but diplomatic maneuvering and shifting alliances with other major naval powers have also served the ultimate purpose of ensuring that in terms of massed fleets the U.S. Navy has been second to none.

In the 1920s that determination led to a single-minded emphasis on battleships, and since World War II it has led to an equally resolute preference for battle groups of large aircraft carriers. In the mid-1980s Secretary of the Navy John F. Lehman, Jr., restated the operational rationale for carrier groups in terms consciously reminiscent of Mahan and Theodore Roosevelt, and this concept of a "maritime strategy" remained the navy's doctrine as the 1990s opened.

In 1989, however, winds of change began to sweep through Europe from the Urals to the Rhine. Overnight the Soviet empire in Eastern Europe dissolved, and the Soviet Union itself stood exposed as economically primitive and politically vulnerable. For the first time since Mahan wrote in 1890, suddenly there was no major continental European power capable of mounting a credible military and naval threat to Anglo-America. The "velvet revolution" immediately called into question the premises of twentieth-century U.S. naval policy and strategy, particularly the expensive battle groups of big warships patrolling the high seas in search of worthy opponents.

If the end of the twentieth century and the opening of the twenty-first continue to be marked by revolutionary geopolitical shifts in Europe as well as in Asia, then the makers of American naval policy will have to calculate carefully their impact on the United States Navy. In the search for a relevant philosophy of sea power, the past may very well offer navigational beacons.

The two-hundred-year history of American naval power demonstrates that certain variables have always been at work. At any given time the task of the navy's leaders has been to assess their relative weight when constructing a policy and strategy. The most prominent of the permanently interacting variables—or elements— include the external political and economic environment; the policies of the president and his advisers, whether in peace or in war; the temperament of the Congress as the putative embodiment of the people's will; the state of warship technology, that is, hulls, propulsion systems, and armament; the attitudes and competence of the officer corps; and the prevailing concepts about the nature of naval warfare.

This book traces the interaction of these variables as they have shaped the American people's navy. What emerges is a broad tapestry woven of many strands of colorful thread. The history of the U.S. Navy from its origins in the mercantile and agrarian age, through its maturity in the industrial age, to its enduring presence in the "postmodern" era is an epic story worthy of the people it has always served with dedication and honor.

1

The American Way of War at Sea

1775 – 1783

O<small>N</small> 3 October 1775, at a session of the Continental Congress, Stephen Hopkins and Samuel Ward introduced a resolution of the Rhode Island General Assembly seeking relief from recent depredations by ships of the Royal Navy. The frigate H.M.S. *Rose* had patrolled Narragansett Bay for months, single-handedly closing those waters to commerce and infuriating the local residents. Convinced "that the building and equipping [of] an American fleet, as soon as possible, would greatly and essentially conduce to the preservation of the lives, liberty and property of the good people of these Colonies," the assembly begged the Continental Congress to fund and build "a fleet [to] contribute to the common defence." The petition failed to move Congress. Christopher Gadsden of South Carolina opposed the "extensiveness of the Rhode Island plan," while Samuel Chase of Maryland angrily proclaimed, "It is the maddest idea in the world to think of building an American fleet; . . . we should mortgage the whole continent." Congress tabled the resolution, but the Rhode Islanders had opened a debate about American naval policy that would last from the Revolution to the present.

The defeat of the Rhode Island resolution sounded the opening gun of one of the periodic outbreaks of that debate over American naval policy. Congress soon learned that on 11 August 1775 two unarmed and unescorted brigantines loaded with weapons and pow-

1

der had left England. If the ships could be captured, those valuable cargos would be diverted from British forces and sent instead to General George Washington's ill-equipped army besieging Boston. The Continental Congress, acting with unaccustomed speed, immediately appointed a three-man committee—John Adams of Massachusetts, John Langdon of New Hampshire, and Silas Deane of Connecticut—to plan the interception of the brigs. Within hours the triumvirate recommended—and Congress approved—a plan authorizing George Washington to obtain an armed schooner and a sloop from Massachusetts and requesting Connecticut and Rhode Island to lend ships for the interdiction. Those raiders were to be "on the continental risque and pay," and their crews would receive prize money. By this action Congress first shaped the national policy toward the American navy under sail, the elements of which can be expressed as emotions: a distrust of fleets, a reluctance to challenge a strong opposing navy, a fondness for attacking the enemy's merchant and cargo vessels, and a desire always to minimize expenditures.

George Washington probably welcomed his instructions to capture the two cargo vessels. In early September, on his own authority, he had converted a Marblehead fishing schooner, the *Hannah*, into a lightly armed commerce raider with orders "to intercept the Supplies of the Enemy." But *Hannah* was a disappointment. She took few prizes, her crew mutinied, and Washington fumed over "our rascally privateersmen [who] go on at the old rate, mutinying if they can not do as they please." The new directions from Congress at least brought the general some hope that the "Capture of an Ordinance [sic] Ship would give new life to the Camp and an immediate turn to the Issue of the Campaign." The two store ships eluded Washington, but he continued to dispatch commerce raiders for the remainder of his siege of Boston, always warning his commanders, "The Design is to intercept the Enemy's supplies, not to look for the Enemy's Armed Vessels."

One of the general's skippers, John Manley of Marblehead, fully understood Washington's intentions. In command of the schooner *Lee*, Manley in November and December 1775 took nine prizes off the Massachusetts coast. His most notable capture was the brig *Nancy*, loaded with muskets, flints, round shot, tons of musket shot, and mortar beds. Washington rewarded Manley with the title of commodore, and the Earl of Sandwich, first lord of the Admiralty, saw the capture of the ordnance ship as "a fatal event." Loss of the *Nancy* and more than thirty other less valuable supply ships led Vice Admiral

Lord Molyneux Shuldham, the British naval commander at Boston in 1775 and early 1776, to recommend "that all Supplies to this Country might be sent in Armed Vessels . . . for however numerous our Cruisers may be or however attentive our Officers to their Duty, it has been found impossible to prevent some of our Ordnance and other valuable Stores, in small vessels, falling into the hands of the Rebels." The leader of those rebels continued to complain of his "plague, trouble, and vexation . . . with the crews of all the armed vessels" under his command, but the reactions of the Earl of Sandwich and Admiral Shuldham show that Britain was stung by the mosquito fleet Washington had created at the behest of Congress and its three-man naval committee.

Adams, Langdon, and Deane had not stopped with the orders to Washington. On 13 October 1775 they spurred Congress to authorize the fitting out of two small armed vessels to ply the western North Atlantic for three months in search of British transports. The delighted Adams pressed his opportunity: "We must excite by Policy that kind of exalted Courage, which is ever victorious by sea and land." Two weeks later, on 30 October, Deane asked Congress to construct a fleet of ten warships, four of them mounting thirty-six guns, at a total estimated cost exceeding $166,000. He shrewdly summarized the strategic dilemma Britain faced in trying to subdue the colonies with ships carrying no more than forty guns: "[I]t is evident if they cruize in a fleet they will not be formidable to Trade, and if single they will be liable to be attacked by an equal if not superior force of the Continental Fleet." By adding ten warships to the six already contributed by Connecticut, Rhode Island, and Massachusetts, Deane hoped

> to form a Naval force equall if not Superior to what the Ministry will think of sending to America the Next season for they dream as little of Our meeting them, on the Sea as of Our invading Canada, and though their Naval power, & resources be ever so great in Brittain, they must inevitably be defeated the Next Campaign in America if We get early to Sea, these Shipps, and with them surprize, & intercept their Transports . . . this effected, the distance between Us & Europe will put it out of their power to recover [from] the blow, until the season is over.

His allusion to invading Canada—made at the moment that Richard Montgomery and Benedict Arnold were moving north to capture Montréal and to attack Québec—placed Deane among the bold, but the majority of delegates in Congress remained cautious. They authorized only four warships, just one of which was to mount thirty-six guns. To oversee construction, outfitting, and deployment of these ships, Congress enlarged the Naval Committee to seven men and somewhat broadened the navy's charter by directing that the vessels be used "for the protection and defense of the United Colonies." Thus, as October 1775 closed, the Continental Congress found itself inching toward the position taken by the Rhode Island General Assembly's resolution earlier that month.

John Adams counted the next two months as "the pleasantest part" of his four years in the Continental Congress. He and the other members of the Naval Committee met every evening at a Philadelphia tavern, "where Governor Hopkins of Rhode Island, above seventy years of age, kept us all alive." That conviviality withstood the grim news of 9 November: King George III had refused to receive Congress's Olive Branch Petition and had proclaimed the colonies to be in open rebellion. Anxiety now marked the Congress at large, permitting the smooth-functioning Naval Committee to overcome sectional differences and speed legislation through the worried body. In a matter of weeks Congress allocated $100,000 for the Naval Committee, authorized two "battalions of American Marines," approved a set of rules for governing "the American Navy," which were modeled on British naval regulations, and "took the decisive step of authorizing the capture of all British vessels employed against the United Colonies, either as armed vessels of war, transports, or supply ships."

To fight at sea the Continental Navy needed ships, officers, men, cannon, powder, and canvas. The Naval Committee purchased four merchantmen and converted them into warships in Philadelphia: two ships, the 30-gun *Alfred* and 28-gun *Columbus*, and two brigs, the 16-gun *Andrea Doria* and 14-gun *Cabot*. Stephen Hopkins guided the committee to select his trusted friends and relatives as commanders. Esek Hopkins, the younger brother of Stephen, was named "Commander in Chief of the Fleet of the United Colonies," although the committee intended the title to confer jurisdiction only over ships in his immediate vicinity. John Burroughs Hopkins, the son of Esek, took command of the *Cabot*. *Columbus* was given to Abraham Whipple, a sea dog from Rhode Island. Silas Deane's brother-in-law, Dudley Saltonstall, became commander of the *Alfred*. His first lieutenant was a twenty-eight-year-old Scots immigrant named John Paul Jones, a former captain in the British merchant marine. Only the *Andrea Doria*'s skipper, Nicholas Biddle, formerly a midshipman in the Royal

Navy and now a resident of Philadelphia, came from beyond the committee's inner circle. Enlistment of sailors and procurement of cannon, gunpowder, and canvas proved difficult in an industrially dependent country where young men placed a high value on personal freedom, so the somewhat desperate committee turned for help to Pennsylvania politicians and Esek Hopkins's friends in Rhode Island.

In mid-December 1775, as conversion of the first four ships of the Continental Navy neared completion, Congress took stock. To the north, Arnold and Montgomery were preparing to attack Québec. Outside Boston, George Washington watched enlistments expire while waiting for Henry Knox to bring him the artillery captured at Fort Ticonderoga the previous May. In Virginia, the rebels had seized Norfolk, "the most horrid place . . . ever beheld"; but the former royal governor, Lord Dunmore, roamed the lower reaches of Chesapeake Bay with a "Fleet [that] is at present Numerous tho' not very powerfull." On 11 December the Rhode Island resolution calling for construction of what Samuel Ward described as "an American fleet" again reached the floor of Congress. This time the legislators acted swiftly. They authorized construction of thirteen frigates at an estimated average cost of $66,666 each, and they established a Marine Committee of thirteen members to oversee the administration of the Continental Navy and direct the deployment of its warships. The committee administered the navy until December 1779. It was then replaced by a Board of Admiralty—a term borrowed from the British—which in turn yielded to Superintendent of Finance Robert Morris, who took control of the navy as Agent of Marine on 8 September 1781 and ran it until the end of the Revolutionary War.

The Naval Committee sought decisive action at sea and sectional harmony ashore. It ordered Esek Hopkins and his Yankee sailors to sail for Chesapeake Bay, to reconnoiter the strength of Lord Dunmore's forces, and if "you find that they are not greatly superior to your own you are immediately to enter the said bay, search out and attack, take or destroy all the naval force of our enemies." If successful, Hopkins was "to proceed immediately to the southward and make yourself master of such forces as the enemy may have in both North and South Carolina." Having single-handedly driven the British from southern waters, Hopkins was to return to Rhode Island "without delay . . . and attack, take and destroy all the Enemies Naval force." Those orders asked the impossible, as the experienced fifty-seven-year-old Hopkins knew. His men lacked the stomach for engaging even the small segment of the Royal Navy controlled by Dunmore or for braving the winter waters off Cape Hatteras, which too often entombed venturesome ships and crews. Hopkins and his men came from a tradition of commerce raiding that valued the preservation of one's own force, the avoidance where possible of combat with a dangerous naval foe, and the seizure of goods and war matériel needed by the parent country.

At once prudent and irresponsible, Hopkins, his fleet now augmented by the small sloops *Providence* and *Fly*, ignored his orders and laid a course for the Bahamas, where on 3–4 March 1776 he attacked Nassau on New Providence Island. Hopkins occupied the city, seized some cannon and gunpowder, and set sail for Block Island channel off Rhode Island. When nearly home, his fleet on 6 April encountered H.M.S. *Glasgow*, a 24-gun frigate commanded by an adroit ship handler, Captain Tyringham Howe. Unaccustomed to fleet maneuvers, Hopkins's captains fought "a typical privateering operation—that is, everyman for himself." *Glasgow* disabled *Cabot* and *Alfred*, outmaneuvered *Andrea Doria* and *Columbus*, then escaped. The 12-gun *Providence* stayed clear entirely, an act of cowardice for which her skipper was cashiered. The Americans slipped into New London and from there into Providence. Hopkins failed to get his fleet to sea again, and for that ineptitude Congress on 16 August 1776 censured him. Still nominally in command, the commodore began to refer to congressmen as "ignorant fellows—lawyers, clerks, persons who don't know how to govern men." The objects of his scorn finally dismissed him from the naval service on 2 January 1778 after passing judgment on him as "an ordinary man who had the misfortune to live in extraordinary times."

In truth, however, Hopkins's cruise to New Providence reflected the best instincts of a man born to the maritime tradition of raiding the enemy for war matériel, and this was the tradition that undergirded most American naval policy for the nation's first hundred years. In a perversely similar way, Hopkins's engagement of H.M.S. *Glasgow* typified the few fleet actions of the Continental Navy on the high seas. They were strategically insignificant, tactically inept, and politically disruptive.

═══

The only successful fleet action of 1776 was fought by the Americans' brown-water squadron on Lake Champlain. As winter gave way to spring, the Americans who had attacked Canada the previous year were falling over one another in disorderly retreat up the Richelieu River and across Lake Champlain toward the relative safety of Fort

Ticonderoga at the lake's southern tip. Major General Philip Schuyler of New York commanded this army-on-the-run. Hampered by the divisive New Englanders and his own ill health, he appeared hesitant and indecisive, a stark contrast with the man to whom he now entrusted the defense of Lake Champlain, Benedict Arnold.

Robust, fearless, intelligent, ambitious, and imaginative, Arnold perfectly understood Congress's instructions to build a squadron "sufficient to make us indisputably masters of the lakes Champlain and George." In desperate need of skilled workers, he appealed directly to George Washington for three hundred carpenters, asserting "the utmost importance that the Lakes be immediately secured by a large number (at least twenty or thirty) of gondolas, row-galleys, and floating batteries." For the next three months, at Skenesboro and Ticonderoga, New York, Arnold and his men feverishly put together what he immodestly described as "a formidable fleet" of one sloop, two schooners, eight gundalows, and four galleys. Mounting a total of about ninety cannon, these vessels were sailed, towed, and rowed by seven hundred men whom Arnold inelegantly characterized as a "wretched motley crew . . . few of [whom] ever met with salt water." On 23 September 1776 these landlubbers arranged their hastily built armada of fifteen green-timbered waterbugs in a crescent-shaped line between Valcour Island and the western shore of Lake Champlain. There they awaited a stronger fleet of British ships put together by Captain Charles Douglas, who had lifted the American siege of Québec in May.

Racing with Arnold, Douglas had reassembled several vessels sent from England as "knock-downs" expressly for this lake campaign. He also transported two schooners from the St. Lawrence overland by road to St. Johns, where Lake Champlain became navigable, and manned all his ships with seasoned veterans of the Royal Navy. When ready for battle, he boasted that "our acquiring an absolute dominion over Lake Champlain is not to be doubted of." He outclassed Arnold in three vital material categories: men, ships, and guns. Only in tactical judgment did the British prove inferior to the Americans.

On 11 October 1776 the British squadron got under way, driven south down the lake by a favorable northeasterly wind. In his haste and overconfidence, the officer to whom Douglas had given command of the squadron, Lieutenant Thomas Pringle, failed to send scouting vessels ahead of his main body, an oversight that the historian Alfred Thayer Mahan would denounce as "a singular negligence." Pringle's entire flotilla thus passed to the east of Valcour Island without sight-ing Arnold's lineup until it was south—meaning downwind—of the Americans. Pringle hauled up, but he initially lay at an extreme tactical disadvantage, having to work to windward in order to engage opponents who, in Mahan's favorite formulation, "were thus permitted a concentration of superior force." Arnold "immediately prepared to receive" the British in an engagement that quickly "became General, & very warm." He "suffered much from Want of Seamen & Gunners" and was forced personally to aim the guns of his galley, the *Congress*, in a losing battle lasting from 11:00 A.M. until dark.

The heavier, more numerous, and better gunned British ships then fell off, with Pringle planning to complete his destruction of the American squadron the next morning. But Arnold took advantage of the night, a heavy fog, and a northeasterly breeze to slip past the anchored Britons. For two nights and a day he eluded the hounds, abandoning and burning his vessels as he fled. Finally cornered on the morning of 13 October, with "the Sails Rigging and Hull of the *Congress* . . . shattered and torn in Pieces, [and] the first Lieutenant and 3 Men killed," Arnold torched his remaining gunboats and raced through the woods to Fort Ticonderoga, only footfalls ahead of "the Savages who way laid the Road in two Hours after we passed."

Throughout the battle Arnold had shown exemplary judgment and bravery, but he had lost ten of his fifteen vessels and had suffered more than eighty casualties. As a result, the British owned the waterways from Québec and Montréal to Fort Ticonderoga. General Sir Guy Carleton stood at the gates of the fort, and the officer most responsible for this British ascendancy, Charles Douglas, sailed for home content that "things" had been "brought to so glorious a conclusion on Lake Champlain" in the campaign of 1776.

Most American commentators, following the lead of Alfred Mahan, reach an entirely different conclusion. In 1898 Mahan interpreted the skirmish between Arnold and Pringle as "a strife of pigmies for the prize of a continent." He reasoned that Arnold's frenzied construction of a squadron, which forced a similar exertion by the British, delayed the Carleton–Pringle advance for at least four weeks. Carleton, always thorough and cautious, decided that it was too late to attack Fort Ticonderoga that year and retired to winter quarters in Montréal. Thus, Mahan concludes: "The little American navy on Champlain was wiped out; but never had any force, big or small, lived to better purpose or died more gloriously; for it had saved the Lake for that year." General John Burgoyne's defeat at Saratoga the next year "led directly to the American alliance with France in 1778, [but] the delay, with all that it involved, was obtained by the Lake campaign of 1776."

Mahan's tempting interpretation has found a universal following among American naval historians, but several other factors insist upon consideration. To the south, in September and October 1776, a British army under General Sir William Howe "jostled Washington's army off Manhattan," but because Howe acted too cautiously in pressing his successive advantages, he failed to conquer the Continental Army that year. In the campaign of 1777 Howe obdurately refused to satisfy the desire of the king and ministry that he cooperate with General Burgoyne in decisively severing New England from New York. Instead, Howe formed "an obsession" with invading Pennsylvania and "provided only meager cooperation with the Canadian army." Finally, and always, George Washington evaded and endured, keeping intact the Continental Army as a force-in-being that no British general could catch and destroy. His integrity of leadership, singleness of purpose, and operational effectiveness were not to be found in the Continental Navy.

===

After the Hopkins debacle of 1776, the navy mounted only two more fleet or squadron operations along the coast of North America, and both came midway through the war. Penobscot Bay, 150 miles northeast of Boston on the Maine coast, supplied timber for the Royal Navy, but because the British did not fully control the surrounding area they suffered harassment at the hands of Yankee privateers. To secure their source of timber and strengthen their line of communications between Halifax and New York, the British in June 1779 occupied and fortified Bagaduce—today known as Castine—a small peninsula dominating the bay. To the south, Newport, Rhode Island, had been in British hands since 1776, and Bostonians began to feel themselves caught in a vise. The Massachusetts Board of War planned a relief expedition with "such armed vessels, State or National, as could be prepared and procured to sail in 6 days."

The Massachusetts navy dispatched its entire fleet of two brigantines, New Hampshire contributed its state ship, *Hampden*, and the Continental Navy added three ships: the 32-gun frigate *Warren*, the 12-gun sloop *Providence*, and the fast brig *Diligent*. Altogether, twenty-two armed vessels, including about sixteen privateers, plus twenty transports brimming with 3,000 militiamen, set sail for Penobscot on 19 July. With Captain Dudley Saltonstall's *Warren* in the van, the fleet gingerly tested the British defenses. The Americans found Fort Saint George too strong to assault with the militia and too well gunned to sail past with impunity. Precious days slid by as the indecisive Saltonstall argued with Brigadier General Solomon Lovell and the other American military officers about whether to "risk my shipping in that d——d hole."

On 13 August the Royal Navy resolved the issue. *Diligent* spotted a British relief squadron of ten ships led by H.M.S. *Raisonable*, a 64-gun ship of the line, and pandemonium ensued. Saltonstall ordered his ships to seek safety wherever they could find it, while his crew blew up *Warren* to forestall capture. The Americans destroyed fourteen of their own vessels and surrendered twenty-eight others. The most ambitious American naval undertaking of the Revolution had ended in a rout. Dudley Saltonstall survived the battle only to face a congressional committee that found him in "want of proper spirit and energy." In early 1780 he was court-martialed and cashiered.

The frustrated Congress looked elsewhere for leadership. In November 1779 the Marine Committee ordered Commodore Abraham Whipple, an aggressive fighter who had commanded the *Columbus* in Esek Hopkins's Nassau expedition, to take four ships south to Charleston to defend South Carolina's leading seaport against an expected British attack. Whipple positioned his ships in the channel of the Cooper River, impotently facing a British force of 14,000 men led by General Sir Henry Clinton and Vice Admiral Marriot Arbuthnot, which blockaded the harbor and besieged Fort Moultrie. On 12 May 1780 Charleston capitulated. In the worst American defeat of the Revolution, more than 5,000 Continental soldiers surrendered. The Continental Navy lost three frigates and a sloop, leaving it with only six ships in commission in 1780. Whipple accepted permanent parole as a prisoner of war.

The disasters at Charleston and Penobscot Bay proved emphatically that the Continental Navy could not defend the American coast against the Royal Navy, a critical point long understood by the astute Philadelphia merchant and delegate to Congress, Robert Morris. In the winter of 1776–77 Morris ran the navy "practically without assistance," because he coolly stayed behind in December when his frightened congressional colleagues fled to Baltimore. General Charles Cornwallis, hoping finally to "bag the fox," was chasing George Washington across New Jersey toward the capital. Buoyed by Washington's stunning counterattacks at Trenton and Princeton, Morris in early February 1777 explained his conception of a proper American naval strategy to John Paul Jones, who by then had an enviable record as a commerce raider, having taken more than twenty prizes while commanding the *Providence* and *Alfred*.

Morris pointed the hot-blooded captain to the Caribbean, Pensacola, and the mouth of the Mississippi River, where he proposed that Jones with five ships could "make a considerable booty." Far more important, with hit-and-run raids on British colonial outposts Jones could "alarm not only the Inhabitants but the whole British nation . . . disturbing their Settlements & spreading alarms." Morris believed that

> forcing the British to defend their extensive possessions at all points is of infinitely more Consequence to the United States of America than all the Plunder that can be taken. . . . It has long been clear to me that our infant Fleet cannot protect our own Coasts & that the only effectual relief it can afford us is to attack the Enemies defenceless places & thereby oblige them to Station more of their Ships in their own Countries or to keep them employed in following ours and either way we are relieved so far as they do it.

Esek Hopkins, still nominally Jones's senior as commodore of the ships in Narragansett Bay, bristled when Jones demanded his "Ready and immediate concurrence" in outfitting vessels for the expedition. He protested that it would be more difficult to man ships under Jones's command "than to do it under any Officer of the Fleet." The Marine Committee listened, and when Congress reassembled in Philadelphia in March it canceled the expedition and ordered Jones to take command of *Ranger*, a swift, ship-rigged sloop-of-war under construction at Portsmouth, New Hampshire. When at last he set sail for Europe on 1 November 1777, Jones carried news of General John Burgoyne's surrender of 5,700 soldiers at Saratoga two weeks earlier. That stunning British defeat transformed a colonial revolution into an international war involving Europe's second greatest naval power, France.

French foreign minister Charles Gravier, Comte de Vergennes, wanted to break the British monopoly of trade and markets in North America. The American Revolution was his great opportunity, and he set his sights on nothing less than the complete separation of the thirteen colonies from Great Britain. In April 1776 he persuaded Louis XVI to order twenty ships of the line made fully ready for sea, in effect doubling the fighting strength of the French navy. For the next eighteen months Anglo-French relations deteriorated as the naval race accelerated and Britain protested French encouragement of American commerce raiding. Vergennes watched and waited until the battle of Saratoga provided him at last with an excuse to abandon neutrality, ally with the Americans, and fight a war at sea designed to strip England of its North American colonies. Signed by Vergennes and Benjamin Franklin on 6 February 1778, the Franco-American Treaty of Alliance gave the Continental Navy a European base of operations from which John Paul Jones could raid the British Isles.

Between 14 February and 8 May 1778 Jones landed on English soil and spiked the defending guns at the Irish port of Whitehaven, the first such intrusion in a British seaport since 1667. He next foraged about St. Mary's Isle hoping to kidnap the absent Earl of Selkirk and exchange him for American sailors held as prisoners by the British. Jones fought, captured, and brought to Brest as a prize H.M.S. *Drake*, a 20-gun sloop-of-war, and returned to France crowing that his short cruise had shown the British that "not all their boasted navy can protect their own coast, and that the scene of distress which they have occasioned in America may soon be brought home to their own shores."

Not everyone shared Jones's enthusiasm. Throughout *Ranger*'s cruise he had been bedeviled by a nearly mutinous crew of homesick Portsmouth men made bitter by nonpayment of prize money. Some of Jones's officers fomented the crew's unrest, notably Lieutenant Thomas Simpson. Unable to convene a court-martial for his disloyal subordinate, Jones finally ridded himself of Simpson and crew by sending them home on *Ranger*.

Jones was kept unemployed for the second half of 1778, while across the Atlantic the Continental Navy was driven from the seas. By the end of 1778 only six American frigates remained in commission, five of which lay at anchor in Boston. Only the French navy saved America from calamity at sea that year. Its Brest fleet pinned down much of the Royal Navy in home waters by threatening a fleet action—*guerre d'escadre*—with ships of the line, as at the Battle of Ushant on 27 June 1778. The Toulon fleet under Vice Admiral Count Charles Hector d'Estaing tested British naval supremacy in the Western Hemisphere, "the vital theater of naval operations." D'Estaing narrowly missed trapping Admiral Howe in the Delaware in July. He failed to break Howe's protective cordon of ships in the dangerously shallow waters off Sandy Hook at the entrance to New York harbor; briefly blockaded Newport, Rhode Island; retired to Boston in early fall; and sailed for Martinique on 4 November. The French admiral did not win the decisive victory that Vergennes sought, but for a brief moment he interrupted the Royal Navy's "almost complete control of American coastal waters."

The year 1779 dawned with another French contribution to the American war at sea: acquisition of a ship acceptable to John Paul Jones. *Le Duc de Duras* was a fourteen-year-old armed French East Indiaman of about 900 tons displacement, measuring 178 feet in length and 39 feet in beam. In early 1779 King Louis XVI purchased her, outfitted her, and paid her crew. John Paul Jones renamed her *Bonhomme Richard*, the French translation of Benjamin Franklin's nom de plume, "Poor Richard," and converted her into a heavy frigate mounting forty guns. At the instigation of the Marquis de Lafayette, Jones's command soon expanded to include the new American-built 36-gun frigate *Alliance*, the French 32-gun frigate *Pallas*, the large 18-gun cutter *Le Cerf*, and the 12-gun brigantine *La Vengeance*.

Lafayette had intended to sail with Jones's squadron and make an amphibious assault on a major British seaport like Liverpool, a prospect that thoroughly alarmed that city's leading citizens. In May the French changed plans, ordering Jones to make a diversionary raid against Scotland or northern England while France and Spain took control of the English Channel, landed at the Isle of Wight, raided Portsmouth, and, it was hoped, destroyed the English fleet at the Spithead roadstead between Portsmouth and the Isle of Wight. With this overly ambitious operation Vergennes would "attack Carthage in Carthage itself." On 3 June the French Brest fleet sailed, but unfavorable winds kept it from a rendezvous with the Spanish until 22–23 July. Once combined, the French and Spanish numbered sixty-four ships of the line mounting 4,774 guns. The best that Sir Charles Hardy could assemble as a protective Channel fleet were thirty-eight ships of the line with 2,968 guns. Blessed with westerly winds and shrouding fog, Hardy sensibly avoided battle as long as possible, until devastating illness and death from a mysterious debilitating disease drove the French and Spanish back to port in early September, a dénouement reminiscent at the fate of Spain's Armada in 1588.

Jones meanwhile struggled to get ready for sea. In July new orders directed him to raid the enemy's commerce rather than make a diversionary landing. He protested, but Benjamin Franklin cut him off, noting that since the French were "at the Chief expense, I think they have the best right to direct." Thus thwarted in his principal object of harassing the enemy's coastal cities, the frustrated captain set sail from Groix roads with his squadron on 14 August 1779. He worked his ships clockwise across the English Channel, north along the west coast of Ireland, northeast off the Hebrides to the Shetlands, and south through the North Sea, where he had a rendezvous with destiny. Along the way he took prizes almost daily. Twice he planned to disregard orders and make raids ashore—once at Edinburgh and again at Newcastle-on-Tyne, where he hoped to cut off London's supply of winter coal—but he was stopped by shifting winds and the timidity of the ships' captains nominally subordinate to him. Then, at 3:00 P.M. on 23 September, off Flamborough Head, Jones sighted H.M.S. *Serapis*. The new 44-gun two-decker was escorting forty-one merchantmen loaded with stores for the Royal Navy. The other ships of his squadron refused to follow him into line of battle, but Jones unhesitatingly engaged *Serapis*, firing his first broadside about 6:30 P.M.

In light winds, with a slower, less maneuverable, and outgunned ship, Jones's only hope of victory or even survival lay in grappling *Serapis* and decimating the British crew with small arms fire. In an act of consummate seamanship, Jones crossed *Serapis*'s bow and literally seized her bowsprit when it became entangled in his mizzen shrouds. Lashed together bow to stern, the two ships lacerated one another until about 10:30, when the mainmast of *Serapis* began to tremble. Captain Richard Pearson lost his nerve and struck his colors. Almost half of each ship's crew had fallen as casualties, many of them victims of three separate broadside attacks by the 36-gun *Alliance*, which inexplicably raked both ships. *Bonhomme Richard* was mortally hulled below the waterline. Two days later Jones, "with inexpressible grief," watched her sink into the North Sea. Pierre Landais, the French captain of the *Alliance*, whom history would judge to have been insane, was subsequently relieved of command.

Jones returned to Europe a hero. Because he had boldly attacked at the very moment when the Franco-Spanish invasion fleet had meekly returned home, Louis XVI awarded Jones the Ordre de Mérite Militaire and presented him with a gold-hilted sword. London's *Morning Post* said that for a month he remained "the most general topic of conversation." When Jones finally returned to the United States in early 1781, Congress voted him "the thanks of the United States . . . for the zeal, prudence and intrepidity with which he has supported the honor of the American flag." The legislators then unanimously made him commander of *America*, the Continental Navy's only ship of the line, under construction at Portsmouth, New

Hampshire. He spent all of 1782 readying her for sea, only to have Congress give her to the French navy as the war wound down and the United States began to discard its navy.

Jones never again commanded an American warship. He served for a time as a rear admiral in the Black Sea fleet of Russia's Catherine the Great, returning to Paris in May 1790. There he lingered in neglect, "like a wine-skin from which the wine is drawn," until his death on 18 July 1792. Only posthumously did this foreign-born American patriot achieve lasting greatness in the United States. In 1905, as the United States Navy redefined its mission and for the first time challenged Britain for supremacy at sea, it brought his remains home. Welcomed by eleven battleships, Jones was canonized for his indomitable spirit in battle and for the inspirational value of his war cries: "I will sink, I will never strike!" "I wish to have no Connection with any Ship that does not sail fast, for I intend to go in harm's way." Above all the navy loves the rebuke he hurled at Captain Pearson: "I have not yet begun to fight."

John Paul Jones's naval contemporaries saw him more as a rival than as a model, and in a fundamental way they disagreed with him. Jones contended that the small Continental Navy should be used to raid the enemy's coast, stir up the population, and politically force a partial withdrawal of the Royal Navy from American shores. The Continental naval officers who had reached Europe before Jones thought and operated as commerce raiders. Lambert Wickes, a Marylander and friend of Robert Morris, transported Benjamin Franklin to France aboard the 18-gun brig *Reprisal* in November 1776. For the next nine months *Reprisal*, in company with the brigantine *Lexington* and the cutter *Dolphin*, chased prizes in the English Channel, in the Irish Sea, and off the coast of Brittany. They seized at least twenty-five merchantmen and irritated the British by bringing the war home. France, however, remained officially neutral and in the fall of 1777 ordered Wickes to stop using French ports as bases of operations.

Like Wickes, Gustavus Conyngham preyed on British commerce in the year before the Franco-American alliance. Sailing a converted English-built cutter renamed *Revenge*, Conyngham in eighteen months took about twenty-five ships as prizes and burned or sank thirty others. Disregarding Madrid's authentic neutrality, he sailed from Spanish ports to ambush British cargo vessels in the Bay of Biscay, off the Canary Islands, and occasionally in the Mediterranean. The Spanish court finally forced him permanently out of Spain in the fall of 1778. On the way home he rampaged about the Caribbean, taking five prizes in three months. Altogether he captured or destroyed more than thirty British merchantmen, making him by one interpretation the Continental Navy's "most successful captain" after John Paul Jones.

The vagaries of patronage nevertheless led to congressional sympathy for the complaints of Conyngham's crew about nonpayment of wages. Congress sold *Revenge* out from under him, and his old Philadelphia mercantile firm purchased the ship. Conyngham left the navy to take command of the now privately owned *Revenge* and sailed her as a privateer. He became in fact what he had been in spirit all along, a privateer, and as such Conyngham was even more typically American than was John Paul Jones as a continental naval officer.

Privateering was an ancient and honorable way to fight at sea. Armed with letters of marque and reprisal, audacious crews set to sea in fast and lightly armed vessels with the sole intention of capturing merchant vessels. They took their captives into ports, where prize courts legitimized the seizures and auctioned them off to the profit of the privateers. This mode of warfare remained popular with American seamen throughout the Revolutionary War, because it promised wealth in the form of prize money, even though the hope was often dashed by British recapture of prizes headed for port or by the prize courts' delayed and confused adjudication of cases. The enduring popularity of privateering facilitated the financing of ships and recruitment of crews. Continental naval officers resented the unfair competition for scarce resources, and congressional critics decried privateering for introducing "Luxury, Extravagance and every kind of Dissipation, that tend to the destruction of the morals of a people." But the more pragmatic John Adams appreciated the American people's predilection for the practice: "Privateering is as well understood by them as any people whatsoever; and it is by cutting off supplies, not by attacks, sieges, or assaults, that I expect deliverance from enemies."

Adam's viewpoint prevailed within Congress, which on 2 April 1776 prescribed a commission for "commanders of private ships of war" authorizing them, "by force of arms, to attack, seize and take the ships and other vessels belonging to the inhabitants of Great Britain." In the course of the war, 1,697 privateers carrying almost 15,000 guns and more than 55,000 men operated under congressional authorization. Massachusetts and Rhode Island licensed 1,000 more privateers on their own authority, and in 1779 a resident of the Bay State rhapsodized, "Privateering was never more in vogue than at present . . .

men seem as plenty [sic] as grasshoppers in the field; no vessel being detained an hour for want of them." Two years later, when the Continental Navy had shrunk to two ships in commission and two others under construction, the Congress issued 559 letters of marque, an increase of 249 over the number issued in 1780. In stark contrast to those figures, the total number of ships making up the Continental Navy's blue-water fleet from 1775 until 1783 did not exceed eighty ships of all classes, including packets.

Privateers took approximately 600 prizes worth about $18 million during the Revolution. They garnered needed supplies for the American armies, disrupted Britain's resupply of its armies, drove up insurance rates for British shipping, and undercut popular support for the war in the mother country. Gardner W. Allen long ago gave the final, definitive evaluation of privateering in the American Revolution:

> It is necessary to look at the events of the past from the point of view of the time and the persons concerned. In this case the temperament of the people, private interests, the sentiment of local independence and fear of centralized military power, the lack of authority on the part of Congress, the hopelessness of raising the necessary money, are at once evident to the student of this period of our history. Privateering, moreover, was thoroughly believed in as a means of striking at the enemy's vitals. Under the circumstances, therefore, it is obvious that a small, weak navy was one of the necessary conditions of the war and that a vigorous offense upon the sea was not in the nature of things.

The "nature of things" included states' sovereignty, which resulted in eleven discrete navies. The largest of those fleets sailed under the flags of Massachusetts, Connecticut, Pennsylvania, Maryland, Virginia, and South Carolina. Of the thirteen states only New Jersey and Delaware failed to commission at least a symbolic navy during the Revolutionary War. The total number of states' ships "greatly exceeded the number of ships in the Continental navy." The states, however, built only a few deep-draft seagoing commerce raiders; they favored small, shallow-draft vessels: "armed boats of various sizes, galleys with and without sails, half-galleys, floating batteries, barges, and fire-ships." This varied assortment of small craft could dart in and out of harbors, rivers, and bays to protect their seaports, coasts, and commerce from raids by offshore ships of the Royal Navy.

They could succeed only at the sufferance of the British, as the Pennsylvania navy learned in 1777–78. Following General Sir William Howe's occupation of Philadelphia on 26 September 1777, the British resolved to open secure communications with the sea by bringing the fleet of Admiral Lord Richard "Black Dick" Howe all the way up the Delaware River. In resistance to a fleet that included four ships of the line, the Pennsylvania navy "did its best fighting" under the command of Commodore John Hazelwood, who also directed the Continental warships in the river. By burning a 64-gun ship of the line, the Pennsylvania sailors slowed the British ascent in October 1777, but the small American fleet was caught in a vise. The desertion rate began to climb, suggesting that the Pennsylvania navy "was without esprit de corps, and that its officers and men were often raw, undisciplined, and insubordinate."

In January 1778 the chairman of the Pennsylvania Navy Board, William Bradford, complained of being "left here alone" and wishing to "be in action with the Militia." As spring approached, George Washington warned Pennsylvania that the British would soon sortie from Philadelphia to destroy all shipping on the Delaware River north of the city. The Pennsylvanians followed Washington's advice and scuttled their fleet to prevent its capture by the British. On 8 March the British army came out and destroyed about forty-five American vessels on the Delaware, including two frigates of the Continental Navy. This inglorious episode demonstrated that states' navies could not fulfill their primary mission of harbor and coastal defense as long as the British retained freedom of movement along the North American coastline.

The British could dominate the American coastline so long as they did not encounter a major French force. Then they were in trouble, because the ships of the British North American Squadron were obsolete in design. French naval architecture by contrast was at its zenith in the late 1770s. That French technological superiority helps explain why the French navy was able to break British domination of the coastal waters twice during the war.

In the summer and fall of 1778 Admiral d'Estaing probed for British weaknesses between the Delaware Bay and Newport, Rhode Island. He returned in September 1779 with twenty ships of the line to besiege Savannah, Georgia, at the behest of the Continental Congress. Although unsuccessful, his attack indirectly led to the British evacuation of Newport, Rhode Island, in early October. For the rest of 1779 and throughout 1780 French and British squadrons skirmished in the Caribbean and traded West Indies islands like pawns. Other British, French, and Spanish squadrons kept the war alive in the English Channel, Mediterranean Sea, and Indian Ocean. In

North America the British captured Charleston, and Charles Cornwallis defeated the southern army of General Horatio Gates at Cam-
den, South Carolina, but in the midst of success the British failed to
guard the approaches to Newport, and on 11 July 1780 Comte de
Rochambeau, with a 5,000-man army convoyed by seven ships of the
line, slipped into Narragansett Bay. They wintered in Newport, quietly nestled behind a British blockade.

Rochambeau joined forces with George Washington in July
1781. Together the French and the Americans marched to Yorktown,
Virginia, where they trapped General Cornwallis between themselves
and the West Indies fleet of Comte de Grasse, who anchored at the
mouth of the York River in Chesapeake Bay with twenty-eight ships
of the line on 30 August. The courageous and energetic de Grasse
beat off a lackluster attempt by Admiral Thomas Graves to relieve
Cornwallis with nineteen ships of the line in the Battle of the Virginia
Capes on 5 September. Five days later six French ships of the line
sailing from Newport under Comte de Barras slipped around Graves
and into Chesapeake Bay with siege artillery and provisions for Rochambeau and Washington. The cornered Cornwallis surrendered
his 7,200 troops at Yorktown on 19 October 1781.

Cornwallis commanded the only major British army not needed
for garrison duty in New York and other occupied positions. By forcing him to surrender in their combined action, a Franco-American
army and an exclusively French fleet broke the British will to fight.
On 27 February 1782 the House of Commons voted to discontinue
offensive warfare against the Americans. The center of the Revolution
then shifted from North America to France, where Anglo-American
negotiations dragged on until the Treaty of Paris was finally signed on
3 September 1783.

Yorktown–Virginia Capes ripped the heart from the eighteenth-
century British Empire. A century later it thoroughly confounded
Alfred Thayer Mahan. For the great American navalist, control of the
seas—ostensibly enjoyed by the global Royal Navy of the 1780s—
necessarily spelled victory in war. To explain away the British loss at
Yorktown–Virginia Capes—and of the Revolutionary War—Mahan
contrived the explanation that in North America the British foolishly
divided their naval forces and thus unwittingly squandered their control of the sea. That thesis ignored the reality that at Virginia Capes
the French navy itself was divided into the two fleets of de Grasse and
de Barras. Ignored also is the shining truth that victory at Yorktown
resulted from the combination of two armies, one French and one

American, and two kinds of forces, one military and the other naval. Achieving such an overwhelming combination had long been George Washington's goal. Delay in its realization can be attributed to many factors, including the fact that the French had other strategic interests in European waters and in the West Indies. North America seemed to Vergennes the key to victory over the British, but apparently it did not seem so to all French strategists.

If it can be said that the Franco-American combination of power at Yorktown–Virginia Capes won the war, it can equally well be said that the Revolution laid the basis for an American naval tradition that would endure for a century. This tradition realistically accepted relative American naval weakness in wars with European powers. From a position of naval inferiority as measured in ships of the line and standing fleets, the Americans worked out a strategy of seeking allies where possible and of devoting their scarce naval resources to small ships—frigates, sloops, and brigs—designed to raid the enemy's commerce and if possible to protect American maritime trade. A corollary of that policy was the defense of coasts and harbors with even smaller vessels—gunboats and galleys—backed by forts and a ready militia. Less formally, the American people relied on privateers to supplement the navy's force of commerce destroyers. In its totality, this was a policy characteristic of most eighteenth- and nineteenth-century continental powers. Its historical roots reached back hundreds of years in Europe and the Mediterranean. It had always coexisted with a tradition of massed fleet engagements contesting for command of the sea.

In the twentieth century the United States accepted fleet engagements as the naval norm, and most commentators began to judge the present and past in those terms. But the truth is that since the Revolution both traditions of naval strategy have characterized the American navy, with one or the other predominating at any given time. In the nineteenth century *guerre de course* predominated; in the twentieth century *guerre d'escadre*. The competition between the two strategies became apparent very early in the national period, and it constitutes the real essence of American naval history from the Revolution to the present.

2

"A Good Occasion to Begin a Navy"

1783 – 1800

In the late eighteenth century the North African powers of Morocco, Algiers, Tunis, and Tripoli—the so-called Barbary States—posed an immediate threat to American commercial expansion. Geographic location and regionally strong navies gave these satrapies of Turkey control over the approaches to the straits of Gibraltar. In exchange for unmolested passage of foreign ships through their coastal waters the rulers of the four states demanded monetary tribute, and compliant European nations signed extortionate treaties in order to secure temporary advantages over their commercial rivals. England especially prospered under this system. It paid tribute while at the same time stationing a few warships in the Mediterranean to temper Barbary rapaciousness.

As a part of the British Empire, the American colonies had benefited from this protective British policy prior to 1776. It provided them with a political base for a lucrative trade, allowed them freedom from tribute, and secured for them immunities enjoyed only by powerful European nations. All of this had swiftly changed with the Revolutionary War, as American merchant shipping fell victim to the unrestrained "Barbary pirates."

In the American mind England had joined the predators. Learning of the narrow escape from Algerine pirates made by two American merchantmen in March 1783, Benjamin Franklin speculated "that those rovers may be privately encouraged by the English to fall upon us, and to prevent our interference in the carrying trade." Franklin was correct. Seafaring Englishmen had a history of close cooperation with the Mediterranean corsairs, and rather than protect American commerce as they had before the Revolutionary War, the British now encouraged raids on American ships by the Barbary navies. John Lord Sheffield summarized his country's case in 1783:

> It is not probable the American States will have a very free trade in the Mediterranean; it will not be the interest of any of the great maritime powers to protect them there from the Barbary States. . . . The Americans cannot protect themselves. . . ; they cannot pretend to a navy.

This attitude, reflected in British policy, would drive the Americans to construct warships once they realized that unprotected merchant vessels in the Mediterranean were subject to capture and their crews liable to interminable imprisonment as hostages of North African potentates. America's European diplomatic and Mediterranean naval policies were therefore interlocked from the outset of the national experience.

Lacking the political cohesiveness and financial resources to build a navy, Congress at first sought a diplomatic solution. On 7 May 1784 it appointed a distinguished triumvirate—John Adams, Benjamin Franklin, and Thomas Jefferson—to negotiate treaties of amity and commerce with Morocco, Algiers, Tunis, and Tripoli. The three diplomats succeeded with Morocco, which Jefferson regarded as "the most important" state because it bordered the Atlantic, into which "the Algerines rarely come . . . and Tunis and Tripoli never." The Mediterranean, however, would remain "absolutely shut to us till we can open it with money. Whether this will best be expended in buying or forcing a peace is for Congress to determine."

Jefferson personally favored force, and from his vantage point as American minister to France he made his case to all who would listen: European diplomats, a few sympathetic members of Congress like John Jay and James Monroe, and his counterpart in London, John Adams. Frustrated by the recalcitrance of Algiers, Tripoli, and Tunis, Jefferson proposed that the United States join Naples and Portugal in a naval confederacy "to effect a peace thro' the medium of war." With "a couple of frigates" the United States and its maritime allies would quickly drive Algiers and Tripoli to the conference table. Jefferson then would lay up his ships in dockyards to eliminate operating costs and minimize maintenance expenses. That course of action, he believed, was demanded by the American people's sense of honor and justice and by a national desire to win the respect of Europe.

A small frigate navy could even affect relations with England, the European power most dangerous to the United States. In the event of another Anglo-American conflict Jefferson foresaw the United States losing its carrying trade to neutral powers and enduring a dreadful suffering "on our coasts, if we have no force on the water." In the face of such a bleak prospect, Jefferson hoped that geography and a navy might combine as an effective deterrent to British aggression. "Our vicinity to their West India possession[s] and the [Newfoundland] fisheries is a bridle which a small naval force on our part would hold in the mouths of the most powerful of these countries."

These early speculations about confronting Britain and fighting the Barbary states foreshadowed Jefferson's presidential naval policies of 1801–1809. For the moment, however, he was blocked by the loose and tentative structure of the government he served.

The roots of Jefferson's frustrations were well understood by the American minister to England, John Adams. Like Jefferson, Adams craved unhindered access to the Mediterranean for American merchantmen, but he wanted to buy his way in. He decried the American refusal to pay tribute as short-sighted and self-defeating. By immediately paying bribes to the Barbary powers the United States could "at this hour have two hundred ships in the Mediterranean, whose Freight alone would be worth two hundred Thousand Pounds." This endorsement of bribery and his reluctance to resort to force rested on politically expedient grounds, a point Adams made abundantly clear to Jefferson:

> Perhaps you will Say, fight them, though it Should cost Us a Great Sum to carry on the war. . . . If this is your Sentiment, and you can persuade the Southern States into it, I dare answer for it that all [congressmen] from Pennsylvania inclusively northward, would not object. It would be a good occasion to begin a Navy.

But as Adams knew, neither Jefferson nor anyone else could persuade the Congress of the Articles of Confederation to build a navy.

As early as October 1785 John Jay, the secretary for foreign affairs with whom Jefferson corresponded regularly, had responded to an Algerine declaration of war against the United States with a proposal to meet "these predatory Enemies in a proper Manner." Jay wanted Congress to arm American merchantmen and build five 40-gun ships, presumably frigates, to be "put under the Direction of a brave experienced Commodore, for the purpose of cruizing in those Seas." In the meantime, he wished to negotiate with Portugal "for such an Alliance, as may provide for a Co-operation of Forces and Mutual Defence against the common Enemy." This remarkably hawkish recommendation for bilateral naval action ran afoul of sectional jealousies and the stipulation in the Articles of Confederation requiring at least nine states "in Congress assembled" to "agree upon the number of vessels of war, to be built or purchased."

On 27 July 1787 the same legislative paralysis doomed Jefferson's proposal to enter a less formal "confederacy with the powers of Europe . . . for the purchase [purpose] of protecting and securing . . . the free navigation of the Mediterranean sea." By then, however, the Constitutional Convention had superseded the Confederation Congress as the policymaking body of the United States.

The nationalists who gathered at the Constitutional Convention in Philadelphia in May 1787 were determined to strengthen the powers of the central government in several vital categories, notably taxation, foreign policy, and military affairs. They were far less interested in naval policy. As a result, they adopted naval provisions with little debate and largely as corollaries of sections providing for an army. The president therefore became "the Commander in Chief of the Army and Navy." To Congress was delegated the power "to declare War, grant Letters of Marque and Reprisal" and "provide and maintain a Navy." Brevity notwithstanding, these sections of the Constitution encountered limited but stiff opposition from Antifederalists in the states during the debates over ratification.

The most incisive challenge to a navy came from William Grayson, a leading Virginia Antifederalist intensely disliked by Jefferson and other supporters of the Constitution. Grayson objected to the Constitution's giving Congress "unlimited power" to build a large navy. "To have a fleet, in the present limited population of America, is, in my opinion, impractical and inexpedient."

A fleet of ships of the line would be prohibitively expensive and would "irritate the nations of Europe against us," Grayson stated. Those countries with "West India possessions, would be alarmed at any extraordinary maritime exertions, and, knowing the danger of our arrival at manhood, would crush us in our infancy." Britain or France would strike, and as the Revolutionary War had proved, the Southern states would lie exposed because "the American fleet would not be competent to the defence of all the states." Grayson had "no objection to such a navy as will not excite the jealousy of the European countries. But I would have the Constitution to say, that no greater number of ships should be had than would be sufficient to protect our trade."

He would tolerate the construction of enough moderately sized warships to guard American merchantmen and their crews from the kind of harassment they were suffering at the hands of the North Africans. But under no circumstances would he try to protect American neutral commerce in a future Anglo-French war: "the profits that might arise from such a transient commerce could not compensate for the expenses of rendering ourselves formidable at sea, or the dangers that would probably result from the attempt."

America's true destiny lay not at sea, Grayson pointed out, but in a thriving agriculture and a growing population of farmers. Sometime in the distant future, perhaps, "when we shall be sufficiently populous, and our situation secure,—then come forward with a fleet; not with a small one, but with one sufficient to meet any of the maritime powers." In the meantime, the sparsely populated and agrarian South faced a special danger from a large navy. "All the vessels of the intended fleet would be built and equipped in the Northern States, where they have every necessary material and convenience for that purpose. . . . The consequence will be that the Southern States will be in the power of the Northern States." He had prophesied the Union Navy's role in the Civil War.

In 1788 Grayson and the Antifederalist opponents of a national navy were drowned out by the Federalists. Led by Alexander Hamilton of New York and James Madison of Virginia, the Federalists defended a strong navy as necessary for a commercial nation that hoped to remain neutral in a war between Great Britain and France, the early outbreak of which Madison "judged probable." America as a neutral and weaker naval power adhered to the doctrine that free ships make free goods; but as a likely belligerent and strong naval power Britain consistently repudiated it, even during the latter stages of the American Revolution when "all Europe was against her." Therefore, Madison quite accurately predicted, the Royal Navy in time of an Anglo-French war would seize American vessels laden with French property. The United States then would "be obliged to relinquish the advantage of a neutral nation, or to be engaged in a war." A more palatable alternative for Madison was "to establish a navy . . . as one reason, out of several, for rendering ourselves respectable."

National respectability also formed the cornerstone of Alexander
Hamilton's plea for "a navy which, if it could not vie with those of the
great maritime powers, would at least be of respectable weight if
thrown into the scale of either of the two contending parties." The
outcome of naval operations in the waters surrounding the West Indies possessions of Britain and France could be determined by an
American navy. In Hamilton's view, "A few ships of the line, sent
opportunely to the reinforcement of either side, would often be sufficient to decide the fate of a campaign, on the event of which interests of the greatest magnitude were suspended." If the United States
would follow this formula for the realistic application of naval force in
the West Indies, Hamilton wrote in *Federalist Number 11,* the American people could hope soon "to become the arbiter of Europe in
America, and to be able to incline the balance of European compe-
titions in this part of the world as our interest may dictate."

Federalists carried the day in the crucial ratifying conventions of
New York and Virginia in the summer of 1788, and they then turned
their attention to electing a president and organizing the new national
government. Naval affairs receded even further into the background.
Britain and France were at peace, however uneasily so. The Portuguese had bottled up the Algerines inside the straits of Gibraltar. The
high seas were therefore tolerably safe for American seamen, although
the Mediterranean remained closed.

One of Thomas Jefferson's early acts as secretary of state in the
first administration of George Washington (1789–1793) was to report
to Congress on the exclusion of American commerce from the Mediterranean and on the state of negotiations with Algiers. He saw those
issues as intimately connected, and he had been troubled by them
since July 1785, when two American merchantmen, the *Maria* out of
Boston and the *Dauphin* out of Philadelphia, were seized by Algerine
corsairs and the crews made prisoners. Numerous attempts by Jefferson and other American diplomats to ransom the hostages had
been thwarted by escalation of the asking price set by the dey of
Algiers. In 1790 Jefferson estimated the cost of bailing out the remaining fourteen American captives at somewhere between $1,200
and $2,920 per man.

To this sum, which Jefferson thought exorbitant, he added $1
million, the estimated Algerine price for negotiating a treaty of amity
and commerce with the United States. Without such a treaty Americans could not safely enter the Mediterranean or hope to resume the
profitable pre-Revolutionary War export trade, which annually had

brought between eighty and one hundred American ships to that sea. Jefferson repeated the opinion he had expressed six years earlier: A treaty without backing would be futile. The Algerines "must see that we are in condition to chastise an infraction of the treaty; consequently, some marine force must be exhibited in their harbor from time to time."

Given inflationary Barbary demands for ransom, the expense of securing a treaty, and the inescapable need for sending warships to Algiers, Jefferson concluded it might be better simply "to repel force by force." The Algerines had one 40-gun frigate "on the stocks." They also commanded six xebecs, each mounting between ten and thirty-six guns, and four galleys. Those vessels were "sharp built and swift, but so light as not to stand the broadside of a good frigate." The ships' guns were of mixed caliber, "unskillfully pointed and worked." The crews were brave men who sought riches by boarding and overwhelming their prey, but they did not maneuver their ships crisply. They could be beaten if the Americans truly wished "to vindicate their commerce by arms," but victory would require a force equal in strength to the entire Algerine fleet. Rather than act alone, the United States ought to arrange "a concert of operation . . . among the powers at war with the Barbary States, so as that, . . . a constant cruise . . . may be kept up before the harbor of Algiers, till the object of such operations be completely obtained." Having expressed his preference for naval action against Algiers, the secretary of state urged Congress "to decide between war, tribute, and ransom, as the means of re-establishing our Mediterranean commerce."

In February 1791 the Senate beat down an administration attempt to declare war on Algiers and advised President Washington to ransom the captives. Senator William Maclay of Pennsylvania, a professed guardian of states' rights, explained his opposition to a fleet on the grounds that paying ransom was practical and that the protracted Algerine imprisonment of a handful of captured American seamen was a "trifling affair," which the administration was using merely as a "pretext for fitting out a fleet to go to war with them." Should "Hamilton's people" succeed in creating a navy, warned Maclay, "farewell [to] freedom in America." A navy, an army, and the revenue-collecting federal apparatus necessary to sustain them would spell "the destruction of the individuality of the States."

The administration took the hint in May 1792. The president sought the prior approval of the Senate for two treaties he hoped to negotiate with Algiers: one ransoming the prisoners for a grand total of $40,000, and the other a peace treaty secured by annual tributary payments of $25,000. The Senate agreed, the House appropriated funds, and the secretary of state appointed a commissioner for the negotiations, John Paul Jones, then living destitute in Paris. The old sailor died before he could act, as did a second minister. All negotiations with Algiers were then entrusted to David Humphreys, the United States minister to Portugal. Humphreys was imbued with a sense of urgency, but the French Revolution was convulsing Europe, and he could not depart from Lisbon for Algiers until December 1793. By then England and France were at war and North Africa took a back seat in American naval and diplomatic policy.

President Washington had issued a proclamation of neutrality toward the war in Europe on 22 April 1793, but Secretary of State Thomas Jefferson undercut him by recognizing the continued viability of the Franco-American alliance of 1778. The unbridled young republican envoy from France, Citizen Edmond Charles Genêt, further compromised American neutrality by outfitting fourteen French privateers in American ports. Washington lost his patience toward the end of 1793 and asked France to recall Genêt. The administration then directed its attention to belligerent violations of American neutral rights on the high seas.

The president sent several messages to Congress in early December 1793 discreetly reminding the members that his proclamation of neutrality the previous April had been directed toward those unspecified European "powers with whom the United States have the most extensive relations." The unnamed European countries could misconstrue the American desire for peace as weakness, and Washington therefore counseled Congress, "If we desire to avoid insult, we must be able to repel it; if we desire to secure peace, . . . it must be known that we are at all times ready for war." Still speaking in generalities, Washington called the legislators' attention to the "vexations and spoliation . . . committed on our vessels and commerce by the cruisers and officers of some of the belligerent powers."

The belligerent power Washington had most in mind was Great Britain, which had outraged many Americans by its diplomatic and naval behavior since the beginning of the war against revolutionary France. The British government, or at least the British consul in Algiers, was held responsible by Americans for a recent truce between Algiers and Portugal that had freed the corsairs to operate beyond Gibraltar and had made the eastern Atlantic dangerous to American commerce. Washington's message of 16 December relating to Algiers included a poisonous accusation against the British submitted by the American consul in Lisbon, Edward Church, who saw a "hellish plot" in the truce. "The conduct of the British in this business leaves no room to doubt or mistake their object, which was evidently aimed at us, and proves that their envy, jealousy, and hatred, will never be appeased, and that they will leave nothing unattempted to effect our ruin. . . . We are betrayed, and many of our countrymen will fall into the cruel snare." Inclusion of such Anglophobic prose in a presidential message to Congress exposed the high level of tension between the United States and Great Britain in 1793–1794 and the fundamental interrelationship between the war in Europe and American naval policy toward Algiers.

On 2 January 1794 Congress met to consider a resolution to provide "a naval force, adequate to the protection of the commerce of the United States against the Algerine corsairs." The resolution narrowly passed the House, 46–44, and a nine-man committee dominated by Federalists was appointed to recommend the exact size of the proposed American fleet. On 6 February the committee made its recommendation to the House: four 44-gun and two 20-gun vessels. The subsequent debate on the committee's recommendation lasted until 10 March and touched nearly every aspect of American naval power in the age of sail: the size and number of ships; the great distance to Europe; the desirability of European allies in remote waters; protection of commerce; fear of England, fear of a navy as an expensive seedbed of tyranny; arming for coastal defense; and the impossibility of maintaining neutrality when a major European land power was fighting the major European sea power.

The opponents of the six-ship navy objected to the cost of a fleet and questioned its effectiveness. Led by James Madison and William B. Giles of Virginia, they favored "assigning a sum of money to buy a cessation of hostilities from the Regency of Algiers." Some of them also hoped to induce Portugal to convoy American merchant vessels past the Straits of Gibraltar into safe harbors in the Mediterranean. Either tribute or Portuguese convoys would prove cheaper, safer, and more effective than the proposed fleet of six ships. The distance to Algiers was too great, they maintained, and the proposed warships too few in number to permit success. Moreover, the warring European nations would not let the American warships operate freely. Giles sketched the danger graphically: "The sending of American armed ships into the midst of the fleets of Europe would certainly produce a quarrel." He predicted that "if an attempt was made to search our ships of war, like our merchantmen, it would infallibly produce a public affront, and consequent hostilities." For this dubious result, the United States was going to incur great indebtedness and a "system of governing by debts," which Giles perceived as "the most refined system of tyranny." Giles's apocalyptic vision of oppression focused on warships. "There is no device which facilitates the expense and debts so much as a Navy."

The supporters of the bill saw the danger facing America as entirely foreign. William Smith feared that the unleashed Algerines "might very soon be on our coast, under the command of British or American renegadoes." Aware of America's historic hospitality to international buccaneers, Smith "could not tell where the danger might end; nor did he know whether Philadelphia itself would be in safety." Fortifications offered no hope; the only chance for safety lay in well-built American warships sent out to attack the Algerines' "old and crazy" ships.

The cost of outfitting the warships was inconsequential when compared with the soaring insurance rates, and in any case, Smith concluded:

> This country is peculiarly fitted for a navy: abounding in all kinds of naval resources, we have within ourselves the means which other maritime nations were obliged to obtain from abroad. The nature of our situation, and the navigating disposition of a considerable proportion of our citizens, evince still more the propriety of some Naval Establishment.

Fisher Ames of Massachusetts echoed Smith—"six frigates at the mouth of the Straits [of Gibraltar] would do the business." To "buy a peace," as Madison was proposing, seemed "shameful" to Ames, and it would not yield security to the United States or its merchant marine. "Our commerce is on the point of being annihilated, and, unless an armament [of ships] is fitted out, we may very soon expect the Algerines on the coast of America."

Whether they opposed the bill or favored it, the great majority of congressmen who took the floor agreed on one fundamental feature of America's troubles with Algiers: Great Britain was the instigator. They blamed Britain for the Portuguese–Algerine truce, which they interpreted as intended by London to keep the American merchant marine from enjoying low insurance rates and picking up profitable cargos normally consigned in peacetime to British carriers. Giles put the matter starkly: "Algiers was but the instrument, Britain was the cause. The reliance of Britain upon the instrument plainly showed that she was not equal to a war [in Europe] and a commercial contest [with the United States]. She has, therefore, turned loose the Algerines upon us—a fact which is pretty generally acknowledged on both sides of the House."

Most of the congressmen saw an even greater and more direct threat in British policy. In a brief paragraph that strikingly foreshadowed his own presidential war message of 1812, Madison succinctly leveled the charge:

> Britain could render very essential service to the Algerines, without embarking in a war. She has not embarked in a war to the Northwest of Ohio, but she has done the same thing, in substance, by supplying the Indians with arms, ammunition, and, perhaps, with subsistence. . . . In the same way that they give underhand assistance to the Indians, they would give it to the Algerines, rather than hazard an open war [with the United States].

The question, therefore, was not whether Britain was an enemy in an undeclared Anglo-American war but rather how best to deal with that nation.

Construction of frigates might prove a provocative liability. One congressman raised the specter of impressment of sailors in the national navy. "It was to be expected that, when they fell in with British ships of war, that the latter would endeavor to search them for prohibited cargoes, and for seamen, because they were in the practice of impressing their own countrymen wherever they could find them. This would produce a quarrel." The anticipated quarrel occurred thirteen years later: the fateful *Chesapeake–Leopard* encounter of 1807.

As the debate over the navy bill reached a climax, the president nudged the House with a message from the new secretary of state, Edmund Randolph of Virginia. Randolph found several of the European belligerents—Britain, Spain, and Holland—reprehensible for seizing American merchantmen trafficking with French ports in the West Indies. He also enumerated complaints against France for interfering with the American merchant marine. But his most serious and extensive allegations fell upon the British, whose practice of maritime warfare violated all the rights of neutrals as the United States understood them.

Randolph indicted the British on six counts: the "plunder" of American merchant vessels by British privateers; the impressment of American merchant seamen into the Royal Navy; the forced exclusion of American corn from all French ports; the overly strict surveillance of American merchant shipping in the British West Indies; the capture of American ships trading with the French West Indies; and confiscatory decisions of British admiralty prize courts in the Caribbean, which Randolph found "impeachable." This long list of grievances outlined precisely the position on maritime neutral rights that the United States would maintain until World War I and that Great Britain, as a belligerent fighting for survival, could never accept.

Randolph's truculent report reached Congress on 5 March 1794, five days before the final House vote on the naval bill. Congressman Giles read the portents: "there remained no doubt but that the bill would pass." The United States, in his opinion, was about to lay "the foundation of a permanent naval establishment." His colleagues in the House fulfilled both predictions on 10 March by a vote of 50 to 39. The president on 27 March signed "An Act to provide a Naval Armament." The statute authorized the purchase or construction of four 44-gun and two 36-gun ships; it provided for the number, pay, and rations of the officers and crews of the ships; and it stipulated that in the event of peace with Algiers "no farther proceeding [shall] be had under this act." The United States had established a national navy.

The administration entrusted the design, construction, outfitting, and manning of the new ships to the secretary of war, Henry Knox, whose office administered the United States Navy until the appointment of a permanent secretary of the navy in 1798. Knox's liberal interpretation of his instructions from Congress set several precedents for the American navy.

He was determined "that this second commencement of a navy for the United States should be worthy of their national character." He therefore made the crucial decision to build frigates that would "combine such qualities of strength, durability, swiftness of sailing, and force as to render them equal, if not superior, to any frigates belonging to any of the European powers." By this decision Knox stepped beyond a literal reading of the naval act, which ostensibly was directed exclusively at Algiers.

Each of Knox's frigates displaced 300 tons more than the type contemplated by Congress. With frames of Georgia-grown live oak, the ships would last at least a half-century, roughly four times longer than vessels built of less expensive and more readily accessible white oak timber. Because of those modifications the ships could not be launched by 1795, as Knox had optimistically promised, and their total estimated cost soon doubled from the $688,888 in the initial congressional appropriation of June 1794 to $1,152,160 in a congressional report of January 1796. But these were indeed ships "worthy of their national character," and the standard of excellence in material design became the hallmark of the American sailing frigate until the class itself was made obsolete by the steam engine in the 1840s.

Three of the six captains appointed by Knox to command the frigates after supervising their construction—John Barry, Richard Dale, and Thomas Truxtun—praised the secretary of war for "laying down the foundation of our infant navy" with full reference to the maritime experience of Europe, "so as to have the ships best equipped for the service of any that was ever built of the kind."

Barry, Dale, and Truxtun wrote Knox while in Philadelphia, where they were collaborating with a local shipbuilder, Joshua Humphreys. Assisting Humphreys was a family friend of Barry, Josiah Fox, recently arrived from England. Both men knew their trade. Humphreys had designed several frigates for the Continental Navy during the Revolutionary War, and Fox had studied shipbuilding and design on the continent of Europe and in England. In a collaboration of high talent marked by a thoroughly human blend of harmony and acrimony, Humphreys and Fox drew up plans for the four 44s and two 36s ordered by Knox.

Humphreys and Fox designed four extremely powerful frigates. The French offered inspiration "in their great experience in naval architecture; they having cut down several of their seventy-fours to make heavy frigates; making them nearly of the dimensions of those [44-gun frigates] of the United States." The firepower of the American frigates gave their commanders the "power to engage, or not, any ship, as they may think proper; and no ship, under sixty-four [guns], now afloat, but what must submit to them."

To enhance this potent advantage Humphreys planned to sheath the hulls with copper below the waterline. The smoother bottoms would measurably increase the frigates' speed. Coppering also cut costs by eliminating the need to clean fouled bottoms every six months by careening the vessels—laying them on one side in shoal water and scraping the exposed opposite side—an expensive process that could delay an expedition and certainly would "strain the ships exceedingly, and injure the hull and rigging more than can be easily calculated."

Humphreys was building a frigate to outsail any ship it could not outfight. This meant that a Humphreys frigate was the equal of anything afloat except a ship of the line. His technical and operational inspiration was France, a continental power that, unable to fund as large a navy as Britain, relied on powerful frigates to raid and harass rather than try to outbuild the Royal Navy in ships of the line. Humphreys envisioned a multiple role for his frigates, one where speed counted. He envisioned the frigates as commerce raiders as well as combatants. Humphreys therefore laid out not only ships, he set down the strategic essence of the American sailing navy: Fight any ship of your class, even the largest; run free when you have to; be ready to sally forth and pounce at will.

The secretary of war meanwhile labored to breathe life into Humphreys's plan. He hired the key supervisors to direct the actual construction of the American frigates: naval agents, constructors or "master builders," and clerks or comptrollers, at the yards. He displayed a healthy awareness of the potentialities of patronage by distributing "the advantages arising from the operation" to privately owned shipyards in six widely dispersed seaports: Portsmouth in New Hampshire, Boston, New York, Philadelphia, Baltimore, and Norfolk, Virginia. At those yards, Knox hoped to collect the timber, sailcloth, cordage, and cannon from which to fashion and fit out his ships by the end of 1795.

He was to be disappointed by the magnitude of the task, particularly the cutting, finishing, and transportation of the huge twisted branches of Georgia live oak used as frames for the oversize frigates. The "infant navy" therefore remained in gestation as Washington's administration dealt with Britain and Algiers in a policy initiative so successful that the frigates began to appear superfluous by early 1796.

George Washington, his cabinet, and Congress achieved peace with Britain and Algiers by brilliantly using every means at their disposal: economic coercion; a steady military buildup, including construction of a navy; and adept diplomacy. In the late winter of 1793 and early spring of 1794 Congress learned that since the beginning of the Anglo-French war British cruisers operating under a secret order in council had seized more than 250 American merchantmen trading with the French West Indies. Information also reached Congress that the British governor general of Canada had directly threatened the northwestern frontier with an inflammatory speech to the Indian tribes of that area. On 25 March, two days before Washington signed the naval act, an indignant House of Representatives retaliated against

Britain with a thirty-day embargo on all American exports. Sensing that in the long run economic warfare would hurt the United States more than England, Secretary of the Treasury Alexander Hamilton and the Federalists in control of the Senate engineered the appointment of John Jay as a special envoy to Britain charged with negotiating a treaty of amity and commerce. Hamilton's Anglophilic instructions placed only two limits on Jay's discretion: The Franco-American alliance of 1778 could not be directly contravened, and the British West Indies must be opened to American trade.

Jay did not succeed in every respect, but he brought home a treaty, signed in November 1794, that ameliorated some of the Anglo-American grievances. Britain renewed its promise to relinquish the northwest forts and also opened the far distant British East Indies to American merchantmen. London also extended most-favored-nation status to Americans trading in the British home isles. But American trade with the nearby British West Indies remained circumscribed in ships' tonnage and type of cargo, and a host of other old irritants were passed on to international arbitrators. Worst of all, Jay made no headway on neutral rights. He conceded to Britain the right to seize goods bound for France on American merchant vessels, thus abandoning the doctrine that free ships make free goods. His acceptance of restrictions on American trade with the West Indies caused such consternation in the Senate and House that President Washington delayed proclamation of the treaty until 29 February 1796.

The largely partisan uproar over the Jay Treaty obscured several concurrent diplomatic achievements of the second Washington administration that undermined much of the rationale for a navy. By mid-1795 Madrid had learned of the Jay Treaty, and the Spanish foreign minister feared the danger of an Anglo-American alliance to Spanish North American possessions should he realize his own hope of switching from the British to the French side in the European war. Don Manuel de Godoy therefore met with the new American minister, Thomas Pinckney, to negotiate safety for Spain's territorial hostages. The result was an enormously popular treaty granting American farmers free navigation of the Mississippi River and the right to deposit their products at New Orleans for transshipment to foreign ports. The treaty also set a northern boundary for Spanish Florida at 31 degrees north latitude. The delighted Senate unanimously approved the pact on 3 March 1796.

At the same time negotiations with Algiers demonstrated that the link between Barbary and European affairs was unbreakable. By

April 1794 Portugal, which had never been wholly enthusiastic, had ended its truce with Algiers and had begun again to convoy some American merchantmen in the Mediterranean. The dey of Algiers became receptive to American overtures for a peace treaty. News of the dey's change of heart presented the Washington administration with the opportunity to renew negotiations, a task entrusted to a team of American agents headed by David Humphreys, the plenipotentiary in Paris and Lisbon, and Joseph Donaldson and Joel Barlow in Algiers. The negotiations were complex, and a fair amount of bribe money changed hands, but on 2 March 1796—the day after Washington's proclamation of the Jay Treaty and just prior to the Senate's approval of the Pinckney Treaty—the Senate advised ratification of a twenty-two-article treaty with Algiers.

The United States obligated itself to pay a sum of $642,500 immediately and $21,600 annually in naval stores. As a further sweetener, Barlow promised the dey a custom-built frigate. In exchange, the dey pledged an end to Algerine attacks on American shipping, release of captive American seamen, humane treatment of Americans shipwrecked in Algiers in the future, the right to sell captured prizes in Algerine ports, and limited extraterritoriality for American citizens involved in judicial proceedings in Algiers. By the summer of 1796 the captives were free, the frigate *Crescent* was under construction in Portsmouth, and Joel Barlow was eulogizing the dey of Algiers as the "father of justice."

Through the patient diplomacy of several men—Barlow, David Humphreys, the former captives Richard O'Brien and James L. Cathcart, and a novice in Barbary affairs, William Eaton—the second Washington administration also secured treaties with Morocco, Tripoli, and Tunis granting American merchantmen immunity from seizure while transiting the Mediterranean Sea. In all three cases immediate and annual cash payments and the promise of military and naval supplies proved indispensable levers for moving the North African potentates. Although formal Senate approval of the treaty with Tunis was withheld until January 1800, the second Washington administration had effectively reopened the Mediterranean to the American merchant marine after a closure lasting more than ten years.

The president now was compelled to consider the terms of the 1794 naval act, which mandated an end to ship construction once peace was negotiated with Algiers. He tried to nudge Congress in the direction of a permanent national navy. In a brief message of 15 March 1796 Washington conceded his statutory obligation to suspend work on the frigates, but he worried that "the loss which the public would incur might be considerable, from the dissipation of workmen, from certain works or operations being suddenly dropped or left unfinished, and from the derangement in the whole system." Washington was referring to a broad network of interlocking economic activity stretching from the live oak forests of Georgia and the iron foundries of industrialized Europe to the American seaports where the six ships were being assembled. Squandering this naval-industrial resource, which had taken two years of painstaking effort to gather, might not "comport with the public interest."

The president's message hit home in the Senate. Estimating that three frigates could be completed for the $688,888 previously thought sufficient to finish all six ships, the Senate on 28 March 1796 passed a bill authorizing completion of two 44-gun frigates and one mounting thirty-six guns. The House of Representatives concurred on 9 April, and on the 20th George Washington signed the measure that led to the completion a year later of the *United States, Constitution,* and *Constellation,* the first warships of a permanent American navy.

On 4 March 1797 John Adams was inaugurated as the second president of the United States. This citizen of maritime Massachusetts believed in naval power. In 1775 he had written the rules and regulations governing the Continental Navy. As minister to Great Britain immediately after the Revolutionary War he tempered his enthusiasm for a permanent naval service, but as vice president of the United States and president of the Senate he had again been true to himself. On 18 December 1796, in the Senate's response to Washington's final annual message, Adams swore his own fealty to a national navy: "We perfectly coincide with you in [the] opinion that the importance of our commerce demands a naval force for its protection against foreign insult and depredation."

France was now the villain. Relations between the revolutionary allies had deteriorated catastrophically since ratification of the Jay Treaty. The Anglo-American rapprochement, however limited, was widely regarded in France as incompatible with the alliance of 1778. In July 1796 the French decreed that henceforth free ships would not make free goods, thus adopting the traditionally restrictive British interpretation of neutral rights that Americans found inimical to their trading interests. The French then unleashed warships and privateers against American merchantmen in the West Indies, taking more than three hundred American prizes within a year. While President Adams was reviewing the growing crisis amid daily reports of additional captures, he learned that the newly appointed American minister to France, Charles C. Pinckney, had been threatened with arrest and then expelled by the French. The outraged president called a special session of Congress.

In his congressional message of 16 May 1797 John Adams showed his anger with a rhetorical flair reminiscent of his best pre-Revolutionary War writing. The French refusal to receive Pinckney "until we have acceded to their demands without discussion and without investigation is to treat us neither as allies nor as friends, nor as a sovereign state." The United States must take measures to "convince France and the world that we are not a degraded people, humiliated under a colonial spirit of fear and sense of inferiority." He proposed both "a fresh attempt at negotiation" and "effectual measures of defense." He would designate a nonpartisan commission to negotiate all outstanding grievances with France. He would ask Congress for legislation to protect the burgeoning American maritime enterprise, which he broadly defined as stretching along 2,000 miles of coastline and embracing "fisheries, navigation, and commerce." Its protection was vital to the wealth, "strength and resources of the nation."

For the defense of this national treasure Adams proposed a comprehensive scheme molded around a navy. "A naval power, next to the militia, is the natural defense of the United States." The British had made "many formidable transportations of troops from one State to another" during the Revolutionary War. Maritime mobility could be denied to a future enemy by "a moderate naval force, such as would be easily within the present abilities of the Union. . . . Our seacoasts, from their great extent, are more easily annoyed and more easily defended by a naval force than any other. With all the materials our country abounds; in skill our naval architects and navigators are equal to any, and commanders and seamen will not be found wanting." But the president realized that "the establishment of a permanent system of naval defense . . . can not be formed so speedily and extensively as the present crisis demands." He therefore sought immediate congressional authority to permit the arming of merchant vessels "engaged in a lawful foreign commerce." As the next step, he wanted funds "to equip the frigates, and provide such other vessels of inferior force, to take under convoy such merchant vessels as shall remain unarmed." For long-term defense in depth, Adams proposed expanding the existing artillery and cavalry, reorganizing the militia, and "forming a provisional army."

These comprehensive measures, Adams assured the Congress, were intended only to defend American commerce and neutrality. In an echo of Washington's Farewell Address of the previous September, Adams reminded the Congress "that we ought not to involve ourselves in the political system of Europe, but to keep ourselves always distinct and separate from it if we can." Therein lay the rub: "However we may consider ourselves, the maritime powers and commercial powers of the world will consider the United States of America as forming a weight in that balance of power in Europe which never can be forgotten or neglected." The safety of American maritime commerce, in other words, depended as much on the attitudes of European chancelleries as on American diplomatic and naval policies.

Congress responded on 1 July 1797 with an act empowering the president, "should he deem it expedient," to man and employ the frigates *United States*, *Constitution*, and *Constellation* as he saw fit. The measure made no mention of arming merchantmen, but it did ordain that the officers and men "belonging to the navy of the United States" would be governed by the rules and regulations adopted by the Continental Congress on 28 November 1775—the author of which was John Adams.

Work on the three frigates was far advanced by the summer of 1797. On 10 May—six days before the president's pro-navy message—the 44-gun frigate *United States* had been launched in Philadelphia, and Captain John Barry began fitting her out while Congress debated naval policy only a stone's throw away. By 16 June Secretary of War James McHenry could advise the House that the hull of the *United States* was sheathed in copper and the carpenters' work nearly finished. She soon would be "in a situation to receive her masts and stores." She was commissioned on 11 July. Meanwhile the caulkers were sealing the wooden hull of the *Constitution*, also a 44-gun vessel, being built at Boston under the supervision of Captain Samuel Nicholson. The secretary of war thought she would be ready for launching in mid-August.

In Baltimore, Captain Thomas Truxtun had brought the 36-gun *Constellation* to "great forwardness." The frigate's bottom was caulked and finished, the lower deck laid, the other decks nearly completed, and the bowsprit ready to mount. Launching was expected in July, and "from the forward state of the masts, yards, and rigging . . . there is reason to conclude she can be completely fitted for sea in one month after she is launched." The only major items for the three frigates yet to be provided by Congress were guns, military stores, and the laborers' final wages.

It now remained to be seen whether these expensive ships would give teeth to diplomacy or serve instead to accelerate the Franco-American slide into open hostilities, and the latter appears to have been the case. French Foreign Minister Charles Maurice de Talleyrand-Périgord, who had lived for two years as an exile in the United States, was quoted in the American press as saying France had nothing to fear from a nation of debaters who had taken three years to build three frigates. He thought a judicious application of maritime pressure could persuade the Americans to honor the 1778 treaties obligating them to relieve France of responsibility for the carrying trade of the French West Indies while the war with England lasted. As one of Talleyrand's diplomatic agents expressed it: "A little clandestine war, like England made on America for three years, would produce a constructive effect."

To set the desired tone for negotiations with John Adams's three ministers, Talleyrand instructed his own agents to demand a bribe for himself and a large loan for the French government. He was a hedonist for whom such demands were not unusual, and the Americans had not altogether rejected similar propositions in their dealings with the Barbary powers, but the move miscarried badly in 1798.

In early March John Adams learned of Talleyrand's demand for blackmail and of a French decree of 18 January directing the seizure of all ships carrying any English goods, regardless of the ships' national registry. The red-hot Adams fumed that "every effort and every resource should be called into action, which cannot be done, unless there be a formal declaration of war." But the country was not behind him, and he decided to temporize, hoping incidents on the high seas would arouse public opinion.

On 19 March Adams sent a relatively mild message to the House, but Republican opponents of all things Federalist blocked action on his proposals until the House had seen all of the dispatches from Paris. Adams compiled on 3 April, after substituting the letters X, Y, and Z for the real names of Talleyrand's lieutenants. The House immediately printed 1,200 copies for public use, and in the resulting furor over the so-called XYZ Affair the press inflated commissioner Charles C. Pinckney's modest patriotic riposte—"No; no; not a sixpence"—into "Millions for defense but not one cent for tribute."

That hue and cry forced Congress again to deliberate naval affairs in an effort to achieve some decisive policy. Secretary of War

McHenry spurred the debate with a letter to Representative Edward Livingston, a letter that could serve as a model for all subsequent executive explanations to Congress of the inevitability of delays and rising costs in construction of weapons systems. McHenry gave five reasons for the "extraordinary expenditures" associated with the three frigates: the politically expedient decision to build the ships at different locations, the use of large quantities of a scarce and expensive material (live oak), normal inflation in the price of materials and labor during the course of construction, certain unforeseen "losses and contingencies," and the large size of these particular ships.

Size was the key to the secretary's explanation, a remarkable rationale considering the fact that in 1794 the frigates were ostensibly designed to intimidate the Algerines, who had no reliable frigates until the Americans built and gave them the *Crescent*. McHenry told Livingston and the House that because of their large dimensions the three frigates "would possess, in an eminent degree, the advantage of sailing; that, separately, they would be supreme to any single European frigate, of the usual dimensions; that, if assailed by numbers, they would be always able to lead ahead; that they could never be obliged to go into action, but on their own terms, except in a calm; and that, in heavy weather, they would be capable of engaging double deck ships." This succinct justification anticipated the strategy and tactics actually used by the Humphreys's frigates during their operational lifetime, a period running through the War of 1812. It persuaded the House to vote immediately a further appropriation of $392,512 to "equip for sea" and operate the ships for one year.

Flushed with success, McHenry pressed his advantage just as the furor over the XYZ Affair crested. On 9 April he wrote to the chairman of a House "committee for protection of commerce and defence of the country" rhetorically asking how the government could "preserve character abroad, esteem for the Government at home, safety to our sea property, and protection to our territory and sovereignty?"

France now was the enemy, McHenry emphasized. The attacks of its privateers on American shipping gave it "the sweets of plunder" and threatened the United States with "the last degree of humiliation and subjection." Unless the nation took "naval and military measures" it would "exhibit to the world a sad spectacle of national degradation and imbecility." He recommended twenty additional ships of sixteen to twenty-two guns and six single-gun galleys "to serve as convoys, [and] protect our fisheries, coasts, and harbors." The price

tag was $2,010,007. To round out his preparations for war, the sec-
retary sought a distinct navy department, formation of a provisional
army, completion of the coastal fortifications, and domestic sources of
cannon and powder. In case of an "open rupture" with France,
McHenry advised the Congress to authorize the purchase of six ships
of the line in Europe.

Congress responded positively. In a series of acts designed to
put the nation on a war footing, the legislature in April created a
separate Navy Department. In May it authorized twelve 22-gun ships
for the protection of commerce, ten "small vessels . . . equipped as
galleys," and the establishment of foundries to manufacture cannon
for the army and navy. It also authorized the president to seize French
privateers "hovering on the coasts of the United States" and subject
them to prize court proceedings in U.S. district courts. In a final
spurt of belligerency Congress in June suspended all commercial
intercourse with France, concurred in the president's decision to arm
American merchantmen to resist "French depredations," approved
the acquisition of twelve more small warships mounting twenty to
twenty-four guns each, and passed the notorious Alien and Sedition
Acts, which abridged the freedom of speech of both citizens and
European refugees.

In its haste to arm the country the House had ridden roughshod
over the protests of men like Albert Gallatin, a representative from
Pennsylvania, who objected to a separate department because "the
head of it would wish to make it of as great [an] importance as possible," and John Williams of New York, who made a similar prediction and noted a dangerous recent precedent: "Soon after the War
Department was established, we had an Indian war." But war was
precisely what many congressmen wanted: war with a European
power, war with France. George Cabot, a staunch Massachusetts
Federalist, minced no words: "It is unfortunate Congress did not
declare war . . . we have much more to fear from peace than war; that
peace cannot be real, and only leaves open a door by which the
enemy enters."

A formal declaration seemed only a matter of time in the super-
charged Philadelphia summer of 1798, but by early fall the president
had resolved to follow a policy of ambiguity, characterized as "neither
peace nor war." John Adams chose that course because he sensed that
the foreign danger was being eclipsed by a greater domestic one.

Alexander Hamilton personified the evil. For months the former
secretary of the treasury had been lobbying the members of Adams's

own cabinet for an appointment as a major general. That would make him the effective commander of the newly formed Provisional Army since General George Washington would not exercise command until war commenced. Hamilton excluded Republicans from the officer corps, and Adams feared that he would use his politicized army to become the de facto head of the federal government and launch an imperial conquest of Spanish Louisiana. To posterity the president explained his stratagem succinctly, if not without bias:

> I have always cried, Ships! Ships! Hamilton's hobby horse was Troops! Troops! With all the vanity and timidity of Cicero, all the debauchery of Marc Anthony and all the ambition of Julius Caesar, his object was command of fifty thousand men. My object was the defense of my country, and that alone, which I knew could be affected only by a navy.

Simply put, Adams would use an undersize army to disarm Hamilton, diplomacy to win Spanish neutrality, and the navy to fight the French without a formal declaration of war.

To head the navy with which he intended to intimidate France, John Adams selected Benjamin Stoddert, a successful shipping merchant from Maryland. The first secretary of the navy oversaw a small office consisting of a half-dozen clerks in Philadelphia, naval agents at several Atlantic ports, and the "Principal Naval Constructor of the United States," Joshua Humphreys. With this minuscule bureaucracy Stoddert built a fighting navy during his tenure from 18 June 1798 through 31 March 1801.

Stoddert had inherited three frigates nearly ready for action; by the end of 1799 thirty-three ships were in service: five 44s, four 36s, seven 32s, three 24s, seven 20s, four 18s, and three 14s. In addition the department acquired nine galleys for coastal defense and eight revenue cutters from the Treasury Department, bringing the number of vessels of all sizes in the navy to a grand total of fifty, a number that remained fairly constant throughout much of the nineteenth century. Those were all relatively small vessels when compared to the standard British ships of the line, which carried 74 guns.

To officer Stoddert's expanded navy, Congress increased the number of captains from three to twenty-eight and enlarged the other ranks proportionately. By 1801 there were 354 midshipmen in the navy, out of a total estimated number of officers and enlisted men of 5,600. Enlistments were short-term—for one year or for a year plus the remainder of a cruise. Young volunteers seeking victory and glory could readily be found to man vessels generally superior to those of the enemy. It typically took only one week to enlist the complement of a frigate, the largest class of ship in the American navy during the Quasi War.

Stoddert wanted bigger ships; he wanted ships of the line. On 29 December 1798 he recommended the acquisition of twelve 74s to Josiah Parker, chairman of the House Committee on the Naval Establishment. Stoddert crafted a shrewd proposal, one that looked beyond the struggle with France without ignoring it. By adding twelve 74s to the United States Navy, Stoddert contended, "an Invasion of any part of our Country would be rendered so difficult, that it would scarcely be attempted."

The twelve 74s, together with twelve frigates and twenty or thirty smaller ships, would do more than prevent a French invasion of the United States, in Stoddert's opinion. His ship-of-the-line navy would also protect American commerce, help win a quick but "proper peace," and "maintain peace hereafter." The result would be salutary and permanent. "Even France with all her Pride, and all her Heroism, will consult her Interest and avoid war with America, and like other Nations she will discover that it will not only be just, but politic to indulge us in our favorite wish of preserving peace with all the world." Lest his intentions be misconstrued, Stoddert hastened to assure Congress that he was arguing "for the Creation of a Navy sufficient for defence, but not for Conquest." Stoddert said his defensive 74s would "Command our own Coast" rather than the high seas, a nice bit of rhetorical camouflage. The first naval secretary knew full well that a ship of the line by its nature is a blue-water, offensive weapons system.

Congress took the bait in early 1799, but only after Albert Gallatin again cut to the heart of the matter. In his strenuous opposition to the ships of the line he focused on two issues: their purpose and their cost. Josiah Parker's committee and the House as a whole had modified Stoddert's request by moving to build "six ships of war" rather than twelve, but even then the final cost would be a staggering $2.4 million, of which at least $1.4 million would be passed on to subsequent congresses. The funding would require a long-term loan and "a perpetual land tax," both of which Gallatin found distasteful. That heavy burden would surely increase, because the six ships now proposed were merely "an entering wedge." Twelve ships of the line would be the next total sought within the Congress, Gallatin predicted, after which the argument would be made that the extensive

American commerce and long coastline required even more than twelve line-of-battle ships.

Gallatin seriously doubted the effectiveness of navies as protectors of commerce, and he used the debate over the 74s to raise issues that remain unresolved in late-twentieth-century American maritime policy. Of all the European powers, he contended, only Britain "had ever derived any advantage from a navy." By contrast, after the Anglo-Dutch wars of the late 1600s Holland had given up "her powerful navy . . . as more expensive than beneficial" without suffering a significant loss in its overseas carrying trade.

More immediately, Gallatin challenged the efficacy of the American navy in protecting commerce. In 1798 American trade in European waters had been made somewhat less hazardous not by any American naval or diplomatic initiative but by London's reaction to fear of a French invasion of the home islands. "The very measures adopted by Great Britain," Gallatin said, "to prevent that invasion, had the effect, by a complete blockade of the French ports, to detain there both their fleets and their privateers."

Even in the West Indies the congressman found the United States Navy superfluous. "Considering the manner in which our trade had principally suffered in the West Indian seas, by row-boats, and other small vessels, there could be no doubt but the armed private commercial vessels had been of much greater service in preserving our vessels from plunder, than our navy." Nonetheless, Gallatin was willing to sacrifice perfect consistency and concede that construction of six small sloops-of-war—one of the provisions of the bill under consideration—might in fact be desirable "for the purpose of protecting our commerce."

Despite Stoddert's rhetoric Gallatin could not construe the 74s as immediately needed or in any way defensive. The proposal to build ships of the line, he astutely pointed out, "was a project of a general nature. The question is, whether it be proper, at the present time, to lay the foundation of a navy, of a fleet, that might be able, thereafter, to give us a certain weight in relation to European nations; which might be able to cope with the fleets of those nations."

Robert G. Harper of South Carolina made the political riposte. He dismissed Gallatin's cost accounting as "the calculation of a schoolboy, not of a statesman" and said his judgment was "warped on this, as on so many other occasions, by his particular political system," a clear slur on Gallatin's Jeffersonian Republican persuasion. Harper denounced Gallatin's assessment of the international naval balance as "most anti-patriotic" and swore that the advocates of ships of the line aimed "not at dominion, but at defence. To dominion we cannot, and ought not, to aspire. To protect our commerce against that portion of the maritime force of Europe which can be brought to act against us, we can and ought to aspire." The Royal Navy set the standard, according to Harper. It guaranteed Britain not only its commerce but also its independence and "her existence as a nation. Every man, who is the smallest degree versed in history, knows that Great Britain, but for her navy, must long since have been a province of France."

Harper, Parker, and Stoddert triumphed on 11 February 1799. By a vote of 54–42 the House passed the bill to build six 74-gun warships. Their triumph was political rather than logical. Harper's anglicized argument that line-of-battle ships were a defensive necessity for the United States ignored essential geographical differences between Britain's island position next to France and that of the North American continent in relation to Europe. Alfred Thayer Mahan would use very similar terms nine decades later, when he laid conceptual foundations for the twentieth-century U.S. Navy, calling the United States an insular nation dependent on battleships.

Harper also ignored the point that the Royal Navy did America's work by holding French warships in check through a blockade of European ports. As early as June 1798 Henry Knox had observed to President Adams that Britain's fleet was the "only preventative" against an invasion of the Southern states by French ships of war and an invading army staging out of the West Indies. Six American ships of the line could hardly deter an unleashed French fleet, and in the event of revived Anglo-American tension they most certainly could not seriously hope to thwart a British naval attack against the United States. Strategic wisdom, prudence, and economy therefore clearly dictated an asymmetrical naval construction policy in which the United States Navy limited itself to frigates and sloops whose purposes were to convoy American merchantmen, harass French—or British, as the case might be—trade in the West Indies, and on propitious occasions to challenge enemy frigates or sloops in one-on-one duels where the fast American ships, bold captains, ambitious officers, and hot-blooded young crews would prove more than equal to the challenge.

Considerably later, in 1808, when Britain again was the nemesis, John Adams would claim to have understood all of this, for he wrote in exculpation, "I never was fond of the plan of building line-of-battle-ships. Our policy is not to fight squadrons at sea, but to have fast-sailing frigates to scour the seas and make [an] impression on the enemy's commerce; and in this way we can do great things." In the autumn and winter of 1798, however, he had abdicated his naval responsibilities. Stoddert's letters to the president, who was at home in Massachusetts much of the time, went largely unanswered, and in his Second Annual Address of 8 December 1798 Adams left to the "consideration" of Congress the precise "manner" by which the United States should "lay the foundation for an increase of our Navy to a size sufficient to guard our coast and protect our trade." With this carte blanche, as has been seen, Stoddert tried to build a navy that owed far more to Hamilton than to Adams in its emphasis on meeting European fleets. Stoddert conceived of a navy in terms of fleet engagements rather than of commerce raiding, and as a result he was less effective than he might have been.

For all of Benjamin Stoddert's imagination and vision, the brevity of the Quasi War compelled his navy to fight with a patchwork collection of revenue cutters, converted merchantmen, and naval vessels no larger than frigates. That wildly mixed order of battle did not discourage the secretary, however, because, as he observed at the time Congress was debating his proposal for 74s, "the vessels which injure our commerce in the West Indies carry one and two guns." The "most useful" ships to meet those attackers would be ones mounting only four to eight guns. Stoddert's favorite frigate captain, Thomas Truxtun, gave emphasis to the secretary's view: Small warships would have "ten times the chance of a frigate, or any other large ship, in making captures." The secretary therefore felt confident of driving French privateers from the Caribbean once he had seen to his "first care," the guaranteeing of "the security of our own coast."

To protect the vulnerable Atlantic coast and the American merchantmen entering and leaving coastal ports Stoddert restricted almost all of his ships to near-shore operations during the first several months of his campaign, and he showed little patience for captains like Samuel Nicholson of the frigate *Constitution*, who left the Southern coast virtually undefended for an entire month while pressing for a favorable prize court decision in Hampton Roads. Stoddert wanted action. "If our officers cannot be inspired with the kind of zeal & spirit, which will enable us to make up for want of great force, by great activity, we had better burn our ships."

Stoddert's anxious concern for coastal defense in part reflected political reality: The American people would not support a war in distant places if left unprotected and subject to attack and invasion at

home. This political calculus was fundamental to every secretary of
the navy's wartime deployment of limited American forces against
European powers from the Quasi War through the Spanish–American
War to the early stages of World War II. Strategic theory was always
less decisive than the voice of the people.

Stoddert himself was not long hobbled. By 27 October 1798
Captain Truxtun, who had spent the months from July to October
cruising between Cape Henry and Havana in the frigate *Constellation*, advised Stoddert, "With respect to French privateers being on
the coasts of the United States, it is folly to suppose it." They were
"all to the southward" in the Caribbean, which Stoddert now made
his primary theater of operations.

He acted sensibly. United States exports to the West Indian
colonies of European powers had more than doubled between 1794
and 1796. By 1797 over one-third of all American exports—a total of
$24 million worth of goods—were annually shipped to the Caribbean,
where the British had failed to establish supremacy and French privateers roamed freely. In 1797 the French raiders took more than 288
American merchant vessels in the Caribbean alone and 58 others
elsewhere on the high seas.

The threat to American commerce thus came not from the occasional French frigate that would slip through the Royal Navy's European blockade but rather from small vessels—Gallatin's "row
boats"—which lay in hiding ready to pounce on passing ships. Under
those circumstances, Caribbean privateering came increasingly to
bear the hallmarks of piracy: "robbery, destruction, evasion, perjury,
cruelty, and insult." In early 1799, for example, an American merchantman out of New York fiercely defended itself against pirates off
Cuba, killing ten of them, with the result that upon finally being
captured the entire crew of the merchant ship was slaughtered.

That episode was extreme, but the palpable danger facing American merchant vessels in the West Indies was understood in every
seaport of the United States, and the merchants of cities like Boston
began to pressure Stoddert to protect their ships. His initial response
was to provide limited convoys, a policy approved by President Adams, who saw the navy's mission primarily as one of protecting overseas American commerce. But as winter approached and the security
of the Atlantic coast from French attack became every day more
apparent, Stoddert began to plan a major operation.

In December 1798 and January 1799 he ordered every American
naval vessel to the Caribbean "to relieve our commerce, from the

picaroons, and pirates." He divided his fleet into four squadrons, the largest composed of nine vessels commanded by Captain John Barry aboard the 44-gun frigate *United States*. With five vessels, Thomas Truxtun, skipper of the 36-gun frigate *Constellation*, commanded the second largest American squadron in the Caribbean. The two remaining squadrons were much smaller. Captain Stephen Decatur, Sr., commanded the 20-gun converted merchant ship *Delaware* and two cutters. Thomas Tingey commanded a single-ship squadron, his fast-sailing converted merchantman, the 26-gun *Ganges*. Stoddert ordered this armada of some seventeen ships to convoy American merchantmen and drive both privateers and pirates from the Caribbean. The secretary maintained that such a massive American effort would give "little short of perfect security . . . to our commerce in those seas; and that the inhabitants of the hostile islands, may be taught respect, and to fear the power of the United States."

Exercising that power could prove highly tedious, because the principal function of the warships was to convoy merchant vessels. That in turn often involved waiting patiently at a port for long periods while merchantmen arrived, offloaded and took on cargos, and gathered in enough numbers to justify being escorted by one or more naval vessels. But the result was impressive, as the cruise of Alexander Murray's 20-gun converted merchant ship *Montezuma* illustrates. Between 20 September 1798, when she left Baltimore for the Caribbean, and her return in late April 1799, the *Montezuma* convoyed more than a hundred merchantmen within the West Indies, and during her homeward voyage she escorted fifty-seven vessels from Havana to the United States.

Bagging privateers—or even a French frigate if one could be found—was more glamorous work. Captain Stephen Decatur, Sr., himself a privateer in the American service during the Revolutionary War, captured the first American prize of the Quasi War, the French privateersman *La Croyable*, twelve guns, taken after a "pretty long chace [sic]" just off the New Jersey coast on 7 July 1798. *La Croyable* was taken into the U.S. Navy as the schooner *Retaliation*, mounting fourteen guns. She sailed for the Caribbean and was surrendered to a pair of French frigates by her skipper, Lieutenant William Bainbridge, the first of four times that he would give up a ship under his command.

Decatur's aggressiveness set the tone Stoddert wanted for ships' captains of the early United States Navy. That pitch was amplified loudly by Thomas Truxtun in the *Constellation*, who on 9 February

1799 overhauled, outmaneuvered, repeatedly raked, and took as his prize the 36-gun French frigate *L'Insurgente* off Nevis in the Caribbean. Understandably flushed with victory, Truxtun boasted to the secretary of the navy, "The French captain tells me, I have caused a war with France, if so I am glad of it, for I detest things being done by halves." A year later Truxtun disabled the 50-gun frigate *La Vengeance*, the largest French warship in the Caribbean. The defeated captain reported he had encountered a ship of the line.

Such bellicosity exposed a spirit of audacity and independence that promised much for individual officers but often impeded the smooth functioning of the navy as a whole. An officer as proud as Truxtun—and most of the senior officers held similarly exaggerated views of their own worth—did not easily subordinate himself to another officer. For these men, rank and precedence meant infinitely more than material reward, often more than life itself. For that reason Stoddert spent a great deal of time trying to adjudicate the claims to precedence of his senior captains. It required enormous tact and patience to avoid reaching a final decision that would not drive one of them to refuse a command or resign his commission. He would not always succeed.

In the summer of 1799 a prolonged dispute between Truxtun and Silas Talbot, the newly chosen commander of the *Constitution*, led to President Adams's intervention on Talbot's behalf and to Truxtun's subsequent announcement to his officers on the *Constellation* that he had "quit." Thus two of the three operational frigates of the United States Navy—the *Constellation* and *Constitution*—were disabled in the middle of a war by a petty squabble between their commanding officers, and three months passed without a single American frigate visiting the Caribbean.

The unseemly dispute between Talbot and Truxtun was not the only reason that Secretary Stoddert's Caribbean operations came unglued in the middle of 1799. Direction and coordination of fleet movements—"command and control" in today's phrase—is always difficult, and Stoddert was innovating as he went along. He had intended for his ships to remain in the Caribbean until about May 1799, but when they began to trickle north to refit and replace crews whose one-year enlistments were expiring, Stoddert was caught unprepared. By the end of May he was reporting to President Adams that there were "too many of our ships in our ports." His "plan of operations" for the West Indies was becoming "somewhat deranged, and I wish our commerce may not feel the effect."

The lull in Caribbean operations was momentary, and the number of ships ready for action would soon increase dramatically through refitting and additions to the naval list. Two newly constructed frigates—the 30-gun *General Greene* and the 28-gun *Boston*—and the recently captured *L'Insurgente* would be outfitted by the end of July. Autumn would see two other new frigates become operational: the 28-gun *Adams* and the 30-gun *John Adams*. Buoyed by this growth, Stoddert toyed with showing the flag in European waters. He knew that the president was "very solicitous to strike some strokes in Europe." But by the end of July the West Indies trade had again asserted its primacy in his mind.

He sketched for the president a commercial and strategic view of the Caribbean that transcended the immediate war with France and anticipated in some ways the hemispheric reach of James Monroe and John Quincy Adams two decades later:

> my impression of the vast importance of securing the West India trade now and laying a good foundation for it in the future is so strong, that I almost consider it treason to employ vessels elsewhere which can be employed in the West Indies while a single French privateer remains to infest those seas.

For the remainder of the war he kept as many ships as possible continuously on station in pursuit of those privateers and as escorts for convoys of American merchantmen. The duty proved frustrating and dangerous; privateers were hard to find and difficult to capture; yellow fever could decimate the crew of any warship that stayed in port any longer than a very few days.

The precise impact of United States naval operations on privateers in the Caribbean during the Quasi War is difficult to determine. Losses of American merchantmen in 1800 nearly equaled the number lost to Caribbean privateers in 1798, when the navy had barely begun to fight. Yet in 1800 the navy captured fifty-nine French attackers, as against only twenty-seven in 1799. By another measurement the Americans clearly were winning: in 1799–1800 they lost 159 merchant vessels to the French, but in the same period they took eighty-six French prizes and recaptured from French prize crews 100 merchant ships. This American naval ascendancy in the Caribbean was reflected in the sharp fall of maritime insurance rates in the same period. Without the naval war against the French commerce raiders, United States merchant vessels would have traversed the Caribbean only at great risk between 1798 and the peace convention of 30 September 1800. The thwarting of commerce raiders is the defensive side of *guerre de course*, and it has remained an important ingredient of American naval strategy ever since the Quasi War.

══════

Throughout America's first undeclared war John Adams had sought peace, but only if he could "get rid of the Treaties of 1778 with France, which had hung like a dead weight on this Country . . . and rendered it a party to all the disputes between Great Britain and France." Neutrality during European wars and free trade as a neutral nation were his goals, as they were of Presidents George Washington and Thomas Jefferson. The judicious use of limited force was his means, and a French change of policy was his deliverance.

On 15 February 1799 Adams learned that France had repealed its decree of January 1798. Widespread attacks on American shipping were no longer authorized. French nationals in the West Indies ignored the change of heart in Paris and continued to prey on American shipping, but Adams felt vindicated in principle. He was also acutely aware of two dissonant and conflicting themes being sounded at home: the growing Republican and mercantile demand for peace, and the war cries of the growing Provisional Army, stimulated by Federalist backers of Alexander Hamilton, whom Adams distrusted as a potential tyrant. He decided that peace posed less danger than the increasing militarization of the nation, and on 18 February 1799 sent a mission to France. The resulting Treaty of Mortefontaine terminated the military alliance of 1778 and reaffirmed the American position on neutral rights. In exchange, the United States dropped all claims against France for maritime damages.

══════

In the Quasi War the Americans had blunted the French attack in the Caribbean with vessels much smaller than 74s. American frigates had successfully challenged French counterparts, and the United States frigates and a collection of converted merchant vessels had made the West Indies relatively safe for American merchant shipping. In all of this activity the hidden ally was the Royal Navy of Great Britain, whose blockade of Europe denied the French navy ready movement to the Caribbean.

Had Britain and France not been at war in the 1790s, there would have been no Franco-American conflict over trade. The issue was one of disparate views about what a neutral merchantman may carry in wartime without becoming subject to capture by a belligerent's warships or privateers. The French finally resolved that issue by accepting the American position that free ships make for free goods. That concession led to a peace which in turn deprived Britain of its quasi-ally, the United States. Whether Britain was prepared to tolerate free trade between its enemy, France, and the United States remained to be seen as the Republicans came to office in 1801.

3

"Strength and Bravery in Every Sea"

1801 – 1815

In March 1801 Thomas Jefferson entered the presidency as the legatee of John Adams. He inherited peace with France and six active frigates. Together, these gave him the opportunity to realize an old dream of extending vigorous naval protection over American commerce in the Mediterranean without endangering the security of the United States. For six years he pursued an active policy of naval diplomacy at the crossroads of European-American-Islamic trade, and his policies set precedents that still influence the United States Navy almost two centuries later.

The rulers of Tripoli, Tunis, and Algiers had been demanding an increasing amount of tribute—in money and naval stores—for several years, and by January 1800 the Adams administration was planning to send a naval squadron to the Mediterranean as soon as peace with France released ships committed to Caribbean and West Indies operations. The Treaty of Mortefontaine came too late for Adams, but it gave Jefferson the chance to follow through. The president made his intentions quite clear: "[W]e mean to rest the safety of our commerce on the resources of our own strength and bravery in every sea." The acting secretary of the navy explained the administration's policy vividly in early April: "It is conceived . . . that such a squadron Cruizing in view of the Barbary Powers will have a tendency to prevent them from seizing on our Commerce, whenever Passion or a Desire of Plunder might Incite them thereto."

The danger to American Mediterranean commerce was clear and present. Reports received from William Eaton, the United States consul to Tunis, and Richard O'Brien, the consul general in Algiers, persuaded Secretary of State James Madison that Tripoli entertained "hostile designs against the United States." Convinced that war with Tripoli was imminent, and fearful that "the contagion" had spread to Tunis and Algiers, Madison advised Eaton and O'Brien that a naval squadron commanded by Captain Richard Dale was on the way. Madison's explanation of the administration's rationale perfectly encapsulated the empiricism, realism, and practicality—perhaps the opportunism—of the great but enigmatic president whom he served as alter ego:

> The policy of exhibiting a naval force on the coast of Barbary has long been urged by yourself and the other consuls. The present moment is peculiarly favorable for the experiment, not only as it is a provision against an immediate danger, but as we are now at peace and amity with all the rest of the world, and the force employed would, if at home, be at nearly the same expense, with less advantage to our mariners.

Madison and his chief were also moved to act by an extraordinary episode involving Captain William Bainbridge of the 32-gun converted merchantman, the U.S.S. *George Washington*. While delivering tribute to Algiers as provided for by the treaty of 1796, Bainbridge had submitted to the dey's demand for the American warship to carry the dey's own tribute to the sultan of Turkey at Constantinople. Madison learned of that humiliation in April, and his outrage underscored the difference between the relatively common raids on merchant vessels and the rare but much more serious affronts to naval vessels: "The sending to Constantinople [of] the national ship of war the *George Washington*, by force, under the Algerine flag, and for such a purpose," the secretary advised O'Brien, "has deeply affected the sensibility, not only of the President, but of the people of the United States." The transgression was "of so serious a nature" as to make imperative some future demand for "a vindication of the national honor."

Commodore Dale—the honorary title denoted command of a squadron, not permanent rank in the navy—thus sailed for deeply troubled waters with what the president disingenuously called "a squadron of observation." Dale's orders, as Jefferson himself noted, included the "strict command" for all hands "to conduct themselves towards all friendly Powers with the most perfect respect and good order." The United States, acting Secretary of the Navy Samuel Smith reminded his squadron commander, was "at peace with all the world" and wished to remain that way. Smith hoped that Dale would find the Barbary Powers "tranquil" upon his arrival at Gibraltar, in which case he was to deliver some of the treaty-stipulated tribute to the rulers of Algiers, Tunis, and Tripoli. The flagship *President* carried $40,000 for this purpose, with "timber & other stores for at least one year's annuity" soon to follow on the *George Washington*.

Payment of tribute was one thing, the acting secretary cautioned Dale, but an exchange of salutes by cannon, the normal courtesy observed by host countries and visiting warships of friendly powers, was quite another. Dale must "be careful not to solicit the honor of a salute from any of those [Barbary] Powers; if you do, they will exact a barrel of Powder for every gun they fire." If he could work his way around these peculiar diplomatic shoals, Dale was to circumnavigate the Mediterranean by sailing east from Tripoli to Egypt, then northeast along the Syrian coast into the Aegean Sea, west to the Adriatic, and around the Italian coast, touching finally at the French Mediterranean port of Toulon, where Smith authorized crews' liberty with the elliptically suggestive observation that a visit to the French city "will be instructive to your young men."

Beneath this velvet lay iron. If upon his arrival at Gibraltar Dale found that the Barbary Powers and the United States had declared war on each other, the commodore was to distribute his "force in such manner . . . as best to protect our commerce & chastise their insolence—by sinking, burning or destroying their ships and Vessels wherever you shall find them." Smith sent Dale a North African naval order of battle showing that only Algiers possessed any significant strength, while the forces of Tunis and Tripoli were "contemptible & might be crushed with any one of the Frigates under your command." Dale was expected to blockade the principal port of any Barbary Power at war with the United States, stationing his ships in a position "to prevent any thing from going in or coming out." If he had warships to spare, which was unlikely in light of the havoc he was expected to wreak with only four fighting platforms, Dale could convoy groups of American merchant vessels to safety across the Mediterranean.

Samuel Smith's guidelines for responding to any European infringement on American neutral rights differed dramatically from the violent reaction expected of Dale in hostile encounters with the Barbary Powers. As a nation, the United States had "suffered as much as any other by the abuse of Neutral rights." While the Jefferson administration hoped neutral rights could be "more justly defined and efficaciously protected," it understood that Europe was badly divided over the rights of neutrals and the legitimate means by which navies of nonbelligerent nations could defend those ill-defined rights. The president and his advisers clearly did not wish to go to war over the issue at that time.

For Dale, this restraint meant permitting the "search of any Merchant Vessel under your convoy [by] a Public armed ship of any Nation." Smith notably did not stipulate that the nation whose naval vessel insisted on searching's Dale escorted merchantmen be at war, a curiously broad concession. Nor did he instruct Dale on whether the object of the search was to be limited to allegedly contraband cargos or if the boarding could include the favorite British practice of searching for British subjects and impressing them into the Royal Navy. But Smith did draw the line at European naval vessels. The right of visit and search was "not to extend to the armed Vessels of any of the Barbary Powers, or the Privateers of any Nation." Should a Barbary vessel or a European privateer attempt to search a vessel under American naval escort, Dale was to resist with force. Moreover, the commodore was not under any circumstance to suffer his "own ships to be entered—or your men examined or taken out, at sea, by any person or power whatsoever." Dale was ordered "to resist such attempt to your uttermost, yielding only to Superior force, and surrendering, if overcome, your Vessel & men, but never your men without your Vessel."

Those instructions of Samuel Smith to Richard Dale of 20 May 1801 established guidelines that would govern American naval operations during the Barbary Wars of the first Jefferson administration, but they reached well beyond the combat of 1801–1807 and well beyond the Mediterranean Sea. They in fact laid down the principles for all routine American naval operations in the nineteenth century— in the Mediterranean, the Indian Ocean, the Pacific Ocean, the South Atlantic, and the Caribbean. They therefore must rank as a major American state paper.

Smith's orders set as the first goal of the navy the protection of American merchant vessels from interference by third- and fourth-rate powers. They decreed that in wars against such powers the blockade of ports would be the American strategy of choice, followed by the resolute seizure or destruction of the weaker powers' ships, whether armed or not. For that purpose a solitary American frigate would usually suffice, because in relation to the naval craft of the nation under attack the United States warship was faster, more heavily armed, and more smartly handled. Non-European peoples and sailors, to judge from Dale's orders, were somehow inferior and deserving of less respect than those of Europe.

Smith's directive repudiated the North Africans' way of taxing offshore trade and fighting at sea, opprobriously branding it piracy. At the same time the secretary incongruously condoned the payment of tribute extorted by the North African threat of renewed attacks on American commerce. Finally, the orders explained that America's national honor could be bent if the alternative was war with a European power. Only one item in the navy's inventory was sacrosanct under every set of circumstances: the crewmen, who must never be given up without the ship. Flawless execution of those intricate orders in the volatile North African political climate of the early 1800s would prove impossible, as Dale and his successors learned.

The commodore arrived at Gibraltar on 1 July 1801 with his flagship, the 44-gun frigate *President;* two lighter frigates, the 36-gun *Philadelphia* and 32-gun *Essex;* and one much smaller ship, the 12-gun schooner *Enterprise.* He learned that Tripoli had declared war on the United States as anticipated, but the United States had not yet passed its own declaration of war. In this no man's land Dale set about trying to do too much with too little. He attempted to maintain surveillance of Tripolitan cruisers at Gibraltar, intimidate Algiers and Tunis with a quick show of force offshore, convoy American merchantmen, and blockade the port of Tripoli. His blockaders frequently had to leave station and return to Malta for fresh water or go to Gibraltar for provisions and stores. That the British allowed Dale to use Gibraltar as his base of operations was fortunate, because American resupply ships refused to enter the Mediterranean.

The geographical overextension of the four-ship squadron soon became apparent, and by the middle of August 1801 Dale was advising the secretary of the navy that an effective blockade of Tripoli would require constant patrol by two frigates and two sloops. He asked for a specially constructed small vessel "to carry a Bomb to heave a few shells in the Town now & then." He also wanted authority to attack armed Tripolitan cruisers and capture them as prizes. The commitment to force was leading to escalation.

While satisfied that Dale's squadron had momentarily "dispelled the danger" posed to American shipping by Tripoli, the president thought he needed congressional authorization to initiate unspecified "measures of offense" for a long-term solution. Thus far Jefferson had limited Commodore Dale to blockading Tripoli and repelling Tripolitan attacks on American warships and merchant vessels. With the imminent expiration of the one-year enlistments of Dale's sailors and a rotation of ships in the Mediterranean unavoidable, the president and Congress took the next step. On 6 February 1802 Congress recognized the existence of a state of war with Tripoli and authorized "acts of precaution or hostility," including the taking of prizes by warships and the outfitting of American privateers to attack Tripolitan shipping. After eight months the Tripolitan *guerre de course* was now bilateral.

The second commodore, Richard W. Morris, sailed to the Mediterranean with a stronger squadron of five frigates and a schooner, but he failed to concentrate all his attention on Tripoli. He diluted his blockade by providing convoys to American merchant ships, and he showed the flag off Morocco, Algiers, and Tunis. None of this dispersed activity contradicted his orders, which directed him to "make such a distribution of the force under your command, as may appear . . . the best adapted to the accomplishment of the views of [the] government." But the administration wanted the war with Tripoli pressed to an early and favorable conclusion, and in June 1803 Secretary of the Navy Robert Smith relieved Morris and ordered him home. A naval court of inquiry censured the commodore for "inactive and dilatory conduct," and he was dismissed from the service.

The stakes of commanding the Mediterranean Squadron were rising when the administration found a better man for the job in the spring of 1803. Edward Preble of Maine was driven by a hunger for military glory. Described by a sailor who resigned from the navy rather than serve under him as "cross, peevish and ill-tempered, surly and proud," Preble stood seventh on the list of the ten captains in the navy in 1803. As an officer in the Massachusetts state navy during the Revolutionary War, he had distinguished himself by boarding and capturing a loyalist privateer with a handful of men in the dark of night. In the Quasi War he had sailed the frigate *Essex* to the Indian Ocean for a year-long cruise escorting American merchantmen. The *Essex* became the first United States naval vessel to round the Cape of Good Hope, but as a result of the voyage Preble missed the chance to capture French prizes in the Caribbean and the West Indies. His record therefore was solid but not stellar when Secretary of the Navy Smith selected him for the choice Mediterranean command.

Preble arrived at Gibraltar in September 1803 on his flagship, the 44-gun frigate *Constitution*, and temporarily joined forces with the remnants of the Morris squadron commanded by John Rodgers. Together they blockaded the coast of Morocco, persuading the sultan to reaffirm the treaty of 1786 with the United States and to halt the attacks on American shipping, which endangered Preble's line of communications. Preble then turned his attention eastward, hoping quickly to end the war with Tripoli. He learned to his chagrin that on 31 October the 36-gun frigate *Philadelphia*, commanded by Captain William Bainbridge, had run aground in a chase outside the harbor of Tripoli. Bainbridge had meekly surrendered his ship and crew before taking a single casualty, thereby cutting Preble's two-frigate force in half. "Would to God," the irate Preble wrote to Secretary Smith, "that the Officers and crew of the *Philadelphia*, had one and all, determined to prefer death to slavery."

Left with only the *Constitution*, three 12-gun schooners, and two 16-gun brigs, Preble felt humiliated, impotent, and endangered. He believed he had a smaller force than had either Dale or Morris, and he exaggerated Tripoli's strength at ten times what it had been the previous year. The *Philadelphia*, now refloated and in the hands of Tripolitans, presented a formidable danger to American warships and merchant vessels. Preble's own deep-draft ships could not enter the harbor to neutralize the *Philadelphia*, but in December Lieutenant Stephen Decatur, Jr., skipper of the 12-gun *Enterprise*, captured an Ottoman ketch allegedly in the service of Tripoli. Remembering his own boarding of an anchored loyalist privateer two decades earlier, Preble renamed his prize the *Intrepid*, disguised her as a Tripolitan craft, and sent her into Tripoli harbor under the command of Decatur. On the night of 16–17 February 1804 Decatur boarded and burned the *Philadelphia* at her moorings. He escaped without losing a man. British Admiral Horatio Nelson lauded Decatur's strike as "the most bold and daring act of the age." He was promoted to captain at the age of twenty-five, to this day the youngest American ever to hold that rank.

The navy had found a swashbuckling hero, but Preble and the administration still had Tripoli on their hands. The feisty commodore promised to "take Tripoly [sic] or perish in the attempt." To ensure success he wanted to beef up his squadron with shallow-draft gunboats and mortar boats, the former to beat back the numerous Tripolitan gunboats defending the harbor, and the latter to lob shells or bombs into the walled city. With the addition of six gunboats and two bomb ketches borrowed from the Neapolitan government, Preble began his offensive on 3 August 1804. The *Constitution* stood offshore and fired into the city and surrounding fortifications; the brigs and schooners provided some general covering fire from deep water; and the gunboats charged in after their Tripolitan counterparts. Stephen Decatur again showed the way, personally accounting for two of the three Tripolitan gunboats taken on the opening day of the campaign. By 9 September Preble was still hammering at Tripoli when a larger squadron commanded by Commodore Samuel Barron arrived from the United States to relieve him.

The blockade and intermittent bombardment of Tripoli continued under Barron and his successor, John Rodgers. Meanwhile the American navy agent William Eaton, seven United States Marines, and some four hundred men of decidedly mixed nationality marched overland from Egypt across 600 miles of Libyan desert in an attempt to topple the pasha of Tripoli by direct assault. On 27 April 1805 they captured the key port of Derna with the aid of Lieutenant Isaac Hull, in command of the *Argus*, *Nautilus*, and *Hornet*. The pasha counterattacked in May, and Eaton was saved from being overrun only by the guns of Hull's small ships. The pasha now realized that Rodgers could complete Preble's work and seize Tripoli with a reinvigorated naval attack, but he admonished Rodgers to "recollect I have upwards of three hundred of your countrymen in my hands; and I candidly tell you that, if you persevere in driving me to the last extremity, I shall retire with them to a castle about ninety miles in the interior of the country, which I have prepared for their confinement and my own security." William Bainbridge and the crew of the *Philadelphia* had become hostages in a deadly game that the United States could not win without paying the pasha's price: $60,000 in ransom. A treaty exchanging the prisoners for money was signed on 10 June 1805.

The Jefferson administration's resort to ransom for hostages signified its reluctant conclusion that force alone could not bring the war with Tripoli to a swift and favorable termination. The squadron would remain in the Mediterranean for two more years, trying to plug holes in the North African dike, but the effort had lost its spark. Within the Navy Department there now was concern that since Preble, Barron, and Rodgers had neither "seen the white's of the enemy's eye" nor returned "covered with laurels," the navy would begin to "lose in popularity." Within the administration as a whole, apprehension was rising over an ominous deterioration in Anglo-American relations, which became so acute in 1807 that all warships were recalled from the Mediterranean.

America's first experiment with maintaining a "naval presence" overseas thus ended with a whimper rather than a bang, but the recall of 1807 was a suspension rather than a cancellation of the policy. Immediately after the War of 1812 Jefferson's Republican successors—among whom was James Madison, who had been present at the creation of the policy—revived it and spread it to the four corners of the earth. Projected naval presence remained the operational mainstay of the United States Navy until 1898. The brief exception was during the Civil War years, when the officers and men of the navy were again called home, this time to fight one another.

The six years (1801–1807) during which the American frigate navy waged war against the Barbary powers witnessed two monumental shifts in the balance of power—one in North America and the other on the Atlantic Ocean. Each was destined to alter the focus and intent of Jefferson's foreign and naval policies.

In the summer of 1801 the administration received bad news: France and England had made peace; Spain had retroceded the vast Louisiana territory to France; and a French army was en route to the Western Hemisphere to suppress a rebellion in Santo Domingo and then head north to occupy New Orleans and control the Mississippi River. The 900,000 Americans living west of the Alleghenies faced the prospect of a strong European nation restricting their navigation of the great waterway which, as Madison put it, "is to them everything. It is the Hudson, the Delaware, the Potomac and all the navigable rivers of the Atlantic States formed into one stream." The president was equally forthright: The moment that France took possession of New Orleans, "we must marry ourselves to the British fleet and nation." In January 1803 he sent a fellow Virginian, James Monroe, to France with instructions to spur along a flagging effort to buy New Orleans.

Napoleon Bonaparte meanwhile was reconsidering his own imperial schemes. His army in Santo Domingo was being ravaged by guerrilla attacks and yellow fever, and the granary of Louisiana began to appear a superfluous liability. The drilling and killing fields of Europe beckoned again, and he started to plan renewed war with England and its continental allies. He dumped the entire Louisiana territory—828,000 square miles of land—on the astounded Americans for $15 million, a cost of three cents an acre. The United States doubled its size in one stroke, and in the words of the American minister at Paris, Robert Livingston, "from this day the United States take their place among the powers of the first rank." To Jefferson the acquisition meant "an empire for liberty" such as man had not "surveyed since the creation." For the balance of power in North America it meant that the United States faced no powerful enemies between the Alleghenies and the Rocky Mountains. Its continental security was unprecedented in scope. Conversely, the withdrawal of Napoleon's army from the West Indies in effect increased the overall British military strength in the Caribbean, an enhancement the United States could not welcome, as France and Great Britain resumed war in May 1803.

For two years neither side seriously assaulted American commerce, and American merchants made enormous profits carrying goods between the continent of Europe and French and Spanish colonies in the West Indies—a trade normally monopolized by the mother countries in peacetime. Then, at midday on 21 October 1805, outside the Spanish port of Cadiz, off Cape Trafalgar, the naval balance in the Atlantic shifted to the Royal Navy, where it would remain until the end of the age of sail. About 11:00 A.M. on that day, in the cabin of his 100-gun three-decked flagship H.M.S. *Victory*, Vice Admiral Horatio Lord Nelson prayed for "a great and glorious victory" and after praying returned to the quarterdeck to direct the fleet engagement he had forced upon the combined French and Spanish fleets under Vice Admiral Pierre de Villeneuve. Nelson's goal was to "annihilate" the enemy by destroying or capturing at least twenty ships of the line. He took eighteen that day, and in the blood bath lost his own life to a sharpshooter firing from the rigging of a French ship. But his colossal achievement put a final end to Napoleon's hope of invading England.

After Trafalgar Bonaparte could win decisive military victories only on land, never at sea. He could attack England only indirectly, by excluding its commerce from the continent of Europe. In 1806 and 1807 he therefore issued the Berlin and Milan decrees establishing the "continental system" by which he hoped to strangle England's export trade, bring it to the brink of financial collapse, and so destroy the fiscal basis of the Royal Navy. His device was to discourage neutral ships from stopping at English ports by threatening to seize them if they subsequently entered a European port under his control.

The continental system hurt American exporters and irritated the administration, but it was less disruptive to shipping or insulting to the national honor than the British violations of neutral rights that followed Trafalgar. At issue was a fundamental difference in the view of belligerent and neutral rights held in London and Washington, a disagreement that dated back to the British Rule of 1756 ordaining that trade not open to a nation in peacetime could not be opened during a war. As a nonbelligerent in the prolonged Anglo-French wars the United States could profit by carrying goods between European ports and European colonies, especially ones in the West Indies. Until just before Trafalgar, Britain tolerated such trade if the cargo vessel "broke" its voyage by touching at an American port and paying duties to convert the cargo into "free goods," that is, the goods of a free or neutral nation.

In May 1805, in a case involving the captured American brig *Essex*, a British admiralty judge declared that such a "break" in a voyage was not evidence of good faith, that the voyage was in fact "continuous," and the ship and cargo hence were subject to seizure under the Rule of 1756. Following Trafalgar the British implemented that decision by stationing cruisers outside American ports in a near-blockade of the coast. Furthermore, a series of orders in council beginning in May 1806 established partial blockades of Europe's coast. The Americans protested these as illegal—or "paper"—because not rigidly enforced by ever present ships of the Royal Navy. In 1807 London again tightened the screws by prohibiting neutral vessels from trading with European ports under French control unless they had previously passed through English ports, where they would be taxed.

As if those restrictions were not enough, the British fully outraged American sensibilities by the practice of impressment. Holding that allegiance was inalienable, Britain denied Englishmen the right of renouncing their loyalty to England. Thus, any British sailor who fled a British warship for an American merchant vessel could be forcibly retrieved by a roving Royal Navy crew, often to be hanged for desertion as a warning to other restless souls. Since country of birth was often impossible to prove, and since Americans and Britons were often largely indistinguishable from one another, the British naval officers interpreted their orders liberally and "impressed" a great many Americans into the Royal Navy. By 1812 James Monroe estimated that 6,257 Yankees had been impressed into the Royal Navy since 1803, and the British conceded at least 1,600.

Britain was fighting for its survival; its weapon was the Royal Navy, and the navy swallowed 10,000 recruits a year. Impressment therefore seemed a regrettable necessity to the British admiralty. Jefferson detested the affront, and Madison condemned it as "anomalous in principle, . . . grievous in practice, and . . . abominable in abuse." Still, as Samuel Smith's orders to Commodore Dale showed, the administration would allow even convoyed merchantmen to be searched if such a genuflection would prevent war.

Jefferson was in a tough spot, one far tougher after Trafalgar than any John Adams had known during the Quasi War. Adams had enjoyed several luxuries denied to Jefferson: a war fought in nearby waters, an enemy that could not dominate the seas, an unspoken but effective alliance with Britain, a political party pressing for naval expansion, and a secretary of the navy who favored construction of ships of the line. By contrast, Jefferson faced the mistress of the seas alone, and he headed a party committed to naval retrenchment. When challenged by much weaker powers in the Mediterranean he could and did use his frigates and smaller ships imaginatively in defense of American commerce, but he was prevented from effectively challenging Britain at sea by his own preoccupation with the trans-Mississippi west, by Republican opposition to naval expansion, and by the sheer magnitude of the Royal Navy. Thus far he had let matters drift, but the audacious attack of H.M.S. *Leopard* on the U.S.S. *Chesapeake* brought the European war into his backyard.

On 22 June 1807, about 10 miles off the mouth of Chesapeake Bay, the 56-gun British ship *Leopard* intercepted the 36-gun American frigate *Chesapeake*, flagship of Commodore James Barron, en route to assume command of the United States squadron in the Mediterranean. Captain S. P. Humphreys of the *Leopard* carried orders from the commander-in-chief of the British North American station requiring any British captain who encountered the *Chesapeake* to search her for deserters. Desertion of British sailors and subsequent enlistment on American warships was all too common, especially around Norfolk, Virginia, where a Royal Navy squadron including two or three 74s lay at anchor in June 1807. The British ships, recently joined by the *Leopard*, procured fresh water and provisions while keeping an eye on a pair of armed French vessels that had sought refuge in the same neutral harbor. It was general knowledge that some of the British sailors had shipped aboard the *Chesapeake*. Humphreys therefore had good reason for hoisting anchor and tagging along with the *Chesapeake* until she was in international waters. He then hailed her and sent aboard a messenger demanding to search the American warship for deserters.

Barron was incensed but unprepared. He had commanded a frigate in the Mediterranean under Commodore Dale, so he knew full well the administration's standing orders that a captain must not surrender his men without also surrendering his ship. But Barron had been tardy in coming aboard the *Chesapeake* and had shown little interest in the condition of the ship, apparently preferring to leave her readiness in the hands of her acting commanding officer, Master Commandant Charles Gordon. As a result, the gun deck was littered with gear—lumber, sails, and cables—and the frigate was far from battle ready when the British messenger presented Humphreys's disconcerting demand. Barron sent him back with the disingenuous reply that he knew of no deserters on board and that in any event he had orders not to allow "the crew of any ship that I command to be mustered by any other but their own officers." After observing a great deal of activity aboard the *Leopard,* it finally dawned on Barron "that it was possible they were serious." He told Gordon to order the crew to battle stations "with as little noise as possible" while he stalled for time. To no avail: *Leopard* "commenced a heavy fire, which did great execution."

The *Chesapeake* took twenty-two shots in her hull and sustained irreparable damage to her main and fore masts. In less than twenty minutes the proud frigate had become a bloody and crippled wreck. Barron struck his colors, permitted the search and removal of four crewmen, and pleaded with Humphreys to take the *Chesapeake* as a prize of war. The British officer refused to compound what was already a warlike act. He returned to Virginia waters, leaving Barron with three men killed and eighteen wounded, including himself.

The hapless commodore had to bring his crippled ship back to Norfolk, past the *Leopard* and the rest of the anchored British squadron. He very soon faced a preliminary court of inquiry, which decided that during the attack he had "manifested great indecision, and a disposition to negotiate, rather than a determination bravely to defend his ship." Armed with this finding, Secretary of the Navy Robert Smith convened a general court-martial which in May 1808 found Barron guilty of not clearing his ship for action when an engagement appeared probable. The court sentenced him to suspension from duty without pay for five years.

The sight of what American naval officers described as "the late United States' frigate Chesapeake" limping into Hampton Roads on 23 June 1807 and disgorging her dead and wounded inflamed the local population. An angry mob destroyed two hundred water casks earmarked for the British squadron. Citizens' meetings unanimously agreed to cease all intercourse with the British warships. Captain Stephen Decatur, commanding officer of the Norfolk Navy Yard, readied a dozen gunboats to prevent the thirsty British from carrying out their threats to obtain water by force. The British commander provocatively moved his squadron from outlying Lynnhaven Bay into Hampton Roads and challenged Decatur with a threat to take the *Chesapeake* and overpower a French frigate, the *Cybele,* undergoing repairs at Norfolk. Decatur shifted the two warships to a mooring protected by coastal batteries and assured the secretary of the navy that he was ready to repel any British attack. None came, but for a few days the unrepentant British did compel all merchant ships entering Hampton Roads to heave to and submit to inspection.

Word of the "British Outrage" against the American warship meanwhile spread rapidly, fanning patriotic anger in every city and uniting the people as no British trespass against merchant shipping could possibly have done. Samuel Smith, now a senator from Maryland, reported the bitter mood of mercantile Baltimore to the president: "There appeared but one opinion—War—in case satisfaction is not given."

The president, however, was resolved upon a patient policy blending diplomatic protest with prudent defense. Thus the cabinet on 2 July approved the symbolic gesture of sending the 12-gun schooner *Revenge* to England with instructions for Minister James Monroe to seek satisfaction. In the next few weeks the administration mobilized part of the Virginia militia, armed coastal fortifications, drew up plans for an invasion of Canada, ordered Congress to convene on 26 October, and protectively recalled all overseas American merchant and naval vessels—thereby interrupting the campaign against Barbary until after the War of 1812.

Jefferson was mildly optimistic about negotiating a settlement, but both he and Madison were determined to achieve "reparation for the past, and security for the future." They therefore included in their demand for redress an insistence that the British government entirely abolish the practice of impressment aboard American merchant vessels on the high seas, a concession the British could not make in mid-1807.

On 7 July of that year—the very day after Madison drafted Monroe's instruction—Napoleon and Tsar Alexander I had signed the treaties of Tilsit ending hostilities between France and Russia. England now stood alone against Bonaparte, and British opinion hard-

ened toward the Americans, whom Britons saw as waxing prosperous
on the high seas by virtue of England's indulgence. The so-called
rights of the neutral upstart could not be honored at the cost of
prolonging a war for national survival. As the former minister to
Spain, David Humphreys, noted when informing Jefferson of the
ominous mood in London: "To maintain the naval superiority or perish as a nation, is the prevalent doctrine of the day." Impressment
therefore became the rock upon which negotiations foundered, and
Jefferson and Madison were largely to blame.

The error lay not in insisting on the abolition of impressment but
in linking the practice with the attack on the *Chesapeake*. As Minister
James Monroe explained from London, it was diplomatically "im-
proper to mingle" other examples of British naval infringements on
American neutrality and sovereignty "with the present more serious
causes of complaint." But he did not persuade the president or secretary of state to disentangle the discrete issues and as a result formulation of an acceptable British apology for the attack on the
Chesapeake was delayed until 1811. By that time the interminably
prolonged Anglo-American dispute over neutral rights on the high
seas and the alleged British incitement of the Indians on the northwest border had made war imminent.

The *Chesapeake–Leopard* affair produced an immediate effect
on Jeffersonian naval and maritime policy in 1807. The American
frigates were withdrawn from the Mediterranean, and on 22 December Congress passed the ill-fated Embargo Act recalling all overseas
American merchant vessels. The *Chesapeake* episode also led to a
renewed commitment to limit sharply the size and number of American seagoing warships, putting finally to rest the remains of Benjamin Stoddert's navy.

In Jefferson's first administration the president and the Re-
publican-controlled Congress neither killed off nor completed the six
74s begun by Stoddert. Construction was simply suspended while the
frigate navy blasted away at the Barbary powers and warring Europeans chipped away at American neutrality. As late as 21 December
1805, two months after Trafalgar, the administration and Congress
were still pondering possible completion of the 74s at an estimated
cost of over $300,000 each and a construction time of three more
years. Without finally deciding that matter, the government began a
modest program of gunboat construction.

The gunboats were small, shallow-draft vessels mounting one or
two guns and propelled by sails or oars. Their purpose was to harass

larger enemy ships by swarming around them and peppering them with small-arms fire and the occasional blast from a cannon. They could not seriously damage an enemy sloop or frigate, much less a ship of the line, but they could annoy and demoralize the crews, especially on hot, humid days when the larger sailing ships were immobilized by lack of wind. They could also prevent landing parties from raiding coastal and river towns for food and water. They were a derivative of the gunboats and the somewhat larger galleys still widely used in the Mediterranean and Baltic at the beginning of the nineteenth century.

At the height of the *Chesapeake* crisis, on 20 November 1807, Secretary of the Navy Robert Smith requested an appropriation of $852,500 from Congress for construction of 188 gunboats in addition to the 69 already authorized and completed. The request reflected the maturation of the administration's naval policy, which the president had explained to Congress in February. Gunboats, said Jefferson, were relied upon by "every modern maritime nation" for the defense of ports and harbors. He listed numerous countries from the Black Sea to northern Europe that found gunboats or galleys an economical and practical means of defending ports and harbors. With a typical ideological flourish he singled out for special praise the small European powers bordering the Mediterranean, "whose system, like ours, is peace and defense." But even warlike England and France—"the two greatest naval Powers in the world"—had included gunboats in their respective arsenals when Napoleon was still planning to invade the British Isles.

With this international testimonial, Jefferson confidently recommended a force of about two hundred gunboats, to be stationed at the major seaports between New Orleans and Boston, most of them in preservative storage, or "in ordinary" as the naval phrase of the day had it. A few would be kept active in each port as a police force to maintain order and discourage insults by visiting foreign warships. The rest would be activated and manned by the "seamen and militia of the port" in times of severe crisis or actual war, but only in numbers proportionate to the severity and immediacy of the danger. This naval policy was purely defensive, an attribute Jefferson valued and stressed in his remarks to Congress:

> It must be superfluous to observe that this species of armament is proposed merely for defensive operations; that it can have but little effect towards protecting our commerce in the open seas, even on our

own coast; and still less can it become an excitement to engage in offensive maritime war, towards which it would furnish no means.

The essentially defensive posture of the United States in the early nineteenth century and the weight of European examples do not fully explain Jefferson's penchant for coastal defense gunboats. Numerous other factors entered into the president's calculus, no one of which would have been determining in itself. As his lucidly persuasive biographer Dumas Malone emphasizes, the president felt constitutionally constrained to defer to the will of Congress in providing for the national defense, and many Republicans in the Congress of Jefferson's presidency favored low-cost gunboats over Federalist-inspired ships of the line. On 25 March 1806, for example, Congress by a margin of more than two-to-one defeated an administration-sponsored measure to spend $660,000 to complete the six 74s while simultaneously voting $250,000 for gunboats and $150,000 for fortification of ports and harbors. Speaker of the House Nathaniel Macon of North Carolina captured the essence of post-Trafalgar naval reality: Forty or fifty 74s would be required to challenge Britain on the high seas; the United States lacked the financial and manufacturing resources to construct such a fleet; to build only six 74s invited national humiliation, because in a war with a major power they would be so heavily outnumbered and outgunned by the enemy fleet that they would have to hide in port.

An even worse fate than that could have befallen American ships of the line, as the American leaders knew. In August 1807, while reporting to Secretary of State Madison that he had read American newspaper accounts of the *Chesapeake* affair, Minister Monroe in London noted the ominous preparations of a British fleet. Some twenty-five ships of the line were about to embark on a raid against Copenhagen, where the Danish fleet lay at anchor. The purpose of the expedition was to prevent Napoleon from seizing neutral Denmark's warships. When the Danish government refused to turn over its fleet to the Royal Navy, the British bombarded the city. In what the Danes still refer to as "the rape of the fleet," the British then seized eighteen ships of the line, eight frigates, eighteen smaller oceangoing warships, and numerous gunboats. As the debates in Congress showed, Americans were quick to draw the obvious conclusion: The same thing could happen to any American fleet that posed a meaningful challenge to the Royal Navy.

During the first two years of James Madison's presidency (1809–

1811), the naval questions facing the national legislature remained essentially unchanged from what they had been in the second Jefferson administration: whether American neutrality could best be served by building a fleet of ships of the line, innumerable frigates for convoying merchantmen, or several dozen gunboats for defense of ports and harbors. The answers of the predominantly Republican body also remained consistent and highly defensive: Make annual additions to the number of gunboats at New Orleans and the Atlantic Coast ports, but build no new frigates and no ships of the line whatsoever.

The most that Congress would do regarding deep-draft vessels in 1809 was to authorize the reactivation of four frigates—the *John Adams, Essex, United States,* and *President*—currently laid up and needing repairs and fresh crews. That modest step was taken reluctantly and only after a protracted debate, which exposed a healthy respect for British naval supremacy and a reasonable fear that by increasing the American navy in any category except gunboats Congress would invite a preemptive attack by Britain, the incorporation of captured American warships into the already swollen Royal Navy, and additional humiliation for the United States.

In 1809 the British navy numbered some 800 ships, a reflection of intense construction and the continual addition of captured French and Spanish warships to the Royal Navy's list. One congressman opposed to "a single additional floating gun" put the issue into perspective: "What had been the consequence of augmentations of naval force in other countries? Were they not perpetually augmenting the British navy?" Representative David R. Williams made a pointed reference to the 1807 British expedition against Denmark: Did the United States really want to build a fleet "and have our towns Copenhagened?"

Williams preferred to place his confidence for the "salvation of his country" in the annihilation "of an invading foe" by an aroused populace rather than invite national bankruptcy and mortification by constructing "fifty fast sailing frigates," which, if sent to sea, must "either carry orders not to fight, or become what the *Chesapeake* has been—a disgrace to us." That view, which Williams thought regrettable but realistic, pervaded Congress in 1809, with the result that the act reactivating the four frigates also directed the president to station them "at such ports and places on the sea coast as he may deem most expedient, or to cruise on any part of the coast of the United States or the territories thereof." This peculiar phrasing meant that America's nine "fast sailing frigates" were statutorily restricted to patrolling coastal waters as offshore adjuncts to the gunboats, which now numbered 176.

Secretary of the Navy Paul Hamilton correctly read the measure as prohibiting him "from sending our vessels . . . beyond our coast." Notwithstanding the tension with Great Britain, Hamilton thought that at least "some of our frigates" ought to be deployed to the Mediterranean, where they could be maintained more cheaply and safely than on the "peculiarly hazardous" Atlantic Coast, whose winter squalls and innumerable shoals made costly and disastrous accidents inevitable. Besides, as Hamilton noted in his mild rejoinder to Congress, in the Mediterranean the United States has "a valuable trade at stake, subject to the depredations of a lawless people, whose disposition might be effectually restrained by the presence of a few vessels of respectable force." The secretary recognized that the United States frigates existed primarily to defend the merchant marine, much of which traversed the Mediterranean at constant risk of seizure by the Barbary Powers, whose wanton disregard of treaties was by 1809 an accepted fact of international life.

As the debates in Congress showed, Republican dogma called for an oceangoing navy with only enough strength to intimidate relatively weak powers. Matthew Lyon, representing Kentucky in 1810, was one of the more ardent House Republicans: In 1798 the Federalists had prosecuted and convicted him for violating the Alien and Sedition Acts, and in the War of 1812 he became a builder of gunboats. The navy's purpose held no mystery for the caustic Lyon: "Awe and chastise the little Powers that would insult and abuse you; for this you want your little navy." Secretary Hamilton's instincts therefore were ideologically and functionally sound, but he could not send his frigates overseas without congressional consent, and the Congress of 1809–1810 considered the danger of losing warships to Britain too great to permit the navy to exercise its by now traditional function of showing the flag in defense of mariners in distant waters.

The likelihood of war with Great Britain increased rather dramatically in the spring of 1811, in part because of a stiffening American posture and in part because of the bellicosity of the senior officers of the United States Navy. On 1 May a British frigate, the *Guerrière*, impressed an American merchant seaman almost within sight of New York Harbor. Less than a week later the outraged administration ordered the heavy frigate *President*, commanded by John Rodgers, to sail from Annapolis and take up station off Sandy Hook in order to discourage further British harassment of American merchant vessels entering and leaving New York.

Speaking for the president, newly appointed Secretary of State James Monroe steadfastly maintained that despite "the excitement . . . produced by previous and recent aggressions, particularly by the impressment of American citizens from American vessels, even on the coast of the United States . . . no order had been given by the Government for the recovery by force of any citizen so impressed from any British ship of war." John Rodgers concurred. The secretary of the navy commanded him to sail to New York, Rodgers said, because "the trade of New York had become interrupted by British and French cruisers." He was not directed to retrieve impressed Americans from British warships.

With his restrictive orders in hand, and aware of the *Guerrière's* impressment of the American mariner, Rodgers weighed anchor on 10 May. He struggled down Chesapeake Bay against headwinds, finally getting to sea on the 14th. On the afternoon of 16 May, about 50 miles northeast of Cape Henry, he sighted a British sloop-of-war, H.M.S. *Little Belt*. Convinced by her appearance that *Little Belt* was a substantial man-of-war, and "desirous of speaking her and ascertaining what she was, I now made sail in chase." Slackening winds prevented Rodgers from coming alongside his prey until after sunset, when darkness made visual identification impossible. By his account, he then hailed the *Little Belt*, asking her identity. The request was answered by cannon fire, and *President* responded in kind.

Little Belt mounted twenty guns; the *President* was rated at forty-four but may have carried as many as fifty, because American commanders habitually overgunned their ships and American naval architects routinely designed overstrength frigates. Secretary of the Navy Hamilton considered the *President* "nearly equal" to a 50-gun ship "in her hull, armament, sails, rigging, etc." The engagement was proportionately brief and one-sided. According to Rodgers, it lasted less than thirty minutes, with the *President* suffering one man slightly wounded and a "little injury . . . in our rigging." The *Little Belt* lost thirteen killed and nineteen wounded, and the Royal Navy surveyors at Halifax described her as "almost a wreck."

The Madison administration could barely contain its glee that the Royal Navy at last had been briskly humiliated in the very waters where four years earlier H.M.S. *Leopard* had mutilated American self-respect. The semiofficial *National Intelligencer* praised Rodgers for "repelling and chastising the attack so causelessly made on the

United States frigate *President*" and assured its readers that the episode evoked "the approbation of the President of the United States." In a letter to Jefferson, Madison showed no inclination to disavow responsibility for the "occurrence between Rodgers & the British ship of war." The clash, which Madison thought likely to be repeated, would "probably end in an open rupture, or a better understanding," depending on "the calculations of the B. Govt."

Madison seemed thoroughly frustrated and fatalistically resigned to a war in defense of American maritime commerce. Economic pressure on the two deadlocked European belligerents—Jefferson's now defunct embargo, the expired Non-Intercourse Act of 1809, and the unwieldly Macon's Bill Number Two—had failed to induce either Paris or London to temper its harassment and manipulation of American trade. Federalist New England was becoming restive after chafing under the yoke of Republican export restrictions for four years. The more ardent Federalists even interpreted the *President–Little Belt* duel as a contrivance of Madison designed to appease France for the burning of a French privateer that had sought refuge in Norfolk.

The accusation was nonsense, but it highlighted the extent to which Madison was being pressed from every quarter to take action. A few months earlier, in phrases strikingly anticipatory of the nontransfer clause of the Monroe Doctrine, Madison had authorized the preemptive occupation of West Florida to prevent either France or England from seizing that strategic salient from an internally divided Spain. Now, in the summer of 1811, he kept the frigates *President* and *United States* at sea, cruising between Cape Henry and Sandy Hook. Because he subscribed to the Jeffersonian-Republican view that Congress was the president's coadjutor in foreign policy, Madison called for an early session to convene 4 November 1811.

Against this darkening backdrop Secretary of State James Monroe coolly parried the British protests over Rodgers's attack on the *Little Belt*. Alleging that Rodgers had "fired a broadside into the sloop without provocation," the British minister in Washington demanded an investigation, punishment of Rodgers, and reparation to the crown. He also sought assurance that the United States had not ordered any of its ships to retrieve impressed mariners from British warships. Monroe facilely responded that "no order had been given by the Government for the recovery by force of any citizen so impressed from any British ship of war." Beyond that formally correct reassurance the secretary of state yielded nothing.

To buttress Monroe's contention that Rodgers was not the aggressor, the administration in July ordered a naval court of inquiry under the presidency of Captain Stephen Decatur. Three years earlier, in January and February 1808, Decatur had served as a member of the court martial that had condemned James Barron for not resisting the attack of the *Leopard*. The president of that court had been John Rodgers, whose aggressive temperament matched Decatur's. On 13 September 1811 Decatur's court of inquiry exonerated Rodgers on no less than eighteen counts of misjudgment or misconduct. It thereby fully underwrote Rodgers's version of the *Little Belt* incident. The very next day Monroe warned the British minister that the affair amounted to "a violent aggression by a British on an American ship." He also reminded the minister that Britain had yet to make reparation for the *Leopard's* attack on the *Chesapeake* in 1807. The linkage between the two events was now formal and firm.

In London the unstable King George III had been replaced by a prince regent anxious to avoid war between Britain and the United States. The acting monarch already had ordered reparation for the *Chesapeake* affair, to consist of repatriation of the two surviving sailors, a formal reminder that the British admiral on the North American station had been immediately recalled because of the episode, and "a suitable pecuniary provision for the sufferers." Secretary Monroe scoffed that the apology "should have been so long delayed" and discounted the transfer of the British admiral as too lenient a punishment. But on 12 November 1811 he grudgingly accepted the British offer as "otherwise satisfactory."

In the remaining seven months of the fragile Anglo-American peace Monroe displayed even less disposition to temporize on the issues of British orders in council and the Royal Navy's practice of impressment. His own truculence, coupled with the hawkishness of the new Congress, contributed significantly to the final breakdown of negotiations and Madison's decision of war.

The 12th Congress, which gathered for its first session in November 1811, was dominated by the newly elected "War Hawks." Those young representatives from the frontier, led by Henry Clay of Kentucky and John C. Calhoun of South Carolina, clamored for redress of multifarious maritime and other wrongs allegedly suffered by their nation at the hands of Great Britain. The president's message to this agitated body was not calculated to cool tempers. Madison opened his address to Congress by complaining of Britain's "more rigorous execution" of the orders in council and of London's threat to retaliate for America's continued nonimportation of British goods. He then turned to the Royal Navy's interference with American shipping along "our coasts, and the mouths of our harbors," a canker which he found thoroughly "derogatory to the dearest of our national rights." The most inflammatory occurrence "produced by the . . . British ships of war hovering on our coasts" was the engagement between the *President* and *Little Belt*, for which Madison now formally blamed the British commanding officer. The *Little Belt*, said the president of the United States, had commenced fire "without cause," and her "commander is therefore alone chargeable with the blood unfortunately shed in maintaining the honor of the American flag."

Faced with such "ominous indications" of British hostility, Madison had ordered completion of coastal fortifications, limited activation of the gunboats, and uninterrupted offshore operations by the frigates "as a cruising guard to the rights of our coast." It was now time for Congress to "feel the duty of putting the United States into an armor and an attitude demanded by the crisis." The president made several specific recommendations for congressional strengthening of the army and militia, but as for the navy he said only that Congress should make "such provisions . . . as may be required for the services to which it may be best adapted."

Madison's vague charge opened the door to the last prewar debate on the composition and strategy of the United States Navy. It began in the House on 17 December 1811 and concluded in the Senate on 5 March 1812. In the end the navy received funds to construct its first dockyard capacious enough to repair frigates without careening them, money to buy timber and "other imperishable materials," and a substantial appropriation for making three of the five mothballed frigates seaworthy. But Congress refused to approve a proposal for ten new frigates and twelve 74s. A naval buildup did not come until January 1813, at which point Congress authorized six new frigates and the navy's first two 74s, the *Washington* and the *Franklin*. Neither of those ships of the line was commissioned until after the war ended.

The prewar opponents of new construction systematically marshaled the arguments that had proved effective in limiting the size of the seagoing navy since the end of the Quasi War. Representative Adam Seybert of Pennsylvania melodramatically portrayed the debilitating cost of large navies: "If the United States shall determine to augment their navy, so as to rival those of Europe, the public debt will become permanent; direct taxes will be perpetual; the paupers of the country will be increased; the nation will be bankrupt; and, I fear, the tragedy will end in a revolution." If a large standing navy did not lead to domestic revolution, then it surely would lead to war, according to Representative Samuel McKee of Kentucky: "Establish a navy . . . and this country may bid farewell to peace; because you thereby organize a class of society who are interested in creating and keeping up wars and contention."

To the argument that the United States should heed the British example of building ships of the line, John Smilie of Pennsylvania replied before the House: "There are two strong reasons for a fleet there which do not exist here. From her insular position, a navy is her bulwark and wall of defense; and it is necessary for keeping up her commerce and communication with her foreign colonies." The United States manifestly had no overseas colonies nor any prospects of acquiring them in 1812, and a navy's efficacy in protecting widely dispersed merchant vessels was seriously questionable. As William Bibb of Georgia noted: "Commerce is neither dependent on such protection nor capable of being maintained by it." But even those congressmen who disagreed with Bibb and thought that a navy could and should protect the American merchant marine did not necessarily endorse a fleet of line-of-battle ships for the agricultural and commercial United States.

By refusing to appropriate funds for an increase of the navy in early 1812, Congress decreed that when open war came the nation would fight Albion's 1,000-ship fleet with the small inventory of vessels on hand at the close of 1811. Secretary Hamilton on 3 December listed in active service three frigates and a brig under the command of Commodore John Rodgers at Newport, Rhode Island. A squadron of two frigates and two lesser warships commanded by Commodore Stephen Decatur lay at Hampton Roads, Virginia. The 44-gun frigate *Constitution* and 16-gun brig *Hornet* were on "foreign service" conveying Minister Joel Barlow to France—a routine, moderately low-profile example of "showing the flag" overseas. Five other brigs were divided among Charleston, New Orleans, and Lake Ontario. In addition the secretary listed five frigates "laid up in ordinary" and requiring six months to be made ready for sea. Finally, Hamilton counted a total of 165 gunboats—of which sixty-two were in commission, eighty-six in ordinary, and seven under repair—spread along the coastal ports from Portland, Maine to New Orleans. Those mosquitoes were concentrated most heavily at the major seaports: New York (54 gunboats), New Orleans (26), Philadelphia (20) and Norfolk (14).

For better or for worse, the United States was wedded to this scattered and inconsequential fleet when James Madison on 1 June 1812 called for war against Great Britain. His enemy's navy, as he and the Congress knew, totaled 1,042 vessels, 111 of which were cruising North American waters. Seven of those deployed British warships were ships of the line, and thirty-one were frigates.

Madison's message to Congress made clear the exasperated president's motives in asking for war against such overwhelming odds. He cited first the "crying enormity" of the continuing British "practice of violating the American flag on the great highway of nations, and of seizing and carrying off persons sailing under it." As a direct result of impressment, "thousands of American citizens . . . have been torn from their country and everything dear to them; [they] have been dragged on board ships of war of a foreign nation . . . to risk their lives in the battles of their oppressors." Almost as outrageous to Madison was the British practice of stationing cruisers just off the American coast to "hover over and harass our entering and departing commerce." Third, Madison protested that "pretended blockades" of Europe proclaimed by the British "without the presence of an adequate force and sometimes without the practicability of applying one."

Those paper blockades, the president cried in an appeal to all sections of the country, were directly "aimed at our agricultural and maritime interests." The British government often announced such ineffective and hence illegal blockades retroactively, despite its own admission "that particular ports must be actually invested [by warships] and previous warning given to [merchant] vessels . . . not to enter." To compound its sins, the British cabinet by 1812 was orchestrating its previously haphazard and intermittent closure of Napoleonic ports with a dangerously "sweeping system of blockades, under the name of orders in council, which has been molded and managed as might best suit its political views, its commercial jealousies, or the avidity of British cruisers." The president thus led the country into a war for neutral rights as defined by Americans since the beginning of the Anglo-French conflict in 1794.

War caught the navy materially unprepared but emotionally fervent. The tone was set at a Fourth of July gala in Washington by a Republican enthusiast who proposed a toast to the navy ghosted by either Madison or Monroe: "An infant Hercules, destined . . . to extirpate the race of pirates and freebooters." Secretary of the Navy Paul Hamilton had not been "anxious for war and bloodshed," he told John Rodgers, but with its declaration by Congress he implored the navy's senior commodore, "For God's sake get ready and let us strike a good blow." Hamilton's immediate targets were two British warships known to be lurking off Sandy Hook, the *Belvidera* and *Tartarus*. Rodgers had been on alert for about three months, and he set sail from New York as soon as he received the secretary's command on 21 June. By acting before the British knew that war had been declared, Rodgers hoped to cut down a few of the Royal Navy's ships in North American waters. He took to sea his flagship, the frigate *President;* the frigates *United States* and *Congress;* the sloop *Hornet;* and the brig *Argus.* The frigates *Constitution* and *Essex* had orders to join him as soon as ready for action. This combination of striking power constituted the bulk of the active American navy, making Rodgers something of a fleet commander.

Two days out of New York, on 23 June 1812, Rodgers fell in with the *Belvidera* and gave chase. The *President,* rated at forty-four guns, had the advantage in speed and weight of broadsides, but as she bore down one of her two bow guns exploded, killing or wounding sixteen men and breaking Rodgers's leg. Partially disabled but seemingly undaunted, the commodore continued his pursuit while the crew of the *Belvidera* peppered the *President* with shot from a battery of stern guns and increased their ship's speed by jettisoning all nonessential gear. To bring his broadsides to bear, Rodgers had to yaw to port and starboard, a maneuver that prevented him from closing on his accelerating target. It also "much surprised" the British skipper because Rodgers commanded the faster ship and "it was fully in his power to have run up alongside the *Belvidera.*"

Rodgers, however, exhibited no taste for grapeshot—the smoothbore cannon's equivalent to a modern antipersonnel cluster bomb—and his overtaking speed was reduced by extensive damage to his foresails, rigging, and spars. About midnight he therefore broke off the war's inconclusive first engagement, rejoined his squadron, and headed to the northeast. He planned to intercept a rich, lightly escorted, 110-ship merchant convoy homeward bound from Jamaica to England. Missing the interception, he kept his squadron at sea in the unrealized hope of bagging a large number of British merchantmen for prize money to enrich himself and his crew. An outbreak of "that wretched disease the scurvy" at last drove him into port empty-handed on 31 August.

In justification of his fruitless seventy-one-day cruise, Rodgers offered a thoroughly patriotic rationale: By cruising well to the eastward as a unit his ships compelled the British to concentrate their own warships for self-defense and for the effective escort of other merchant convoys traversing the North Atlantic. Rodgers contended that the British could not safely disperse themselves as blockaders of American ports so long as he remained at sea. But many within the navy seriously doubted the prudence of concentrating America's few warships in a single squadron, the loss of which would strip the United States of its entire seagoing navy. Foremost among the skeptics was Stephen Decatur, who reluctantly sailed under Rodgers's command as a subordinate commodore commanding two frigates and a brig.

Decatur and Rodgers had received identical letters from Secretary Hamilton in May asking them to propose "a plan of operations, which in your judgment, will enable our little navy to annoy in the utmost extent, the trade of Great Britain while it least exposes it to the immense naval force of that Government." Decatur's reply was characteristically audacious and intelligent: Send the frigates "out with as large a supply of provision as they can carry, distant from our coast, & singly, or not more than two Frigates in company, without giving them any specific instructions as to place of cruising, but to rely on the enterprise of the officers." Significantly, he alluded to a similar strategy "recently adopted by the French, & with the greatest success." Frigates operating singly or in pairs would be harder for the enemy to detect than if they operated as part of a larger squadron; "their movements would be infinitely more rapid, they would be sufficiently strong in most cases to attack a convoy, & the probability is that they would not meet with a superior cruising force." Should one or two frigates unhappily encounter a stronger British force from which they could not escape, at least "we would not have to regret the whole of our marine crushed at one blow." Distant cruising had one further strategic advantage: It would force the enemy to search for the frigates with ships that might otherwise blockade the American coast, thus permitting American merchantmen to leave and enter home ports unscathed. With that formula Decatur articulated the classic justification for commerce raiding or *guerre de course*. Such a strategy is followed almost instinctively by the relatively weaker naval power in any major maritime war, and it perfectly suited the United States Navy in 1812.

In contrast to Decatur, Secretary Hamilton favored caution and worried more about protecting returning American merchantmen than attacking British commerce. Therefore, on 22 June he ordered Rodgers and Decatur to sail in two separate squadrons not too far off the American coast and to cooperate whenever necessary to ensure the safe arrival home of the "great bulk of our returning commerce." Rodgers could disperse or concentrate the ships of his own squadron as he saw fit, but Hamilton did "intimate" his opinion "that it may not be prudent, for the vessels to sail singly." Rather overcome by timidity, the secretary also counseled an occasional return to port by Rodgers's entire squadron "for further instructions." As a final demoralizing counsel, Hamilton, "from prudential considerations," warned Rodgers "that, possessing as you do, every belligerent right of capture, attack & defence, still, you are not voluntarily to encounter a force superior to your own," although, of course, he was "not to fly from an equal."

Fortunately for Rodgers's peace of mind, these largely ambiguous orders reached New York after he had departed on his ten-week cruise in company with Decatur's attached squadron. He learned of them only upon his return in September, by which time a fellow officer, Captain Isaac Hull of the *Constitution*, had answered President Madison's prophetic challenge: "It is victories we want; if you give us them and lose your ships afterwards, they can be replaced by others."

On 5 July 1812, freshly refitted but with a dangerously green crew, the *Constitution* had set sail from Annapolis, headed for a rendezvous with Rodgers's squadron off New York. Instead, Hull encountered a British squadron consisting of a ship of the line, several frigates, and some smaller ships. The wind died, but the sailors manned the longboats and towed the ship until freshening winds enabled the *Constitution* to break away and dash for Boston. Hull stayed in port only long enough to replenish his food and water. Fearing blockade by the British at any moment, he grabbed the first westerly wind and headed for the open ocean without orders from the secretary of the navy or communications from his nominal squadron commander, Commodore Rodgers. He planned to cruise the fishing banks off Newfoundland, hoping "to intercept some small convoys that are now about to sail for England." But commerce raiding was not to be Hull's destiny.

While watching the shipping lanes that led directly into the Gulf of St. Lawrence, Hull learned of a solitary British "Ship of War standing to the Southward." Not a man to hesitate, he "made sail . . . intending if possible to fall in with her." Fortune favored him. On 19 August he caught up with H.M.S. *Guerrière*, the 38-gun frigate whose skipper had helped trigger the war by impressing a seaman in American coastal waters. She was headed for Halifax for refitting, and she sailed alone because the British squadron commander had dispersed his squadron in early August, once he knew that Rodgers's squadron was still sailing eastward toward the English Channel.

The 44-gun *Constitution* was a heavier and faster platform, and her skipper could handle a ship as well as any man afloat. Finding himself astern of his prey and under fire, much as Rodgers had been when chasing the *Belvidera,* Hull courageously "ordered the Main-topGallant sail set, to run up alongside her." Once the two ships lay side by side, Hull's heavier broadsides did the job quickly. In less than thirty minutes, he reported to the secretary of the navy, "She was left without a Spar Standing, and the Hull cut to pieces, in such a manner as to make it difficult to keep her above water, and the *Constitution* in a State to be brought into action in two hours. Actions like these speak for themselves." The message implied that a strategy of dispersion and single-ship engagements promised laurels for the United States Navy and the fortunate skippers in command of victorious ships. The *Constitution* herself, whose stout planking withstood the British shot with little penetration, earned the affectionate nickname "Old Ironsides."

News of the *Constitution*'s triumph served as "a national tonic, invigorating the whole war effort" in Washington, where mortifying news from the northwest was disconcerting the Madison administration. On 16 August General William Hull, Isaac's uncle, had surrendered 2,500 men to an inferior British army without firing a shot. By then British troops had captured Fort Michilimackinac on Lake Huron and Fort Dearborn on Lake Michigan. The thoughtlessly bold plan of the War Hawks to decide the war quickly by invading Canada lay in shambles, and Madison now had to fear a British invasion from the north as well as the inevitable blockade of Atlantic Coast ports. The president summoned the full cabinet to debate the next step, tersely noting his mistakes: "The failure of our calculations with respect to the expedition under [General William] Hull needs no comment. The worst of it was, that we were misled by a reliance, authorized by himself, on its securing the command of the lakes." For that control and the security it would bring, Madison now turned to the navy. He ordered Commodore Isaac Chauncey to defend Lakes Erie and Ontario and Lieutenant Thomas Macdonough to do the same on Champlain.

Chauncey's orders of 31 August 1812 left no room for doubt about Madison's northern strategy: "The President of the United States has determined to obtain command of the Lakes Ontario & Erie, with the least possible delay." Chauncey should consider himself "unrestrained, minor interests must yield to the greater. The object must be accomplished; and all the means which you may judge essential, must be employed." At the time commandant of the New York Navy Yard, Chauncey quite properly used his carte blanche to strip his command—including the frigate *John Adams* and the coastal defense gunboats—of officers, men, "cannon, carriages, shot, powder, small arms and every other munition of war." In three weeks of frenzied activity the new commodore of the lakes dispatched northward 140 carpenters, 700 sailors and marines, and more than 100 pieces of large-bore ordnance.

On 26 September he set off for Sackets Harbor, New York. That strategic junction was located on the eastern shore of Lake Ontario, where the St. Lawrence flows from the lake, directly across from the British base at Kingston. Chauncey immediately established the base of operations for his fleet, commenced a naval buildup, and set out to destroy "the principal naval force of the Enemy." In the gales of early November he engaged several British warships, which escaped by running before westerly squalls and fleeing into Kingston, where the heavy guns of the fort sheltered them from Chauncey. As ice formed and bitter winter closed in, Chauncey accurately boasted to the secretary of the navy: "I think I can say with great propriety that we have now the command of The Lake and that we can transport Troops and Stores to any part of it without any risk of an attack from The Enemy." More important, the British no longer could safely move men and matériel westward toward Lake Erie.

Chauncey's remarkable sweep of Lake Ontario coincided with Madison's message of 4 November, which publicly stressed the administration's "expectation of gaining command of the Lakes" and its determination to establish "on them a naval force superior to that of the enemy." Upon reading Madison's challenge, the British North American naval commander, Admiral Borlase Warren, urgently advised General Sir George Prevost to build frigate-sized ships on the inland waterways, for "unless the *superiority upon the Lakes is preserved* . . . all the Indian force will be destroyed," and Madison might successfully "wrest the Canadas from the British Empire." A shipbuilding race for naval superiority on Ontario followed. It lasted for the duration of the war, with temporary predominance seesawing back and forth. Neither Chauncey nor his British counterpart, Sir James Lucas Yeo, was willing to risk his fleet in less than overwhelmingly favorable odds, which never materialized. At war's end Yeo commanded a 104-gun flagship—about the same number of guns as

Nelson's *Victory*, though not comparable in draft, cube or seawor-thiness—and Madison had just ordered Chauncey to compete by building two 94-gun ships of the line and a 44-gun frigate.

The inflated size of those ships and Chauncey's failure to force a decisive naval battle or to assault Kingston frontally has been criti-cized by Mahanian naval historians for whom aggressiveness carried to the point of recklessness is a touchstone of fine naval leadership. Their criticism is highlighted by comparing Chauncey's plodding per-severance on Ontario with the spectacular victory of Oliver Hazard Perry on Lake Erie and the heroically decisive defense of Lake Cham-plain by Thomas Macdonough. Yet Chauncey had his reasons, and they were good ones. In building a naval base at Sackets Harbor he had created a liability as well as an asset. If he strayed too far, the British—emerging from Kingston or the St. Lawrence—could over-run his base and cut his supply lines. Alternatively, if he forced Yeo into a major engagement and lost, British logistics and communica-tions could flow from Halifax to Detroit without interruption, making possible an invasion of the United States anywhere in the upper Ohio Valley. Madison, for one, appreciated Chauncey's protective role in a war of defense. When it was over, the president appointed him com-modore of the revived Mediterranean Squadron and personally in-spected his flagship, the spanking new 74-gun ship of the line *Washington*—commissioned on 26 August 1815—before she sailed from Annapolis, Maryland.

By maintaining his fleet-in-being in 1813, Chauncey had pro-vided a shield—however imperfect—for Oliver Hazard Perry on Lake Erie. On 8 February of that year, following Chauncey's personal intervention, the new secretary of the navy, William Jones of Phila-delphia, appointed twenty-seven-year-old Master Commandant Perry commander of American naval forces on Erie. Perry's father had seen naval combat in the American Revolution; his three brothers became officers in the navy (Matthew Calbraith, nine years his jun-ior, would command a squadron during the Mexican War and later "open" Japan to the West); and two of his three sisters married naval officers. With the navy literally and figuratively in his blood, Perry resented his confinement in Newport, Rhode Island, where he com-manded an idle flotilla of defensive gunboats he had helped construct. The secretary's orders gave him his chance to win glory, and he sped to Presque Isle, on the southern shore of Lake Erie, with 150 of his best-trained gunboat sailors. His task was to build a fleet in the wil-derness and win control of the lake. His scarcest resources were sailors and skilled workers. As he wrote to Chauncey, his immediate senior in an admittedly loosely linked chain of command, if provided with enough men he would "acquire both for *you* and myself honor and glory on this lake, or perish in the attempt."

Perry was as good as his word. He scrounged matériel and workmen from every conceivable source. General William Henry Harrison collaborated in a rare instance of interservice harmony. By September Perry had built a fleet of nine ships mounting a total of 54 guns. He named his flagship the *Lawrence* after his closest friend, James Lawrence, the skipper of the *Chesapeake*, who had died in a losing battle against the British frigate *Shannon* two months earlier.

The gifted builder Noah Brown, who had supervised construction of the brig *Lawrence* and her sister ship, the *Niagara*, pronounced Perry's ships good for one battle but no more. The ships were fashioned from green timber, but Perry's unrelenting drive had produced a fleet numerically superior to that of his tough British antagonist, Captain Robert H. Barclay, a one-armed veteran of Trafalgar. Barclay's sole advantage lay in longer-range guns, which meant that Perry would have to seek close engagement in order to bring his larger-bore cannon into play.

Perched precariously at the end of an extremely long supply line often cut and always threatened by Chauncey's Ontario fleet, Barclay on 6 September decided he had to open Erie to the free flow of food and equipment desperately needed by British troops and their Indian allies. He sailed south to meet Perry, and the two fleets joined on the morning of 10 September. The action was a classic fleet engagement. Favored by a windward position, Perry bore down on the British ships. Beneath a banner streaming Lawrence's inspirational last words, "Don't Give Up the Ship," Perry's crew of the *Lawrence* fought until their vessel lay dead in the water. Only nineteen of 142 men remained fit to fight. Perry survived because he had dressed as an ordinary seaman to fool sharpshooters such as the one who had shot down Nelson at Trafalgar.

His second in command, Jesse D. Elliott, who had inexplicably kept his ship, the *Niagara*, well clear of the two-hour bloodletting, now gingerly approached the flagship. Perry jumped into his gig, was rowed over to the *Niagara* through a rain of British bullets, ordered Elliott rowed toward the smaller ships, and smartly sailed his undamaged new flagship into battle. He managed to cross the British line perpendicular to its direction of advance, a maneuver called "crossing the T" and much favored by battling fleet commanders because it enabled them to fire their broadsides at the nearly defenseless bows or sterns of their opponents. Each shot so fired traveled the length of its victim, "raking" it. Barclay knew that raking fire was unanswerable, and so about 3:00 P.M. on 10 September 1813 he became the first commander in history to surrender an entire British squadron.

Perry's terse message to Harrison said it all: "We have met the enemy and they are ours." The British position in Michigan and Ohio was now untenable; the Northwest was safely American. Transported by the fleet and joined in battle by the commodore, General Harrison swiftly moved across Lake Erie and broke a British army at the Battle of the Thames on 5 October. By then an elated president had already ordered the young naval officer promoted to captain—the navy's highest permanent rank prior to the Civil War. Congress voted $250,000 in prize money for the victorious officers and men, a very handsome recognition considering that the crew of the frigate *Constitution* had received only $50,000 for its victory over the *Guerrière*.

Those members of Congress who favored a large seagoing navy saw Perry's victory as an augury and an opportunity. William Lowndes of South Carolina praised Barclay and his crews in order to exalt Perry even further: "They were skillful officers, subdued by the ascendancy of still superior skill. They were a brave foe, who yielded to one yet braver." Not only was Perry the bravest of the brave, he mattered more to the victory on Erie than had Horatio Nelson at the battles of the Nile (1798) and Trafalgar (1805). Nelson fell at Trafalgar, but "victory never for a moment fluttered from what was then her chosen eyry—the British mast." If Perry had faltered or fallen, "his associates . . . must have shared his fate. The battle was lost." Instead, Perry transferred his flag to the *Niagara* "when his ship was a defenceless hospital" and thereby gave "us victory in one quarter" while showing his countrymen "how to obtain it in another yet more important. How deep is now the impression on every mind that we want but ships to give our fleet on the Atlantic the success which has hitherto attended our single vessels!" Then came the oratorical *coup de grâce*. Henry Clay stepped from the Speaker's chair to sing the West's appreciation of blue-water fleets: "Our ships on the ocean, commanded by the most gallant officers in the world, had already shown what American tars could do, ship to ship. It remained for the hero of Erie to exhibit to them an awful lesson of our capacity to fight in a squadron against, not only an equal but superior force."

The belief in a strategy of fleet actions was spreading in early 1814, but only as a result of a battle in which the Americans had been favored by the limits geography and logistics placed on an opponent far removed from his great industrial and maritime base. In the north woods Perry had been able to improvise a fleet to match Barclay's, but the Atlantic Coast yards of the United States could not win a shipbuilding race with Liverpool. The blue water was Britain's as long as its industrial base remained supreme.

The national euphoria engendered by Perry's triumph proved short-lived. By April 1814 Napoleon had been defeated, and the British, already strangling the East Coast of the United States with a naval blockade, now began a concerted three-pronged assault aimed at capturing New Orleans, disrupting the Chesapeake Tidewater, and splintering the Northeast by moving an army down the Lake Champlain–Hudson River corridor. Madison had entrusted the defense of Champlain to Lieutenant Thomas Macdonough, a thirty-one-year-old veteran of the Barbary Wars who had accompanied Stephen Decatur on the raid against the *Philadelphia*. His mission resembled Perry's and Chauncey's: to build a fleet large enough to repulse any British effort to establish naval command of the lake. It differed from theirs in one important respect: In addition to a rival naval squadron, he and the small American military contingent on the lake's western shore faced an invading army of 11,000 hardened veterans from the Duke of Wellington's European army. Their commander, General Sir George Prevost, fortunately concluded that his soldiers could not safely sweep south until the Royal Navy had won control of the lake. He therefore paused in his attack on the hopelessly outnumbered American garrison at Plattsburgh, New York, to observe the outcome of the naval contest shaping up in the bay bordering that city.

By September 1814 Macdonough had built a fleet whose weight of broadside fire equaled that of the British, but his ships and crews were green. He therefore anchored his vessels in a north-south column at the mouth of Plattsburgh Bay so that prevailing northerly winds and a prominent protective peninsula would force the British ships to attack him bow-first, enabling him to rake the attackers with his broadsides. With a touch of tactical genius, he also set his anchors on "spring lines" so that by hauling on cables his men could rotate their ships to keep the British more or less continuously under fire. Such maneuvering required brute strength, but it did not demand the complicated sail-handling teamwork lacking in his inexperienced crews. The steadiness provided by the anchors gave Macdonough's unseasoned sailors an additional advantage: stability of gun platforms, which permitted more accurate fire.

The British obliged Macdonough on the morning of 11 September 1814. Captain George Downie, with four ships and twelve gunboats, rounded Cumberland Head and made for Macdonough's four ships and ten tiny galleys. Downie of necessity sailed close-hauled, line abreast—the worst possible formation for square-rigged sailing vessels engaging an enemy fleet. The British ships were totally vulnerable as they approached Macdonough's waiting broadsides. Within fifteen minutes Downie and several of his officers were dead. Within two hours the decimated British survivors had surrendered. That night Prevost began a ragged retreat back to Montréal. Once again— as with Benedict Arnold in 1776—a jury-rigged flotilla manned by untested crews had parried a deadly British thrust at the heart of America.

Macdonough's victory was historic in several respects. It rested in part on Macdonough's own study of Horatio Nelson. In the Battle of the Nile of 1798 Nelson had drubbed an anchored French fleet by anchoring his own ships and maneuvering them with spring lines. Macdonough admired Nelson as a leader of men and went into battle with flags mimicking Nelson's famous signal at Trafalgar: "England Expects That Every Man Will Do His Duty." Macdonough's chauvinistic paraphrase was: "Impressed Seamen Call on Every Man To Do His Duty." He even borrowed words from Nelson's triumphant announcement after the Battle of the Nile. His own victory message to the secretary of the navy proclaimed: "The Almighty has been pleased to grant us a signal victory." In England the Battle of Lake Champlain was called "the false Nile," and Macdonough's tactics were studied as models. The British naval historian William Laird Clowes praised Macdonough's victory as "a most notable feat, one which, on the whole, surpassed that of any other captain of either navy in this war." All major nineteenth-century American naval historians of the war—James Fenimore Cooper, Theodore Roosevelt, and Alfred Thayer Mahan—agreed.

So did James Madison, whose adamant insistence on rushing Macdonough's 20-gun *Eagle* to completion had tipped the balance of firepower in the American's favor. Word of the decisive victory on Champlain reached the president almost coincidentally with the equally exhilarating news that the British, having failed to subdue Fort McHenry with a prolonged naval bombardment, had lifted their siege of Baltimore and were withdrawing down Chesapeake Bay. They had burned the national capital, but they had not taken a major seaport or split off restive New England from the rest of the country.

Two of the three prongs of the British attack had been blunted by Americans fighting bravely on the defensive, and Madison's message to the reassembled Congress gave ample recognition to the pivotal strategic accomplishment of Macdonough "and his intrepid comrades," whose "illustrious victory"—like Perry's on Erie—had "established at a critical moment our command of another lake."

The expansive president also expressed his pride in the "gallantry and good conduct" of the officers of the blue-water navy, most notably David Porter, who had carried the war against British shipping into the Pacific Ocean. As skipper of the 32-gun frigate *Essex*, Porter captured twelve British whalers in a six-month period, a blow from which the British whaling industry never recovered. He then chose to ignore the rules of *guerre de course*, hunted the Royal Navy, and was forced to surrender his ship after a copious bloodletting just outside Valparaiso, Chile. Madison discounted the loss of the frigate because of the "blaze of heroism" with which Porter had "maintained a sanguinary contest against two ships, one of them superior to his own, . . . till humanity tore down the colors which valor had nailed to the mast." While the navy's solitary cruisers were thus adding "much to the rising glory of the American flag," privateers were busily capturing British merchantmen and bringing their prizes home as a clear demonstration of "the incompetency and illegality" of the British blockade of the American coast.

Madison was being charitable about his navy's war on the high seas. In 1812 the American blue-water navy had captured five British ships—three frigates and two sloops—while losing only one brig and a sloop, but in 1813 the Americans lost a 36-gun frigate, the ill-fated *Chesapeake*, and three brigs in a poor swap for two British brigs and a 5-gun schooner. In 1814 the high seas navy managed to defeat three British brigs and one schooner, but it lost a sloop and a brig in the Atlantic as well as the frigate *Essex*, the only American warship in the Pacific.

The commanding officers of the *Essex* and all the other blue-water ships went to sea with standing orders from the secretary of the navy stating that "the commerce of the enemy is the most vulnerable point we can attack, and its destruction the main object; and to this end all your efforts should be directed." But taking prize vessels could endanger a skipper's own ship if he sought to enhance his own "fame, and the national honor, by hazarding a battle after the reduction of your officers and crew by manning prizes."

Privateers, by contrast, could safely dilute their crews by de-

taching men to sail prizes into port. Unlike the square-rigged warships, privately owned "close-winded schooners" could slip past the
"British watchdogs" hugging the Atlantic coast. In 1814, 200 of the
526 registered privateers penetrated Britain's blockade with one or
more cruises and took more than 1,300 English prizes. Those losses
annoyed "Britain's politically powerful merchant class, contributed to
the unpopularity of the war in England and, consequently, to the
negotiated peace."

There could be no doubt about the British inability to subdue
the Americans on the North American continent. Their impotence,
coupled with the repeal of the orders in council and the general peace
in Europe, which had brought a de facto end to impressment, meant
there was hope that peace could now be concluded.

The challenge of extricating the United States from an unpopular war against an uncompromising enemy that could be held off but
not defeated fell to a distinguished delegation. The principal American negotiators were John Quincy Adams, Albert Gallatin, and
Henry Clay, and their prospects brightened measurably when Secretary of State Monroe in June 1814 authorized them as a last resort
to "omit any stipulation on the subject of impressment." But the
British continued to make demands for territorial adjustments until
news of the Plattsburgh-Champlain debacle reached London in late
October. At that juncture England's most respected soldier, the Duke
of Wellington, strongly advised the government to seek peace on the
basis of the *status quo ante bellum.* Less than two months later, on
Christmas Eve 1814, Adams and his colleagues signed the Treaty of
Ghent, which restored peace without settling the issues of neutral
rights that had plagued Anglo-American relations for two decades.

The treaty reached Washington a few days after the capital
learned that Andrew Jackson had smashed the third prong of Britain's
1814 offensive with his victory at New Orleans. In the resulting euphoria the Senate approved the Treaty of Ghent by a unanimous vote,
and the long-term French minister in Washington, Louis Sérurier,
caught the significance of the national mood at war's end: "Finally the
war has given the Americans what they so essentially lacked, a national character founded on a glory common to all." The naval element in this new spirit of national cohesiveness could not be mistaken:
"The United States," wrote Sérurier, "are at this moment, in my
eyes, a naval power. . . . Within ten years they will be masters in
their waters and upon their coasts." More than this, the U.S. Navy
was about to become a global agent of American policy.

4

Extending the Empire of Commerce

1815 – 1846

ALGIERS had begun to harass American merchant-
men and to demand immediate payment of all tribute owed almost as
soon as the United States withdrew its warships from the Mediterranean in consequence of the *Chesapeake–Leopard* affair of 1807. In
1812 the dey initiated an unrestricted naval war against American
commerce, no doubt encouraged to strike by the British prince regent, who promised to protect the Algerine "capital with his fleets"
but also warned the dey that "the British fleets are masters of every
sea and are the terror of all maritime states and that whoever attempts
to oppose them will be subdued."

A combination of mercantile prudence, naval blockade, and offshore interceptions by the Royal Navy kept most American merchantmen out of the Mediterranean during the War of 1812, so the dey
enjoyed slim pickings. But his insolence earned him the wrath of
President James Madison, who struck back as soon as he could. On 25
February 1815—only days after the Senate approved the Treaty of
Ghent—Madison asked Congress for a declaration of war against Algiers. He also ordered two naval squadrons to sail to the Mediterranean.

In New York Stephen Decatur rushed his squadron of three
frigates and seven smaller warships to readiness, while in Boston the
more senior William Bainbridge prepared his 74-gun flagship *Inde-*

pendence and seven lighter ships for sea at a less frenzied pace. The intramural naval race was won by Decatur, who set sail for the Mediterranean on 20 May 1815. He touched briefly at Gibraltar and then flew into the Mediterranean in pursuit of an Algerine frigate, the 46-gun *Mashuda*, which he overwhelmed on 17 June, taking the ship as a prize and more than 400 Algerines as prisoners. Anchoring off Algiers on 28 June, Decatur and the new American consul general to the Barbary States, William Shaler, initiated peace negotiations with the startled dey, who suddenly faced an aroused America and a formidable blockading force.

Decatur and Shaler demanded a commercial treaty with a most-favored-nation clause—precisely the kind of pact that the United States sought in its dealings with most of the world throughout the nineteenth century—and abolition of payment of "any tribute to Algiers under any form whatever." Decatur insisted that the negotiations be conducted on his flagship, a 44-gun frigate. To the dey's request for a truce and safe passage for his offshore cruisers during the talks Decatur characteristically replied: "Not a minute. If your squadron appears in sight before the treaty is actually signed . . . ours will capture them." Faced with imminent loss of his navy and heavy bombardment of his capital, the dey signed Decatur's treaty on 30 June 1815.

Decatur's boast to the secretary of the navy that the settlement had "been dictated at the mouths of our cannon" was echoed with understandable bitterness by the Algerine minister, who complained to the British consul: "You told us that the Americans would be swept from the seas in six months by your navy, and now they make war upon us with some of your own vessels which they have taken." When the new commodore of the permanent American squadron, Isaac Chauncey, arrived off Algiers on 8 December 1816, the American message was unmistakable. Chauncey sailed on board the 74-gun ship of the line *Washington* and carried a letter from President Madison declaring "the settled policy of America, that as peace is better than war, war is better than tribute."

The golden age of American "gunboat diplomacy" had dawned. It was characterized by an unprecedented sense of Anglo-American cooperation on distant stations, and it lasted until steam displaced canvas as the motive force of naval vessels.

The principal architects of the new naval policy were President James Monroe and John Quincy Adams, who served as Monroe's secretary of state from 1817 until he succeeded to the presidency in

1825. Monroe had acquired a realistic understanding of naval power as American minister to the Court of St. James's at the time of the *Chesapeake–Leopard* affair. It was Monroe who had first warned President Jefferson of the British intention to capture the neutral Danish fleet at Copenhagen in 1807, the cold-blooded episode that frightened many members of Congress. As secretary of state in 1811 he had suavely interpreted John Rodgers's attack on H.M.S. *Little Belt* as self-defense, while brushing off British protests with reminders that London had yet to repatriate the sailors impressed from the *Chesapeake*. Monroe therefore came to the presidency with a mature sense of the potential utility and inherent limits of the United States Navy.

In his first inaugural address of 4 March 1817 the president outlined a naval policy that took into account the relevant facets of domestic and international politics. The United States, he said, had just passed "with glory" through a difficult war and was now in a "highly favored condition," but permanent peace could not be guaranteed. Blending economic self-interest with Republican ideology he limned the danger of foreign war:

> Many of our citizens are engaged in commerce and navigation. . . . Many are engaged in the fisheries. These interests are exposed to invasion in the wars between other powers, and we should disregard the faithful admonition of experience if we did not expect it. We must support our rights or lose our character, and with it, perhaps our liberties. . . . National honor is national property of the highest value.

To protect the nation against invasion the president proposed inland and coastal fortifications, a well-drilled militia, and a "moderate, but adequate" army and navy. Upon the advent of war the navy would be augmented with "the great naval resources . . . which should be duly fostered in time of peace." This enlarged navy "would contribute essentially, both as an auxiliary of defense and as a powerful engine of annoyance, to diminish the calamities of war and bring the war to a speedy and honorable termination." Monroe's prescription for a belligerent naval strategy fitted neatly into the traditional American mold of coastal defense and commerce raiding. Such a strategy relied primarily on coastal fortifications and floating gun batteries on the one hand, frigates and smaller cruisers on the other. Ships of the line existed only to drive off heavy enemy blockaders long enough for American frigates, sloops, brigs, and schooners to slip to sea in search of prize merchantmen.

Monroe also spelled out a precise nationalistic role for a properly limited peacetime navy: It could "aid in maintaining the neutrality of the United States in the wars of other powers and in saving the property of their citizens from spoliation." Two years later the president detailed how and where the navy was guarding the seaborne property of Americans. "For the protection of our commerce in the Mediterranean, along the southern Atlantic coast, in the Pacific and Indian Oceans, it has been found necessary to maintain a strong naval force, which it seems proper for the present to continue." To withdraw "any portion of the squadron heretofore stationed in the Mediterranean" would result in the interruption or outright destruction of "our intercourse with the powers bordering on that sea."

In the other regions mentioned, the hazard came from "the growth of a spirit of piracy . . . by adventurers from every country, in abuse of the friendly flags which they have assumed." An American failure "to protect our commerce there would be to abandon it as a prey to their rapacity." Pirates captured by the navy on the high seas were to be brought to the United States for trial, conviction, and execution. Similarly, Monroe energetically prosecuted the slave trade: "Orders have been given to seize all vessels navigated under our flag engaged in that trade, and to bring them in to be proceeded against in the manner prescribed by . . . law."

The global pattern of deployment of American warships established by Monroe was documented in 1820 by Secretary of the Navy Smith Thompson. He reported that the new 74-gun *Columbus*—commissioned on 7 September 1819—together with a 24-gun corvette and a brig were patrolling the Mediterranean "to keep the Barbary Powers in awe." The 36-gun frigate *Constellation* was "cruising in the Pacific Ocean for the protection of our trade and whale fisheries." The frigate *Congress*, also a 36, was roaming "the India seas, and the several straits, to afford convoy and protection to our trade to and from China, and to give security against the native pirates." Three ships, each mounting twenty-four guns or less, hunted slave traders and pirates off the coast of Africa. On the way home they would snoop around Guiana and the West Indies. The brig *Enterprise*, with fourteen guns, and two schooners hunted slavers and pirates in the West Indies, the Gulf of Mexico, and along the southern coast of the United States.

Whenever possible, these ships were relieved on station by replacements of the same class, so that identifiable squadrons soon took shape, with the largest vessel becoming the flagship and her skipper assuming the honorific rank of "commodore," even though the squadrons rarely sailed as units. By 1826 Secretary of the Navy Samuel L. Southard routinely referred to four squadrons by name: the Mediterranean, West India, Brazilian, and Pacific. With the addition of the East India—later the Asiatic—Squadron in 1835, peacetime cruising organization changed only marginally throughout the rest of the century.

For Monroe's purposes, ships of the line were inefficient by their very nature. Their great cost of construction, maintenance, and operation prevented more than two—the *Franklin* and the *Columbus*—from reaching the high seas in his administration; their commanding firepower was concentrated in a small arc around each ship; their cumbersomeness prevented rapid maneuver and fast chase of small antagonists whose rigs enabled them to sail close to the wind; their deep keels precluded pursuit of shallow-draft prey into shoal waters. Monroe's navy needed only a few frigates backed by a score of 18-gun sloops, 12-gun brigs, and 8-gun schooners.

The president permanently transformed the United States Navy from an episodic scourge of North Africa into a worldwide policeman. He refused to create a battlefleet to challenge European navies. He had no use for such an armada. Instead he sent his ships to distant stations, where they often cooperated with European warships in the enforcement of Western standards of maritime behavior. His was a naval policy well calculated to meet the needs of a secure continental power with extensive maritime interests. It was especially useful as an adjunct to diplomacy in the West Indies, where nationalist revolutionaries were tearing down the Spanish Empire.

Monroe and Secretary of State John Quincy Adams conceived two diplomatic instruments to cover American penetration of former colonies of Spain in the Western Hemisphere: the Adams-Onís Treaty, signed in 1819 and jointly ratified in 1821, and the Monroe Doctrine of 1823. Together, these documents established a claim to American penetration of Latin American markets, particularly those in the Caribbean. But Monroe and Adams clearly felt that given the power vacuum created by Spain's withdrawal from the region, diplomatic initiatives must be backed with force.

As early as 1815 United States trade with the West Indies was second only to Great Britain's. Many American merchants became dependent upon it, and some of them also sought to enrich themselves by outfitting privateers—manned by unemployed American sailors—for service with the rebels in the wars against Spain. The

Spanish understandably resented this Yankee entrepreneurship. They protested to the United States, and whenever possible they captured the offending privateers and imprisoned the crews. The indignant Spanish also began to outfit their own privateers to seize American merchantmen in reprisal, hauling them to remote ports where they were condemned as legitimate prizes and auctioned off to the profit of the captors and judges alike. As Spanish authority deteriorated throughout the region and Spanish letters of marque and reprisal became legally meaningless, the erstwhile Spanish privateers became outright pirates, whose villainy knew no bounds, at least in the opinion of American congressmen. Pirate nests flourished from Venezuela to the Gulf Coast of the United States. Their chief target was the burgeoning western commerce of the Mississippi Valley through the port of New Orleans, second only to New York as the nation's busiest.

An exasperated Monroe turned to the navy. On 2 March 1819 he approved an act of Congress intended "to protect the commerce of the United States and punish the crime of piracy." It directed United States naval vessels to capture any armed vessel "which shall have attempted or committed any piratical aggression, search, restraint, depradation, or seizure upon any vessel of the United States." Secretary of State Adams denounced pirates for their "outrages and depredations" and shrugged off Spanish blockades as paper-thin and therefore "unwarranted by the laws of nations" because unenforced by warships in the immediate vicinity. The navy sent Captain Oliver Hazard Perry on a mission to dissuade Venezuela from wholesale licensing of privateer-pirates. The hero of Lake Erie died of yellow fever on the return voyage.

As soon as the Adams–Onís Treaty was ratified by both Spain and the United States in 1821, Monroe unleashed a campaign against commerce raiding, which cleared Spain's Caribbean islands of buccaneers in less than two years. The West India Squadron was created for this purpose. It was the navy's largest command, with 1,300 men and an initial fleet of four 12-gun schooners, two 18-gun brigs, an 18-gun sloop, and the flagship *Macedonian*, a 36-gun frigate. That force was later augmented by the secretary of the navy and Congress with a $44,000 appropriation for ten schooners, five cutters, and a converted river steamer, the *Sea Gull*—all shallow-draft pirate-chasers.

For the squadron's permanent headquarters, Secretary Thompson chose Key West, fortified a year after Thompson had directed

Lieutenant Matthew C. Perry—Oliver Hazard Perry's younger brother—to claim the strategically located Gulf island for the United States. To command the squadron the secretaries of the navy and state hand-picked two of the navy's most capable and aggressive captains: James Biddle, followed by David Porter.

As skipper of the sloop *Ontario* in 1818 Biddle had earned Adams's approval for asserting the rights of U.S. neutrals against the conflicting claims of Spanish and revolutionary governments on the Pacific coast of South America. Now focusing on Spanish Cuba and Puerto Rico, his new squadron's blue-water hunters captured some twenty-seven pirate vessels in 1822. He burned the small ones and brought the rest back to United States ports as prizes. His cooperation with the Royal Navy extended to joint landing parties in pursuit of buccaneers along the Cuban coast, an invasion of sovereignty resented by Spain but defended as regrettably necessary by Secretary of State Adams.

Captain Biddle would continue a long and distinguished career, but in December 1822, only eleven months after assignment to the West India Squadron, he was replaced by the even more aggressive David Porter. Already famous for his 1812–1814 *guerre de course* in the Pacific as skipper of the frigate *Essex,* Porter was also familiar with the hoary practices and politics of Caribbean piracy from a prior tour as commander of the naval station at New Orleans. Having demanded and received shallow-draft vessels, he used his enhanced squadron to complete the task of driving freebooters from the coast of Cuba by pursuing them into the inshore refuges where Biddle's heavier vessels could not go. Porter often operated from the side-wheeler *Sea Gull,* a precedent for subsequent commodores, who would forsake their deep-draft ships in coastal and riverine operations. He also turned his prisoners over to the Royal Navy for summary execution rather than send them back to the United States, where they were often pardoned and permitted to return to their grisly trade. "The patriotic zeal and enterprise of Commodore Porter" were praised by President Monroe in his annual message of 2 December 1823.

The president also called attention to the "significant cooperation of the government of the island of Cuba" and "the corresponding active exertions of a British naval force in the same seas." Antipiracy operations in the Gulf and Caribbean were now international ventures sanctioned and limited by the Monroe Doctrine, which warned Europeans that any attempt to "extend their political system" into the Western Hemisphere would endanger "our peace and happiness" and as a *quid pro quo* pledged United States respect for Europe's existing American colonies.

Commodore Porter's failure to grasp this nuance caused his downfall. In November 1824 he led two hundred armed men into Fajardo, a town in the Spanish colony of Puerto Rico, demanding at bayonet's point an official apology for the mistreatment of one of his officers who had been arrested as a trespasser while chasing thieves. Porter naïvely bragged to the secretary of the navy about his three-hour punitive expedition: "There is no doubt that our persons and our flag will be more respected hereafter . . . by the authorities of Porto Rico."

The president suspended Porter from command and recalled him to stand trial in a court-martial on the charge of disobeying orders. Found guilty in what was a show trial staged for diplomatic purposes, Porter was leniently sentenced to six months' suspension at full pay, because his intentions had been praiseworthy: "to maintain the honor and advance the interest of the nation and the service." A victim of Monroe's discreet policy and his own hubris, Porter railed against "an unrighteous sentence" and resigned from the United States Navy to become for a time commander of the Mexican navy.

David Porter was succeeded on the West Indies station by Commodore Lewis Warrington, whose meticulously correct relations with Spanish authorities and exemplary cooperation with the Royal Navy facilitated the final eradication of buccaneering in the Caribbean and the Gulf of Mexico in 1826. The West India Squadron, having completed its mission, was absorbed into a new Home Squadron in 1841.

For nearly three centuries the Caribbean had been ruled by international piracy, although under nominal Spanish sovereignty. Within a few years this Spanish lake had been transformed into a part of the coastal waters of the United States, where Anglo-American naval portals ensured safe transit for merchant vessels of all countries. A geopolitical revolution had been effected.

Anglo-American naval cooperation likewise prevailed in the Pacific Ocean, where Monroe and Adams again displayed their astute awareness of the synergistic relationship between naval force and commercial expansion. The naval instrument of their policy was the heroic former skipper of "Old Ironsides," Isaac Hull. On 27 March 1824 Commodore Hull arrived at Valparaiso with the 44-gun frigate *United States*. On board was the first United States minister to Chile, Heman Allen, the new commodore's brother-in-law. Both Allen and Hull acted under identical instructions drafted by Secretary of State

Adams and approved by President Monroe during a heated cabinet meeting, which debated those segments of the annual message to Congress of 1823 later known collectively as the Monroe Doctrine.

Secretary of the Navy Samuel L. Southard therefore spoke for the entire administration when he enjoined Hull, "Our relations with the government of Chile and Peru are of the most friendly character. . . . Your conduct must, on all occasions, be such as those relations require; at the same time full protection must be afforded to our citizens and their interest." In other words, Hull must protest if nationalists seized American merchant vessels for trafficking with isolated Spanish outposts, but he must restrain his naval officer's instinct to settle a dispute with cannon. Hull lamented his dilemma to his brother-in-law: "I am much at a loss how far I should be justified in using force when remonstrance is found to be unavailing."

Particularly irritating to Hull was the illegal seizure and taxation of ships by the four vessels commanded by Peru's semi-autonomous vice admiral, an English sailor of fortune named Martin George Guise. Hull worried that "were I to use force and disable his ship and General [Simón] Bolívar should fail in establishing the independence of Peru, it would be said that America was the first to acknowledge their independence and the first to injure their cause when endeavoring to regain it."

Commodore Hull did not experience a similar compunction regarding ships of the nearby Spanish squadron, whose operations he once impeded by anchoring in their line of fire and whose commander he loathed: "I do not believe he is either a Sailor or Soldier, nor do I believe that he is a man of honour or honesty." His contempt for the Spanish contrasted sharply with the mutual respect Hull shared with the officers of the Royal Navy. In a passage that goes a long way toward explaining the warmth of Anglo-American cooperation on distant station, a British officer aboard a ship of the line caught the essence of Hull and the American sailing navy at their prime:

> [Hull's] honest tar-like habits, the substantial fittings of the ship—her shrouds, stays and rigging generally possessing more scantling than that of the *Cambridge*, an 80-gun ship—the physical strength and excellent discipline of her crew. . . . All brought forcibly to my mind the Golden Days of our irresistible Navy before the Peace of Amiens. The *States* is a tremendous frigate.

With admirers like that alongside, Hull was not alone as he strove to carry out a delicate national policy.

Benevolent neutrality toward one belligerent or the other has never been an easy policy to enforce with warships, especially in a civil war, but Hull walked the tightrope gingerly enough to avoid official censure after the nationalists finally captured Callao in January 1826. Pacification of that busy port freed the commodore to send the two smaller vessels of his three-ship squadron—the sloop *Peacock* and the schooner *Dolphin*—on cruises far to the westward in compliance with Southard's general orders.

The secretary asked the impossible of Hull's modest force: to operate principally from Callao while keeping an eye on Valparaiso, some 1,700 miles to the south; and occasionally to drop an anchor along the coast of California, at the mouth of the Columbia River, and in the Sandwich (Hawaiian) Islands. From time to time Hull received more specific directives, one of which ordered him to search for mutineers from an American whaling ship. *Dolphin* led the way, touching at the Galápagos, Marquesas, and Mulgrave islands before reaching Honolulu.

The *Dolphin*'s arrival at Oahu in January 1826 exposed the bifurcated view overseas Americans had of the navy in the nineteenth century. Merchants welcomed the ship as a policeman able to intimidate native Hawaiians and maintain some order among the crews of whalers and merchantmen in port. Under the command of the fiery Captain John "Mad Jack'" Percival, *Dolphin* oversaw a mushrooming business; during her four-month stay American whalers and traders with a total value exceeding $2 million visited Oahu. Local missionaries, on the other hand, disliked the navy for encouraging a revival of prostitution, which had been recently outlawed. Their antipathy was very common throughout the nineteenth century, and it was reciprocated by commanding officers like Percival, who knew that a ship's morale improved when a "liberty" including sexual release was in sight. They had scant incentive to heed Southard's informal plea to cooperate with the missionaries and "receive the benediction of the pious for the good you may perform."

Sloop-of-war *Peacock* was next out, sailing in June 1826. Commanded by Thomas ap Catesby Jones, she called at the Marquesas—abortively claimed for the United States by David Porter in 1813—and pressed westward to the Society Islands. The first American warship to reach Tahiti, *Peacock* next headed north to the Hawaiian Islands. In Tahiti and Honolulu Jones drew up treaties with native potentates intended to ensure safe treatment of shipwrecked American sailors, and the treaty with King Kamehameha III included a most-favored-nation clause. Although neither document was ratified by the United States, the provision for trading on a most-favored-nation basis had roots in the Model Treaty drafted by John Adams in 1776. The goal of safe treatment for mariners stranded in remote and inhospitable places was consistently pursued by diplomats, naval and civilian alike, until superseded by the birth of late-nineteenth-century imperialism. Both concepts were part and parcel of American foreign policy in the age of sail.

No ship from Hull's squadron reached the Columbia River, a point for checking British imperial ambitions in the Pacific Northwest, but James Biddle had staked a firm claim to the river's mouth as skipper of the 22-gun sloop *Ontario* in 1818. The pattern of operations and the composition of the Pacific Squadron therefore had been thoroughly established when Hull's "Old Wagon" weighed anchor for the last time at Valparaiso on 23 January 1827. The *United States* set sail to the accompaniment of a 13-gun salute fired by the British flagship *Cambridge*. Her replacement, the fast frigate *Brandywine*, joined in rendering honors and then settled down to routine patrols of the area circumscribed by "Uncle Isaac's" scouts.

From the flagship's normal station in Callao or Valparaiso—the most frequented ports of call for American merchantmen heading to or from the Pacific—the squadron's smaller ships were assigned to cruise to the Society and Hawaiian islands, touch at lesser South American ports and Panama, and occasionally probe farther northward toward Mexico and especially California. In 1829, under orders from President Adams and Secretary Southard, the sloop *Vincennes* returned home to New York from Honolulu by way of the Portuguese colony of Macao, the East Indies, the Indian Ocean, and the Cape of Good Hope. This first circumnavigation by an American warship put the western Pacific within relatively safe reach of the United States and marked the way by which American warships would look after commerce, ships, and sailors from China to Africa once the East India Squadron was established in 1835.

By the time the *Vincennes* reached New York, the federal government had changed hands. Andrew Jackson—"Old Hickory"—was as rough-hewn, pugnacious, and vulgar as John Quincy Adams had been polished, diplomatic, and sophisticated. A freewheeling son of the South and West, the hero of New Orleans opposed "standing armies as dangerous to free governments in time of peace." He thought that "the bulwark of our defense is the national militia, which in the present state of our intelligence and population must render us invincible." This sensible viewpoint did not cause him to oppose the navy, "whose flag has displayed in distant climes our skill in navigation and our fame in arms." He understood, however, that in time of peace the United States needed "no more ships of war than are requisite to the protection of our commerce."

The ships of the line that had been partially completed under the provisions of the naval act of 1821 lay rotting at dockside in the navy yards. The cost of commissioning them would be prohibitive, and Jackson therefore had "little doubt that our best policy would be to discontinue the building of ships of the first and second class." Instead the navy should stockpile timber and other materials for the construction of large warships in a national emergency with a European power. He gauged the stockpiled materials rather than the number of ships afloat "as the index of our naval power." A navy of 5,000 officers and men—precisely the complement of one modern supercarrier—seemed adequate for the nation. This Monroe-like prescription guided Jackson throughout his first term and most of his second. Conservative in terms of expenditures, manpower, and construction, it did not preclude an aggressive use of the navy on distant stations, where Jackson unsheathed the sword more readily than his predecessors.

Two examples—one in the Pacific, the other in the South Atlantic—illustrate the bellicosity of Jackson's naval diplomacy. In 1831 the cargo vessel *Friendship* out of Salem, Massachusetts, was captured by armed natives while in the port of Quallah Battoo (Kuala Batu) on the Dutch-claimed East Indies island of Sumatra. Three of her crewmen were killed in the raid, but her skipper escaped, rallied American sailors from other ships, recaptured his vessel, and returned to the United States screaming for blood. The *Friendship* was one of hundreds of American merchantmen to visit the "pepper coast" between 1795 and 1832 in a profitable trade controlled by merchants of Salem and Boston. The unprecedented assault upon her was probably stimulated largely by drug-lust. As was unfortunately common with American merchantmen in the nineteenth century, she carried a valuable cargo of opium, which the raiders quickly grabbed. One of her owners was a United States senator, and he wrote directly to the president demanding redress.

The heavy frigate *Potomac*, carrying fifty guns, was preparing for sea under the command of Captain John Downes, so Jackson and Secretary of the Navy Levi Woodbury ordered Downes to Sumatra by way of the Cape of Good Hope, the preferred passage to the western Pacific. Woodbury instructed Downes to verify the account of the attack reported by the *Friendship*'s commander before exacting retribution. But British army and navy officers at Cape Town warned Downes that the people of Quallah Battoo were treacherous and dangerous pirates, precisely the admonition that this protégé of the trigger-happy David Porter needed. On 6 February 1832, without warning, he landed sailors and marines at Quallah Battoo, killed more than a hundred Sumatrans in hand-to-hand fighting, and then lobbed a few broadsides at the remaining defenders. He sailed on to Java, China, Hawaii, and Tahiti before taking up command of the Pacific Squadron at Valparaiso.

Downes's aggressiveness caused a partisan uproar in Washington, where the new Whig party censured the Democratic administration for waging war without a congressional declaration. Downes was baffled, thinking himself justified by the nature of the Sumatrans and the size of his ship: "I could not believe for a moment that my Government had dispatched a vessel of such dimensions, and through seas so dangerous, without attaching to her movement expectations of National importance." Woodbury reassured Downes that President Jackson had "the highest consideration for the coolness, firmness, and skill evinced by yourself, officers, and men." In December 1832 President Jackson publicly praised Downes for inflicting a suitable "chastisement" on a "band of lawless pirates," the effect of which was "an increased respect for our flag in those distant seas and additional security for our commerce." To spare itself and Downes the embarrassing ordeal of a court-martial, the administration prudently let him finish his two-year tour as commodore of the Pacific Squadron while the political storm subsided at home.

Jackson was equally determined to advance American commercial interests in the South Atlantic. The Falkland Islands, claimed by Argentina but located 1,200 miles south of Buenos Aires and some 300 miles east of the Straits of Magellan, comprised a rich seal rookery in the early nineteenth century. Louis Vernet, the leading colonist and resident Argentine governor general, had declared the habitat off limits to American hunters in order to prevent depletion of the fur-bearing herds. In July 1831 he seized an American vessel, the *Harriet*, whose crew had been slaughtering seals ashore despite repeated warnings. The ship was taken to Buenos Aires for condemnation as a prize, but when word of the detention reached Captain Silas M. Duncan of the 24-gun sloop *Lexington* at Montevideo, he decided to step in without awaiting special orders from the Navy Department.

Duncan sailed south and issued an ultimatum at Buenos Aires demanding the trial of Vernet as a pirate and thief. When properly rebuffed, he stormed off to the Falklands. There he landed, spiked the local fort's cannon, and arrested several colonists.

The colony never regained its tenuous viability, and two years later Britain administered the *coup de grâce* by permanently occupying the Falklands. Buenos Aires severed diplomatic relations with Washington, a rupture that lasted for more than a decade. Despite the reprehensibility of the *Harriet* and Duncan's unwarranted impetuosity, the Jackson administration backed him after the fact. According to Secretary of State Edward Livingston, "Vernet and his band" were indistinguishable from pirates, and "the President has signified to Captain Duncan that he entirely approves of his conduct."

The episodes at the Falklands and Quallah Battoo were symptomatic of national policy, but the Jackson administration showed its unambiguous resolve to expand the navy's commercial-diplomatic mission in a number of other less sensational instances. In 1830 James Biddle, by then commodore of the Mediterranean Squadron, helped through his sagacious commentary to win Senate approval of the first Turkish–American treaty of amity and commerce. Long desired by the United States as a protective umbrella over an annual trade exceeding $1 million in value, the 1830 pact set a standard for nineteenth-century American diplomacy outside Western Europe. It provided for most-favored-nation status, opened the Black Sea to American merchantmen, permitted the stationing of American consuls in Turkish ports, confirmed the principle of extraterritoriality—Americans accused of crimes committed in Turkey would be tried under American law by presumably sympathetic consular courts—and guaranteed humane treatment to shipwrecked American sailors.

The Senate's lopsided endorsement (42 to 1) and Jackson's enthusiastic ratification gave irrefutable evidence of a bipartisan continuity of naval-diplomatic policy. Regardless of the domestic differences dividing conservative anti-Jacksonians—of whom Biddle privately was one—and the egalitarian followers of "Old Hickory," neither faction was impractical enough to let political ideology interfere with the pursuit of profit through a well-regulated and expanding overseas commerce. That lesson was not lost on less senior naval officers, notably Master Commandant Matthew C. Perry, the skipper of one of Biddle's Mediterranean ships in 1832. Perry's penetration of Japan two decades later merely completed work in the western Pacific begun by the navy in the age of Jackson.

In 1832 Secretary Woodbury, pleased with Captain Downes's action at Quallah Battoo, ordered a detachment of two ships to Sumatra and "such places in India, China, and on the eastern coast of Africa, as may be conducive to the security and prosperity of our important commercial interests in those regions." The secretary selected Master-Commandant David Geisinger to command the ship-rigged sloop-of-war *Peacock* and a new schooner, the *Boxer*. Sailing aboard the *Peacock* under the guise of a captain's clerk was Edmund Roberts, a businessman from New Hampshire who had persuaded Woodbury that the time was ripe for negotiating commercial treaties with kingdoms bordering the Indian Ocean and South China Sea. Woodbury ordered Geisinger to treat Roberts "as a Gentleman having the confidence of the Government and entrusted with important duties in India, Arabia, and Africa." The Navy Department paid one-third of Roberts's salary, and the State Department provided the other two-thirds from a "contingent fund for Foreign Intercourse."

This was a well-conceived national mission looking to treaties that would promise humane treatment of shipwrecked American sailors awaiting repatriation. It also sought to put American commerce "on the footing of that of the most favoured nations." Yankee trade in the western Pacific was extensive. In 1831–1832 thirty American merchantmen called at Chinese ports. Others regularly brought cargoes to Cochin-China (part of Vietnam), the Philippines, and the East Indies, while American whalers hunted off Japan. None of this activity was protected by treaties with local rulers, although vessels calling at ports in the Philippines, the Dutch East Indies, India, and Ceylon (Sri Lanka) were shielded from arbitrary treatment by United States pacts with the respective colonial masters: Spain, the Netherlands, and Britain.

Fluent in Spanish and French and personally familiar with Arabia and the east coast of Africa, Roberts was the right man for an important job. He and Geisinger logged 43,150 miles in 412 days under sail between February 1832 and May 1834. They visited Sumatra, Manila, Whampoa (Huangpu), Canton (Guangzhou), Cochin-China, Bangkok, Singapore, the Gulf of Aden, the Red Sea, Yemen, and Mozambique. Roberts brought home commercial treaties with Siam (Thailand) and the sultan of Muscat, whose territories stretched from the Persian Gulf to Zanzibar. Both were easily ratified, and Roberts was again sent out on a warship as America's roving diplomat, this time to exchange articles of ratification in Muscat and Bangkok before heading north to try his hand with the reclusive Japanese. On

23 April 1835 he sailed, once more aboard the *Peacock* and now accompanied by the *Boxer*'s sister ship, the *Enterprise*.

The new secretary of the navy, Mahlon Dickerson, broke fresh ground in his orders to the new commanding officer of the *Peacock*, Captain Edmund P. Kennedy. Unlike Geisinger, who had remained technically subordinate to another squadron commander, Kennedy was his own boss: "As this is to be a separate and distinct service from that of any of the Squadrons now employed, the Commander will be allowed to hoist his broad pendant and receive the allowances incident to the command of a Squadron." At very little cost to itself, the navy through this designation enhanced its own prestige in the Orient. By bearing the honorary rank of commodore, Kennedy was entitled to the same salutes and honors accorded to European squadron commanders in Asian waters and thus, it was hoped, would appear more intimidating in the eyes of local authorities. The possible impact he and Roberts might have had on Japan unfortunately cannot be determined, because the envoy succumbed to cholera and dysentery in Macao.

Lacking credentials to negotiate alone, Kennedy turned east and headed home to Norfolk, Virginia, via Honolulu, Mexico, Callao, Cape Horn, and Rio de Janeiro—another circumnavigation for an American warship. He returned to a country whose sensitivity to the navy was running high following a war scare with France. Congress as a result made specific recommendations regarding the number of ships in each squadron, including the East India. The legacy of Roberts, Geisinger, and Kennedy therefore was not so much the two treaties as it was a new and permanent squadron whose commodores in the next two decades would extract commercial treaties from two proudly reluctant nations: China and Japan.

In March 1837 Andrew Jackson bequeathed to his chosen heir, Martin Van Buren, a modestly expanded navy that fitted the national purpose like a comfortable shoe. Its twenty-one ships in commission included one ship of the line and five frigates as principals—the remainder being sloops, schooners, and brigs. Distributed among five squadrons, all those ships operated away from the Atlantic coast, which could remain defenseless so long as the unwritten Anglo-American understanding endured.

Van Buren showed little interest in the navy, and in any event his administration soon was preoccupied with the financial panic and serious economic depression of 1837. Mahlon Dickerson remained at the navy's helm until 30 June 1838, when he was replaced as secretary by James K. Paulding, who served for the remainder of the Van Buren presidency. The new secretary preferred writing literary works to administering the Navy Department. He lamented to his friend Washington Irving that "to a gentleman of leisure like myself, it comes rather hard to work like a horse and be abused like a pickpocket for my pains." At the next level down, John Rodgers retired as chairman of the Board of Navy Commissioners in 1837. His immediate replacement was Isaac Chauncey, who had served with Rodgers as a senior officer in the War of 1812.

Paulding took over a navy whose officer corps was moody and discontented. From his viewpoint, Dickerson had been too lenient and as a result "a low, dirty, sordid feeling . . . seems to pervade all ranks of the Navy. . . . Not an officer can lift his hand, or perform any, the most trifling duty, . . . without foisting up a claim for remuneration." His "young Midshipmen & Lieutenants too, are extremely Bilious at this Season of the year, and when I order them in Service, answer me by a request for permission to accompany mamma to the White Sulphur Springs for their health." He dismissed a few midshipmen, insisted that a call to duty came before personal convenience, and concluded that tightened discipline had improved the officers' morale.

Paulding continued the limited naval expansion begun under Dickerson, so that by the time he left office in 1841 the annual budget exceeded $5 million, nearly double the yearly fiscal figure for 1829 to 1835. The naval register now listed twenty-six commissioned ships distributed worldwide: three each in the permanent squadrons—Mediterranean, West Indies, Pacific, and East Indies—with most of the remainder cruising between Brazil and Africa as part of an intermittently assiduous antislavery patrol. From Paulding's perspective, therefore, his tenure as secretary of the navy during the unhappy one-term administration of Martin Van Buren was productive, if indeed "laborious, vexatious, and thankless."

Others viewed Paulding's work quite differently. The critics focused on two shortcomings of the navy of the late 1830s: its resistance to steam and the alleged incompetence of the Board of Navy Commissioners. The most caustic foe of the board was Lieutenant Matthew F. Maury, who in 1840 and 1841 wrote a withering series of articles in the *Southern Literary Messenger* under the pen name "Harry Bluff." Maury later had a brilliant career as a meteorologist and oceanographer and a less distinguished one as an officer in the Confederate States Navy, but during Paulding's stewardship he devoted himself to attacking the "bad" organization of the board and the malevolent influence of its head: "Some will tell you that the Navy Board is a power behind the Secretary greater than the Secretary himself—that there is a Master-Spirit in that board, which rules the Navy. Others will tell you that the evil genius of the Navy presides at that board."

Maury laid virtually every defect of the navy at the feet of the commissioners. He wrote so passionately and compellingly that Congress revamped the entire administrative system of the navy shortly after Paulding left office. Yet the record shows that on all matters of policy the board's functions were purely advisory. The policies themselves originated with the presidents and their cabinets, appropriations to carry them out came from Congress, and movement orders for ships were written and signed by the secretary of the navy in consultation with the secretary of state. The record shows also that the sailing navy of 1816–1842 realistically met the national purposes with ships designed for the conditions they encountered.

Maury's real frustration was rooted in an abysmally slow promotion system that kept talented young officers like himself in subordinate positions throughout their most energetic years. In a way, Maury wanted Isaac Chauncey's job, not abolition of the board. That was implicitly recognizd by supporters of Maury who briefly touted him as a candidate for secretary of the navy on the basis of the "Harry Bluff" articles. But despite the success of Maury's attack on the board, promotion based on merit rather than strict seniority did not come to the navy until passage of the Naval Personnel Act of 1899.

The full integration of steam into the navy took an equally long time. The United States had launched its first steam warship, the *Fulton*, in 1814. An invention of Robert Fulton, the strange craft mounted a paddle wheel between protective twin hulls. She was designed to defend New York but never saw active service, because the War of 1812 ended before she was completed. The next steam-propelled American warship was the *Fulton II*, begun in 1835 at the direction of Secretary Dickerson and launched at the navy yard in New York in 1837. A hybrid driven by both sails and steam, she too was intended for harbor defense and was not meant to be oceangoing. But Matthew C. Perry, an advocate of steam power, won assignment as her first commander and prepared the way for the integration into a ship's company of two entirely new species: the steam engineering officers and their enlisted counterparts. He extended honorary membership in the wardroom mess to the *Fulton*'s steam engineer.

From 1837 to 1842 Perry's *Fulton II* attracted attention in coastal cities, and Secretary Paulding was appalled by the "steam fever now raging among us." He would yield enough ground to "keep the steam enthusiasts quiet . . . but I will never consent to let our old ships perish, and transform our Navy into a fleet of sea monsters." It took an act of Congress to force the secretary to convene two special naval boards charged with establishing the guidelines for oceangoing steam-driven warships. The panels met in Washington in 1839 and conceived of two large steam-wheel frigates, the *Mississippi* and *Missouri*, which were completed in 1842.

Paulding's disdain for steam-driven warships derived from an aesthetic appreciation for the potent beauty of a square-rigger flying before a stiff wind under full sail. But his intransigence also had pragmatic roots. Sailing ships of the old navy typically remained on distant station for two years or more. During that extended cruise they spent much time in foreign ports watching over American maritime and mercantile interests. The crews went ashore almost daily for fresh provisions and water, for their greatest enemies were the diseases bred by bad food and the stifling air of cramped and soggy quarters—cholera, generalized dysentery, scurvy, and, in the West Indies, yellow fever. While in port the sailors drilled at hauling out the guns, caulked the leaky seams of wooden hulls, replaced rotted or damaged spars, tightened slack rigging, and restitched frayed sails. They effected this essential maintenance largely with supplies carried in their ships, sometimes with materials borrowed from other vessels, and rarely with supplies purchased ashore.

The U.S. Navy soon would learn that steam-driven warships were not as self-sufficient as the old square-riggers. For upkeep and repair steamers required workshops and coal depots on distant station. The technology that was making ships free of the winds was tying them to overseas bases, and the United States had not a single colony in the entire Pacific Ocean.

Paulding saw the vast Pacific basin as a proper operating area for the navy, and his cruising orders to Commodore Alexander Claxton of 9 May 1839 succinctly expressed the operational rationale of the United States Navy at the crest of the age of sail. It was symbolic that Claxton's flagship was America's most beloved sailing frigate, "Old Ironsides," the U.S.S. *Constitution.* "The primary objects of the Government of the U.S. in maintaining a naval Force in the Pacific Ocean," Paulding reminded his squadron commander, "have always been, and still are, the protection of our commerce and the improvement of discipline, by affording active service to the officers of and crews of our vessels." Claxton was to remain at sea for as much of the time as possible, "without losing sight of other objects; frequently exercising your guns; clearing the Ships for action . . . and as often as they shall be together, passing them through such maneuvers as their limited number will permit, so that should it ever be their fortune to be called upon to act in concert, the officers and men will not be taken altogether by surprise."

The Pacific Squadron continued to pivot around Callao and Valparaiso, the principal seaports of mutually antagonistic Peru and Chile. Paulding deplored the "great confusion and uncertainty" in the two countries, but he did not intend to abandon the important American interests in South America. "Revolutions of rulers rather than principles still agitate these regions so favored by nature, and the commerce of neutrals continues to require the protection of a competent naval force." Without diverting his attention from the west coast of South America between Valparaiso and Panama, Claxton should detach ships as necessary "for the protection of the interests of the U. States at the Sandwich [Hawaiian] or Society Islands."

Those guidelines reaffirmed existing policy, but Paulding broke precedent in setting the northern limits of Claxton's squadron: "The increasing commerce of the U. States, within the Gulf [of California] and along the coast, of California, as far as the Bay of San Francisco, together with the weakness of the local authorities and their irresponsibility to the distant Government of Mexico, renders it proper in the opinion of the Department, that occasional countenance and protection should be afforded to American enterprize in that quarter." Claxton should send a sloop, a smaller vessel, or both north to the California coast "as occasion may require."

Acting under this general directive, in June 1840 Commander French Forrest showed the American flag and the twenty guns of the sloop-of-war *St. Louis* to the Mexican rulers of Monterey, who had imprisoned a group of British and American citizens on charges of attempting to set up an independent government. The Anglo-American troublemakers were promptly released from jail. In praising Forrest for carrying out his orders, Paulding's successor, Abel P. Upshur, fired the opening volley of the coming war for the conquest of Mexico:

The atrocities committed on American and English residents of Monterey and its neighborhood, by the Mexican authorities, are well known. Under the unfounded pretence of a conspiracy among the foreigners to wrest the country from Mexico, and to set up a separate and independent Government of their own, they were attacked by armed soldiers in the night, wounded, beaten, imprisoned, sent in chains to a distant place, and their property destroyed, without even the forms of trial.

The "prompt and spirited interposition" of Commander Forrest "vindicated and secured the rights not only of American citizens, but of British subjects in California."

The accolade from the navy's senior official, made in a report to the president, demonstrates the contempt of nineteenth-century Americans for the Mexican government. Moreover, regardless of the intensifying Anglo-American rivalry for possession of the Pacific Northwest, British and United States naval officers would continue their policy of mutual protection of one another's nationals whenever threatened by other governments or peoples in remote areas of the world.

The most complex case of "gunboat diplomacy" to concern Paulding involved China during the Opium War (1840–1842), the effect of which was a drastic reduction in Chinese–American trade. Faced with a deterioration of the American commercial position in China and numerous recommendations for a permanent naval presence on the China coast, Paulding on 2 November 1840 ordered Captain Lawrence Kearny to sail for Macao via the Cape of Good Hope with the proud old frigate *Constellation* and the sloop *Boston*. Kearny's remarkable orders enlarged the geographical scope of the East India Squadron substantially, iterated a precise policy regarding blockades by belligerents, anticipated a sophisticated and somewhat duplicitous level of exchanges with the Chinese, and required astute intelligence-gathering by the commodore.

At Macao Kearny's task would be complex and important: "to protect the interests of the United States & their citizens on the Coast of China, most especially during the existence of the war of that Country with England." Kearny must scrupulously observe any "legal blockade established by the British force." Simultaneously, he had to ensure that the British naval commander had not "illegally molested" Americans or their property, and if so he was to gain redress through "an appeal to the law of nations, combined with firm, yet temperate remonstrances." He was to conform to "the usual Etiquette" in his "intercourse with the British Commander," an injunction made pointed by the fact that the British had on station more than twenty warships. If the Chinese gained the reasonable impression that Kearny's solicitude for the Royal Navy's goodwill constituted cooperation with the attacking power, the commodore was to assure them that he had come only "to protect our citizens from Pirates [and] to prevent and punish the smuggling of opium into China either by Americans or by other nations under cover of the American Flag." While performing this diplomatic balancing act, Kearny should also report "regularly & promptly" to the Navy Department on

> the nature & extent of the force employed by the British Government, as well as the demands it has made on that of China. Also whether it is likely this [British] force will be sufficient to accomplish the objects aimed at, & if not whether it is probable reinforcements will be sent.

When the Anglo-Chinese war abated, Kearny was to turn to the secondary objects of his squadron's cruise. By sailing to New Zealand and along the western coast of Australia, he would encourage and protect American whalers from unspecified dangers. On his return home he was to stop at "the Sandwich, Society, and other Islands, which are daily becoming more & more frequented by our whale ships, and where the frequent appearance of our vessels of war is considered of great benefit to those growing interests." From Hawaii he would proceed to "the Coast of California, with the same objects in view," and then along the western flank of South America, finally to reach Boston via Cape Horn in mid-1843.

Paulding's expansive orders did not establish a permanent naval presence in Chinese waters as urged by many petitioners, but they did dramatically expand the putative operating area of the East India Squadron southward, northward, and eastward.

======

In the Pacific Ocean proper, another American squadron had its limits stretched between 1837 and 1841. The Pacific Squadron assumed the boundaries it would patrol until the twentieth century: "All of the west coast of America, and westward from the meridian of Cape Horn to the 180th degree of longitude; and southward between those meridians to the South Pole." The squadron's northern extremities lay in the uncharted Arctic, and ships of the U.S. Navy now routinely crisscrossed the Pacific Ocean.

To embellish those expanding operations, Paulding sent forth the United States Exploring Expedition of 1838–1842. The idea of organizing a naval expedition to explore the southernmost latitudes of the Atlantic and Pacific Oceans had originated a decade earlier during the administration of John Quincy Adams, but it was not funded by Congress until 1836. Then, after a good deal of bureaucratic fumbling in the Navy Department, President Martin Van Buren had ordered Secretary of War Joel R. Poinsett to get it started. Poinsett reached deep into navy ranks for a leader, picking a forty-year-old junior lieutenant, Charles Wilkes. Known for his scientific interests and belief in stern naval discipline, Wilkes was an inspired choice. By July 1838 the Wilkes expedition was a going concern, which Paulding smoothly integrated into his own scheme for enlarging the role of the navy in the Pacific. "The Expedition is not for conquest, but discovery," Paulding suavely reminded Wilkes. "Its objects are all peaceful; they are to extend the empire of commerce and science; to diminish the hazards of the ocean, and point out to future navigators a course by which they may avoid dangers and find safety."

Wilkes set sail from Hampton Roads, Virginia, on 18 August 1838. Under his command were six small ships, forty-seven commissioned officers, 342 enlisted men, and several civilian scientists, most notably the geologist James Dwight Dana and the naturalist Titian Peale. Entering the Pacific by way of treacherous Cape Horn—where one ship was lost with all hands—the squadron worked its way northward to Callao, turned west to Tahiti and Samoa, then south to Sydney, Australia. From Sydney the ships sailed dangerously farther south toward the unknown, and on 19 January 1840 made the first authenticated discovery of Antarctica. They returned to Hawaii via Sydney, New Zealand, and the Fiji Islands. In Fiji the group encountered its only serious trouble with islanders: The natives killed two officers—one of them Wilkes's nephew—for which savagery Wilkes razed a village and slew eighty-seven inhabitants. From Hawaii the squadron headed to North America, where Wilkes surveyed three potential naval harbors: Puget Sound, the Columbia River, and San Francisco Bay. The sloop *Peacock* was wrecked on the bar at Columbia's mouth, a loss that colored Wilkes's subsequent recommendations to the secretary of the navy. In November 1841 the remaining ships headed west again, to Honolulu, Wake Island, Manila, Singapore, and home via the Indian Ocean and the Cape of Good Hope.

The sloop *Vincennes*, flagship of the United States Exploring Expedition, arrived at New York on 10 June 1842, after logging 87,000 miles in a cruise lasting 1,392 days. To Wilkes's great chagrin, the Whig President John Tyler and Secretary of the Navy Abel P. Upshur received him with cold indifference, perhaps seeing him as a vestige of the recently defeated and much vilified Democratic administration. But Wilkes could as well blame his own prickly personality. For nearly four years he had played the role of martinet, assuming the title and uniform of a captain although only a lieutenant. His insistence on strict discipline harshly enforced alienated many of the officers, including some who had volunteered for the expedition out of admiration for its commander. An ugly round robin of mutual accusations and courts-martial ensued. Wilkes was "publicly reprimanded" by Secretary Upshur for "illegally punishing or causing to be punished, men in the squadron under your command."

Chastened but not subdued, Wilkes devoted most of his next twenty years to publishing the results of the expedition, beginning with a five-volume narrative in 1845 and culminating in twenty-one published volumes of scientific findings on topics ranging from ethnography through zoology. The thousands of specimens and artifacts collected by the expedition led directly to the establishment of the Smithsonian Institution in 1846, and a century later the charts published by Wilkes proved accurate and useful during the U.S. Navy's Pacific campaigns of World War II.

More immediately, Wilkes helped nudge the United States toward an empire on the Pacific with a confidential report to the secretary of the navy and with public lectures attended by Upshur, John Quincy Adams, Thomas Hart Benton—a lifelong advocate of a maritime "passage to India"—and members of the cabinet, among others. Wilkes delivered resounding endorsements of San Francisco Bay and Puget Sound—the one held by Mexico and the other claimed by both Britain and the United States—as possible ports for American warships. He denigrated the mouth of the Columbia River with equal fierceness. Of the strategic importance of San Francisco he left no doubt: "The Bay of San Francisco is well adapted for a naval depot. . . . Its possession ensures us the command of the Northern Pacific." To guarantee free American access to the open waters of Puget Sound he recommended that the final boundary of Oregon be drawn above the 49th parallel.

Lieutenant Charles Wilkes had returned to the United States at a time when the foreign and naval policies of the nation were in ferment. Americans had begun their great westward migration over the Oregon Trail, leading President Tyler in 1843 to remind Britain that the United States had always claimed rights to "the entire region of country" between 42 degrees and 54 degrees, 40 minutes north latitude. "Fifty-four forty or fight" would become a Democratic battle cry in the presidential election of 1844, but by then Tyler had already staked out an American claim for the high ground of the Pacific Northwest, just as he had for San Francisco and Hawaii.

In 1842 Tyler sounded out Mexico about ceding the great California bay to the United States. He also publicly warned the world that because of the propinquity of the Hawaiian Islands to North America and because "five-sixths" of the merchant and whaling vessels annually visiting the islands were American, the United States must feel "dissatisfaction . . . at any attempt by another power . . . to take possession of the islands, colonize them, and subvert the native Government." To back his claim for Pacific hegemony, the president proposed to increase the number of naval vessels in commission from twenty-five to forty-one and "to build 12 ships of a small class."

Tyler's secretary of the navy, Abel P. Upshur of Virginia, was an avid naval reformer, modernizer, and expansionist. He was attuned to the contemporary criticisms of the old order voiced by fellow Virginian Matthew Fontaine Maury in the same journal to which he himself contributed articles. His first annual report of 4 December 1841 showed a sharp awareness of the navy's shortcomings and a determination to remedy them. As a working premise, Upshur asserted "that it is now the settled policy of the Government to increase the navy as rapidly as the means at its disposal will admit."

Upshur's main justification for enlarging the navy was the nation's burgeoning overseas commerce, which he "regarded as our principal interest, because, to a great extent, it includes within it every other interest." Just as Alfred Thayer Mahan would argue fifty years later, Upshur contended: "Wars often arise from rivalry in trade, and from the conflicts of interests which belong to it." But unlike the prophet of sea power, who decried commerce raiding as indecisive, Upshur hoped that a plethora of small cruisers—sloops, brigs, and schooners—roving the commercial sea lanes would prevent escalation "by promptly redressing the injuries" inflicted on overseas American commerce by another power.

Regardless of the commercial imperative, by "ranking in the first class of nations" the American people came "under an absolute necessity to regulate our policy by that of other countries." Since for several years "the considerable maritime Powers of Europe" had been increasing their navies, "we should make similar preparation." Here again, Upshur appears to anticipate Mahan's emphasis on naval strength as a true index of national greatness, and like Mahan he wrote at a time of technological transition. But Upshur's conclusions about the tactical nature of a European–American naval war in the nascent age of steam and iron had more in common with Thomas Jefferson's gunboats than Mahan's battleships.

As a slaveholder, Upshur feared a foreign invasion aimed at inciting revolution among the slave population. Such an assault, "horrible in its effects" and previously unthinkable, had become dangerously possible as a result of the "application of steam power to vessels of war, and the improvements which have recently been made in artillery." In the past, when "maritime wars were conducted in vessels of large size and great draught," the relatively few deep-water harbors of the East and Gulf coasts created topographical security, but with the advent of shallow-draft steamers most of the American coastline now lay defenseless. "Steamboats of light draught, and which may be easily transported across the ocean in vessels of a large class, may invade us at almost any point of our extended coast, may penetrate the interior through our shallow rivers, and thus expose half our country to hostile attacks."

Upshur's friend, Virginia Representative Henry A. Wise, said the greatest danger came from the British, who were establishing "another Gibraltar at Bermuda . . . where they had laid up abundant stores of coal and every other requisite for their ships in time of war." By staging out of the Royal Navy's base at Jamaica, Britain could demolish the social foundation of the South with a black-manned army of liberation. Such fears presaged the Confederacy's dilemma of naval defense during the Civil War.

Upshur's strategy was thoroughly conservative and traditional. He would build a substantial number of "steam vessels of a smaller class, destined for the defence of our own coast and harbors." Those gunboats would prove especially suitable for the Gulf of Mexico, where the only deep-draft harbor was Pensacola. To meet the enemy at sea, Upshur would extend government subsidies to privately built steam "packets" for conversion into commerce raiders in a crisis. He would razee the navy's half-dozen ships of the line and convert them into heavy frigates, and he would construct a new class of heavy frigates to replace the grand old 44s. His proposed ten new small seagoing ships—sloops, brigs, and schooners—would raid the enemy's commerce according to the classic American formula for *guerre de course* in wars against stronger powers.

The limited Anglo-American rapprochement occasioned by negotiation of the Webster–Ashburton Treaty in 1842 permitted Upshur to clear his mind. No longer faced with the appalling prospect of a war that conceivably could prove fatal to his section of the country, the secretary could concentrate on reforming and modernizing a navy whose peacetime functions\were well understood. He sought four major reforms: establishment of a naval academy; statutory delimitation of the number of officers occupying each of the three commissioned ranks (lieutenant, commander, and captain); creation of the additional rank of admiral; and abolition of the Board of Navy Commissioners. Congress, however, was frustratingly indifferent. It was only by working closely with his ally, Representative Wise, chairman of both the Ways and Means and Naval Affairs committees, that Upshur extracted a single reform from the House: replacement of the Board of Navy Commissioners with five "bureaux."

By legislative intent each of the new bureaus constituted a highly specialized administrative apparatus whose chief—usually a very senior captain—acted in the name of the secretary of the navy. Each chief of bureau therefore exercised extraordinary but limited power downward and outward from his office in Washington, D.C. This aura of authority, coupled with good pay, modest and regular hours, a fixed residency, and freedom from sea duty, attracted middle-aged men anxious to settle into a comfortable and respected pattern of living. The second chief of the most powerful antebellum bureau, Joseph Smith of the Bureau of Yards and Docks, held tenaciously to his office for almost a quarter of a century. As head of that bureau, Smith oversaw the construction and maintenance of all facilities at the eight navy yards and disbursed as much as $2 million annually. The line officers commanding the yards reported directly to him, which meant that he could at least influence if not dictate their future careers.

Heady stuff, but strictly circumscribed. Neither Smith nor any of his fellow bureau chiefs individually or collectively ordered senior officers to the command of squadrons or ships, assigned ships to the squadrons, or directed the deployment of ships to meet crises. Those crucial operational powers were reserved to the secretary, who communicated directly with squadron commodores, often in the name of the president and frequently as a result of consultation with the secretary of state.

The authority of the bureau chiefs was further diluted by a raging feud between line officers and staff officers, especially the engineers. Then as now, command of a major ship was the ultimate goal of every line officer. Prior to the advent of the steam engine, the commanding officer in theory was the most skilled sailor aboard a warship, the man whose experience and expertise enabled him to fly the suit of sails that would impart the maximum thrust in whatever direction he wanted to go. The same knowledge, born of instinct and nourished during a lifetime at sea, enabled him to trim the sails quickly when he wanted to maneuver the ship in combat. The senior line officer knew everything about taut lines and billowing canvas, but nothing about coal-blackened boilers and hot steam engines. Yet in the new age, the man who understood the steam engine was the man who could extract the maximum speed and maneuverability from the fighting platform. For a navy without overseas coaling stations, the maxim was that a ship cruised under sail and fought under steam. That was tactically sensible but psychologically dispiriting to the commanding officer, who now was dependent upon his chief engineer for the power to propel and maneuver his warship in battle.

The engineering officers presented a special problem, because they did not hold congressional "commissions" as did "line" officers, nor did they carry naval rank. Moreover, the old salts—the line officers—resented the new competitive breed for very human reasons. The new propulsion systems were dirty, noisy, and explosively dangerous, and by their technical competence the steam engineers displaced the seasoned line officers as the absolute masters of their ships, the men whose consummate seamanship literally made ships move and maneuver. Friction between the two classes—the new specialist who knew only his machinery and the traditional generalist who knew the entire ship from stem to stern and the oceans on which it sailed—persisted throughout the navy until the two groups were formally amalgamated by the Naval Personnel Act of 1899.

During the overhaul of the navy's administrative structure in 1842, Secretary of the Navy Upshur also established several policies bearing directly on the American challenge to Mexican primacy in Upper California. He estimated the value of the current American whaling activity in the Pacific Ocean at $40 million, noted that "American merchants have formed establishments in different parts of the coast, from Chili [sic] to [the] Columbia river," and warned that Americans residing in volatile Upper California "cannot be safe, either in their persons or property, except under the protection of our naval power." For those reasons, he proposed "a large increase of the Pacific squadron."

To support the squadron he recommended acquisition of a naval base somewhere between the Columbia River and Guayaquil, Ecuador. He put his case cogently:

Our public vessels cruising in that ocean àre generally absent from the United States not less than four years; within which time they necessarily require a variety of supplies which cannot now be obtained without very great difficulty and expense. Any considerable *repair* is almost impossible, with all the means which can be furnished by all the nations of the coast.

He mentioned to Congress that "a naval depot at the Sandwich [Hawaiian] islands would be of very great advantage."

The secretary professed to believe that a suitable harbor on the West Coast could be purchased from Mexico, but his selection of a contentious Welshman from Virginia to be the Pacific Squadron commander suggests that Upshur was ready to use more than dollars to achieve his ends.

Commodore Thomas ap Catesby Jones took command of the Pacific Squadron in May 1842, shortly after Britain had preemptively seized New Zealand to prevent France from occupying it and precisely the time when a large French naval force was headed west from Valparaiso to colonize the Marquesas and the Society Islands. Jones tried to fathom France's intentions in mounting "so formidable an expedition, fitted out with so much secrecy as to have eluded the observation even of Great Britain, her ever-watchful rival." He considered New Zealand, Tahiti, the Marquesas, and the Sandwich Islands, before quite erroneously deciding that California was the most likely French target.

Jones had hardly learned of his error when he was hit with disquieting rumors that a state of war existed between Mexico and the United States and that in exchange for a British guarantee of the security of Lower California Mexico had ceded Upper California to Great Britain. The abrupt and unscheduled departure of the British flagship from Callao on 5 September 1842 convinced Jones he must act to keep California out of Britain's grip.

Thinking himself in a race with the British, Jones ordered the flagship *United States* and two smaller ships to set sail for Monterey. At an under way conference in the commodore's cabin the three ships' commanding officers paid deference to the Monroe Doctrine "as the avowed and fixed policy of our country" according to which "we should consider the military occupation of the Californias by any European Power, but more particularly by our great commercial rival, England, . . . as a measure . . . decidedly hostile to the true interest of the United States." They therefore must preclude a British takeover of San Francisco or Monterey by themselves "supplanting the Mexican flag with [that of] the United States."

The squadron slipped into Monterey Bay without opposition, and on 20 October 1842, while riding quietly at anchor beneath the walls of the old fort, Jones accepted the Mexican surrender of the city. The next day he learned that Mexico and the United States were at peace. He immediately hauled down the American flag, reembarked his occupying force, and tried to explain his precipitousness to the secretary of the navy. It was too late. The protests of Mexico compelled Upshur to recall Jones from his command. The secretary tried to assuage Jones's anxiety by assuring him that the recall was "not designed to prejudge the case, nor even to indicate any opinion as to the propriety or impropriety of your conduct." Jones could "return to the United States in such mode as may be most convenient and agreeable to yourself." Once back in Washington, Jones was spared the indignity of a court of inquiry, but he was consigned to ignominious duty as the commanding officer of a hulk that served as a receiving ship in New York.

Commodore Jones had interpreted the British squadron's departure from Callao as evidence of rapacious designs on Upper California, but in fact the British in 1842–1843 showed a keener interest in Hawaii, if indeed a somewhat preemptive one. The British were aroused by the evident French imperialism in the Pacific, as were elements of the ruling groups in Hawaii. To thwart French plans, the Hawaiian Prince Timoleo Haolilio—lustily nicknamed "Timothy Hallelujah" by President Tyler's future wife—journeyed to Washington, where his presence helped gestate the Tyler Doctrine of noncolonization of Hawaii on 30 December 1842. That was none too soon, for on 25 February 1843 the Hawaiian king bowed to the demands of an imperious British naval officer, Lord George Paulet of H.M.S. *Carysfort*, and ceded his kingdom to Britain.

A naval brouhaha soon threatened with the arrival in Honolulu of the American sloop *Boston* from the East India Squadron. In July the same squadron's homeward-bound commodore, Lawrence Kearny, arrived aboard the frigate *Constellation*. Kearny formally protested Paulet's takeover but remained coolly tactful until the arrival of the British Pacific commander, Rear Admiral Richard Thomas, who promptly disavowed the cession as excessively preemptive and returned the islands to their native king. The retrocession of Hawaii confirmed the Hawaiian policy of British Foreign Secretary

Lord Aberdeen, who required only "that no other Power should exercise a greater degree of influence than that possessed by Great Britain." Britain's self-denial complemented the restrained American assertiveness, and the issue of ultimate Hawaiian sovereignty was laid to rest for the next fifty years, until the bloodless revolution of 1893— engineered with the active participation of men from another warship named the *Boston*.

Kearny had arrived in Honolulu fresh from a modest triumph in China, the domestic reaction to which exemplified the continuity of Pacific policy between administrations of different parties and the depth of Tyler's commitment to enlarging the American presence throughout the Pacific basin. Capitalizing on China's preoccupation with the Opium War, Kearny's squadron had penetrated as far as the merchant ship anchorage at Whampoa (Huangpu), directly below Canton (Guangzhou) and much farther up the Hsi (Xi) River than warships had previously been allowed by the hermetically minded Chinese.

The commodore had forwarded to Washington copies of the benchmark Sino-British Treaty of Nanking (Nanjing) of 29 August 1842. The pact ended the war, ceded Hong Kong to Britain, and opened five Chinese ports to British trade. Kearny's covering letter to the secretary of the navy urged that the United States dispatch a diplomatic agent to negotiate a most-favored-nation treaty. To demonstrate American seriousness, the emissary should be accompanied by several warships:

> The presence of a fleet of United States ships appearing here would do more to obtain a favorable treaty than any other measure; for unless the Emperor and officers of the Chinese government are convinced of our power, they will not fail to be governed by that policy which the British . . . will be inclined to carry out in opposition to the interests and trade of the United States.

Once again a naval officer had expressed the prevalent ambivalence toward Great Britain: It was both partner and rival.

Kearny was preaching to the choir. On 30 December 1842 Tyler informed Congress of the existence of the treaty, observed that China's "spirit of nonintercourse" appeared to be breaking down, and requested authorization to send a fully empowered commissioner to China. Reporting for the House Committee on Foreign Affairs, Representative John Quincy Adams, who had first hinted at the commercial possibilities of the Pacific in the 1819 Adams–Onís Treaty, pronounced "the present moment auspicious" for placing Sino-American relations on "a footing of national equality and reciprocity." The president nominated Caleb Cushing, a former congressman from Massachusetts, and Upshur put at his disposal the East India Squadron, now composed of a frigate, a sloop, and a brig.

The flagship *Brandywine* dropped Cushing off at Macao in February 1844, and on 3 July he signed the Treaty of Wanghia (Wangxia) granting the United States extensive privileges of judicial extraterritoriality in criminal cases and guaranteeing it the status of a most-favored nation in all commercial matters involving China and Western countries. For the benefit of the East India Squadron the treaty stipulated, "And the said ships of war shall enjoy all suitable facilities on the part of the Chinese Government in the purchase of provisions, procuring water, and making repairs if occasion require." A half-century later, when the United States was taking a more fateful step toward the heart of Asia, Secretary of State John Hay coined the phrase "open door" to describe the policy begun by Cushing in the wake of Commodore Kearny's opportune probing of an empire under siege.

Abel P. Upshur did not live to see Cushing's handiwork. In July 1843, with great reluctance, he left the Navy Department to become secretary of state and President Tyler's point man in the battle to annex Texas. Still deeply interested in the navy, he cruised the Potomac River on the newly completed U.S.S. *Princeton* with a presidential party on 28 February 1844 and was decapitated by the explosion of a prototype cannon during an exhibition firing. The bitter irony was that the *Princeton* owed its existence to Upshur, who as secretary of the navy had judiciously sponsored the advancement of two key naval technologies: steam propulsion and ordnance.

In April 1841 Secretary Upshur had received a model of a proposed steam warship from Captain Robert F. Stockton, a highly intelligent and versatile officer who had persuaded the gifted Swedish naval engineer John Ericsson to immigrate to the United States and help him introduce steam warships into the United States Navy. Stockton and Ericsson envisioned a full-rigged ship of 954 tons displacement that used a steam-driven propeller as auxiliary power. The idea, quite simply, was to cruise under sail and fight under steam.

Up to that point the navy's few experimental steam vessels had been driven by paddlewheels. This was the case with both *Fultons* and with the much larger seagoing sister ships *Mississippi* and *Mis-*

souri, begun in 1839 and completed in early 1842. Classed inconclusively as a "steam-frigate," the *Mississippi* was constructed under the personal supervision of Matthew C. Perry and reflected his experience with the second *Fulton.* With a length of 229 feet and a displacement of 3,220 tons, this bark-rigged ship spread 19,000 square feet of canvas. She devoured coal so voraciously that Upshur condemned her as "unsuited to cruising in time of peace." Although she served Perry well as a flagship during the Mexican War and in his expedition to Japan in the 1850s, the paddlewheels were a tactician's nightmare: 28 feet in diameter and 11 feet wide, the wheels were so positioned that the steam engines had to be mounted on deck in line with the wheels' shafts, thus exposing the entire propulsive mechanism to enemy fire.

The trick of the day was to design an efficient, wholly submerged screw—or propeller—driven by a shaft and engines mounted securely below the waterline. Ericsson and Stockton achieved precisely that feat with the *Princeton,* as Upshur's successor, Secretary of the Navy David Henshaw, recognized. He praised her as "most beautiful" and confidently predicted "a new era . . . in the use of war-steamers. Vessels that can move, at the pleasure of their commanders, against wind or tide, and whose machinery is beneath the reach of an enemy's fire, will be able easily to overcome and destroy any war-vessels of the ordinary structure." Henshaw was right. The death knell had been sounded for the square-rigger, the ship that had dominated naval warfare since the Spanish Armada in 1588.

American naval architecture did not follow the linear trail seemingly marked out by Upshur and Henshaw, and part of the reason was that Stockton egotistically overreached himself. For the *Princeton* both he and Ericsson designed a monster 12-inch diameter wrought-iron cannon reinforced by metal bands, but Stockton's was essentially a poor copy of Ericsson's. The explosion of Stockton's weapon— named the "Peacemaker"—and the death of Upshur and five others on 28 February 1844 led to a great deal of recrimination between Stockton and Ericsson, with the latter refusing to shoulder any blame for the disaster. Embittered and desperate about his suddenly tarnished reputation, Stockton saw to it that Ericsson was never paid for his work on the *Princeton.* As a result the United States Navy lost the talents of the nineteenth century's premier naval inventor until 1861, when Secretary of the Navy Gideon Welles dragooned him back into service to design the revolutionary Civil War *Monitor.*

A single public disaster had delayed a major national program.

In the intervening years American naval ship design, which had set the world standard in the heyday of the sailing frigate, faltered for want of inspired guidance. Only in the ordnance expert John A. Dahlgren did the antebellum navy recognize a spark of innovative technological genius in the period following the *Princeton* explosion, and even Dahlgren's best work did not come until the very eve of the Civil War. Nonetheless, the operating navy of the 1840s proved preponderant in the war against Mexico, the only formally declared American war fought between 1815 and 1898.

5

Brown-Water War for a Blue-Water Empire

1846 – 1860

PRESIDENT James K. Polk wanted an empire on the Pacific, and he blended diplomacy and bluster to force Great Britain and Mexico to give him what he wanted. Fortunately for him, British Foreign Secretary Lord Aberdeen remained as conciliatory in 1845–1846 as he had been at the time of the Webster–Ashburton Treaty. In the spring of 1846 he sent Polk a draft treaty drawing the final segment of the Canadian–American boundary along the 49th parallel and midway through the Strait of San Juan de Fuca to the Pacific Ocean. Polk accepted the compromise, which gave both nations maritime and naval access to the channel assayed by Lieutenant Charles Wilkes as exceedingly beautiful and safely navigable for even the largest warships.

Proud Mexico proved a tougher nut to crack. It was unwilling to negotiate its own dismemberment but impotent to garrison its seemingly limitless frontier with the United States. Polk began to force the issue in July 1845 by ordering Colonel Zachary Taylor to move from Louisiana through Texas toward the Rio Grande. By October Taylor commanded 4,000 men, fully half of the regular army of the United States. The hoped-for incident occurred on 25 April 1846 with a clash between Taylor's troops and Mexican cavalry on the north side of the Rio Grande. News of the encounter reached Washington on 9 May, persuading the last cabinet holdout, Secretary of the Navy George

Bancroft, to change his mind and counsel war. By an overwhelming bipartisan vote of Democrats and Whigs the Congress on 13 May recognized the existence of a state of war with Mexico. The unequal contest would last for almost two years; at its conclusion the United States would stand firmly astride the continent of North America, with sovereign right to every Pacific coast port and harbor from San Diego to Puget Sound.

The navy that fought the Mexican War was essentially the navy of Abel Upshur. During the first year of the Polk administration Secretary of the Navy George Bancroft made only one lasting innovation: establishment of the U.S. Naval Academy in Annapolis, Maryland. In the short run, however, Bancroft's school for midshipmen had no operational significance. The officers who fought the navy's first two-ocean war came from the old school where obedience, seamanship, and navigation were learned at sea.

David Conner was such a man. Able, brave, conversant in French and Spanish, and one of the navy's best sailors, Conner assumed command of the Home Squadron on 30 December 1843. His operating area was the Gulf of Mexico. Washing the shores of the United States, Mexico, and precariously independent Texas, the Gulf became the principal theater of operations during the Mexican War (1846–1848).

Whatever misgivings Bancroft may have had about a conflict with Mexico, the various orders he sent Conner in 1845 clearly envisioned a war of aggression. The secretary's precautionary directive of 11 July 1845—written a week after Texas accepted American annexation—set the tone: "Should Mexico declare war, you will at once dislodge her troops from any post she may have east of the mouth of the Del Norte [Rio Grande River]; take possession of Tampico; and *if your force is sufficient*, will take the castle of San Juan d'Ulloa [sic]."

A month later Bancroft ordered the commodore to blockade most of Mexico's ports on the Gulf coast if Mexican troops crossed the Rio Grande in numbers or if Mexicans attacked an American ship. Conner responded that he was equipped to blockade Mexico and protect American maritime commerce in the Gulf, but he requested shallow-draft steamers for assaults on upriver ports and several heavy ships for attacking the fort at Veracruz. By 5 April 1846—the very eve of war—Conner commanded the formidable steamer *Mississippi*, two frigates, three sloops, and three brigs. At sea all was in readiness as the navy awaited the final provocation of Mexico by Zachary Taylor's troops along the Rio Grande.

The naval preparations of Bancroft and Conner emphasized offensive operations—blockade, bombardment, and amphibious assault. Completely absent from the scenario was the traditional American reliance on commerce raiding and coastal defense. Furthermore, Conner took for granted his ability to protect American merchantmen adequately in his theater of operations. The commodore's facile but accurate assumption about his squadron's prowess underscores the obvious but fundamental difference between the Mexican War and the War of 1812. In the earlier contest the United States was the weaker power, but in 1846–1848 the United States was disproportionately stronger than its opponent. By instinct it therefore adopted a naval strategy associated with relative strength.

When war finally came in May 1846 Secretary Bancroft reiterated his earlier instructions. He ordered Conner to "effectually blockade the principal Mexican ports, protect our commerce from the depredations of privateers, [and] assist the operation of our army." Initially the wartime Home Squadron was composed of two heavy frigates, three sloops, five brigs, a schooner, and the powerful deep-draft steamers *Mississippi* and *Princeton*. To augment the squadron Bancroft purchased five steamers drawing less than 8 feet from a New York yard that was building them for the Mexican navy. Conner in the meantime established a blockade, pivotally positioning his flagship off Veracruz, where he could concentrate the entire squadron "when required to operate on that point."

It was a blockade established in conformity with historic American doctrine regarding neutral rights, a viewpoint often disregarded in the past by Britain's Royal Navy. To be legal the blockade must be effective, and therefore its extent was limited to those ports where Conner could actually station ships. In the words of Bancroft's successor, John Y. Mason, the blockade was designed "to interfere, in as small degree as possible, with neutral commerce." Thus Conner ordered his commanders to hew to the twin tenets that "free ships make free goods" and "enemy's ships, enemy's goods" when deciding whether to confiscate a merchantman. They could properly capture anything Mexican, but vessels flying neutral flags must be allowed to pass the blockade unless laden with contraband cargos.

Conner's flag lieutenant, Raphael Semmes, later explained the vital importance of scrupulously maintaining a legal blockade:

> As a commercial nation, interested in the freedom of the seas, it behooved us, to set an example of liberality in this war . . . and to show

. . . that the principles we had so long contended for, in vain when a neutral, we were willing to carry out in good faith, now that we had become a belligerent.

The Home Squadron carried out Conner's exacting instructions extremely well; the validity of all of its captures was sustained by admiralty courts. And as wearisome and boring as it was, maintaining the blockade constituted the navy's principal contribution to the war in the Gulf. The threat of privateers never materialized, the Mexican navy did not send a single ship into the Gulf, and the Home Squadron's cooperation with the army for the most part was limited to supporting Major General Winfield Scott's textbook-perfect assault on Veracruz in March 1847.

President Polk had suggested an attack on Mexico's second largest city to his cabinet in August 1846 as a means of launching a decisive thrust toward Mexico City. The plan of operations was developed by Major General Scott, the commanding general of the army, who proposed a sequence of naval bombardment, amphibious assault from army transports, occupation of the city, neutralization and capture of the Castle of San Juan de Ulúa, and an overland march to the Mexican capital. Scott estimated that the attack would require at least 10,000 men and enough small flat-bottomed landing craft to put ashore 2,500 soldiers at one time.

This was an army operation conceived and executed by Scott, and Conner's role was limited to reconnaissance, recommendation of landing sites, and the last-minute transfer of some of the troops from army transports to the assault vessels. It took place on 9 March 1847 and it came off flawlessly: The Mexicans elected not to defend the beach, and in less than five hours the Americans landed more than 8,600 men without the loss of a single life. The landing contrasted brilliantly with the Revolutionary War disaster at Penobscot in 1779, and in the opinion of the military historian Russell F. Weigley it constituted "a model operation which might well have aroused the envy of many of those who conducted similar landings in World War II."

For David Conner, the assault on Veracruz came as a bittersweet climax to the inevitable frustrations of squadron command in the early stages of a war. On 21 March, the very day Scott planned to begin his artillery bombardment of the surrounded city, Matthew C. Perry relieved Conner as commodore. Conner was ill and past due for routine rotation out of command, but his extraordinary replacement figuratively in the heat of battle was the result of Perry's sedulous politicking with Secretary of the Navy John Y. Mason while his ship, the *Mississippi,* was laid up at Norfolk for overhaul of her boilers in early 1847.

Perry was a master of the old art of naval intrigue and the new technology of steam. He was also vigorous and decisive. One of his officers later recalled that when the new commodore was ceremonially rowed under the sterns of his ships, "Cheer after cheer was sent up in evidence of the enthusiasm this promise of a release from a life of inaction we had been leading under Perry's predecessor inspired in every breast."

Perry had won command of what the secretary of the navy proudly described as "the largest squadron" ever to be "collected under the American flag." His armada included a sailing ship of the line, the *Ohio*; the steam frigate and flagship, *Mississippi*; two sailing frigates; six sloops-of-war; two brigs; six small steamers; seven schooner-gunboats; four volcanic bomb barges; and assorted store and supply vessels. His opponent, as Mason tartly noted, had "no vessels of war afloat, and can hardly be said to have a commercial marine." Commodore Perry's primary tasks therefore were to maintain "a vigorous blockade" of Mexico's Gulf ports and to "attack and capture such places as in your judgment will promote the success of our operations against the enemy."

Once the city of Veracruz and the forbidding fort at San Juan de Ulúa—"the alleged Gibraltar of America"—capitulated on 29 March, Perry took the offensive. Lacking an enemy to fight at sea, "Old Matt" became a commander of amphibious landings. He sent the *Ohio* home. With a keel plunging 26 feet below the waterline, the vintage sailor was useless for brown-water operations. He retained his favorite ship, the steam frigate *Mississippi,* as the command and communications center.

By early April the most important port on the Gulf coast not under American control was Tuxpan, situated midway between Tampico and Veracruz. Lying 8 miles upriver from the coast, the town was protected by a sand bar and by guns taken from the U.S.S. *Truxtun,* which the Mexicans had captured. On 18 April 1847 the commodore attacked in an operation remarkable for its use of steam-powered vessels. The shoal at the river's mouth forced Perry to anchor the *Mississippi* offshore. He led the expedition from a comparatively tiny temporary "flagship," the shallow-draft paddle-wheel steamer *Spitfire.* The *Spitfire* and two similar steamers each towed a sail-driven gunboat and ten barges loaded with sailors organized as a landing party.

The future defender of Mobile Bay, Commander Franklin Buchanan, leapt ashore at Tuxpan and led his foot sailors in a charge against the battery commanding the highest promontory. Another future Confederate naval strategist, Raphael Semmes, later remembered the engagement as "a little serious." When the firing stopped in midafternoon, the Americans had effectively disarmed Tuxpan. Four days later Perry withdrew to the *Mississippi* to prepare the Home Squadron's final major operation of the war: the raid on Tabasco, the last significant Gulf port in Mexican hands.

In the three-day attack on Tabasco in June 1847 Perry won the respect of all hands by conspicuously exposing himself to enemy small arms fire while steaming upriver aboard the expedition's temporary flagship, the side-wheeler *Scorpion*, and by charging ashore with drawn sword at the head of the 1,000-man landing party. Commander Buchanan wrote at the time, "He is at present certainly the man for the navy; in many respects an astonishing man, the most industrious, hard working, energetic, zealous, persevering, enterprising officer of his rank in our navy." Lieutenant David Dixon Porter, the executive officer of the *Spitfire*, agreed with Buchanan: Perry was "one of the finest officers we ever had in our navy—far superior to his brother Oliver."

For Lieutenant Porter, Tabasco had an additional tactical significance; it was here that he learned how to force his way upriver past obstructions, experimenting with techniques that he would employ to help dismember Buchanan's Confederate navy when he became commander of the Union's Mississippi Squadron in 1862. The Tabasco raid therefore constituted more than a mere reprise of Tuxpan; it involved a demonstration of inspirational naval leadership at the top and a tactical rehearsal for the Civil War battles in the Gulf and inland waters. Perry's officers were being schooled in steam's revolutionary potential for amphibious operations along coasts characterized by shoaled river mouths and recessed towns or cities. The topographic similarity of the United States Southern seaboard was not lost on them.

But not even the most heroic nineteenth-century commander could master yellow fever, and an epidemic in the occupying garrison compelled Perry to withdraw his troops from Tabasco in July. For the rest of the wet season, yellow fever and malaria laid waste the squadron, abating finally with the coming of cool, dry northerly winds in

October but returning with deadly effect in April 1848. The fleet surgeons blamed the rats and cockroaches infesting filthy bilges for creating a "putrescence" that induced fevers, and they were not far from the truth, for the unsuspected fever-bearing mosquitoes also bred in those wet holds. The *Mississippi's* bilges had not been scrubbed in six years, and Perry himself was stricken with yellow fever, as was one of his two sons serving with him. They survived, as did many others, but the debilitation demoralized the men and cut the squadron's effectiveness. Fortunately for the Home Squadron all of the action was past by mid-1847, and thereafter Perry had only to maintain his blockade while Winfield Scott's army pressed toward the enemy's heart from the terminus of his lifeline at Veracruz.

———

Preparation for the navy's campaign in the Pacific had begun two years before the actual declaration of war. At that time the commander of the Pacific Squadron was John D. Sloat, an officer made cautious by thirty years of service in a peacetime navy and by chronic ill health. The skipper of Sloat's flagship, the frigate *Savannah,* was Captain James Armstrong, who had commanded the flagship *United States* during Commodore Thomas ap Catesby Jones's premature occupation of Monterey in 1842. Jones had lost his command, a fate naval officers regard as the ultimate disgrace. Twenty-one years earlier Sloat had personally witnessed a similar humiliation as commanding officer of the *Grampus* during the attack on Fajardo that led to the recall of Commodore David Porter.

No wonder, then, that Sloat bewailed his situation as "anything but pleasant" when Secretary of the Navy Bancroft repeatedly directed him to concentrate his ships "off the coast of Mexico and Oregon" but forbade him to act unless he ascertained "beyond a doubt, that the Mexican Government has declared war against us." Certitude about formal decisions by Mexico or the United States was a scarce commodity in a region long infested with rumors of war and not yet blessed with extensive telegraphic communications. Hamstrung until he knew for certain that a state of war did exist, Sloat at that point was instructed "at once [to] possess yourself of the port of San Francisco, and blockade or occupy such other ports as your force may permit."

While peace prevailed, the officers of the Pacific Squadron were expected continually to measure the attitudes of the American settlers in Monterey toward the alternative suzerainties of Mexico, the United States, and Great Britain. Similarly, by visiting the Columbia

River basin and mingling with the white inhabitants, they could assess "the relative strength of those friendly to the United States and of those friendly to Britain." That information would help the Polk administration persuade Great Britain to compromise over Oregon and to accept the inevitable American conquest of California, but the secretary's orders had the unintended side effect of heightening Sloat's Anglophobia to the point where for a time he feared Britain more than Mexico.

To facilitate the conquest of California, the Navy Department reinforced the Pacific Squadron with its largest frigate, the *Congress*, and the sloop-of-war *Cyane*. In October 1845 the two ships sailed from Norfolk under the charge of Captain Robert F. Stockton, whom Bancroft designated as Sloat's second in command and standby replacement should the commodore's health fail. The cunning secretary was providing backbone with a vengeance, and the parallel with the Perry–Conner duality in the Gulf is obvious. In both theaters Bancroft assured himself of aggressive leadership by putting hesitant commodores under the watchful eyes of ambitious subordinates who enjoyed the important symbolic advantage of arriving on station aboard the most powerful ships in their squadrons. In each case the subordinate acceded to command and claimed the laurels of victorious conquest, callously and irreparably tarnishing his predecessor's reputation in the process.

It took Stockton more than eight months to rendezvous with the Pacific Squadron, and when the *Congress* stood in to Monterey Bay on 15 July 1846, Commodore Sloat had already seized the port. Having read enough reports from Mexico City to convince himself that a war was on, Sloat acted on Bancroft's discretionary orders of 24 May 1845. He occupied Monterey and San Francisco without encountering resistance in early July. Proclaiming his friendship to the people of Monterey, he predicted that "henceforward California will be a portion of the United States." He also prohibited the sale of liquor, and warned his sailors not to act like sailors: "Let every man . . . avoid that eternal disgrace which would be attached to our names and our country's name by indignity offered to a single female even let her standing be however low it may." In a reprise of his ceremonial performance during Commodore Jones's 1842 occupation, Midshipman William P. Toler again hoisted the Stars and Stripes over the Monterey customhouse.

The conquest had been as bloodless as it was swift. To Sloat's pleasant surprise the Royal Navy tacitly assented to his easy victory.

The day after Stockton arrived at Monterey aboard the *Congress*, British Admiral Sir George F. Seymour sailed in with the 80-gun ship of the line *Collingwood*. Sloat took sensible steps to defuse tension: He sent an officer to pay a courtesy call, offered Seymour full use of the facilities of the port, and supplied the *Collingwood* with replacements for some missing masts and spars. When Seymour sailed for Hawaii a week later, Sloat interpreted the admiral's visit as

> very serviceable to our cause in California, as the inhabitants fully believed he would take part with them, and that we would be obliged to abandon our conquest; but when they saw the friendly intercourse subsisting between us, . . . they abandoned all hope of ever seeing the Mexican flag fly in California again.

This interpretation serves as further evidence of the extent to which the Royal Navy was always a ponderable, and often a friendly, factor in the calculations of nineteenth-century American naval officers.

While Sloat was capturing the northern California coast, a brevet captain of the U.S. Army Topographical Engineers, John C. Frémont, incited alienated whites to rebel and establish the Bear Flag Republic in the Napa and Sacramento valleys. Between them, Sloat and Frémont controlled all of Upper California north of Santa Barbara when the commodore relinquished command of the squadron and sailed for home at the end of July 1846.

Sloat's aggressive successor, Robert F. Stockton, promoted Frémont to a major in command of the "California Battalion of United States Troops" and shipped him south aboard the 20-gun sloop *Cyane* for the unopposed occupation of San Diego. Leaving a frigate to guard San Francisco and a sloop at Monterey, Stockton himself sailed south on the flagship *Congress*. He organized most of the crew and shipboard marines into a 368-man landing party, stopped off to claim Santa Barbara for the United States, and headed on to San Pedro for debarkation and the march overland to Los Angeles. On 13 August he followed the blaring brass band of the *Congress* into the militarily deserted Ciudad de Los Angeles. Frémont and his men arrived later that day, after an uneventful trek overland from San Diego. The American conquest of Upper California was complete.

Fancying himself the "Commander-in-chief and Governor of the Territory of California," Stockton organized a civil government and proclaimed a blockade of the entire west coast of Mexico. Both actions ran contrary to American tradition. Under the Constitution the authority to establish a civil government is delegated to Congress, and throughout the nineteenth century paper blockades were anathema to the United States. But Robert F. Stockton had empire rather than legal nicety on the brain. He was planning to seize Acapulco, which he conveniently considered a breeding ground for Mexican privateers fitting out "to prey upon our commerce," and then march on to Mexico City for the final victory. He was eager "to leave the desk and the camp and take to the ship and to the sea." His sidekick, Frémont, would serve as governor of his new territory in his absence.

Stockton conveyed these romantic plans to Frémont on 24 August 1846, about the moment he first learned for certain "that war has been declared both by the United States and Mexico." Until then he and Sloat had known only that hostilities had begun south of the Rio Grande, and even now Stockton's source was "the Mexican newspapers." But in taking California before definitely knowing that their nation was at war the two commodores acted fully in concert with the desires of the Polk administration, which in turn was completely in the dark about the state of affairs along the Pacific coast.

Secretary of the Navy George Bancroft made his ignorance and perplexity palpable in a series of dispatches written precisely as Stockton was bagging Los Angeles. Mistakenly convinced that Sloat had "remained in a state of inactivity" even though aware of the onset of hostilities, Bancroft castigated him for not understanding that "actual hostilities" constituted more convincing evidence of a Mexican–American conflict than "the mere declaration of war." Hesitation was unacceptable: "The Department willingly believes in the purity of your intentions. But your anxiety not to do wrong, has led you into a most unfortunate and unwarranted inactivity." The exasperated Bancroft ordered Sloat to surrender his command, but to whom? To James Biddle, en route home from China, perhaps. To Stockton, if he had arrived but Biddle had not. If neither was present, "to the oldest officer" at hand.

Within a three-week period Bancroft addressed instructions to "Commodore James Biddle, or Commo. R. F. Stockton, or to the senior officer in command," passed the command to William B. Shubrick aboard the 54-gun *Independence* at Boston, and ordered Sloat to "re-hoist your broad pendant, and again assume command of the Squadron." The issue by then was moot, since Sloat had already relieved himself in favor of Stockton.

Although ignorant of his agent, Bancroft retained absolute consistency of purpose: "to take and keep possession of Upper California, especially of the ports of San Francisco, of Monterey and of San Diego, and also if opportunity offers . . . of San Pueblo de Los Angeles." The hope was that the peace treaty would be made on the basis of *uti possidetis,* with the United States thereby acquiring all of Upper California. In the meantime Sloat or whoever was in command should establish "a civil administration" throughout Upper California while simultaneously taking possession of, or blockading, "all Mexican ports as far as your means allow."

The secretary's flurry of correspondence makes it clear that Stockton, who had left the United States well after the department had issued its contingency plans for the conduct of the war in the Pacific, read the administration accurately in occupying San Diego and Los Angeles, in establishing a civil government within occupied California, in expanding the blockade, and in planning to carry the war to the heart of Mexico.

In September Mexican-Californian insurgents recaptured Los Angeles, forcing Stockton to abandon his planned attack on Acapulco. He did not drive the Mexicans out of the city until mid-January 1847, and then only with the help of Frémont and Brigadier General Stephen Watts Kearny. After marching from Kansas through New Mexico, Kearny's small but pretentiously named "Army of the West" was attacked and nearly annihilated by a band of Mexicans. The survivors pushed on and linked up with Stockton at Los Angeles.

Immediately after the final pacification of Upper California, Stockton and Kearny had a falling-out. Both martinets claimed to govern the territory. The impasse was resolved in February and March with the arrival of first Shubrick and then Biddle, as well as fresh orders from the new secretary of the navy, John Y. Mason. Kearny became the governor of California, Biddle took over the Pacific Squadron, and Stockton languished in California until heading home in June.

Under Biddle the squadron's activity tapered off for several reasons. Stores and provisions were exhausted. As one observer noted: "Our ships, as far as sea-service is concerned, are of about as much use as so many nautical pictures. They look stately and brave, as they ride at anchor in our bay; but let them go to sea, and they would carry famine with them." Store ships were on the way, but the dangerous passage around Cape Horn took months. Second, with the nearest admiralty courts located on the Atlantic Coast, taking prizes was unprofitable and militarily inconsequential. Finally, Mason's stringent orders regarding the blockade of Mexican ports inhibited audacity.

Secretary Mason did not disavow Stockton's vaguely worded proclamation, which seemed to include every Mexican seaport in the Pacific, but he insisted that the new squadron commander issue an unambiguous edict reaffirming the historic American principle that "a lawful maritime blockade requires the actual presence of a sufficient force, stationed at the entrance of the port, sufficiently near to prevent communication." The secretary was writing with one eye on Great Britain, whose naval officers had protested the illegality of Stockton's paper blockade. He was prudently reaffirming the classic American position on blockades in anticipation of future conflicts in which the United States might again be a maritime neutral and Britain a belligerent. His mild rebuke, if it can be classified as such, signified consolidation and clarification, not moderation, of the administration's imperial war aims.

Polk was riding a crest of expansionism. In June 1846 the Senate had approved the Anglo-American treaty settling the Oregon boundary, and in December the United States signed a treaty with New Granada (Colombia) establishing an American right-of-way across the strategic isthmus of Panama. Now Polk wanted a peace treaty with Mexico reflecting military conquest. "The President," said Mason in January 1847, "foresees no contingency in which the United States will ever surrender or relinquish the possession of the Californias." The problem was that Stockton and his friends had secured Upper but not Baja (Lower) California—the second California to which Mason alluded—and the orders to take and hold at least one port in Baja California did not reach Monterey until May 1847.

The naval high command remained divided in the Pacific, with Biddle the senior commodore and Shubrick his second in command. Biddle had been at sea aboard the 74-gun *Columbus* since June 1845. He was returning to California from the East India Squadron, where he had suffered a humiliating rebuff while attempting to "open" Japan. He had first seen Monterey Bay in 1815, almost thirty years earlier. He was an old man on his last cruise: "I have become heartily tired of the sea, and all its anxieties and all its discomforts. I am aware that life at sea is just what it was forty-six years ago, when I first knew and liked it, and that the change is not in it but in me." He did the gracious thing for the younger, ambitious and frustrated Shubrick: He put him in charge of the campaign against Baja California and in July sailed for home, knowing that a ship of the line was useless for amphibious operations against an enemy without a navy.

With the large frigates *Independence* and *Congress* and three sloops, Shubrick occupied La Paz, the capital of Baja California, and Mazatlán, the busiest port on Mexico's west coast. He kept constant pressure on other towns with hit-and-run raids and attacked Mexican merchantmen wherever he found them. But Shubrick lacked men for an army of occupation, and the secretary of state did not include cession of Lower California as a *sine qua non* in his instructions to negotiator Nicholas P. Trist, so the Treaty of Guadalupe Hidalgo (February 1848) left Mexico in possession of Baja California. But the United States gained the area encompassing the present states of California, Nevada, Utah, New Mexico, Arizona, and parts of Wyoming and Colorado.

President Polk well knew that he had acquired "a great empire . . . second only in importance to that of Louisiana in 1803." More to the point, he perfectly articulated the maritime significance of his grab:

> The possession of the ports of San Diego and Monterey and the Bay of San Francisco will enable the United States to command the already valuable and rapidly increasing commerce of the Pacific. The number of our whale ships alone now employed in that sea exceeds 700, requiring more than 20,800 seamen to navigate them. . . . The excellent harbors of Upper California will under our flag afford security and repose to our commercial marine, and American mechanics will soon furnish ready means of shipbuilding and repair, which are now so much wanting in that distant sea.

What was true for the merchant marine was equally true for the navy. In the nascent age of steam-driven ironclad warships, shipyards and coal depositories firmly under American control and safely out of reach of a potential enemy's hands were the keys to an active Pacific navy.

The navy's own unvarnished valedictory on the Mexican War was pronounced best by Lieutenant Raphael Semmes, an apostle of Manifest Destiny who epitomized the midcentury American naval mind as perfectly as anyone in uniform. In reflecting on the war shortly after its conclusion, he made two points about its national and international significance: It was the irresistible work of God, and it destined America for supremacy in the Pacific. However much flawed by chauvinism, his was the grand vision:

> [I]t is only necessary to remark that our Pacific front opens to us, and will enable us to monopolize, almost all the commerce of the East

Indies, and the west coast of America, north and south. This will make us the carriers and the factors of the world. Twenty years hence, and it will no longer be Britannia, but America "rules the waves."

This immodest peroration touched every base of nineteenth-century American nationalism and navalism. By the Mexican War the United States had become a vast continental empire, but naval officers like Semmes were still looking overseas, much as their peers in the Royal Navy were doing. The American officers were confusing the imperatives of a small insular nation with those driving a continental power, but their dream had great potency. In the twelve years between the Mexican War and the firing on Fort Sumter, a decentralized but vigorous and self-confident United States Navy tried to give life to Semmes's vision of a global American maritime empire.

=====

Like the disintegrating nation it reflected, the navy of the final antebellum decade lacked a unifying center of gravity. Power and authority were diffused among several centers, and Congress held the purse strings. Determined naval committee chairmen like Senator Stephen R. Mallory of Florida did not hesitate to legislate the kind and number of ships they believed appropriate for the navy. Mallory, for example, strongly favored shallow-draft vessels for coastal defense and nothing larger than sloops or frigates for blue-water operations. For Mallory, who would become secretary of the Confederate States Navy, the inspirational single-ship engagements of the War of 1812 set the model. As late as June 1858 Mallory, speaking on the floor of the Senate, extolled those memorable American naval actions of almost a half-century earlier "in which frigate was matched against frigate, sloop against sloop, and brig against brig."

This disposition has been consistently criticized by Mahanians like Harold and Margaret Sprout. They denounce it as hopelessly antiquarian because it did not challenge the great naval powers of Europe, notably Great Britain. But in fact Mallory spoke with a wisdom born of respect for the traditional American reliance on single-ship encounters and *guerre de course*. As naval secretary of the Confederacy—the vastly weaker power in the Civil War—he would follow his instincts as a matter of inescapable necessity. As a United States senator in antebellum America, he followed them because he understood that a sprawling agricultural nation with a continent to pacify and settle could not match the world's leading industrialized sea power in capital ships—not in design, and certainly not in number.

The secretaries of the navy who depended on congressional largess for the administration of their department constituted the next most readily identifiable nexus of power in the navy of the 1850s. Probably more than congressmen in general, and certainly more than senators, the naval secretaries bent with the prevailing political winds, and in the decade before the Civil War those winds were highly variable. As the decade opened, an internally divided Whig administration experienced the unsettling death of President Zachary Taylor and the succession of Millard Fillmore. At the same time Congress was debating a series of laws regarding slavery that came to be known as the Compromise of 1850. With the election of Democrat Franklin Pierce in 1852, one divided political party replaced another. That irresolvable factiousness led to the formation of the Republican party and the displacement of Democratic President James Buchanan by Abraham Lincoln in 1861.

In such an unstable milieu presidents gave even more attention than usual to the partisan qualifications of candidates for secretary of the navy, and the secretaries in turn concerned themselves as much with the political future of their patrons as with the administration of the Department of the Navy. The rate of turnover was correspondingly high.

Five men served as secretary in the decade of the 1850s, and this rotation further militated against firm civilian direction of the farflung service. The three secretaries who served Whig Presidents Taylor and Fillmore (1849–1853)—William B. Preston, William A. Graham, and John P. Kennedy—submitted similar proposals to reform the navy's moribund officer promotion system and institute a humane system of discipline in place of the flogging of enlisted men. But because the secretaries lacked tenure in office and clout with Congress, their recommendations for reform came to nothing.

Their two Democratic successors fared better. James C. Dobbin, who served for the entire Pierce administration (1853–1857), extracted from Congress two significant reform measures. One created a naval board of review that scrutinized the qualifications of every officer and recommended the dismissal or furlough of 201 considered unfit for duty ashore and afloat. The other act of Congress instituted a regular system of courts-martial and punishment to replace flogging of the sailors. But Dobbin's main achievement was the construction of six first-class propeller-driven steam frigates, authorized by Congress in April 1854 and launched in 1856. The most famous of the group was the U.S.S. *Merrimack*, the namesake of the class.

Dobbin modernized the fleet in order to maintain "our proper and elevated rank among the great powers of the world." But he also thought in the traditional terms of coastal defense and protection of the expanding merchant marine. His Whig predecessor, John P. Kennedy, conceived of the navy very similarly, but Dobbin had the advantage of longer tenure and a somewhat more stable administration and party.

The fortuitous circumstance of the Crimean War added force to the secretary's recommendation that Congress upgrade a thinly spread navy of forty serviceable vessels if the nation wanted to husband its neutrality during European wars and otherwise act like a major maritime power. Dobbin's success left a lasting impression on two midshipmen, George Dewey and Alfred T. Mahan, both of whom more than a half-century later glowingly recalled the Dobbin secretaryship as the last great period of American naval awakening and expansion prior to the Civil War. Dobbin may therefore be considered a godfather of modern American sea power.

James Buchanan's secretary of the navy, Isaac Toucey (1857–1861), held a thoroughly conventional conception of the proper size and function of the United States Navy. He entered office after the Crimean War and understandably saw less peril abroad than had Dobbin. It was "not the policy of our government," he wrote, "to maintain a great navy in time of peace." With a Jeffersonian flourish he advised the president that it was against "settled policy to burden the resources of the people by an overgrown naval establishment." Nor should the maritime powers of Europe be models for American naval policy, however much they might be commercial rivals of the United States: "It is universally admitted to be inexpedient to endeavor to compete with other great commercial powers in the magnitude of their naval preparations." The modest and appropriate need of the United States Navy was for shallow-draft steam sloops-of-war to complement the heavier frigates. Screw sloops could chase suspected slave traders into coastal waters, where otherwise they would escape the deeper-draft ships.

Toucey understood that technology was changing the nature of ships, but he did not believe that technology or anything else had altered the historic position of the navy in American life or the mission of the service. One of his explicit purposes in sending four steamers to Cuban waters in 1858 was to protect American merchant vessels from harassment by the Royal Navy, a mission as old as the navy itself. He sought, he explained to President Buchanan, to "put the deck of an American vessel on the same footing as American soil, the invasion of which under foreign authority is to be as strenuously resisted in the one case as in the other." Only the means of protection was changing, as Toucey understood. In what may be considered the last annual report by a secretary presiding over the American sailing navy, Toucey pleaded for "the universal introduction" into the navy of "the motive power of steam." But by December 1860 South Carolina's secession from the Union made all rational considerations of naval policy irrelevant.

In theory the bureau system created in 1842 might have compensated for the uncertainty at the top echelon of the department in Washington during the 1850s. But to function effectively the five bureaus required the very firmness of secretarial guidance that the constitutional crisis made impossible.

Outside of the bureaus, the commodores constituted the next tangible level of substantial power in the navy of the 1850s. They commanded the six squadrons of active ships with a degree of autonomy and absolutism unthinkable in the late twentieth century. As the confusion over command of the Pacific Squadron during the Mexican War had shown, commodores moved about and took action without direct control from Washington or from any representative of the government. On station they could send an insubordinate officer home in disgrace to stand trial by court-martial. Until the congressional reform of 1850 they and the ships' commanding officers could order miscreant enlisted men flogged senseless. It was not until 1855 that Congress established a system of summary courts-martial, and even then the commodores and ships' captains had the power to prescribe the dishonorable discharge of enlisted men or their "solitary confinement in irons, on bread and water or diminished rations."

For those exalted senior captains nothing mattered, and everything mattered: nothing because they had reached the pinnacle of their profession and could look forward to no greater perquisites in the remainder of their lifetimes than sailing beneath their own unfurled broad pennant; everything because one serious operational misstep or hesitation—Porter at Fajardo, Jones at Monterey, Conner in the Gulf, Sloat in the Pacific—could cost them their command and plunge them into retirement without honor.

In the 1850s six operating squadrons divided the world into large areas, which they patrolled on behalf of overseas American commercial activity. The Mediterranean Sea was patrolled by a squadron of the same name. The Pacific Ocean was divided between the Pacific Squadron, which ranged from California to Hawaii, and the East India Squadron, which operated between Hawaii and the China coast. At Rio de Janeiro a small squadron protected the transit of ships heading to the Pacific Ocean around Cape Horn or the Cape of Good Hope. East of the Brazil Squadron, the African Squadron scoured the Atlantic for slave traders, while the Home Squadron kept a watchful eye on the Gulf of Mexico.

The six squadrons varied in composition, function, and desirability as commands. None of the six constituted a coordinated operating entity comparable to modern American overseas fleets. They were more in the nature of administrative units than organized fighting forces. Dispersion of the squadrons' ships rather than concentration of firepower was the rule, a feature much criticized by twentieth-century Mahanians but quite sensible given the absence of a strong enemy throughout most of the nineteenth century. The commodore's ship was always the "flagship" and almost always the largest vessel in the squadron, but like the other ships she typically sailed from port to port unaccompanied by escorts.

The Mediterranean Squadron headed the list in attractiveness. French imperialism had brought an unprecedented degree of submissiveness to the states of North Africa in the 1830s, leaving the ships of the American squadron with little to do but make lazy summer cruises along the Mediterranean littoral, sometimes providing taxi service for itinerant American diplomats and consuls. Such placidity was magnetic. As Matthew C. Perry remarked in his rejected appeal for the command, the Mediterranean Squadron offered senior officers the chance to blend service on a congenial station with frequent visits from wives and families making the grand tour of Europe.

The squadron had been deactivated on the eve of the Mexican War but reconstituted immediately after Perry effectively ended the American naval offensive in the Gulf of Mexico with the capture of Tabasco in March 1847. The first ship past Gibraltar was the screw-frigate *Princeton*. Burning smokeless anthracite coal, this state-of-the-art ship momentarily revived European respect for American naval architecture. She was followed on station by the flagship *United States*, a classic frigate from the age of sail. Both ships would be made equally obsolete when the British launched H.M.S. *Warrior* at the end of the next decade.

The arrival of the *Princeton* and *United States* coincided with an outbreak of popular liberal uprisings throughout Europe. Many Americans thought that the stirring revolutions of 1848 heralded the birth of American-style democracy in the Old World, and Whig Secretary of the Navy William B. Preston strengthened the squadron to meet the opportunities. He posted the razeed two-decker *Independence*, rated as the largest frigate in the world, as the flagship of a force including three other frigates and three less consequential vessels. In 1849 Preston bragged that the Mediterranean Squadron was "larger and more efficient than at any previous period in our history, with the exception, perhaps, of the years 1804 and 1805, during the Tripolitan War."

The senior officers of the squadron welcomed the anticipated birth of freedom and hoped that soon "the whole worthless tribe of kings, with all their myrmidons, will be swept from their places." Sentiment aside, they had American commerce to protect and American citizens to shelter all along the turbulent Italian peninsula. They therefore damped their revolutionary ardor, attempting, in the words of Commodore George C. Read, to observe "the law laid down by Mr. Monroe, 'we will not meddle in your affairs, nor shall you in ours.' " But they often bent Monroe's "law" by giving sanctuary on American warships to revolutionary refugees fleeing the restoration armies of Austria and France.

The two most celebrated cases involved Lajos Kossuth and Martin Koszta, two nationalists espousing Hungarian independence from Austria. To the disgust of the Austrian government, Kossuth and some fifty compatriots were rescued from Constantinople by the large steam frigate *Mississippi* and transported to America for a triumphal propaganda tour in 1851. Two years later Koszta was freed from imprisonment on an Austrian brig in the Turkish harbor of Smyrna (Izmir) when the visiting sloop-of-war U.S.S. *St. Louis* cleared for action and faced down several armed Austrian ships. Congress by joint resolution awarded her skipper, Commander Duncan N. Ingraham, a special medal.

The final burst of revolutionary enthusiasm in the Mediterranean was a pale reminder of the decade's opening. On 7 November 1860 the newly launched steam-powered sloop-of-war *Iroquois* gave a last symbolic blast for liberty. She was the only foreign warship in the harbor of Naples to exchange gun-for-gun salute with the victorious Piedmontese squadron of the Italian unifier, Giuseppe Garibaldi. Six months later, on 4 May 1861, Flag Officer Charles H. Bell received orders to return with all his ships to the North American war zone. The Mediterranean idyll had ended.

The Ingraham episode represents the peak of American naval activity in the Mediterranean during the 1850s. The vigorous American Mediterranean trade remained an object of protection for the rest of the decade, but the Pacific Squadron increasingly became the cutting edge of democratic "gunboat diplomacy." The Oregon compromise with Britain in 1846 and the imperialistic war with Mexico gave the United States an imposing geopolitical presence on the great ocean's eastern rim. Discovery of gold and the admission of California to the Union in 1850 underscored the unlimited maritime potential of San Francisco Bay. As the London *Times* noted: "From so favorable a harbour the course lies straight and obvious to Polynesia, the Philippines, New Holland, and China, and it is not extravagant to suppose that the merchants of this future emporium may open the commerce of Japan." The 1844 Treaty of Wanghia (Wangxia) with China had already given the navy five new ports to patrol on the distant Asian coast. But between San Francisco and Canton (Guangzhou) lay 70 million square miles of water whitened by the sails of clipper ships and bloodied by American whalers.

Immediately after the Mexican War, the flagship of the Pacific Squadron was permanently moved to San Francisco Bay from its historic de facto base at Valparaiso, Chile. The Navy Department insisted that from this point ships of the squadron regularly visit ports in North, Central, and South America. Their mission was the traditional one, as explained to the commanding officer of the sloop-of-war *St. Mary's*: The "objects of our government in keeping a Naval force in these Seas [are] to afford aid and protection to our commerce and to look after the interests of our Citizens generally, where engaged in their lawful pursuits, more especially our whaling interest, which is by far the most extensive and important we have in the Pacific."

Not all of the American activity on the Pacific station was "lawful," and in the 1850s the squadron had to cope with unsatiated expansionists, many of them Southerners who still coveted Mexican territory for the extension of slavery. The most famous armed expansionist, or "filibuster," was William J. Walker, the "grey-eyed man of destiny." In 1854 he tried and failed to liberate Baja California and the province of Sonora from Mexico, and when he fled back to California left comrades in Mexico to be rescued by the U.S.S. *Ports-*

mouth. In 1855 Walker set himself up as ruler of Nicaragua and quickly became embroiled in a war with Central American mercenaries fronting for the steamship magnate Cornelius Vanderbilt. Again the navy was called in, this time to intervene and stop the fighting. The delicate diplomatic mission was accomplished by Commander Charles H. Davis of the *St. Mary's* in May 1857. Walker seemed to thrive on extrication from risky ventures, but in 1860 there was no American warship near enough to rescue him from a Honduran firing squad intent on cutting him down before he once more invaded neighboring Nicaragua.

In the late 1850s Walker was one reason, but not the only one, that Commodore John C. Long often kept his flagship, the new steam frigate *Merrimack*, near Panama. The 1846 treaty with New Granada (Colombia) obligated the United States to maintain order in the Isthmus of Panama in exchange for the right of transit, and in 1855 the American Panama Railroad Company completed a rail line across the Isthmus. New York and San Francisco were thus linked overseas by steam and iron, and Panama took on added importance as the Pacific transfer point for passengers and mail traveling between the East and West coasts of the United States. The railroad—a scant 50 miles long from ocean to ocean—speeded communications with the Navy Department and made it possible to rotate a ship's crew without sending the vessel around Cape Horn on a voyage that was always dangerous and could take as long as six months.

Panama thus became the southern point of a strategic arc bounded to the west by Hawaii and to the north by Puget Sound. The lines of radius converged at California, specifically the squadron headquarters in San Francisco Bay. From the new navy yard at Mare Island—opened in 1854 by Commander David G. Farragut—the squadron's ships fanned out on regular patrols in all directions, concentrating mostly on Panama City, Hawaii, and the Pacific Northwest. Sloops-of-war sometimes dropped anchor as far west as Samoa and Fiji, where American whalers depended on the islanders for fresh water and provisions. Other small ships of the squadron maintained some order among the merchant seamen loading guano at the rich deposits of Peru's Chincha Islands.

In addition to the flagship—typically a frigate in the 1850s—the number of ships operating with the squadron averaged about five. With luck, one of them mounted an auxiliary steam engine, but another would surely be a lumbering merchantman converted into an awkward warship—not an impressive array of firepower by a European standard, yet a clear measure of United States hegemony in the eastern Pacific when set alongside the merchant and whaling fleets and the new political presence in California, where the discovery of gold accounted for early statehood.

The interdependence of California gold and the Pacific Squadron was vividly demonstrated by the fact that it was the only distant station not abandoned during the Civil War. Rear Admiral Charles H. Bell, a seasoned naval diplomat who assumed the command in 1862, understood the squadron's critical importance to the Union's financing of the war. Treasure ships of the Pacific Mail Steamship Company annually carried $40 million in gold and silver from San Francisco to Panama for transshipment across the Isthmus and reshipment to New York City. Early in the war a petition from New York bankers and merchants raised the specter of "depredations by Southern privateers" and darkly threatened that an interruption of gold shipments would "necessarily incommode our Government in any future loans it may . . . apply for." Secretary of the Navy Gideon Welles reacted by alerting the Pacific Squadron, but the decade of the 1850s had already made the point that at the end of the age of sail bullion had become the real economic *raison d'être* of the Pacific Squadron. In that respect the command differed fundamentally from its counterpart on the other side of the Pacific Ocean.

=====

Since 1842 the collection of warships nebulously described as "the force employed in the Indian and China seas" had been formally designated the East India Squadron. In 1844, when Caleb Cushing negotiated the Treaty of Wanghia (Wangxia), the squadron comprised three ships: the frigate *Brandywine*, the sloop-of-war *St. Louis*, and the new brig *Perry*, all sailing vessels. In 1851, at the beginning of the squadron's busiest decade, Secretary of the Navy William A. Graham augmented it by ordering out the new paddle frigate *Susquehanna*, a highly significant addition facilitating patrols against pirates in the rivers and estuaries of the newly opened treaty ports of China. But steam-driven warships brought special problems of their own. Unlike their self-reliant sail-driven sisters, they depended on machine shops and foundries for repairs, which were available only at British or French yards in Hong Kong, Whampoa (Huangpu), and Shanghai. Equally critical was the American dependence on foreign sources for coal, a dependency not remedied until the acquisition of the Philippines in 1898.

Secretary Graham's greatest impact on the East India Squadron came from his choice of Matthew Calbraith Perry as the commodore beginning in 1852. Renowned as the combat commander of the Home Squadron in the Mexican War, the younger brother of the hero of Lake Erie was a bona fide member of the American "naval aristocracy" and in a position to haggle with the Navy Department over the terms of his command. He was promised twelve vessels—a tripling of the squadron's size—and a role in selecting his subordinates and writing his own orders. He was given one primary mission: to negotiate a treaty with Japan guaranteeing safe treatment and repatriation of shipwrecked American sailors and opening Japanese ports to American commercial penetration.

The expedition has been treated by historians as a last vestige of the expansionism of the 1840s, but it must also be interpreted as the culmination of a historic American naval and commercial desire to "open" Japan to the West. David Porter had proposed such a mission to President Madison in 1815; Edmund Roberts was under orders to visit Japan when he died in Macao in 1836; and Perry's Mediterranean mentor and predecessor as a commodore of the East India Squadron, James Biddle, had tried to unlock the "double-bolted land" with warships in 1846.

Those precedents were familiar to Secretary of State Daniel Webster and Secretary of the Navy Graham. Webster especially was anxious that the American merchant marine be allowed to purchase Japanese coal, which the secretary of state in a typical flight of rhetoric described as "a gift of Providence deposited by the Creator of all things in the depths of the Japanese islands for the benefit of the human family."

Perry received his orders to command the squadron on 24 March 1852 and began to plan carefully for what he later described as the "great object of my life." He built his enlarged squadron around the *Mississippi*, his old favorite, and the *Susquehanna*, another sidewheel steamer. Four sailing sloops-of-war and three store ships made up the rest of the contingent. To officer the expedition he turned to men who had served under him in the Mexican War, including Commander Franklin Buchanan, who would later command the Confederate States Navy.

Perry forwarded Webster's announcement to the shogunate via the American minister to the Netherlands, the only Western nation permitted access to Japan under the Tokugawa Shoguns' rigid exclusionist policy. He read extensively and collected an elaborate assortment of gifts intended to awe the Japanese with American technology.

In addition to clocks and a daguerreotype camera, he packed guns from Samuel Colt, a telegraph system from Samuel F. B. Morse, and a specially built quarter-size steam train with tracks from Philadelphia. Since the Navy Department regarded the mission as primarily a diplomatic one, he was not permitted to engage a large battery of well-paid civilian scientists, as Lieutenant Charles Wilkes had done in 1838. In other respects the expedition was a microcosm of the United States at midcentury.

Perry's instructions originated in the state and navy departments. Webster died of cirrhosis of the liver while they were being drafted, but President Millard Fillmore actively participated in the planning. In November Fillmore made Perry an envoy extraordinary and minister plenipotentiary, and the expedition became a diplomatic mission of the highest order. Its goal was to arrange "for the protection of American seamen and property wrecked on these Islands" of Japan, to permit American ships to replenish and refit in Japanese ports in emergencies, "to establish a depot for coal," and to open a Japanese port to commercial intercourse. Steam navigation lay near the heart of the mission, and Perry was instructed to convince the Japanese that California, with all its gold and riches, lay only twenty days' steaming time to the east.

This was not a Decatur-like sortie. Perry had to impress upon the Japanese "the power and greatness" of the United States, but he was to "bear in mind that as the President has no power to declare war his mission is necessarily of a pacific character." Perry could "resort to force" only for "self-defence in the protection of the vessels and crews under his command." The treaty was to be imposed through pomp, circumstance, bearing, and dignity, not at the cannon's mouth. It was a delicate task, for which Fillmore was convinced he had the right man. In his annual message of 6 December 1852 he lauded Perry as "a discreet and intelligent officer of the highest rank known to our service." Fillmore by then was a lame-duck president, the Whigs having lost the election of 1852. But Perry was a lifelong Democrat and since the Mexican War a friend of President-elect Franklin Pierce. His expedition therefore did not succumb to the vicissitudes of politics but on the contrary took on a truly national character as the *Mississippi* sailed from Norfolk on 24 November 1852.

Perry held several advantages denied to his predecessor, James Biddle, less than seven years earlier. Given ample time to prepare, Perry enjoyed the president's enthusiastic endorsement, full diplomatic powers, and steam-driven ships. He arrived in Edo (Tokyo) Bay in July 1853 confident of his prowess. The Japanese, who had never encountered steamers, were overawed by the *Susquehanna* and *Mississippi*, which became legendary in Japan as the "black ships." For almost two weeks Perry jousted diplomatically with shogunate officials, each side trying through colorful military pageantry to persuade the other to alter its national purpose. To allow time for impressions to sink in, Perry left Japan on 17 July, promising to return for formal negotiation of a treaty in the spring of 1854.

The second visit was anticlimactic. On 8 March, with eight American warships anchored offshore, Perry and the Japanese began negotiations in a specially constructed treaty house at Yokohama, then a village south of Edo. Perry landed five hundred men, paraded in full dress uniform, and unveiled products of American ingenuity— the Colt revolvers, the train, and the telegraph system. On 31 March 1854 he signed the Treaty of Kanagawa, opening two ports for the emergency provisioning and resupply of American merchantmen and whalers, guaranteeing safe treatment to shipwrecked sailors, and granting the United States most-favored-nation status. That last provision was mostly of academic interest since the Japanese had not consented to trade with the United States.

Perry had barely opened the door of Japan. It took two more years of persistent effort by consul Townsend Harris—backed initially by the screw frigate *San Jacinto*—to negotiate a second treaty actually initiating commercial intercourse between the two nations. But Congress was pleased with the commodore. It voted him a bonus of $20,000, and the Senate unanimously ratified his pact.

Perry himself captured the meaning of the treaty for a generation of expansionists whose untamed spirit would be turned violently inward five years later:

> It requires no sage to predict events so strongly foreshadowed to us all; still "Westward" will "the course of empire take its way." But the last act of the drama is yet to be unfolded; . . . to me it seems that the people of America will, in some form or other, extend their dominion and their power, until they shall have brought within their mighty embrace the Islands of the great Pacific, and placed the Saxon race upon the eastern shores of Asia.

In the westward maritime march Perry perceived a partner whom he had once seen as a rival: Great Britain. The unstinting hospitality recently shown to the East India Squadron—under Perry the U.S. Navy's largest seagoing command—by overseas colonial officials and officers of the Royal Navy had begun to pay off. In remarks before the American Geographical and Statistical Society of New York, the fledgling Anglophile reported, "And I cheerfully take occasion here to remark, that wherever I have found the British flag, in whatever part of the world, there I have always found a courteous and hospitable reception." Rear Admiral Sir James Stirling, commander of the British East India Squadron, saluted Perry's achievement with a mild reservation: "The Commodore is said to have conducted his mission with wisdom, Temper and Firmness, and probably accomplished all that could have been done." Stirling offered the sincerest form of flattery by heading off to Nagasaki to negotiate an Anglo-Japanese treaty modeled after Perry's. At the highest operational level, at least, an Anglo-American naval rapprochement clearly had taken place in the 1850s.

The solidarity of the informal naval union was demonstrated in Shanghai, where the *Plymouth* stood guard while Perry was winding down his mission to Japan. Anti-Western attacks on the international settlement had come not from the Taiping rebels but from Chinese imperial troops. A conference of Western consuls and commanding officers agreed on a joint response, which took the form of deploying landing parties of marines and sailors from the *Plymouth* and two British warships, the *Encounter* and *Grecian*. On 4 April 1854 a brief encounter with artillery and rifles forced the imperial soldiers to withdraw, leaving behind three American dead and seven wounded. Perry approved the bilateral intervention shortly before he departed for the United States in September 1854.

After Perry's departure the East India Squadron shrank to about three ships, a more typical size. Commodore Joel Abbot continued the practice of Anglo-American naval cooperation with attacks against Chinese pirates operating from armed junks off Canton (Guangzhou). Lieutenant George H. Preble of the chartered paddle steamer *Queen* joined with H.M.S. *Encounter* and several other armed vessels in attacking the junks with ships' guns and boarding parties. In one action late in 1855 the Anglo-Americans destroyed fifty junks, three villages, and three shore batteries. In a letter to Secretary of the Navy James Dobbin, Abbot pronounced Preble a "most excellent and valuable" officer and bragged of his own "most friendly and harmonious" relationship with Admiral Stirling.

The East India Squadron closed out the decade of the 1850s in this same spirit. In November 1856 Commander Andrew H. Foote exercised the guns of the *Portsmouth* and *Levant* in a victorious duel with the formidable European-designed Chinese "barrier forts" between Canton and Whampoa, on the Pearl (Zhu) River above Hong Kong. Foote had provoked the encounter by deploying sailors and a howitzer to defend the American and French consulates in Canton at the very time that a nearby British amphibious force was attacking Chinese positions in the opening stages of a second Anglo-Chinese war. He was incited to act by the consul, Oliver H. Perry, a former naval officer and son of the recent commodore.

The current squadron commander, James Armstrong, prudently removed himself to the flagship *San Jacinto,* whose deep draft kept her out of riverine operations. From this retreat he negotiated with the Chinese about their failure properly to recognize and honor the American flag. Some junior officers denounced Armstrong as an "old woman," and American merchants at Canton called for more vigorous protection, but Secretary Dobbin commended him for discouraging the Chinese from "trifling with our flag" and praised the squadron for the "gallantry, good order and 'intelligent subordination' displayed by all in the various conflicts." The United States government, of course, was eager "to cultivate and maintain friendly relations with the people and Government of China." The secretary did not attempt to reconcile this national goal with the belligerency of Foote, who came out unscathed. His men cheered his aggressiveness, and he gained combat experience to be used in attacking the Confederate river strongholds of Fort Henry and Fort Donelson six years later.

Between Foote's engagement in Canton and the squadron's dissolution in January 1862 America's unneutral collaboration with the Royal Navy reached new heights. Joined by France, Britain seized on questionable pretexts to declare war on China. Anglo-French forces captured Canton in January 1858, and the Western diplomats began the now standard negotiations to extort from China an indemnity for the war forced upon it. The United States government elevated the American minister, William B. Reed, to the rank of envoy extraordinary and minister plenipotentiary and ordered the commodore to the East India Squadron to deploy his ships as Reed directed. The powerful new screw-frigate *Minnesota* was sent out to highlight the Buchanan administration's serious interest in China.

By late spring 1858 Reed was in Tientsin (Tianjin) negotiating with the Chinese mandarins alongside the ministers of Britain, France, and Russia. The *Minnesota,* commanded by Captain Samuel

F. Du Pont, lay off the mouth of the Pei Ho (Hai) River, the imperial capital's artery to the sea. British and French gunboats cleared the river of barriers and neutralized its forts before mooring at Tientsin. Thereafter unarmed charter steamers of all four powers plied the river between the deep-draft offshore blockaders and diplomats ashore. They were escorted by specially designed, heavily armed, light-draft British screw-steamers. The Chinese commissioners got the point and agreed to open eleven more ports to the West. The Sino-American Treaty of Tientsin, signed on 18 June 1858, duplicated its British counterpart, just as the Treaty of Wangxia had copied the Treaty of Nanking (Nanjing). Subsequent negotiations legalized the opium trade, giving foreigners a monopoly on the sale of the debilitating drug in treaty ports.

Ingeniously adept at passive resistance, the Chinese fortified the Pei Ho while awaiting the Westerners' reappearance to exchange ratifications of the treaties. In June 1859 the British and French once again faced the river forts, and this time they paid heavily, suffering an estimated total of 450 casualties. During the riverine fusillade the American squadron commander, Flag Officer Josiah Tattnall, busily steamed about on a small, unarmed, chartered paddlewheeler, the *Toey-wan*. At one point he conferred with the badly wounded British commodore while American sailors reinforced a gun crew on the battered British flagship, H.M.S. *Cormorant*. Tattnall excused his actions on the grounds that "blood is thicker than water," and his limited but distinctly unneutral intervention was approved by President Buchanan and Secretary of the Navy Isaac Toucey. The Sino-American exchange of ratifications took place two months later, and the Chinese government opted not to protest Tattnall's violation of the Treaty of Wangxia's prohibition against neutral protection of "vessels engaged in the transportation of officers or soldiers in the enemy's service."

Tattnall had acted with calculation. The British were rarely as embarrassed in their chastisement of the Chinese as they were in the summer of 1859. The next year they returned to the Pei Ho and overwhelmed the forts. The Royal Navy's ships—thirty of them— were again supreme in Far Eastern rivers, ports, and harbors. Because Tattnall and his predecessors had consistently reciprocated British goodwill, the Navy Department could count on those ships to protect Americans during crises in the event that no American warships were nearby.

The East India Squadron dwindled to three ships deliberately selected with coastal and river work in mind. The *Saginaw*, part of the Toucey buildup of 1858 and the first warship built at Mare Island Navy Yard in California, was a side-wheeler specially designed for the East India Squadron. Larger than the British gunboats, which evoked the envy of the squadron's officers, the *Saginaw* was expected by Secretary Toucey to "be particularly useful in suppressing piracies, as her light draught will enable her to reach the retreats of those who commit them." Catching Asian marine outlaws apparently presented the same tactical problems that Caribbean pirates had posed in the days of David Porter. They fled to shallow bays and river mouths, where blue-water ships could not follow without grounding and in turn becoming the prey. Matthew C. Perry learned the same tactical lesson in the Mexican War: Lightly armed, shallow-draft paddlewheel steamers were far more useful in coastal waters than deep-draft, screw-propelled, blue-water warships.

The wisdom of special designs was confirmed one final time in the East India Squadron in May 1861, when the *Saginaw* steamed 700 miles up the Yangtze Kiang (Chang Jiang), a prototypical expedition anticipating the much romanticized "Yangtze Patrol" of the early twentieth century. She was accompanied for a short part of the ascent by the new flagship, the screw-sloop *Hartford*, a good steamer with shallow draft.

While the ships were on that expedition, Captain Frederick Engle was en route to Hong Kong with orders to assume command of the squadron. On 22 July 1861 he relieved Flag Officer Cornelius K. Stribling, a veteran of almost fifty years' active service in the U.S. Navy. A South Carolinian, Stribling was politically suspect in the eyes of President Lincoln's secretary of the navy, Gideon Welles of Connecticut. With the commodore's ignominious recall, the once-proud East India Squadron effectively ceased to exist. The age of American "gunboat diplomacy" under sail ended with a whimper, and the *Hartford* came home to become the flagship of David G. Farragut in his operations in the Gulf of Mexico and on the Mississippi River.

===

While Josiah Tattnall was collaborating with the Royal Navy in the Far East, the prevailing spirit of Anglo-American naval harmony was being sorely tested in the South Atlantic and the Gulf of Mexico. The divisive issue was the slave trade, which London began to prosecute vigorously at the end of the Crimean War (1854–1856). The British revived the claimed right to board and search suspected slavers, even if they flew the American flag. The United States contended that a vessel flying the national ensign was immune to boarding by foreign naval officers. The disputed interpretation of international law recalled the unresolved issue of impressment, so prominent as a cause of the War of 1812.

The administration of James Buchanan genuinely desired to combat the slave trade, but Southern congressmen were moving to repeal the legislation of 1819–1820 that had made slave trading by vessels flying the American flag an act of piracy punishable by death. Repeal would eliminate the statutory basis of the already imperfect American antislaver campaign. Buchanan could not risk alienating Northern legislators by surrendering the historic American principle of national maritime inviolability. Secretary of State Lewis Cass therefore shored up Northern partisan support by protesting British searches of merchantmen flying the American flag, while Secretary of the Navy Isaac Toucey tried to convince Britain of America's sincere commitment to the war against slave traders.

Toucey added four new shallow-draft steamers to the African Squadron and ordered the commodore to cooperate with his British counterpart without conceding the historic American insistence on the sanctity of any vessel flying the Stars and Stripes. Contending that England shared this interpretation of limited rights of visit and search, and wishing to give teeth to the antislavery patrol, Toucey formally ordered Commodore William Inman to operate jointly with the British, a rare instance of prior endorsement of a widespread operational practice. "I would consider it highly desirable," Toucey instructed Inman, "that a vessel of each nation should, as far as possible, cruise in company with a vessel of the other, so that each might be in a condition to assert the rights and prevent the abuse of the flag of its own country. In this way . . . the harmonious cooperation of the two powers will go far to insure the full accomplishment of the common object of suppression of the slave trade." The secretary was overly optimistic about the efficacy of Anglo-American naval cooperation in the antislavery patrol on the African coast and rather naïve about Britain's readiness to abandon its claimed right to search any vessel on the high seas.

By 1859 Toucey had four steamers circling Cuba in addition to the four cruising off the west coast of Africa. His target was still the slave trade, and here again the Royal Navy complicated matters. Prime Minister Lord Palmerston had decided that the British campaign against slave ships should be concentrated in the West Indies and the Caribbean. With a large base in Jamaica, the Royal Navy could patrol Spanish Cuba, a notorious landing place for slavers, far more easily and effectively than it could the African coast. The Americans therefore were impaled on the horns of a dilemma. Toucey's four steamers could hardly blockade the Cuban coast, and it was especially unpalatable to contemplate British inspection of American cargo ships in waters so close to home. But the surveillance took place, and in at least one instance the skipper of a coastal vessel bound from Mobile to New York reported that the British officer boarding his vessel had not suspected him of being a slaver but was acting under ominously general orders authorizing the boarding of all vessels traversing the Gulf of Mexico.

In the summer of 1858 the American minister to the Court of St. James's was compelled to advise the British ministry that the American public had "been abruptly startled by the sound of British cannon near their own shores." He warned that the practice threatened to "establish over the commerce of an independent community a system of foreign police." The *Times* of London concurred and cautioned restraint in the exercise of a questionable policy in a geographic area deemed vital to the United States:

> Let us . . . frankly admit that we have not the right to challenge the American flag upon the open sea at a time of profound peace. . . . The Americans will say that they are quite competent to watch over the honour of their own flag, and to take care that it is not applied to the protection of the slave trade. Now, whatever our opinion may be as to their sincerity, it would be idle to contest the point. They are a sovereign people as we are ourselves, and have a perfect right to assert their resolution to resist all foreign dictation.

The Admiralty soon restrained its overzealous captains as part of the continuing adjustment of Anglo-American relations in the Caribbean and the West Indies that characterized the 1850s.

London and Washington were jousting for predominance in two spots: Central America and Cuba. American hunger for Cuba dated back to the Monroe administration. It was reawakened by Cuban slave revolts against Spain in the 1830s and 1840s and kept alive by growing Cuban–American commercial ties. President Polk tried to buy the island after his conquest of Mexico, but France and Britain blocked him. To a subsequent Anglo-French proposal for a tripartite pledge of self-denial, Secretary of State Edward Everett in 1852 haughtily replied that the island's destiny was "mainly an American question." By mid-decade the impending crisis over the expansion of Southern slavery dampened the Northern appetite for the island, but as late as 1859 the Senate Foreign Relations Committee seconded a recommendation to buy the island made by President James Buchanan, an unregenerate Cuban annexationist. Only Republican abolitionist resistance thwarted a congressional appropriation that might have advanced the final expulsion of Spain from the Caribbean by a half-century.

The Central American isthmus assumed a vital strategic importance to the United States with the acquisition of California in 1850, but Great Britain did not at first back off easily or gracefully. To neutralize the transit rights across Panama ceded to the United States in the treaty with New Granada, Britain in 1848 seized Greytown. This Nicaraguan town controlled the mouth of the San Juan River and gave access to one of the two most promising routes for a canal across Central America. Checked by the new British presence, Secretary of State John M. Clayton proposed Anglo-American construction of "a great highway" to benefit all nations. Lord Palmerston recognized American strength in the region and wanted American raw cotton far more than conflict with the United States. The upshot was the Clayton–Bulwer Treaty of 1850, stipulating nonmonopolization and nonfortification of any canal built by either power across Central America. The treaty was destined to last for fifty years, and the bilateral spirit of compromise behind it explains why the two nations weathered the provocations of unscrupulous American filibusters who quite literally descended on Cuba and Central America in the 1850s.

Because of the fluidity of Anglo-American diplomacy regarding the area, the history of the Home Squadron in the Caribbean was episodic and hesitant in the 1850s, a contrast to the systematic and programmed operations of the squadrons in the Mediterranean and Pacific. In 1849 it briefly blockaded a filibustering expedition on an island off the Louisiana coast. Commander Victor M. Randolph of the sloop-of-war *Albany* contemptuously described the men led by Narcisco López as "reckless and abandoned adventurers." In 1854 the squadron sat on the sidelines as the State Department demanded Spanish indemnification for seizing the merchant vessel *Black Warrior* in Havana. The squadron's passivity in that instance contrasted with the bombast in Congress, where Representative Caleb Lyon shouted that "Cuba should have been taken in, sir, and satisfaction demanded afterwards." That same year the skipper of the U.S.S. *Cyane*, overreacting to an insult to an American diplomat, bombarded

Greytown, and the British fortunately looked the other way. In 1856 the navy landed 160 sailors to occupy the railroad station at Colón, the Atlantic terminus of the Panama railroad, in retaliation for a riot in which several Americans were killed. At the very end of 1857 Commodore Hiram Paulding risked his reputation by landing three hundred men near Greytown, where the ever elusive William Walker was again filibustering. Paulding captured Walker and shipped him home, only to endure a presidential rebuke for committing a "grave error," though admittedly out of "pure and patriotic motives."

Paulding knew what he was doing. A veteran of the War of 1812 and sixty-one years of age, he was holding the "twilight" billet reserved by the nineteenth-century navy for senior officers on the eve of retirement, a squadron command. Like so many others, he fell under the spell of "this lion-hearted devil" and took the prisoner into his cabin as a guest. In a letter to his wife the commodore shrewdly appraised Walker and the impact of grabbing him on a foreign shore: "We laugh and talk as though nothing had happened, and you would think, to see him with the captain and myself, that he was one of us. He is a sharp fellow and requires a sharp fellow to deal with him. I have taken strong measures in forcing him from a neutral territory. It may make me President or may cost me my commission." Three years later, when the captain of H.M.S. *Icarus* turned Walker over to Honduran authorities for execution, American naval officers must have welcomed the elimination of so charismatic a menace to international order and personal careers.

While by no means an arbiter of global empire, the United States Navy of the 1850s was octopus-like in its operations. In addition to its regular squadrons, whose domain was worldwide, the navy dispatched scientific and technical expeditions to areas as remote as the Dead Sea and the Arctic Ocean. The unprecedented scope of naval exploration was one facet of the intense American nationalism of the 1840s and 1850s. It was an attempt to convince Americans and Europeans that democratic science was superior to that of the aristocratic and elitist Old World. In the mid-1840s the federal government sparked the nationalization of American science with special appropriations. Congress chartered the Smithsonian Institution in 1846 as a national center for research in the physical sciences and to house the specimens of the Charles Wilkes expedition. Within the navy itself structural evolution facilitated scientific exploration, and several naval officers of the antebellum period devoted substantial portions of their careers to science, or at least to naval technology.

By 1844 the Navy Depot of Charts and Instruments had evolved into two scientific agencies, the Naval Observatory and the Hydrographical Office, both headed until 1861 by the industrious and erratic Matthew Fontaine Maury. Maury's greatest achievement lay in popularizing and harnessing hydrography and meteorology rather than in conducting or sponsoring abstract research. He concentrated on mapping the winds and currents of the high seas, most notably the Gulf Stream. By collating the innumerable tracks of merchant vessels recorded in ships' logbooks on deposit in his office, Maury charted the swiftest courses and in five years radically shrank the sailing time between ports. The first vessel to travel his "Fair Way to Rio" cut thirty-five days from the round trip between New York and the principal port-of-call in Brazil.

Permanently consigned to shore duty by a lame leg, Maury tirelessly encouraged other naval officers to go where he could not. He sponsored scientific expeditions to the Dead Sea, the Rio de la Plata, and the Amazon River; to the Arctic in search of a northwest passage; and to the Isthmus of Panama to survey for a canal route. The North Atlantic soundings he ordered in 1849—confirmed in 1853 by a bottom sampling device invented by one of his Hydrographical Office lieutenants—found the submarine plateau route where American and British naval vessels laid the first transatlantic telegraph in 1858. Although his two offices did not exert operational command or control over any of those naval-commercial-scientific expeditions, Maury played a catalytic role in each one, and he was at the center of this aspect of midcentury American naval globalism.

After Maury and Charles Wilkes, the most prominent of the naval scientist-technicians was John A. Dahlgren, chief of ordnance at the Washington Navy Yard from 1847 until named commandant of the yard in April 1861. Like Maury, Dahlgren built an international reputation from an obscure position as a relatively junior officer assigned to shore duty in Washington. Like Maury, he capitalized on the proximity of his duty station to the nexus of national power. He created an infrastructure of supporters, including President Abraham Lincoln. Proficient in Latin and Spanish, and a master of careful mathematical calculation, Dahlgren was intellectually more precise than Maury. A native of Philadelphia, Dahlgren became the sixth-ranking rear admiral in the United States Navy in 1863.

The guns Dahlgren designed at the Washington Navy Yard marked an important step in the mid-nineteenth-century transition from historic muzzle-loading smoothbores, which threw round shot against wooden hulls, to modern breech-loading, rifled cannon firing shaped explosive shells that blast through iron and steel hulls. Challenging the navy's preference for the 32-pound shot-firing gun, he developed shell guns varying in size from howitzers for gunboats to large-caliber weapons for frigates. He wanted safe guns, that is, ones unlikely to burst and kill their crews when firing, as had the "Peacemaker" in the disastrous demonstration cruise of the *Princeton* in 1844. In his quest for reliable and effective ordnance he studied the French Paixhans shell gun, the gunnery duels of the Crimean War, and the 1856 bombardment of the Chinese barrier forts by his friend Andrew Hull Foote. From Foote he learned that shot still had utility against forts. From the British he learned appreciation for "concentration of fire." From all his sources he deduced the "axiom, that the utmost simplicity is indispensable in all the arrangements of the [gun] battery."

The result was the 11-inch smoothbore, which Dahlgren hoped would set the national standard for concentrated fire by large-caliber guns mounted on uniform carriages and serviced by efficiently arranged powder magazines. Bulging like a soda-water bottle to prevent explosion at the breech, the muzzle-loader could fire either shot or shell. A perfect hybrid, the 11-inch Dahlgren constituted part of the battery of the *Merrimack*-class steam frigate. A brace of them constituted the entire armament of the *Monitor* in the historic engagement at Hampton Roads.

By the outbreak of the Civil War Dahlgren's name had become synonymous with American naval ordnance. One newspaper bragged that Dahlgren had "rendered obsolete much of the existing naval armament of the world." He had "shorn the large fleets of Europe of much of their strength, and has compelled the great maritime Powers *to start with us* for the dominion of the sea." No scarcity of jingoism here, and a faint echo sounded in the annual report of Secretary of the Navy Isaac Toucey for the year 1858: "In the Dahlgren gun we have found what we want." Judging by the crucial qualities of "strength, range, accuracy and power," there was "no gun in any service that surpasses it." Perhaps, but the same could not be said of the decks beneath the guns.

Three ships symbolize the state of American naval architecture in the blue-water navy of the 1850s: the *Mississippi, Princeton,* and *Merrimack.* A creature of the 1830s and the brainchild of Matthew C. Perry, the *Mississippi* was old and obsolescent. Her oversize paddlewheels were highly susceptible to disabling fire from enemy ships, and they limited the number of guns that could be placed in broadside batteries. The *Princeton*, authorized in 1842, was driven by a propeller linked to engines mounted safely below the waterline. She entered the Mediterranean in 1847 as a fine example of contemporary naval craftsmanship, but she was really a "hoodoo ship" from the beginning. The explosion of one of her experimental guns, the "Peacemaker," in 1844 inhibited technical development in the U.S. Navy for a decade. In 1852 her evil star finally set when her two engines deteriorated beyond repair while Perry was outfitting her for his expedition to Japan.

The full-rigged screw-frigate *Merrimack*, the prototype of a class, "had been considered the epitome of American naval architecture" at the time of her commissioning in 1856. About 260 feet in length and displacing 4,500 tons, she carried forty Dahlgren guns. But her sleek lines hid two 600-horsepower engines of uncertain reliability. They decayed quickly, and in 1860 she had to be taken to the navy yard at Norfolk for complete overhaul and refitting.

The *Merrimack*'s engineering collapse coincided with the launching of H.M.S. *Warrior*—"the black snake among the rabbits." Classed as the first modern battleship, the *Warrior* had an all-iron hull, not one of iron sheathing over wood. She was impervious to the shot and shell of the day and was the catalyst of tempestuous changes in naval architecture. *Warrior* ushered in a thirty-year era in which American warship design was totally eclipsed by the Royal Navy.

The incipient obsolescence of the American warships was obscured by their success in the war with Mexico and the vigor of the global "gunboat diplomacy" in the decade and a half following the war. The United States had ascended to a higher plateau of international power as a result of annexing the Pacific Coast, acquiring the wealth of the California gold fields, and covering the seas with its clipper ships and whaling fleet. In that rush of prosperity and power, the relative technological decline of the U.S. Navy was hidden. It would be hidden for a few more years, during the Civil War, when the industrial base of the North and the genius of the inventor John Ericsson gave the Union navy an unquestionable quantitative and qualitative edge over the Confederate States Navy.

6

A Navy Divided Against Itself

1861 – 1890

THE War Between the States pitted friend against friend. Officers who had served together in the Mexican War and on distant station in the decade between wars now looked across cannons at one another. David Dixon Porter and his step-brother, David Glasgow Farragut, stayed with the Union navy. Franklin Buchanan, Raphael Semmes, and Matthew Fontaine Maury went home to their states and helped form the Confederate States Navy. The band of brothers was split asunder.

Two hard men ran the North's navy, Secretary of the Navy Gideon Welles and Assistant Secretary Gustavus Vasa Fox. The Confederate navy was directed by equally talented and resolute men, Secretary Stephen R. Mallory and Matthew Fontaine Maury, nominally the chief of the Submarine Battery Service. In addition, the Confederacy dispatched a naval agent, James D. Bulloch, to London for the crucial purpose of purchasing ships and war matériel, something the industrially stronger Union did not have to do.

The civilian directors and the officers on both sides drew from a common naval heritage. They knew that the war would not be one in which fleets of line-of-battle ships met one another in a Trafalgar-like contest for command of the sea. Neither side had such a fleet at the war's beginning; the South lacked the industrial base to build one; the Union did not need one since the Confederacy had none. Those facts were self-evident, yet fundamental to the conduct of the war at sea from 1861 to 1865.

The absence of line-of-battle fleets in the naval equation meant that this was an *American* war in strategy and operations. Each side, North and South, drew on the American experience in the War of 1812 and the Mexican War, both of which had occurred in the lifetimes of the more senior participants. Those two wars had taught that a blockading navy could mount stinging amphibious assaults on the enemy's coastal cities, that coastal defense was difficult if not impossible if the opponent were truly preponderant at sea, but that regardless of its preponderance at sea the stronger power could win the war only if its army successfully invaded and occupied the opponent's politico-economic heart. The War of 1812 taught two final lessons: commerce raiders could elude blockaders, and their attacks on the stronger power's merchant marine could dampen his morale even if by themselves they might not win the war.

The war opened on 12 April 1861 with the Confederate bombardment of the U.S. Army garrison at Fort Sumter, on an island in the bay of Charleston, South Carolina. Serious planning had begun on both sides two months earlier, when the seceding states adopted a constitution for the Confederate States of America. On 21 February President Jefferson Davis appointed Stephen R. Mallory the Confederate secretary of the navy, and on 7 March Gideon Welles assumed office as the Union secretary.

In April, as soon as Fort Sumter surrendered, President Davis took the step characteristic of weaker naval powers in the nineteenth century. He urged Southern entrepreneurs to outfit privateers, and on 6 May the Confederate Congress authorized the issuance of letters of marque and reprisal. The Union, of course, preferred to regard Southern privateers as pirates eligible for hanging as international outlaws, but as late as the Paris Declaration of 1856, in which most industrialized nations declared privateering illegal, the United States held to the traditional American position that the practice was a legitimate means of fighting at sea. The tables now were turned on Washington.

Within hours of Davis's call for privateering President Abraham Lincoln and Secretary of State William H. Seward responded with the proclamation of a blockade of the Confederate coast. The blockade ran contrary to the American conception of legitimate war at sea on two counts. First, a blockade is an act of war, and to prevent European assistance to the South the Union denied that this was an international war. It was merely a "civil war" in which foreign nations had no right to interfere. Second, the United States historically had contended that to be legal a blockade must be effective, that is, the blockading power must station intercepting ships off the enemy's ports as visible evidence of the blockade. Otherwise neutral nations need not abide by the proclamation of blockade. In 1861 the United States Navy numbered about 42 operational ships, most of them on distant station. The Confederate coastline from Texas to Virginia stretched over 3,000 miles and was riddled with innumerable bays and inlets. An effective blockade was beyond imagination.

Those legal interpretations became far more than moot questions in May 1861, when Stephen Mallory sent Commander James D. Bulloch to London as the Confederate naval agent. Suave, tactful, and well versed in the complexities of international trade, Bulloch was "the perfect person for finding and exploiting loopholes in European neutrality laws." His task was overwhelming: "to create a navy in foreign shipyards for an unrecognized country that had neither money to build ships nor open ports to sustain them." Queen Victoria's Proclamation of Neutrality of May 1861, various parliamentary acts, and Admiralty regulations all created an ambiguous field of play for Bulloch. It was clear that Great Britain had recognized Confederate belligerency but not the South's sovereign independence. It was equally clear that Britain would tolerate the profitable construction of ships for the Confederacy in its yards, but their ultimate ownership and purpose would have to be disguised.

Bulloch constantly pressed the ministers and judges for liberal interpretations of English neutrality. His opposite number, the American minister to the Court of St. James's, Charles Francis Adams, pressed for stringent neutrality and confiscation of Bulloch's ships. These well-matched adversaries depended on the outcome of combat in North America to determine which of them would ultimately carry the day.

One episode, Captain Charles Wilkes's removal of two Confederate envoys from the British packet *Trent* in November 1861, nearly brought the incensed British into the war against the Union. But Secretary of State William H. Seward crafted a near-apology satisfactory to the cooler heads in London, and the crisis passed. In October 1862, following General Robert E. Lee's defeat at the Battle of Antietam, all hope of Britain's intervention on the side of the Confederacy vanished. His people, said Prime Minister Lord Palmerston, "must continue to be lookers on." By the fall of 1863, following the Union victories at Gettysburg and Vicksburg, the British foreign minister concluded that he must confiscate the Confederate ironclads then under construction at the Laird Brothers yard in Liverpool.

Mallory initially had directed Bulloch to obtain two types of vessels for the Confederate States Navy: wooden commerce raiders powered by sail and steam, and ironclad rams with rifled guns mounted in turrets. The raiders would follow the traditional American strategy of *guerre de course*, and the rams would pursue the corollary strategy of defending the Southern coast by breaking the Union blockade. Toward the end of the war the Confederate naval secretary added a third item to Bulloch's shopping list: swift, shallow-draft blockade runners to carry cargos from Southern ports to points of transfer in the Caribbean and West Indies.

The most famous British-built raiders were the *Florida*, *Alabama*, and *Shenandoah*. They slipped to sea ostensibly as cargo vessels, only to take on guns and be recommissioned as ships of the Confederate States Navy in neutral ports less closely watched than those in Britain. Together they destroyed more than a hundred Union merchantmen, turning the world's oceans into "a furnace and melting pot of American commerce."

Blockade runners, which proved highly profitable to private owners, continued to slip through the Union cordon until war's end. Of an estimated 2,742 attempts to slip through the blockade during the war, some 2,525 runners—92 percent—got through, a clear demonstration of the steam engine's potential for changing warfare at sea. The British continued to build these greyhounds without compunction, because as unarmed and unarmored vessels they did not contravene any neutrality restrictions.

While Bulloch and Adams dueled diplomatically for the favor of the English government, the Union began to transform its paper blockade into wood, iron, and guns. Secretaries Welles and Fox built and purchased blockaders as fast as possible, so that by the end of 1861 there were 264 vessels in commission. This was an improvised force composed of barges and ferryboats as well as frigates, sloops, and brigs. Many of the craft featured steam engines, at least as an auxiliary means of propulsion. The Mexican War had shown the utility of steam-powered vessels to a blockading and invading force, but as all naval officers knew, steam-driven vessels required regular resupply of coal, which was arduous when done by colliers. Steam-powered blockaders also depended on shore facilities for maintenance and upkeep far more than did sailing ships. It was imperative to seize bases for naval operations along the Confederate coast.

The first targets were two forts guarding Hatteras Inlet, a North Carolina waterway favored by blockade runners. They fell to a small army–navy expedition commanded by Flag Officer Silas H. Stringham and Major General Benjamin F. Butler in late August 1861. Next came a much bigger operation against Port Royal Sound, midway between Charleston and Savannah, Georgia.

In early November Flag Officer Samuel F. Du Pont attacked Port Royal Sound with a seventy-seven-ship expedition composed of eleven deep-draft warships; an assortment of small, hastily built gunboats; and more than thirty transports loaded with 16,000 army soldiers. Anchoring the transports safely out of range, Du Pont neutralized the Sound's two earthen forts with gunfire from his 46-gun steam frigate *Wabash*. The Confederate defenders abandoned their positions, and the Federal troops landed without opposition. The operation set the pattern for Atlantic and Gulf Coast operations, and for the rest of the war Port Royal served as a major base of operations for the blockading fleet.

Fully appreciating the danger posed by the blockade, Mallory in June 1861 began converting the refloated 40-gun steam frigate *Merrimack*, burned and sunk by Union forces as they abandoned Norfolk Navy Yard, into a blockade-destroyer. The masts and superstructure of the original ship were replaced by a sloped iron casemate to protect the engines and crew from Union shot, and she was rechristened the C.S.S. *Virginia* on 17 February 1862. The new warship carried eleven guns and an iron ram mounted on the bow below the water's surface. Mallory hoped that the *Virginia* would be able to destroy the Union's wooden blockaders or drive them from the mouth of Chesapeake Bay, secure control of Hampton Roads for the Confederacy, and prevent the Union army from ascending the James River to attack Richmond.

Upon learning of the intended conversion, Gideon Welles and Gustavus Fox had convened a special "Ironclad Board" to meet this unanticipated threat to the blockade. The board recommended three types of vessels, but only the *Monitor* design proposed by the Swedish naval architect John Ericsson was truly revolutionary. It was a vessel without a model. Ericsson made detailed drawings and as many as forty patentable inventions as he supervised the construction during a hectic hundred-day period. Commissioned on 25 February 1862, the original *Monitor* featured a single turret with two 11-inch Dahlgren smoothbore guns. Iron plating protected her hull from cannon fire above the waterline, and her deck was fully armored. She drew only 12 feet and presented an extremely low silhouette to enemy gunners.

In her totality—steam, turret, and armor—she has been seen as "a prototype for the future battleship navies of the world," and there is some truth in this contention. The first great battleship of the U.S. Navy, the *Oregon*, authorized in 1890, would resemble the *Monitor* in low-lying silhouette and apparent predominance of turrets. But the *Monitor's* extremely low freeboard and shallow draft made her unseaworthy and incapacitated her for duty on the ocean. She was a coastal gunboat, intended to fight in the bays and river mouths of the divided Republic. She was, in fact, the steam-driven embodiment of Thomas Jefferson's ideal defensive vessel.

Sea trials, crew training, and gunnery practice were out of the question in the race to confront the *Virginia*. Commanded by Lieutenant John L. Worden, the *Monitor* left New York under tow for Hampton Roads, arriving on the evening of 8 March 1862—none too soon. Earlier that day Captain Franklin Buchanan had driven the *Virginia's* ram into the 32-gun Union sloop *Cumberland* and then turned his guns on the 52-gun frigate *Congress*. The two blockaders were destroyed; the United States could not encircle the Confederacy with a wooden fence; the *Virginia* was on the verge of realizing Stephen Mallory's latest dream for her.

In a letter delivered to Buchanan on 7 March, the Confederate navy secretary proposed that the *Virginia* make her way to New York City, where "she could shell and burn the city and the shipping." Mallory believed that

> peace would inevitably follow. Bankers would withdraw their capital from the city. The Brooklyn navy yard and its magazines and all the lower part of the city would be destroyed, and such an event, by a single ship, would do more to achieve our immediate independence than would the results of many campaigns.

Mallory's apocalyptic vision haunted American naval strategists long after the Civil War. As late as the early twentieth century it influenced United States planning for war against Germany.

The fortuitous arrival of the *Monitor* in Hampton Roads ended any Confederate menace to the Union's financial hub. On 9 March 1862, in one of history's most celebrated one-on-one gun duels, the *Monitor* and the *Virginia* pounded each other for more than four hours. Neither ship was seriously damaged; each partially achieved its strategic aim. The *Monitor* saved the remaining wooden blockaders from certain destruction. The *Virginia* protected Norfolk and the James River until her new skipper, Josiah Tattnall, blew her up during a Union attack two months later. The victor of Hampton Roads, the *Monitor*, was swamped while under tow off Cape Hatteras on 31 December. But both ships became prototypes, and Union monitors spearheaded the invasions of many Confederate ports, while the Confederacy commissioned twenty-two imitations of the *Virginia*. The *Virginia*s were plagued with design and mechanical problems that severely inhibited their fighting characteristics. Their principal contribution was psychological. They generated a "ram fever" that "raged through Union naval circles throughout the war."

The protracted naval war thereafter subdivided itself into three theaters: the Atlantic and Gulf coasts, the great inland rivers, and the blue water over the horizon. The Union was victorious in the first two, the Confederacy in the third.

On 9 January 1862 Flag Officer David G. Farragut was assigned command of the West Gulf Blockading Squadron and charged with taking New Orleans. The nation's leading exporter of cotton prior to the war, and second only to New York in total exports, New Orleans was the key to the South's "King Cotton" strategy of coercing Great Britain into full diplomatic recognition and military assistance. Located 100 miles up the Mississippi River from the Gulf of Mexico, New Orleans controlled the exit and entrance of the greatest maritime highway in North America. Assistant Secretary of the Navy Fox and Commander David Dixon Porter concluded that the navy could take the city. They would send mortar boats from the Gulf to knock out the two forts, Jackson and St. Philip, 10 miles above the river's mouth. Then deep-draft warships could steam past and threaten New Orleans itself.

In February 1862, Farragut assembled a fleet of four first-class steam sloops and twelve gunboats. His flagship was the powerful sloop *Hartford*, a veteran of the East India Squadron built for coastal and riverine operations prior to the war. Farragut placed Porter in subordinate command of twenty-one schooners that had been converted into mortar boats for lobbing 13-inch fused shells into the wooden and earthen forts. Porter began his attack on 18 April. He failed to knock out the forts, but two gunboats commanded by Captain Henry H. Bell cut a narrow path through the massive log obstruction the Confederates had placed in the river just under their guns. With characteristic impatience and audacity, Farragut on 24 April ordered his sloops and gunboats to charge through the gap opened by Bell and past the forts Porter had not fully silenced. New Orleans surrendered to the fleet the next day. Stunned by the reversal, the defenders of the navy yard at Pensacola followed suit on 10 May. On 16 July Congress created the rank of rear admiral to honor Farragut for capturing the South's major entrepôt and the gateway to the Mississippi.

The Union goal now was to win control of the entire Mississippi River in order to cut off the Western states, notably Texas, from the rest of the Confederacy, and to restore the export trade of the upriver corn belt states. It took the army and navy more than a year to achieve that objective. The Confederacy had several strongholds between New Orleans and the Ohio River, notably Memphis, Tennessee, and Port Hudson, Louisiana. The South also controlled key tributaries flowing into the Mississippi, which could be used to resupply or reinforce Confederate troops or to outflank Union operations. Principal among these was the Red River, which drained Texas and western Louisiana. But the nearly insurmountable obstacle to wresting control of the Mississippi was the great fort on the bluffs of the eastern bank at Vicksburg.

The navy's operations on the Mississippi River from April 1862 until 4 July 1863 became a two-man show masterminded by the stepbrothers David G. Farragut and David Dixon Porter. Farragut directly commanded the deep-draft steamers operating on the river, and Porter held semi-autonomous command of the smaller gunboats and mortar boats. A combination of army troops and navy gunboats took Memphis in early June 1862, leaving Farragut the dubious opportunity to dash past Vicksburg with his big ships to satisfy the secretary of the navy's orders for some decisive move on the Father of the Waters. Three of his eleven ships were turned back by artillery fire from Vicksburg. Farragut's *Hartford* and eight others made it past, but the navy's first rear admiral concluded from the operation that naval gunfire could not reduce this particular bastion.

Isolated above Vicksburg, Farragut began to worry that Confederate sorties to the south could threaten the entire Union naval force on the river. He charged past the fort once more and returned to his base of operations at New Orleans. He and his heavy ships remained there until March 1863, when they pressed north one last time. The Confederate batteries at Port Hudson stopped all but the *Hartford* and one gunboat, but those two got through to establish a permanent blockade at the confluence of the Red and Mississippi rivers. Farragut established direct communications with Porter, now a rear admiral, who together with Generals Ulysses S. Grant and William Tecumseh Sherman was trying to unlock the back door of Vicksburg.

Porter assembled a flotilla of army transports and escorted them south past Vicksburg with his gunboats. While Sherman made a convincing feint against the fort's northern salient, Porter ferried the bulk of Grant's army from the western to the eastern shore of the river about 30 miles downstream. Once on the eastern side, Grant's troops laid siege to Vicksburg from its rear. The surrender came on 4 July 1863, at the same time as Lee's defeat at Gettysburg. Grant and Sherman had split the Confederacy along the Mississippi. Porter and Farragut had provided three essential elements of naval support for the operations along the river's banks: gunfire, troop transport, and logistical reinforcements. If one conceives of the Mississippi operations as analogous to naval operations along an extended enemy coastline, one can see that the Union navy acted as a traditional blockading force, just as its senior officers had during the Mexican War a decade and a half earlier.

The reopening of the Mississippi in July 1863 was followed in March 1864 by a strategically pointless army–navy expedition up the Red River toward Texas. David Dixon Porter's ironclad gunboats led the way, as an army under Major General Nathaniel P. Banks advanced along the shore. Banks was stopped by a Confederate army, and Porter was blocked by a sunken steamer in early April. The withdrawal of the gunboats was imperiled by the falling level of the river and Confederate harassment, but in May Porter finally got all of his ships but one back to the Mississippi. The sortie, described by one historian as "the greatest fiasco of the war," diverted energy from renewed large-scale offensive operations in the Gulf of Mexico.

On the Mississippi, Farragut and Porter found that they could establish a local blockade and seize relatively minor settlements pretty much at will, but the active cooperation of the Union army was absolutely essential in taking well-garrisoned strongholds.

The blue-water navy learned the same lesson about the same time. In 1862 Union blockaders based in Port Royal and Hilton Head, South Carolina, cut blockade running from Charleston to a trickle. The city itself, the most strongly defended port in the Confederacy, lay untouched. Secretary of the Navy Welles pressed the commander of the South Atlantic Blockading Squadron, Rear Admiral Samuel F.

Du Pont, to use his new monitors to bombard and take Fort Sumter, the taunting symbol of rebel insolence. The question was whether well-armored gunships could batter heavy forts into submission. On 7 April 1863 Du Pont, in the *New Ironsides*, led eight monitors into Charleston harbor for a point-blank fifty-minute slugfest with the forts. Du Pont's ironclads took more than 325 direct hits; none sank immediately, but all were damaged.

The question was answered. Ships could survive a vicious pounding from forts, but they could not silence or capture them. The army would be needed to mount a conventional siege from the rear or flanks of coastal forts. Du Pont yielded command to Rear Admiral John A. Dahlgren, who opened a joint army–navy siege of the Charleston forts with Brigadier General Quincy A. Gillmore in July. Despite their best efforts, the city held out for 567 days. It was evacuated by its defenders only when General William T. Sherman's army approached it in February 1865 at the end of the march from Atlanta to the Atlantic.

In the Gulf of Mexico, planning for a serious offensive had intensified once Rear Admiral Porter extracted himself from the unfortunate diversion on the Red River in May 1864. For some time Farragut had wanted to hit Mobile, Alabama, "the last Gulf Coast port of any consequence left in Southern hands." With General Sherman calling for a diversion to prevent Confederate units in Mobile from reinforcing his target of Atlanta, Washington finally gave Farragut the go-ahead. In July, at the Pensacola Navy Yard, he assembled a fleet for the stroke that earned him immortality.

Just before dawn on 5 August 1864, Farragut's force of fourteen wooden ships and four monitors began its approach to Mobile Bay. The combination of a fort, submerged pilings, and buoyed mines forced the attackers into a narrow passage under a second fort on the eastern side of the channel. In the bay itself waited the *Tennessee*, a new Confederate ironclad improvement on the ill-fated *Virginia*, supported by three light gunboats. The squadron mounted a total of sixteen guns against the Union's 159.

Farragut's *Hartford* was second in column behind another screw-sloop, the *Brooklyn*, but the monitor *Tecumseh* dashed past the older ships and headed straight toward the Confederate flagship *Tennessee*. Hitting one of the submerged mines—called torpedoes at the time— *Tecumseh* went down almost instantly. Eighty of the crew of one hundred perished in a catastrophe that suggested for the first time the real vulnerability of ironclads to weapons lurking below the waterline.

The frightened *Brooklyn* went dead in the water, blocking the *Hartford* and the other ships in column astern. From the port rigging where he was lashed for visibility, the old firebrand in command shouted to the *Hartford*'s helmsmen and all others who would hear, "Damn the torpedoes! Full steam ahead." *Hartford* cut left through the mines, some of which bounced off her hull without exploding. The ensuing four-hour melée ended only when the South's Rear Admiral Franklin Buchanan squandered the *Tennessee* in a singular attack on the *Hartford* and seventeen other Federal warships. The heavy Confederate ram could have been a potent threat to lighter ships outside the bay or in night attacks, but "Old Buck" wanted to duel with his antagonist personally. Farragut's ships and monitors hammered the unwieldy *Tennessee* into submission, and by 10:00 A.M. Mobile Bay was in Union hands. Although the city and its forts did not succumb to the besieging Union army until 12 April 1865, this naval victory closed the last major Gulf port to Confederate blockade runners.

The Battle of Mobile Bay coincided with Sherman's sack of Atlanta, which in turn set the stage for his sweep to Savannah and subsequent foray north into the Carolinas. While Dahlgren was giving Sherman some token help in coercing Charleston into surrendering, the navy and army were mounting a joint assault on Fort Fisher, the seaward protector of Wilmington, North Carolina. Wilmington's rail line to Richmond, Virginia, carried supplies for Robert E. Lee's army, and General Grant was willing to divert troops to cut off Lee's resupply from the rear.

Farragut declined command because of battle fatigue, so Porter took charge for the navy. At Hampton Roads he assembled almost a hundred ships, everything from new screw-frigates to ferries converted into gunboats. His plan was to soften Fort Fisher with naval gunfire and then cover about 8,000 troops landing in a frontal assault. The first attempt, on Christmas Day 1864, failed when General Benjamin F. Butler concluded that he could not safely assault the fort, which "was left substantially uninjured as a defensive work by the navy fire."

The army removed Butler, and Grant assigned Brigadier General Alfred H. Terry to cooperate with Porter. The new team tried again on 12–15 January, and this time they succeeded. Terry's men went ashore north of the fort, which was situated on a peninsula. They cut it off from the land link with Wilmington and moved on it from behind. Porter's ships kept the installation under fairly continuous fire, and a landing party of about 2,000 marines and bluejackets tried a frontal attack. They fell back in bloody confusion, and just as the Confederate defenders were shouting their victory Terry's men came at them from the rear. The Confederates held on as long as possible, but by 10:00 P.M. on 15 January they had surrendered to Terry as an alternative to being pushed into the sea at the tip of the promontory. The navy lost three hundred men on the beach that day, the army almost seven hundred, and the Confederacy more than seven hundred. But Wilmington was now Union property, and Lee could not draw supplies from its railhead.

One historian concludes that with the fall of Fort Fisher, "The Navy's war was over." But it is important to emphasize that the major battles in the "navy's war" on the Atlantic and Gulf coasts and along the banks of the Mississippi were won only with the full cooperation of the army. New Orleans was the only major Confederate city to fall exclusively to the navy.

While Du Pont, Dahlgren, Farragut, and Porter could maintain ships off strongholds to interdict blockade runners, they proved generally unable to take the ports or forts in front of the blockade. Until they were taken and in fact occupied, the South's ports and harbors could not be said to be permanently and irrevocably closed to foreign commerce. In the Civil War blockade, therefore, the navy's function was essentially supportive of the army.

This indispensable requirement for full-fledged army–navy cooperation in capturing major enemy positions from the sea had been demonstrated negatively by the British failure to subdue the United States in the War of 1812 and positively by General Winfield Scott's invasion of Mexico along the Veracruz–Mexico City axis. It was an unpleasant lesson to contemplate, and its unpalatability explains to some degree why after the Civil War United States naval officers preferred instead to dwell on the apparent promise for the future revealed in the short happy life of the C.S.S. *Alabama*, the greatest American commerce raider of all time.

Confronted with a stronger opponent, the Confederacy instinctively turned toward the historical American way of fighting at sea: coastal defense and commerce raiding. Coastal defense was only marginally in its navy's bailiwick. For the South, as for all mid-nineteenth-century powers, the backbone of coastal defense was a system of large forts built of earth and stone and perched on protective bluffs overlooking the channels and harbors they were guarding. The Union's inability to overcome many of those forts until very late in the war and the Confederacy's consequent retention of such crucial cities as Wilmington, Charleston, and Mobile shows conclusively that the South's coastal defense program worked.

What did not work was the naval component of coastal defense, and therefore the Union navy was able to maintain an effective offshore blockade of the Southern ports it could not physically occupy. The C.S.S. *Virginia* and Rear Admiral Buchanan's *Tennessee* epitomized the Confederacy's doomed attempt to disrupt the Union blockade. The concept was sound; there simply were not enough ironclad gunboats to do the job. The ironclads that might have succeeded, the Laird-built rams, were confiscated by a British government under threat of war for complicity in breaking the Union blockade. A similar point can be made about other innovations with which the defenders experimented: the submarine *Hunley* and the semi-submersible *Davids*, which mounted a spar torpedo for blasting a hole in the opponent's hull in the vulnerable area beneath the waterline. But both were primitive in design and too few in number to affect the blockade.

The South's naval men had luck with coastal defense in only two areas: mines and blockade runners. Matthew Fontaine Maury, chief of the Confederate Submarine Battery Service, built enough good mines to destroy thirty-one Union blockaders, the greatest single cause of Northern naval losses in the war.

Blockade runners generally are not classed with coastal defense, but by carrying war matériel and goods in and out of ostensibly closed ports they undermined the comprehensiveness of the North's blockade to the very end of the war. These were small, fast, shallow-draft vessels of limited range. They ran only from Confederate ports to sanctuaries in the West Indies and Caribbean, where they dumped their loads of cotton or tobacco and took on whatever arms or ammunition Europe was willing to sell. The great profitability of that trade attracted Southern entrepreneurial capital from the beginning of the war and drew it away from the other capitalistic system of naval warfare: privateering.

In any event, privateering had lost much of its attraction because of the 1856 Declaration of Paris, which outlawed this means of fighting at sea. Since the declaration ran counter to the American tradition of oceanic warfare, the United States had refused to sign. Although Secretary of State William H. Seward promised to adhere to the prohibition when the Civil War opened, the issue by then was largely moot, because Great Britain had banned prize courts throughout the empire, and France had followed suit.

In 1861, while the Union blockade still existed mostly on paper, the European proscription meant very little. Southern privateers could send prizes back into Confederate ports for condemnation and auction. Confederate privateers captured more than fifty Union merchantmen in the first five months of the war, showing the potential for harm in a traditional American maritime offensive. But the increasing effectiveness of the offshore blockade made passage in and out of Southern ports increasingly hazardous. Privateers had to run the gauntlet, search for prey, and capture the victims. The privateer then put a small prize crew on board the captured vessel. Each prize crew had to keep the regular crew from mutinying and retaking the vessel. With this restive manpower, the prize masters had to navigate their way past the blockaders in an unfamiliar vessel whose handling characteristics and maneuverability were unknown.

By contrast, a blockade runner carried a cargo for profit in a swift run to a relatively nearby port. It then swapped cargos and with a load of valuable goods dashed back under the full control of a dedicated and experienced crew. For those reasons, after 1861 the South sent very few of the traditionally American, privately owned sea rovers out to prey on Union merchant shipping. Commerce raiding became the exclusive preserve of the Confederate States Navy, and the record here was so strikingly successful that for a generation afterward American naval officers could think of no better way to conduct offensive warfare at sea.

There were a number of commerce raiders—the *Sumter*, the *Florida*, the *Shenandoah*—but there was only one *Alabama*. This barkentine-rigged, 230-foot-long rover mounted eight guns and could make better than 13 knots under steam. Built for Bulloch, she sailed from Britain under the guise of a merchant vessel on her first sea trial. She never returned. Instead, her skipper, Raphael Semmes, took her to the Azores for arming and outfitting and then commissioned her at sea. In August 1862 she set out on a twenty-two-month campaign of commerce destruction.

The Declaration of Paris and the Union blockade denied prize courts to Semmes, so he routinely stripped captured U.S. merchantmen of whatever he wanted, took the crews and passengers on board the *Alabama* for safety, and blew up the prizes. When overloaded with prisoners, he would strip a prize, designate it a "cartel ship" and send it ashore. He operated first in the North Atlantic, where he made twenty captures, and later rampaged on the world's oceans from the Gulf of Mexico to the South China Sea. In all, he took sixty-eight Union vessels, contributing to what has been called "the flight from the flag" by the American-owned merchant marine and driving maritime insurance rates sky-high.

In June 1864 Semmes dropped into Cherbourg, hoping to refit in one of the French docks. The American consul spotted him and cabled the U.S.S. *Kearsarge*, anchored in Holland. U.S. Navy Captain John A. Winslow had let the cruiser *Florida* slip by him off Brest in February. Not wanting to miss this second chance to bag one of the two deadliest Confederate ships then in action, Winslow brought his screw-sloop down to Cherbourg in a hurry. Semmes threw down the gauntlet, and Winslow readily accepted, knowing that his superior ship gave him the advantage. The *Alabama* had not been built to fight a warship; her crew had not drilled regularly at their guns, because powder and shot were irreplaceable, and her machinery was worn out.

In full view of cheering spectators lining the shore, the two protagonists circled one another hoping for the raking shot, which the tired *Alabama* could not achieve. She was gunned down in an hour, but in sinking she denied the Union the satisfaction of taking her prisoner. Semmes jumped over the side without surrendering. He was picked up by a watching British yacht and whisked to safety in Britain. As a replacement, Bulloch in October commissioned the *Shenandoah*, which in the remaining months of the war took thirty-six prizes to become the second-ranking Confederate commerce raider in terms of kills. But it was the *Alabama* that caught the world's imagination and seemed to set the pace for America's future *guerre de course*.

Raphael Semmes formed a transitional link between commerce raiding in the age of sail and modern submarine warfare. He was denied the ancient motivational power of enriching his crew through prize money, although at one point he did hope to capture one of the treasure ships racing from the Isthmus of Panama to New York City with California gold. His steam engine gave him advantages in running down prey denied to earlier commerce raiders fully dependent on the winds. Compelled to destroy his captures rather than auction them off, he refused to harm their passengers and crews. He conducted his commerce destruction with humane gallantry. In this fundamental regard he differed from the U-boat skippers of World War I or the submariners of World War II. In Raphael Semmes's raider *Alabama* the Confederate States Navy truly distinguished itself.

═══

With the Confederate naval threat—except that posed by commerce raiders—subdued by the end of 1864, Secretary of the Navy

Welles began a partial demobilization even before Robert E. Lee surrendered to U. S. Grant at Appomattox. By late 1865 he had sold half of the navy's 671 ships, mostly the converted merchant-men used on the blockade. With no intention of eviscerating the navy, he thought in the traditional terms of cruising squadrons and ships in reserve, the combination of which in an emergency would provide "for the prompt reestablishment at any time of our great naval force in all its efficiency." Like most of his prewar predecessors, Welles glimpsed "true wisdom" in a policy of cherishing and husbanding the navy so as "to hold within prompt and easy reach its vast and salutary power for the national defense and self vindication."

The Civil War had witnessed an anomaly of offensive naval operations as part of a campaign of conquest. The future promised to resemble a more typical past, wherein the United States Navy deployed its active vessels on distant station and maintained a reserve fleet theoretically suitable for rapid recommissioning should war with a European power seem imminent. Welles's ironclad "floating batteries" were to be laid up in noncorrosive fresh water at League Island, the new navy yard in Philadelphia. The *Army and Navy Journal* predicted they would "be a grand and imposing sight." The screw-driven and side-wheel steamers, rotated through the several reconstituted and globally dispersed squadrons, would protect overseas Americans and their commerce.

For Welles it was to be business as usual, and for two years he was remarkably successful. In December 1867 the secretary described a navy of 238 ships and 1,869 guns. There were 103 vessels mounting 898 guns in commission, an active force numerically more than twice the strength of the navy of late 1860. More than half of the commissioned ships—a total of fifty-six—were deployed with the six operating squadrons, until then the largest overseas peacetime force in American history. Some 2,000 officers and 11,900 enlisted men remained in uniform.

Welles's secret in retaining an unprecedentedly large peacetime navy was his large hoard of unexpended wartime funding, which he parceled out as supplements to the lean annual appropriations for 1866 and 1867. In 1867 he actually returned unspent funds to the Treasury Department. But his overture did not appease budget-cutters like the Republican congressman from Ohio, William Lawrence, who declared in 1870, "It is time . . . to come back to the peace establishment." Because that sentiment represented an emerging consensus within the Congress, the year 1867 was the navy's high-water mark for the next decade.

In 1867, as in 1783 and 1815, the great question was whether there would soon be war with Britain. American policymakers felt a deep resentment toward England for having constructed Confederate commerce raiders. The U.S. government's case for indemnification for the damage done by the British-built commerce raiders and the alleged consequent prolongation of the Civil War became known as the "indirect" or *Alabama* claims, which totaled $2.125 billion. This altercation sharply divided Britain and the United States from 1865 until Senate acceptance of the 1871 Treaty of Washington, a compromise by both sides. Britain expressed its regret that the *Alabama* and the other raiders had escaped the Crown's jurisdiction. That admission stopped short of an apology, but it satisfied the Americans, ended the prolonged dispute, and ushered in two decades of amity in Anglo-American relations. After Senate acceptance of the Treaty of Washington, and until the last nineteenth-century Anglo-American war scare over the Venezuelan boundary in 1895–1896, the two nations resumed their pre–Civil War stance of cooperation in keeping Europe out of the Western Hemisphere and competition in exploiting the markets of Latin America, Africa, and Asia. The theme of naval collaboration on distant station also reappeared within the texture of Anglo-American relations.

Although some ardent navalists tried to use Britain's Civil War policies and the specter of an Anglo-American war to revive the idea of England as a naval rival and potential maritime enemy, the Congress correctly understood that Britain was more a friend than a foe. In 1870 Aaron F. Stevens, representing the maritime and naval state of New Hampshire, exorcised the bogeyman in phrases that could have been uttered on the floor of Congress by the small-navy men of Jefferson's time. "And so it is, sir," said Congressman Stevens,

> because we are in danger of war with England or some other foreign Power, that we are urged to build up a great Navy at an expense of many millions of dollars which should go into the Treasury to pay the public debt, or which should be taken from the burdens of taxation that now oppress the people. War with England, sir! Why England today stands upon her good behavior toward the United States and toward all the world bound to it by a commerce which whitens every sea.

Jefferson's secretary of the treasury, Albert Gallatin, could not have put the case for fiscal responsibility and elimination of the national debt any more succinctly. Of equal vintage was Steven's faith in the potency of maritime commerce as a guarantor of international peace.

Key members of Congress grasped the essential geopolitical and naval differences between England and the United States. With keen insight Cadwallader C. Washburn of Wisconsin distanced the United States from Europe. "It has never been the policy of the United States to maintain a large navy or standing army in time of peace," stated Washburn, because we "have no balance of power on this continent to maintain." Europe was a different case. Concern for the balance of power had recently led England and France to put "afloat a class of monster ironclads, which will be very good to fight each other." But as Congressman Stevens added, the Anglo-French naval race did not set the standards for the United States Navy. As a member of the House Committee on Naval Affairs, he confessed to

> but one desire in the discharge of my official duties as connected with the Navy, and that is to render it respectable, powerful, and efficient. I use these terms in their American and not in their British sense. I do not speak of a British navy or of a French navy; I speak of an American Navy such as it has been to our fathers, and such as it should be to us in time of peace.

Insofar as the makers of naval policy entertained ideas of war with European powers—and most of them repeatedly emphasized the American "career of peace to which our interests and our traditions impel us"—they thought as had the pre–Civil War generations: Coastal defense and commerce raiding embodied the American way of war at sea. The *Army and Navy Journal* accurately described the small-navy man's image of American naval defense policy:

> Our immense coast line . . . our rivers, on which an inland trade without parallel plies its daily course; our foreign policy, which desires as little to interfere with other nations, on other continents, as it brooks interference by none in the affairs of this; . . . all these considerations make the question of *coast defence* one of more importance to us than perhaps to any other people.

The fact that coastal defense required forts and guns for the army and monitors for the navy also increased its allure to legislators eager to gain maximum political mileage by benefiting both services equally without spending large sums on either.

If the brown-water strategy remained traditional during the 1870s and 1880s, so did its blue-water counterpart. The Union navy had made a vital contribution to victory in the Civil War with the coastal blockade, capture of Southern ports, and riverine operations. But the Union navy seemed irrelevant to those few postwar Americans who contemplated war with a European power. The Confederate States Navy set the model. Confederate naval weakness in relation to Union naval prowess resembled the United States in its relation to the one truly dangerous European opponent, Great Britain. For that reason the dramatic success of the Confederate commerce raiders, most notably the C.S.S. *Alabama*, caught the collective imagination and gave a new lease on life to the century-old American strategy of *guerre de course*.

Even Admiral David Dixon Porter remained steadfast in the belief that steam and steel had not vitiated the old way of fighting. Throughout the 1870s Porter reiterated his opinion that in time of war the United States must rely principally on commerce raiding by fast, independently operating cruisers constructed of steel frames and wood sheathing. Those would be relatively large ships of some 5,000 tons displacement, with a length of 350 feet and a sustained speed of 14 knots. But they were not to contest for mastery of the seas. They were "simply to destroy commerce and to avoid an action with superior or equal forces."

The American posture vis-à-vis enemy warships was to be strictly defensive. As Porter wrote in his annual report for 1874, contests between hostile fleets of powerful ironclads, whatever the outcome, would not determine victory in war. Only by destroying the commerce of the opponent could the United States bring him to terms. Thus, "one vessel like the *Alabama* roaming the ocean, sinking and destroying, would do more to bring about peace than a dozen unwieldy iron-clads cruising in search of an enemy of like character." Porter retained this conventional view of blue-water strategy and his confidence in the effectiveness of forts and monitors until 1890.

The governing assumption among policymakers was that the nation would remain at peace with the major powers, but soon after the Civil War Spain began to trouble the defenders of the Monroe Doctrine. In Spanish Cuba an intermittent nationalist revolution elicited brutal repression, which periodically evoked widespread American sympathy for the revolutionaries and calls for humanitarian intervention to secure the independence of the Cuban people. The Spanish method of suppressing revolution also had the quite unpredictable effect of fundamentally altering the history of the United States Navy, since it was the Spanish-caused *Virginius* crisis of 1873 that led directly to intensive and ultimately successful lobbying for a "new navy."

The *Virginius*, built in Britain as a Confederate blockade-runner, was a side-wheel steamer operating under American registry. Beginning in 1870 she regularly ran guns to Cuban revolutionaries. The national ensign entitled her to United States naval protection, even though she and her kind had been declared pirates by a Spanish decree of 1869. In 1872 and 1873 American warships routinely escorted the *Virginius* on her runs to Cuba from Aspinwall, on the Panamanian Isthmus. Twice the escort vessels encountered Spanish warships and faceoffs resulted. In each case the Spanish skipper backed down.

Unhappily for the *Virginius* and those on board, no American warship was in the vicinity when she met the Spanish corvette *Tornado* on 31 October 1873. The Spaniard overtook the gun-runner and towed her into Santiago de Cuba. After a cursory naval court-martial, forty-nine men were "shot, against a stone wall." Some of them were American citizens who thought of themselves as filibusters. Their skipper, Joseph Fry, fell on the first volley. A graduate of the U.S. Naval Academy and former Confederate officer, Fry was a misfit adventurer typical of restless Civil War veterans with nowhere to go after the war. He had led many of his men to death. More would have followed had not the executions been stopped by the arrival of H.M.S. *Niobe*, hastily despatched from the Royal Navy base on Jamaica.

A full-blown war scare erupted, and the bellicose reaction of the Navy Department contrasted sharply with what the fleet actually was able to accomplish. Secretary of the Navy George M. Robeson put workers at the nearly dormant navy yards on full schedules, hired new laborers, and raised the ceiling of the enlisted ranks to 10,000 men. A cabinet meeting of 14 November instructed him to concentrate the fleet at Key West. Two weeks later he reported "that a respectable force of war-vessels and monitors is already on the sea . . . that our whole available iron-clad fleet is in hand, and every wooden war-vessel that will float, in active preparation." Robeson had transferred the entire American squadron from the Mediterranean to Florida.

The secretary's senior uniformed adviser, Admiral David Dixon Porter, tallied up Spanish and American naval orders of battle and concluded that by 30 December the United States could threaten Cuba with thirty ships mounting 414 guns. Borrowing a leaf from an

1855 recommendation by Commodore Joel Abbot that the East India Squadron seize Manila in the event of a Spanish–American war over Cuba, Admiral Porter counted twelve ships with 134 guns "in the Pacific and China sea that could be brought to bear upon the Spanish possessions in that quarter."

Robeson and Porter had doubts about the outcome of the mobilization and subsequent conflict. The secretary rightly worried that the navy was an "inadequate . . . force . . . and greatly at [a] disadvantage . . . in respect of number and character of vessels in a contest, with the fleets of any respectable naval power." He could only hope that the "activity, skill, science, and experience" of his officers would compensate for material inferiority. Porter later conceded, "There is not a navy in the world that is not in advance of us as regards ships and guns, and I . . . feel an anxiety on the subject which can only be appreciated by those who have to command fleets and take them into battle." His misgivings about the "incongruous set of vessels as we now possess" put him at his "wit's end," but that despondency naturally did not stop him from claiming the right "to command the naval forces of the United States, in case of hostilities."

The doubts were valid, but they were as irrelevant to the outcome of the crisis as the navy itself. Hamilton Fish, President Grant's secretary of state, swiftly negotiated a solution with Madrid. He was moved by visions "of the tens of thousands of wives who might have been made widows, and of the hundreds of thousands of children who might have been made orphans, in an *unnecessary* war undertaken for a dishonest vessel." Spain promised an indemnity for families of the dead, and by 18 December the 102 survivors of the *Virginius* were safely on board the U.S.S. *Juniata*, en route for New York. The gun-runner herself was turned over to the United States Navy. She foundered while under tow and sank off Cape Fear, North Carolina, on 26 December 1873. The crisis passed a week before the officer designated to command the retaliatory fleet arrived at Key West.

With an armada, however obsolescent, assembled in one place for the first time since the Civil War, the Navy Department decided to "drill" the fleet in tactics and "those naval maneuvers so assiduously practiced every year by the great naval powers, and so highly valued by all naval men as a preparation for war." The two-month exercise was divided into three segments, one each for "unarmored ships," monitors, and a landing brigade of almost 3,000 men. Robeson pronounced himself well pleased with the results, but in truth the exercise was a fiasco that fueled the cries for naval reform.

Commodore Foxhall A. Parker, "chief of staff of the united fleets," had published two books on naval tactics under steam. They were somewhat pedestrian pieces that glibly equated a fighting steam fleet to an army in combat. Referring to himself in the third person, he had written in the preface to his first book:

> He contends that the winds, waves, currents, and tides of the ocean present no more serious obstacles to the movements and maneuvers of a *steam*-fleet than the inequalities of the surface of the earth present to the movements and maneuvers of an army. He therefore regards a fleet as an army, whose divisions, brigades, regiments, and companies . . . have each their appropriate representatives afloat.

The simplistic extension of useful metaphor into direct parallel was a mistake Alfred Thayer Mahan later made, and it echoes Oliver Cromwell's generals-at-sea, but criticism after the fact does not detract from Parker's contemporary status as an expert whose opinion regarding the fleet maneuvers off Key West carried weight in the navy.

In his after-action report, Parker concluded that the month-long exercise of the fleet in February revealed fundamental weaknesses. As a unit, the top speed of the fleet was 4.5 knots, a "slowness" Parker understatedly described as "disheartening." He blamed the ships' age and their decrepit boilers and engines for this figure, which Rear Admiral C. R. Perry Rodgers was "loath to believe . . . of any fleet of the United States Navy."

Reactions such as Rodgers's encouraged Parker to depict his ideal new American navy in detail. After giving lip service to construction of mine defenses and a torpedo-boat force to defend "our long line of seaboard" and drive off blockaders, Parker was

> forced . . . to the conviction that, for the maintenance of our national dignity at home and abroad, the protection of our commerce upon the high seas and our citizens in foreign lands, a sea-going fleet is absolute[ly] necessary for us—not a large fleet like that of England, but one which shall be complete in itself, and serve as a safe nucleus to rally around when the hour of trial comes.

Parker's blue-water, steam-driven fleet would be composed of three classes of vessels: rams, torpedo boats, and "artillery-vessels." He identified the ram as the most deadly. The fatal and decisive ramming of the *Re d'Italia* by the Austrian flagship at the Battle of

Lissa, fought in the Adriatic on 20 July 1866, and the sinking of the U.S.S. *Cumberland* by the C.S.S. *Virginia* proved that "for fleet-fighting, it is the most terrible engine of war that a navy can possess." The torpedo boat was useful "for creeping stealthily upon a large vessel at night, in thick weather or amid the smoke of battle." The "artillery-vessel" would attack forts, and for this reason her guns would have to be of the largest possible caliber. But the "artillery-vessel" also had a distinctive role in fleet engagements, where Parker believed "the shot of mammoth guns" would be highly effective.

Parker envisioned the naval battle of the future as analogous to a cavalry attack, with the rams beginning "the action by charging the enemy . . . then the artillery-vessels would open fire with some effect, and the torpedo-boats . . . proceed stealthily but swiftly to complete the work of devastation inaugurated by the charge." He was ambivalent about the value of armor plating, believing that advances in ordnance continually gave the edge to guns over iron plating. He thought rifled ordnance probably more promising than smoothbores, but he was not sure. And he recommended "ships of the *Alabama* and *Shenandoah* type" to cut up an enemy's commerce. But a commerce raider was just that; it was not a "fighting-vessel."

Parker's fighting vessels must be deployed as a well-drilled fleet organized as "*a unit of force acting under one head.*" For success in battle, this fleet must possess a reliable system of tactical signaling, speed, and maneuverability. The old commodore with the eye of a prophet concluded by exhorting the navy's future leaders "to read diligently the naval history of the past . . . and to imitate Nelson in his close study of naval tactics." Parker's prescription is significant in several ways. He anticipated the all-big-gun battleship of the early twentieth century, although he underestimated its central role in fleet engagements. He overestimated the ram, but so did the naval architects who shaped the bows of late-nineteenth-century capital ships into rams. The torpedo's great impact on naval warfare awaited the advent of an operational submarine, when the submerged weapons system would achieve lethal force in commerce raiding rather than in fleet actions. Parker clearly misjudged a great deal, but in proposing the construction of an American battlefleet to act as a unit of force under one head and in enshrining Horatio Nelson as the ideal naval tactician he laid the foundation for Alfred Thayer Mahan's writing at the end of the next decade.

The commodore's message was enhanced by his platform. He delivered his evaluation of the Key West exercise to a meeting of the reformist U.S. Naval Institute at the Naval Academy on 10 December 1874. The institute had been organized in October 1873 to advance "professional and scientific knowledge in the Navy." Its constitution designated the secretary of the navy as its "patron" and Admiral Porter as president. The roster of the "council of regents" read like a "who's who" of senior and flag officers of the United States Navy, and the list of founding members included most of the officers who would leave their imprint on the "new navy" and its testing grounds in the Philippines and Cuba. The innovative and cerebral Charles Belknap, French E. Chadwick, and Caspar F. Goodrich had joined, as had Commanders Winfield Scott Schley and William T. Sampson. Of the triumvirate of flag officers who would lead the navy in battle in 1898, only Commander George Dewey's name did not appear, but he was a member by 1877. Captain Stephen B. Luce had joined by early 1876, and Commander Alfred Thayer Mahan was the vice president in 1878.

The significance of the early institute and its membership is that professional men had created a forum where they could cast off the inhibiting restrictions of their hierarchical subculture in order to debate their collective future. Officers as senior as rear admirals might disagree with the conclusions of lieutenants but at the same time thank them for "valuable" papers containing "a great many ideas . . . worthy of consideration." At the institute and in the pages of its *Proceedings*, the navy at least for a moment had found a neutral ground where free expression took precedence over gold braid.

Parker and other officers might persuade a sympathetic audience at the institute of the need for naval rebirth, but Congress remained impassive. The speedy diplomatic resolution of the *Virginius* crisis undercut Secretary Robeson's request for $4 million in emergency funding. Long-term calculations in Congress stressed national fiscal restraint during a depression that would last for several years. Partisanship caused Democrats to oppose Republican expansion of the navy, and the unfinished Reconstruction of the South kept many eyes turned inward. Those who did look outward scanned a peaceful horizon. Senator Eli Saulsbury of Delaware enjoined America's youth

> to read upon the shield of Achilles the desolating power of war and the happiness and blessings that follow in the train of peace. I would take them to the battlefields of earth, and point them not to the crowns that deck the victor's brow, but to the emaciated forms of the wounded.

The men of Saulsbury's generation who had experienced the Civil War preferred to build "castles of peace" in their minds rather than follow the "unerring star of destiny," which Representative Charles Hays of Alabama saw "slowly rising in the Gulf Stream and pointing with the relentless finger of fate to that little gem of an island that nature has made to hug our southern shores, and which sooner or later must be ours." Cuba would have to wait for its liberation until a younger generation of Americans seeking excitement and glory took up the righteous sword and carved out an overseas empire.

The introspective and peace-seeking Congress of the 1870s did not dissolve the navy, as had the post–Revolutionary War legislators. It merely limited the service to its pre–Civil War status as the guardian of American overseas enterprise. That old shoe fitted the navy quite well until midway through the 1880s, when a combination of political, technological, and intellectual changes began to transform the service into a fleet modeled after the Royal Navy.

After 1885 fundamental changes in the world balance of power seemed to render a commercialistic American navy obsolete and impotent. The Berlin Congo Conference of 1884 signaled a new age of European imperialism, closing markets previously open to Americans. In 1890 Kaiser Wilhelm II dismissed his cautious chancellor, Otto von Bismarck, and initiated a seriously destabilizing naval race with Britain. A national census in the United States that year recorded the disappearance of the frontier, a demographic and statistical awakening that contributed to a collective "psychic crisis" and a reordering of national goals. As if sensing that change was in the air, the United States Navy in the 1880s retooled its hardware and rewrote its strategic theory to make itself into a European-style force ready for combat with the navies of other major powers.

The revolution in American naval hardware began in October 1882, when reformist Republican Secretary of the Navy William E. Chandler appointed Rear Admiral Robert W. Shufeldt chairman of the Naval Advisory Board. Shufeldt was a visionary exponent of commercial expansion who had taken the U.S.S. *Ticonderoga* on a two-year global cruise in search of markets for American manufactured products and had "opened" Korea in 1882 with a treaty fashioned after Perry's pact with Japan. His vision cohabited with a sharp sense of the politically possible.

As chairman of Chandler's board, Admiral Shufeldt decided that the "first thing" to be done was "to make a Navy with reference to the protection of our people and our commerce abroad. . . . Then afterwards I would like, perhaps, in the not very distant future, to build larger ships." Shufeldt was too shrewd a politician to jeopardize a naval renaissance by asking the impossible of Congress, so he asked for a mere five ships, a move whose wisdom would soon be demonstrated to the great good fortune of the United States Navy.

Shufeldt and Secretary of the Navy Chandler were fortunate to have a sympathetic Naval Affairs Committee in the House. After an extensive investigation, the committee concluded that the United States Navy should be composed principally of two classes of ships: monitors for coastal defense and fast seagoing cruisers for *guerre de course*. Since the navy already had several monitors in various stages of completion—or decay—the need for cruisers was more urgent. The committee's chairman, Benjamin W. Harris of Massachusetts, felt there was an "immense moral power in a 15-knot ship," and the United States needed "all the moral power which can be crowded into iron and steel." Congress decided that the security and economic well-being of the country also demanded the immediate development of the industrial expertise required to build steel warships. On 3 March 1883 a bill was approved appropriating funds for four warships to be built entirely of American steel.

Shufeldt's board immediately began designing three cruisers and a small "despatch" boat. Named to garner popular support in their respective sections of the country and known collectively as the *ABC* cruisers, the *Atlanta, Boston*, and *Chicago* were classed as "protected cruisers." Their hulls were made of easily pierced thin steel, but their engines and boilers were protected by an overhead main deck of armor plate and coal bunkers outboard of the machinery. Hulls and gun housings did not have armored plate, as would the fully armored cruisers built at the end of the decade. In place of smoothbore guns, the new ships mounted breech-loading rifled cannon. Propulsion of the cruisers was by means of sail and steam, each ship carrying about two-thirds the canvas of a fully rigged vessel of the same displacement. The largest of the three, the *Chicago*, displaced 4,500 tons. Shufeldt and his board demanded high speed, defined as about 14 knots for both the cruisers and the despatch boat, but all four vessels failed to meet that crucial expectation, at least in the early sea trials.

The ships that Shufeldt built were too lightly armored and too few in number to stand in line of battle before a first-rate European fleet. But their anticipated speed, endurance, and modern armament made them, in theory at least, the ideal vessels for the protection of American commercial interests in the distant ports of the world. There the danger usually came from pirates or weakly armed native populations fitfully contesting Western encroachments on their customs and lands. The *ABC* cruisers, therefore, were a pre-Mahanian means of accomplishing the navy's historic peacetime mission: stimulation and protection of overseas commerce. During war the same characteristics theoretically would enable them to descend upon and destroy the oceangoing merchantmen of the enemy. But their ultimate significance lies in the simple fact of their birth. For the first time since the Civil War the Congress had voted to build a small number of substantial new ships, and once the legislative resistance was overcome further appropriations followed almost automatically. Popular enthusiasm for the *ABC*s soon fueled bipartisan political support for a "new navy."

William C. Whitney, a wealthy conservative Democrat from New York City, took advantage of the fresh enthusiasm for rebuilding when he became Grover Cleveland's secretary of the navy on 7 March 1885. His most important additions were the protected cruiser *Baltimore*, similar to the *Chicago* but much faster; the armored cruisers *Maine* and *Texas*, later reclassified as second-class battleships; and two war horses destined for fame in 1898, the large armored cruiser *New York* and the smaller protected cruiser *Olympia*. All of these ships sported rifled, breech-loading cannon usually mounted off the center line in the belief that ram bows were the ultimate weapon in surface engagements and the guns' purpose was to fire dead ahead as the ship charged into the enemy with its lance-like bow. With the invention of the self-propelled "automobile torpedo" by Arthur Whitehead about that time, the would-be ramming vessels became vulnerable as they raced toward their targets. The emphasis returned to guns, which now were relocated in main batteries along the centerline fore and aft. Here they could rotate through a wide arc of fire to both sides of the ship without encountering shipboard obstacles or excessively shifting the center of gravity.

Secretary Whitney contributed ships to the "new navy," but he added nothing to the theory of naval warfare. Most of the uniformed hierarchy seemed largely impervious to the possibly revolutionary implications of a runaway technological transformation of the fleet. No fresh strategic or tactical theory was needed. One typically crustaceous admiral brusquely dismissed novelty: "Teach the art of war! Well, I'll be damned! You have [James Fenimore] Cooper's *Naval History* and [Foxhall A.] Parker's *Fleet Tactics*; what more do you want?"

By 1885 the answer was being formulated, largely as a result of the inspiration of Rear Admiral Stephen B. Luce, the intellectual link between Foxhall Parker's early musings about American battlefleets and Alfred Thayer Mahan, the thinker who brought the Royal Navy's way of fighting home to America. A gifted sailor, Luce was convinced that steam had made obsolete the tactical maneuvers of the age of sail. A warship under sail was limited by prevailing wind and sea conditions. To a great extent, steam-driven warships were independent of those factors and hence could attack or retire in a variety of new ways. That technological revolution persuaded Luce that the fleets and squadrons of the future would "perform military movements" with the same precision as armies—the same conclusion reached by Parker a decade earlier and one that Mahan would later reiterate. Luce described future naval battles as "military operations conducted at sea." In order to devise tactics for those engagements, naval officers would need to perfect a "true scientific method of studying naval warfare under steam."

In the late 1870s Luce had begun to agitate for the establishment of a postgraduate school to teach naval officers the higher refinements of the art of war. Faced with entrenched bureaucratic opposition, he invoked the aid of his old superior, Admiral David Dixon Porter, and bent the newly formed Naval Institute to his purposes. In 1877 the institute announced an annual prize for the best essay on naval education. The following year Lieutenant Commander Caspar F. Goodrich won the prize by proposing the foundation of a naval college for the postgraduate education of officers.

In 1884 Secretary of the Navy Chandler gave in to Luce's campaign. He appointed Luce, Commander William T. Sampson, and Lieutenant Commander Goodrich as members of a board to "report upon the whole subject of a post-graduate course . . . giving in detail the reasons for establishing such a school, the scope and extent of the proposed course of instruction, and an opinion as to the best location therefor."

None of the three, Luce, Sampson, or Goodrich, thought that steam had totally altered naval realities. As late as 1889 Sampson took for granted that "the defense of our coast is the most important end to be secured . . . for the first care of any nation is to secure its integrity." Goodrich emphasized the conventional peacetime functions of the navy. Protection of the merchant marine, including aid to shipwrecked sailors, and oceanic exploration were foremost. To the navy, "in time of peace, the people look for routes across tropical isthmuses and to the North Pole; for new continents discovered, fresh outlets for trade." All three officers agreed that the new navy, like the old, would be composed of "independent cruisers and fast 'commerce destroyers,' " but it must also have "fighting ships" and "a system of steam tactics devised with special reference to battle."

In their report to Chandler, the three officers argued that establishment of a naval war college would offer an unparalleled opportunity "to bring to the investigation of the various problems of modern naval warfare the scientific methods adopted in other professions." Forced to serve on obsolescent ships that usually operated independently of one another, the American naval officer—unlike many of his European counterparts—was denied an opportunity to practice fleet or squadron maneuvers and amphibious landings. A war college would at least partly alleviate this handicap. To theoretical or academic studies could be added experimentation with the assembled North Atlantic Squadron. In other words, Luce, Sampson, and Goodrich were proposing a curriculum of war games to make American naval officers masters of their craft.

On 6 October 1884 Secretary Chandler approved the report of the three officers and ordered the establishment of the Naval War College at Newport, Rhode Island. He also appointed Luce the first president of the college. One of Luce's first acts was to name Captain Alfred Thayer Mahan to the faculty.

From the outset the Naval War College encountered stiff opposition from naval traditionalists opposed to Luce's intellectualism in particular and to advanced study by naval officers in general. Luce responded with a political counterattack, enlisting such powerful supporters as Senator Nelson W. Aldrich of Rhode Island and William E. Chandler, who returned to Washington in 1887 as New Hampshire's Republican senator. In February 1888 Luce wrote to a rising star of the reform wing of the Republican party, Theodore Roosevelt, praising him for his book *The Naval War of 1812* and inviting him to the War College to meet its second president, Captain Mahan. Roosevelt at the time was staying with his "great friend" Henry Cabot Lodge, whose sister-in-law was married to Luce's son. The future assistant secretary of the navy took the bait hungrily. Roosevelt replied to Luce that he could not remember receiving "any letter which gave me more genuine pleasure than yours did; it gives me a real pride in my work. Praise coming from you is praise which may indeed be appreciated." Roosevelt knew "Captain Mahan by reputation very well; it is needless to say that I shall be delighted to do anything in my power to help along the Naval College." The Roosevelt–Mahan axis, around which would pivot so much of the history of the American battleship navy, had been formed.

Between 1885 and 1889 Alfred Thayer Mahan wrote and delivered his lectures on "sea power." In 1890, after Mahan had added a prefatory first chapter to awaken the general reader to the significance of eighteenth-century Anglo-French naval history to the new American navy, the Boston house of Little, Brown & Company published Mahan's ideas as *The Influence of Sea Power upon History, 1660–1783*. Never has one book on naval history and strategy meant so much to so many.

Mahan's work was a blend of history and propaganda. In the preface, Mahan readily admitted that he was "a naval officer in full sympathy with his profession." He was writing naval history because he believed

> the study of the sea history of the past will be found instructive, by its illustration of the general principles of maritime war, notwithstanding the great changes that have been brought about in naval weapons by the scientific advances of the past half century, and by the introduction of steam as the motive power [of ships].

Mahan was making a subtle but fundamental distinction that he repeated throughout his book. He theorized that naval history illustrates general and unalterable strategic principles, while tactical conditions vary to some extent with technology. The warrior's milieu is strategic before "hostile armies or fleets are brought into contact." Thereafter the environment is tactical, where history remains useful but is far less trustworthy as a guide.

Mahan's delineation between strategy and tactics was extremely convenient. It allowed for changes in naval warfare brought about by the continuing technological revolution and simultaneously permitted him to disregard those developments in his subsequent writing. Other matters interested Mahan far more than naval technology. The cursory manner in which he passed over the millennial changes from oar to sail and from sail to steam reflects that indifference. "The best-planned schemes might fail through stress of weather in the days of the galley and the sailing-ship; but this difficulty has almost disappeared. The principles which should direct great naval combinations have been applicable to all ages, and are deducible from history; but the power to carry them out with little regard to the weather is a recent gain."

Strange indeed, given the above, that in his subsequent work Mahan enshrined Admiral Horatio Nelson as the tactical model nonpareil, a reverence that was more unthinking than it was original. David Glasgow Farragut had been praised as "the American Nelson" for his Civil War victories. Foxhall A. Parker had urged young officers to emulate Nelson. Mahan's own biography of the British admiral, published to transatlantic acclaim in 1897, was equally laudatory. Nelson, the subtitle proclaimed, was "The Embodiment of the Sea Power of Great Britain." Especially attractive to these American navalists was Nelson's dictum that "no captain can do very wrong if he places his ship alongside that of the enemy."

What was strange about this hero worship on the part of Parker and Mahan is that while they were both grappling with the implications of steam and steel for naval warfare, they were citing as their ideal tactician a master mariner from the age of canvas sails and wooden hulls. Nelson's brilliance at Trafalgar shone because he split his line of battle into segments to maximize firepower at discrete points. But the epochal victory owed at least as much to his tenacious holding of the weather, or windward, gauge so that he could descend upon the French and Spanish fleets at the moment and place of his choice. That persistence mirrored British tactical doctrine. Yet, according to both Parker and Mahan, the windward gauge was irrelevant to battle in the age of steam. Therefore it necessarily follows that Trafalgar was largely irrelevant to the new American navy of steam and steel. An anachronistic hypothesis demonstrates the irrelevance of Nelson's greatest victory: Had the French and Spanish fleets been steam-driven, Admiral Villeneuve could have maneuvered his leading ships to meet the British admiral's divided battle line at the time and place of *his* choice. Independent of the wind, his van could have turned through it rather than be cut off from the action.

Mahan never bothered to square this circle, preferring instead to concede candidly his amateur status as a tactician from the outset. In December 1891 he wrote his mentor, Stephen B. Luce, that "in studying problems of a certain character . . . chiefly *tactical*, I have to admit disadvantages owing to no opportunity for studying such questions. I bring to them no special knowledge of details, only a few general principles." His overriding interest in "general principles" was fortuitous for the new author. It won him great acclaim as a popular writer of history and contemporary strategy.

Mahan's principal thrust as a naval strategist was to lay to rest once and for all the ghost of the C.S.S. *Alabama* and American confidence in *guerre de course*. He insisted that commerce raiding, while useful as a subordinate means of striking the enemy, could not determine the outcome of a war. Naval wars could be decided only by battlefleet engagements.

That proposition was not original. Small-navy congressmen had long recognized that England owed its survival to the line of battle, but they also understood that unlike the United States England lay just off the coast of Europe, where other great nations could build threatening battlefleets and amphibious invasion forces. Mahan's emphasis on the paramount importance of the battlefleet to any great maritime power had the effect of discrediting the small-navy men's well-considered appreciation that England's geopolitical position was quite different from that of the United States.

A geographic and military reality of the American Civil War and its expansionist precursor against Mexico was that they were continental wars in every sense, including that proclaimed by Mahan. The naval role in both wars was specifically consistent with conflicts between continental powers. Both wars confirmed that the United States was a continental power for which the congressional naval policy of small budgets and commerce raiding made sense. Mahan and other American naval officers advocating battleships had to try to make the United States appear insular to justify a battlefleet navy. As Geoffrey Symcox, the premier historian of *guerre de course*, makes clear:

> Only the renunciation of privateers and the *course* would clear the way for the attainment of Mahan's real goal, which he publicized with single-minded zeal—the creation of a great battle fleet, to make the United States Navy "second to none." Once his countrymen had been convinced of the futility of commerce-destroying, the chief obstacle would have been removed from the path of naval and imperial expansion.

With *The Influence of Sea Power upon History*, Captain Alfred Thayer Mahan removed that obstacle.

7

"Not Merely a Navy for Defense"

1890 – 1898

The *Influence of Sea Power upon History* was the right book at the right time for the U.S. Navy. The year 1890 ushered in a decade of geopolitical realignments destined to transform the United States from a continental power with a modest navy and virtually no overseas territorial possessions into an imperial power with major holdings in the Pacific and undeniable hegemony in the Caribbean and Gulf of Mexico. After proving itself in two decisive actions against the Spanish navy, the new imperial American navy would permanently divest itself of the apparently outmoded strategy of commerce raiding and coastal defense in favor of the fashionable Mahanian strategy of fleet engagements. Whereas before the 1890s planning for a naval war with a major European or Pacific power seemed quixotic, by the decade's end American naval strategists planned exclusively for possible wars with Germany in the Caribbean and Japan in the western Pacific. By 1899 Rudyard Kipling was exhorting the United States to "Take up the White Man's Burden" in a poem subtitled "The United States and the Philippine Islands." The unstated corollary was that the United States Navy had taken up the Royal Navy's mantle.

The first hint of this geopolitical transformation had appeared in Samoa, a Pacific archipelago strategically positioned in the central southwest Pacific, midway between Hawaii and Sydney, Australia.

On the Samoan island of Tutuila lies the fine natural harbor of Pagopago, long of interest to American naval officers. Lieutenant Charles Wilkes investigated the commercial possibilities of Samoa and advertised the value of Pagopago's great natural harbor after his expedition of 1838–1842. The desirability of overseas coaling stations for the new steam navy also led Commander Richard W. Meade of the U.S.S. *Narragansett* to conclude a treaty granting the United States the exclusive right to a naval station in Pagopago in 1872. The treaty died in the Senate but was replaced in 1878 by one conferring most-favored-nation trading privileges on the United States and affirming a more generalized right to build a naval station. There followed a troubled decade of Samoan suffering while the consular agents of three Western powers—the United States, Great Britain, and Germany—jockeyed for positions of ultimate influence in the islands.

By January 1889 the German chancellor, Otto von Bismarck, had concluded that Samoa was not worth a war with the United States and proposed a high-level conference in Berlin to partition the archipelago. Meanwhile the navies of the three powers had assembled in the Samoan harbor of Apia to glower at one another while the diplomats wrangled. On 15 March 1889 "a hurricane of monumental proportions" struck. Only one warship escaped. H.M.S. *Calliope*, driven by large engines and skippered by a masterful seaman, fought her way to sea while three German ships were dashed on the reef or beached alongside the bulk of the American Pacific Squadron, the *Trenton, Vandalia,* and *Nipsic*—all steam-driven, wooden-hulled relics of the transitional "old navy."

The tragedy accelerated the transatlantic drift toward accommodation, and in June 1889 delegates from the three nations created a tripartite government for Samoa without infringing on existing American treaty rights to a naval base at Pagopago. Congress cooperated by appropriating $100,000 for the station. But the true significance of the disaster was that it provided grist for the mill of the new Republican secretary of the navy, Benjamin F. Tracy, an ardent imperialist and navalist of the Mahanian stripe.

Tracy's annual report for 1889 marked the official beginning of the American battleship navy and the formal adoption of an offensive naval strategy directed principally at major European powers. It featured the American naval loss at Samoa as a vivid illustration of the weakness of the United States Navy in the Pacific and as a graphic demonstration of the need for more powerful steam-driven warships.

The secretary would not be happy with unarmored or lightly armored cruisers such as had been built since 1883. Even "with all the additions authorized by the legislation of the last seven years, the country will . . . be absolutely at the mercy of states having less than one-tenth of its population, one-thirtieth of its wealth, and one-hundredth of its area." By Tracy's reckoning, the United States Navy, with no more than forty-four ships in service or under construction, stood twelfth among the naval powers, immediately after Austria-Hungary and somewhere below Turkey and China. Great Britain, as always, led the world with a phenomenal total of 367 warships, seventy-six of which were armored.

The staggering disproportion between the British and American navies had always troubled American statesmen, but in the nineteenth century they had come to accept it as an inescapable result of the peculiar British geopolitical need for European and imperial security. The great Royal Navy could be a threat, but it also served as a shield for the American Republic, insulating it and the Western Hemisphere from unwanted intrusions by continental European powers. By midcentury the Navy Department routinely sanctioned the informal cooperation with Royal Navy squadrons on distant station. But in 1889 Tracy frontally challenged that status quo by insisting on armored battleships. The secretary was not calling for a navy second to none—President Woodrow Wilson would take that step in 1916—but was laying the foundation for the next generation's bid for parity with the world's greatest naval power. Henceforth, said the voice of modern American sea power:

> We must have a fleet of battleships that will beat off the enemy's fleet on its approach, for it is not to be tolerated that the United States . . . is to submit to an attack on the threshold of its harbors. Finally, we must be able to divert an enemy's force from our coast by threatening his own, for a war, though defensive in principle, may be conducted most effectively by being offensive in its operations.

Tracy concluded with an explicit reference to President John Adams's message of 1800, a direct way of applying the line-of-battle ship standards of Benjamin Stoddert to the new era of steam-driven battleships. "Until the United States has a fleet of twenty battleships," said Tracy in echoing the first secretary of the navy, "the country cannot consider that it possesses a Navy; and a Navy it can never afford to be without."

The Congress was receptive. For the first time since 1875 the Republicans controlled both houses. Among their number were disciples and friends of Rear Admiral Stephen B. Luce, whose patient and persistent politicking now paid off handsomely. Most notable was Charles A. Boutelle of Maine, chairman of the House Naval Affairs Committee. The second ranking member of that committee was Henry Cabot Lodge of Massachusetts, intimate of Civil Service Commissioner Theodore Roosevelt and a navalist and imperialist in his own right. Across the aisle, many Democrats supported naval expansion as a nonpartisan issue. One of them, Hilary A. Herbert of Alabama, succeeded Tracy as secretary of the navy in 1893. A second, William G. McAdoo of New Jersey, served as Herbert's assistant secretary. In the Senate, the number two man on the naval committee, Eugene Hale of Maine, could be counted on to support naval expansion enthusiastically in the Tracy years. A congressional consensus was gathering. Agitation for a battleship navy and a policy or strategy of command of the sea was no longer the peculiar bailiwick of naval officers.

A few proven friends of the navy did not beat the drum for battleships. Former Assistant Secretary of the Navy Gustavus V. Fox and former Secretary of the Navy William E. Chandler, the father of the *ABC*s and now a Republican senator from New Hampshire, remained true to the American tradition of commerce raiding and coastal defense. In December 1889 the prestigious *Army and Navy Journal* endorsed Fox's theories of *guerre de course.* Chandler favored the inexpensive policy of coastal defense with monitors, although he remained a steady friend of the Naval War College.

Tracy and his congressional stalwarts met the challenge politically. They persuaded President Benjamin Harrison's son, the editor of a leading New York newspaper, to publish an editorial counterattack:

> It is desired to build . . . battleships which can go to sea and stay there; can fight an enemy at all times and wherever . . . encountered; can prevent a blockade . . . and keep a hostile fleet so far from our coast that it cannot shell our cities. . . . None of these requirements can be met by the low-freeboard monitor. She is a . . . harbor defender but not a coast defender.

House Naval Affairs Committee Chairman Charles Boutelle pared down the number of battleships in the 1890 appropriations bill, cut their cruising radius so they would seem less offensive in nature, and shrewdly redefined them as "three seagoing coastline battleships." In a letter to Rear Admiral Luce he explained the political deceptiveness of his compromise: "By building such ships, we should avoid the popular apprehension of jingoism in naval matters, while we can develop the full offensive and defensive powers of construction as completely as in foreign cruising battleships in all but speed and fuel capacity."

The stratagem worked. The naval act of 30 June 1890 provided for three battleships, one protected cruiser, a torpedo cruiser, and one light torpedo boat. At the unprecedented cost of more than $3 million apiece, each battleship displaced more than 10,000 tons, two thousand more than the *Maine* or *Texas*. Those big warriors mounted heavy main batteries: four 13-inch and eight 8-inch rifled cannon. The large turrets and low freeboard might remind the unwary citizen of giant monitors, and to widen their sectional appeal the ships were named the *Indiana, Massachusetts,* and *Oregon,* a political gambit reminiscent of the naming of the *ABC*s in 1883.

Any resemblance between the *Indiana*-class battleships and earlier American warships was purely deceptive. Their builders exceeded the 5,000-mile range Congressman Boutelle had stipulated to pacify the isolationists. Their armor plate was heavier than that carried by the British *Majestic* class, rated the world's most powerful battleships at the time. At a London meeting of the Institute of British Naval Architects in June 1891 a leading British designer praised them as "distinctly superior to any European vessels of the same displacement, and . . . quite a match for any ships afloat." The Admiralty's chief constructor noted that the ships' plans were wholly American in conception and execution, another first for a "new navy" previously dependent on European naval architects for many of its designs. The United States Navy had declared its independence from European designers. At the same time it had discarded its earlier confidence in a ship peculiarly fitted to the American geopolitical position, the frigate, in favor of one conceived to meet the exigencies of great-power naval rivalry in European waters.

In his annual report of December 1891, Secretary Tracy explicitly dismissed the modern equivalent of the sailing frigate. Light cruisers displacing less than 4,500 tons, the size of the recently commissioned *Chicago,* "perform useful service in time of peace in carrying the flag about the world. . . . But when opposed to armored ships these vessels cannot be counted on as an element of force."

Only "sea-going armored vessels" could resist the attack of similar vessels, already in the inventory of many foreign nations. To meet the threat the United States Navy would need several armored cruisers at least as heavy as the nearly completed *New York*, which displaced 8,150 tons; but the backbone of the new fleet was the three *Indiana*-class battleships then under construction. Those ships alone met all of Tracy's criteria for heavy guns, thick armor plate, and extreme cruising range.

Range of ships was a crucial consideration for Tracy, and in his discussion of the *New York* as the ideal heavy cruiser the secretary disclosed the offensive implications of his stress on endurance under steam. He was explicitly worried by the potency of the Chilean navy, whose modern cruiser *Esmeralda* "appeared in April last, without warning, close to the California coast." He noted that the distance from San Francisco to Callao, Peru, where the fleet might recoal before charging on to attack Valparaiso, Chile, was 3,900 miles. Ships smaller than the *New York* could not cover that distance in a single step. Less explicitly, he sensed enemies across the Pacific. Yokohama, Japan, lay 5,000 miles from San Francisco, a journey beyond the capacity of any light cruiser "were it not for the possibility of breaking the voyage and coaling at the Hawaiian Islands." He would welcome the chance to acquire those strategic islands when it came in 1893.

Tracy's elliptical reference to the *Esmeralda* concealed the administration's anxiety that a revolution in Chile might soon involve the United States in a war with that distant country. Two crises nearly led to hostilities. The first involved a near engagement between the 4,000-ton cruiser *Charleston*, based in Mare Island, and the *Esmeralda*. The two warships met and cleared for action off Acapulco Bay when the *Charleston* was chasing a gun-runner loaded with arms purchased in San Diego. The *Esmeralda* had been commandeered by Chilean insurgents anxious to protect their cache, and an engagement was avoided only because the renegade steamer passed well to seaward of the two cruisers on her run to Valparaiso.

The second crisis was more celebrated in the United States. Even after the success of the Chilean revolution and the withdrawal of other foreign warships in the summer of 1891, Tracy elected to keep one watchdog at Valparaiso. The U.S.S. *Baltimore* was commanded by Commander Winfield S. Schley, who had reported: "Everything quiet. The presence of a vessel is no longer demanded." But the quiet ended with Schley's decision to grant liberty ashore to a crew after their long confinement to the ship. Chilean resentment collided with the sailors' boisterousness at the True Blue Saloon on 16 October 1891. Two Americans were killed and several badly injured after a riot that spread across the waterfront as the sailors fled to their ship. Schley tried to take the high moral ground. He devoted most of his attention to arguing the implausible case that his men had been the totally innocent and sober victims of a prearranged attack. Secretary Tracy was not interested. He ordered the *Baltimore* out of the harbor, to be relieved by the gunboat *Yorktown*, commanded by Commander Robley D. "Fighting Bob" Evans.

Known for his bellicosity, Evans grasped what Schley had not: the assertion of sobriety was as irrelevant as it was dubious. He later recalled:

> [I]t was not an issue worth discussing. [Schley's] men were probably drunk on shore, properly drunk; they went ashore, many of them, for the purpose of getting drunk. . . . When in this condition they were more entitled to protection than if they had been sober. . . . Instead of protecting them, the Chileans foully murdered these men, and we believed with the connivance and assistance of armed policemen. That was the issue—not the question of whether they were drunk or sober.

The *Yorktown* sat in Valparaiso with Chilean torpedo boats making practice runs on her while Evans awaited the verdict of the local courts and the results of diplomacy. "Taking all things under consideration," Evans noted in his diary, "the crew of the *Yorktown* will sleep at the loaded guns tonight and every night until I get better news." He had a while to wait.

With talk of war sweeping Washington in December 1891, Sir Cecil Spring-Rice, secretary of the British legation and an intimate of Theodore Roosevelt, wrote home, "The President [Benjamin Harrison] and the Secretary of the Navy [Tracy] wish for war; one to get re-elected, the other to see his new ships fight and get votes for more." Roosevelt publicly enthused, "The United States is absolutely in the right and Chile absolutely in the wrong!" Europe did not agree. Former Chancellor Otto von Bismarck could not understand why "a nation as powerful as the American Union did not show more moderation and respect for a nation as small as Chile." In Chile itself, the British minister criticized the U.S. Navy's "defiance."

The crisis peaked when Harrison issued a virtual ultimatum demanding an apology for the *Baltimore* incident and on 25 January

1892 went so far as to ask Congress to consider a declaration of war. Within five days Chile capitulated, and the body of one sailor, Boatswain's Mate Charles W. Riggin, was brought home for a massive hero's welcome in Philadelphia. The *Philadelphia Inquirer* jingoistically exulted that "a great principle has been vindicated—that the flag of the Union is to be respected everywhere, on land and sea alike." And apparently in wharfside saloons.

Chile's compliance with Harrison's demands may be explained in part by Secretary Tracy's extraordinary mobilization of the navy in preparation for war. The president of the Naval War College, Alfred Thayer Mahan, thought so. On 28 January 1892, immediately after a meeting with Tracy, Mahan wrote to his most trusted naval colleague, Rear Admiral Luce, that the secretary "feels, and I think justly, that the energy with which he has pushed naval preparations has had much to do with the final pacific outcome. I believe myself that Chile simply temporized to see how much we would stand, and had our naval effort been less vigorous and sustained there would have been a collision."

During the crisis Mahan had been in Washington and had seen Tracy frequently. He had waited "impatiently and somewhat anxiously the outcome of the Chilian [sic] trouble." Chile's new warship, the *Captain Prat*, displacing 6,900 tons and ringed with a 12-inch-thick belt of steel armor, could prove "formidable. . . . We are so confident in our bigness and so little realize the great extra load entailed by the distance of Chili [sic], in case of war. The ultimate result, I suppose can be little doubtful, but we may first get some eye openers." Captain Mahan was not released from duty in Washington until the threat of war passed.

The war plan that Tracy developed corresponded closely to the captain's strategic thinking. It also enjoyed the prior approval of the chairmen of the House and Senate Naval Affairs Committee, elicited by Tracy at the outset of the crisis. At the end of the decade Tracy remembered the essential elements:

> According to this plan, the first order to be issued was to concentrate the fleet. A point of concentration was agreed on, and this was to be telegraphed to the three fleet [i.e., squadron] commanders with the orders sent to them to begin operations. . . .
> According to the plan laid out, after the fleets had concentrated, they were to proceed to Chile, drive the Chilean men-of-war under the guns of the fort at Valparaiso, and then attack the whole coast of Chile. The coal mines in the southern part of that country were to be seized,

thus cutting off the coal supply for the warships of the enemy, and all other details were to be looked after.

Theodore Roosevelt cheered from the sidelines: "From the moment when hostilities became possible, the Navy Department had been quietly preparing a thoroughly adequate naval force with an energy and success that argues well for the conduct of this department in any future crisis." As assistant secretary of the navy during the showdown with Spain in 1898, Roosevelt would show that he had studied the naval preparations of 1891–1892 closely. Like Tracy, Roosevelt would insist that the first objective of the new battleships must be to neutralize the enemy's battlefleet. He also would use the telegraph to ensure that Washington called the shots.

The men who transformed the United States Navy in the 1890s commonly blended imperialism with enthusiasm for capital ships, and they cited the need for coaling stations as their immediate motive for advocating overseas expansion. The Samoan crisis of 1889 had warned them that the increasing tempo of European imperialism endangered American access to possible coaling sites and markets in the Pacific. Secretary Tracy in 1891 noted, "The rapid extension of commercial relations has doubled the importance of our interests, especially in the Pacific." And in the Pacific, Hawaii was the keystone.

Hawaii attracted the new navalists because the islands seemed ideal as a western sentinel for the proposed Central American canal, which the Harrison administration hoped to build through Nicaragua. Tracy was especially keen on a canal as a means of rapidly moving warships from one ocean to another. At the moment, the secretary advised the president with palpable cogency,

> the two seaboards are so remote that each requires its separate system of naval defense. Each has its vulnerable points, and each has neighbors that are well prepared for offensive movements. There is a circle of insular fortresses facing our Atlantic seaboard, the sole object of whose existence is to maintain naval outposts at our doors. There are States in the Pacific, and not large States either, whose fleets are more powerful than any force we could readily bring to meet them. To protect either seaboard, even when our present authorized fleet is completed, will involve stripping the other at a critical moment.

But if a canal were constructed through Nicaragua, "the strategic situation would be largely modified." Major combatant ships could then be shifted from the Atlantic to the Pacific so rapidly, and returned so swiftly, that no debilitating naval power vacuum would form in their absence. Appreciation of the strategic significance of a canal through Central America was not original, but Tracy stated it in terms of modern warships and contemporary naval orders of battle.

President Harrison had appointed an annexationist crony of Secretary of State James G. Blaine as minister to the Hawaiian kingdom. The direct implication of either the president or the secretary of state is impossible to establish, but Minister John L. Stevens actively participated in the revolution that toppled Queen Liliuokalani in January 1893. Stevens encouraged the islands' wealthy white planters to overthrow the native monarchy and honored their request for naval intervention the moment they seized power in Honolulu.

The flagship of the Pacific Squadron, the protected cruiser *Boston*, was docked at Honolulu when the uprising began on 16 January 1893. Captain Gilbert C. Wiltse tersely reported his quick reaction to Secretary Tracy: "At 4:30 P.M. landed force in accordance with the request of U.S. Minister Plenipotentiary. Tuesday afternoon the Provisional Government was established, the Queen dethroned, without loss of life." Some 164 bluejackets and marines were brandishing Gatling guns and rifles outside the royal palace. The secretary did not question Wiltse's action.

Minister Stevens immediately recognized the new provisional government, declared Hawaii an American protectorate, and urged the administration to annex the islands before Great Britain plucked the "Hawaiian pear . . . now fully ripe" from the American grasp. Harrison hastily negotiated a treaty of annexation and rushed it to the Senate in the last hours of his presidency. His administration expired before the Senate could act, and the new Democratic president, Grover Cleveland, withdrew it for reconsideration. Swallowing of the ripe pear would await the Spanish–American War, and even then opposition to overseas colonies made the final annexation take the form of a joint resolution of Congress rather than a treaty requiring two-thirds approval by the Senate.

The *Boston*'s landing party had been helpful, perhaps essential, in preventing bloodshed, but the presence of the *Boston* in Honolulu was not in itself unusual. Ships of the Pacific Squadron had routinely made the town a port of call for half a century or more. The fact that the flagship was now made of steel only reflected the upgrading of a crucial squadron with modern vessels as they became available.

Grover Cleveland's rejection of Hawaiian annexation broke with his Republican predecessor's imperialistic foreign policy, but the naval policy of the two administrations displayed a striking continuity. In his first annual report, the new Democratic secretary of the navy, Hilary A. Herbert of Alabama, took direct aim at the lingering influence of the C.S.S. *Alabama.* He discredited the strategy of *guerre de course* by pointing to the failure of Confederate commerce raiders to counterbalance the stranglehold of the Union blockade. He denounced unarmored cruisers—the modern equivalent of the sailing frigate—and called for immediate congressional authorization of "at least one battleship" and a half-dozen protective torpedo boats. He wanted a navy ready "to give weight to whatever policy it may be thought wise on the part of the government to assume." The unspecified but clearly assertive and expansionist policies could require battleships anywhere in the Pacific or off the coasts of Latin America.

This was a bold cast of mind for a cabinet officer in an avowedly anti-imperialist administration, and President Grover Cleveland prudently vented his skepticism by withholding endorsement of Herbert's expensive building program. The president was busy extricating the United States from his predecessor's treaty of annexation with Hawaii, and as a fiscal conservative he wanted no part of a $3-million increase in naval expenditures during an economic recession. Cleveland's caution matched the mood of Congress, which authorized only three light gunboats and an experimental submarine in 1894.

Herbert was undaunted. He ordered the South Atlantic Squadron to break a rebel blockade of Rio de Janeiro, Brazil. In the course of the action the U.S.S. *Detroit* exchanged fire with the insurgents' flagship. Assistant Secretary of the Navy William G. McAdoo bragged of his boss's aggressiveness at a meeting of Boston Democrats. Mahan's theories were now universally accepted, said the assistant secretary, and the United States had become "a factor in the affairs of our neighbors. During the recent trouble in Brazil, the United States . . . put into Brazilian waters the most powerful fleet which ever represented our flag abroad." McAdoo had been profoundly stimulated by "the sight of that splendid squadron . . . carrying our flag with pride over decks cleared for action, as it steamed up the Bay of Rio."

For McAdoo vigorous naval intervention in a neighbor's home waters was but a beginning. He anticipated "constant upheavals" in the Far East and throughout Latin America, and those could be met only by creating a two-ocean fleet. That proposal contravened the nineteenth-century American navy's deployment of ships in five widely dispersed squadrons. It marked the first official call for concentration of the navy's ships in two major battlefleets, the deployment pattern characteristic of the first half of the twentieth century. That it was made by a Democrat rather than a Republican shows the bipartisan appeal of Mahanian thinking about strategic rearrangement of the nation's warships. But this Democrat was special: McAdoo became the son-in-law and secretary of the treasury to President Woodrow Wilson, and he was at the president's side when Wilson in 1916 issued the battle cry for "incomparably the greatest navy in the world."

Herbert, too, took to the hustings to advance a Mahanian navy in 1894. The secretary visited Newport to welcome the new president of the Naval War College, Captain Henry C. Taylor, whose appointment was sanctioned by Mahan. Herbert took the occasion of his visit to outline an expanded role for the school. In addition to devising strategic theory for the battleship navy, Newport was amassing a body of "practical information . . . without which the Navy Department cannot possibly, in the event of war, utilize the naval resources of our country." Taylor, at the close of the 1894 session, elaborated on Herbert's themes. Classroom problems in naval strategy and tactics, combined with war games employing vessels from the North Atlantic Squadron, were generating "a backlog of operational programs of great value in the event of sudden aggression in the future." The college, in other words, was becoming an ad hoc planning board, and it was using the growing volume of reports from the relatively new Office of Naval Intelligence to make realistic assessments of foreign orders of battle. It would continue in this function until the Naval War Board was created in 1898 to plan the operations of the Spanish–American War.

Great Britain was the favorite hypothetical enemy, a logical choice because the Royal Navy was the toughest opponent and England was America's most formidable overseas economic competitor. In an 1894 lecture at the college, Captain Charles H. Stockton glumly predicted that "when the overproduction of this country is relieved by free commerce and lower prices, a rivalry will begin with Britain for the markets of the world."

A few months later Grover Cleveland's meddling in the festering boundary dispute between British Guiana and Venezuela almost gave the navy a chance to pit itself against the world's best. The president in July 1895 approved Secretary of State Richard Olney's strong protest that British incursions into Venezuela violated the Monroe Doctrine. Proudly christened Olney's "twenty-inch gun" by Cleveland, the note generated war hysteria among jingoists like Theodore Roosevelt, who characteristically put his finger on Britain's strategic military weakness vis-à-vis the continental United States: "Let the fight come if it must; I don't care whether our sea coast cities are bombarded or not; we would take Canada."

At sea the prospects were grim, a fact well understood by Captain Henry Taylor, who was called to Washington from Newport for war planning. The United States Navy had in commission only one first-class battleship, the *Indiana*, to oppose a fleet boasting more than forty battleships. The numbers had changed since 1812, but the Anglo-American naval imbalance had not, and this naval reality compelled the Americans to shape a traditional strategy regardless of their dreams of blue-water battlefleet engagements.

Taylor's staff planned to concentrate the navy's armored vessels, including several monitors—the conceptual descendants of Jefferson's gunboats—in Nantucket Sound for the defense of New York and southern New England. From their sanctuary the armored ships might attack portions of a British fleet under cover of darkness or bad weather. If somehow victorious, they would subsequently assault and neutralize the naval base at Halifax, the historic launching point of British operations against the American coast. Then the navy would convoy an army of invasion northward, a move anticipated by Canadians since the 1830s. Meanwhile, fast cruisers and armed merchantmen would raid British commerce. The offensive operations depended on luck; the plan itself was essentially defensive, for as Taylor reminded the secretary of the navy, "the wars for which we must plan, at least for the next few years, are defensive on our part and [are] to be waged against enemies probably superior to us on the sea."

The United States Navy emerged untested but triumphant from this final great Anglo-American war scare because Her Majesty's government agreed to arbitration. Isolated in Europe, and engaged in an ominous dispute with Berlin over South Africa, London dared not further antagonize the United States, however contemptible the Monroe Doctrine might seem. The Admiralty's margin of superiority over France and Russia, let alone over Germany, was insufficient to permit even a precautionary reinforcement of the British squadrons in the Western Hemisphere. Britain's recognition of its naval and diplomatic overextension, coupled with sober second thoughts in America about the wisdom of fighting one's cultural and ethnic kin, led rather directly to a major diplomatic rapprochement that settled issues dating back to the Revolutionary War. For the U.S. Navy, the gains were monumental. By 1902 Britain had acquiesced to the idea of a Central American canal totally under United States control, and by 1906 the Admiralty had closed its naval bases at Halifax, Nova Scotia, and on Jamaica in the West Indies. The ascension of the U.S. Navy to parity with the Royal Navy was well under way, even if not realized at the time.

The highly favorable long-term outcome to the Venezuelan boundary crisis could not be predicted in 1895 and 1896, a time when the U.S. Navy saw enemies in almost every ocean. Far across the Pacific, near the Yalu River, a modern Japanese navy had just badly hurt a Chinese fleet containing two European-built battleships, each displacing 1,000 tons more than the U.S.S. *Maine*, then undergoing steam trials. Theodore Roosevelt, a Republican without portfolio, relayed to Democratic Secretary Herbert the principal conclusion of a European attaché who had seen the riddled Chinese fleet straggle into Port Arthur: Unarmored cruisers were obsolete. That deduction was conveniently congenial to Roosevelt, a proponent of battleships.

Intrigued by the chance to study the effects of combat between modern warships, Secretary Herbert cabled the commander of the Asiatic Squadron: "Afford every facility for intelligence officers of our fleet to obtain information." As a result, the Sino-Japanese War witnessed the most extensive intelligence-gathering activity by the American navy in the entire nineteenth century. One of the main investigators was Lieutenant William S. Sims, who within a decade would prove to be the navy's most alert student of the implications for technological change on warfare at sea.

Sims's report and others provided by the Office of Naval Intelligence made Herbert well aware of Japan's blossoming naval might. He prudently reinforced the Asiatic Squadron and designated certain ships on the Pacific coast as scheduled reinforcements for vessels returning from the Far East for overhaul in San Francisco.

Soon after the war Japan ordered six battleships from European and English yards and two cruisers from American shipbuilders. The augmentation was in anticipation of revenge against Russia for the tsar's key role in forcing Tokyo to retrocede the Liaotung Peninsula (Liaodong Bandao) to China, but the United States had to take heed. By 1895 Japan stood second only to Great Britain as a Pacific naval power, and two of the battleships on order from Britain would outclass everything in the U.S. fleet, including the *Indianas*. The emergence of Japan put a new strain on American primacy in the Hawaiian

Islands, where a large Japanese population attracted the patronage of Tokyo. Impotent to resolve the dilemma of an unattached Hawaii and an expansionist Japan, the Democrats passed it along to their Republican successors as unfinished business.

Secretary of the Navy Herbert also handed down the more immediate crisis over Cuba, where Spanish brutality in suppressing nationalist insurgents had become a prime object of American popular and naval attention from the moment of the Cuban revolution's rebirth in 1895. The New York newspapers of Joseph Pulitzer and William Randolph Hearst sensationalized real and alleged Spanish atrocities in a media circulation war that helped lead to the shooting war of 1898. Herbert was increasingly concerned for the security of the Caribbean, but he and Secretary of State Olney were reluctant to provoke Spain by honoring the request of Fitzhugh Lee, the American consul general in Havana, that "a man-of-war" be held ready "at Key West under a discreet officer, with a full complement of marines."

Herbert's assistant secretary, William G. McAdoo, maintained that the Cuban crisis underscored the need for a board of officers to advise the secretary on the interrelationships between naval strategy, tactics, and technology. He had the British Board of Admiralty in mind as a model, and he envisioned ultimately a second, interservice board to advise the secretaries of the navy and war on national military and naval strategy. He would call it the "Board for the Military Defense of the United States."

The idea of a naval war board dated back to the imperfect Board of Naval Commissioners, formed after the War of 1812. It was a concept often advanced by officers, perhaps most earnestly by Admiral David Dixon Porter during the post–Civil War doldrums. It reached fruition in 1900, in the form of the General Board of the Navy. The idea of an interservice strategy board was new, and it was realized with the establishment of the Joint Army and Navy Board in 1903. The institutionalization of McAdoo's ideas by Republican administrations demonstrates once again the bipartisan or nonpartisan nature of turn-of-the-century American navalism.

McAdoo's advocacy of an increased role for officers in national war planning, necessarily achieved at the expense of the autonomy of the civilian secretaries, was characteristic of a man enthusiastic about a more centralized capital-ship navy, a man who chafed at being number two in the department. His immediate successor, Theodore Roosevelt, displayed the same temperament. Typical also was Mc-

Adoo's use of an agency of the Royal Navy as a model for the United States Navy, a tendency of Mahanians from that time to the present.

If the Navy Department seemed somewhat bifurcated at the very top, the Naval War College and the Office of Naval Intelligence added to the uncertainty by disagreeing on how to fight Spain. Newport studied the strategic options from 1894 to 1896, finally concluding that the optimal thrust would consist of an immediate combined military and naval attack on Havana, "the natural objective" and "the commercial and military center of the Island." Citing the two years it took for the Union blockade to become effective in the Civil War, the college staff rejected a blockade strategy as ineffective and as a dangerous dispersal of the fleet into vulnerable "blockading detachments." In contradiction, Lieutenant Commander Richard Wainwright's Office of Naval Intelligence proposed a blockade of Cuba and "harassment and descents on the enemy's colonies." Specifically targeted was Manila, which the Asiatic Squadron "should reduce . . . at the earliest possible opportunity."

Faced with divided counsels of war, Herbert played the bureaucratic card: He convened a departmental review board in Washington, and it in turn came up with its own variation. Although the departmental planners rejected a descent on Manila, they advocated an immediate blockade of the deep-water ports in Cuba and Puerto Rico, a central feature of the Wainwright scheme. More significant in light of the actual course of the campaign in 1898 was the addition of a novel recommendation that American battleships ought to "destroy the depots and arsenals at Havana [Cuba] and San Juan [Puerto Rico] by bombardment, compelling at least their temporary abandonment or surrender." In the judgment of Captain William T. Sampson, the chief of the Bureau of Ordnance and the future wartime commander of American naval forces off Cuba, the bombardment of Havana, the political capital of colonial Cuba, promised an immediate and almost bloodless American naval victory over Spain. But before Herbert could extract a unified opinion from his uniformed advisers, time ran out, so he forwarded all three plans to the next administration.

Herbert might appear to have bequeathed mostly foreign crises and discordant advice to his successor, John D. Long, and Assistant Secretary of the Navy Theodore Roosevelt in March 1897, but that was not so. He also passed along an enormously strengthened navy, one that had risen in four short years from ninth place to sixth among the world's fleets and one that was fully modern in ship-type and ordnance. The credit for the expansion and modernization began with the Republican Benjamin F. Tracy, as Herbert graciously noted when inviting the former secretary to participate in a German naval review aboard one of the new cruisers: "Certainly you are entitled if anyone is, to be upon these ships when they are presented to the world." But the Democrat had used every opportunity to add firepower of his own, most successfully in June 1896, when he goaded a Congress shaken by the recent war scare with Britain and anxious about the future of Cuba to authorize three battleships and ten torpedo boats.

In 1897, for the first time in American history, the battleship sat at the core of the United States Navy. The second-class battleships *Texas* and *Maine* had made their shakedown cruises in 1895; the first-rate battleships *Indiana*, *Massachusetts*, and *Oregon* began active service in January 1897. Five more battle wagons authorized during Herbert's tenure were under construction and scheduled for commissioning in late 1899: *Kearsarge*, *Kentucky*, *Illinois*, *Alabama*, and *Wisconsin*. Backing the capital ships were seven new cruisers. In addition, a miscellany of smaller vessels was under construction or newly completed: four monitors, an armored ram, an experimental submarine, sixteen torpedo boats, and six 1,000-ton gunboats. The monitors were vestiges of an earlier era, the era in which coastal defense was one of the two legs of American naval strategy, the other being commerce raiding. The battleships were hallmarks of a new era, destined to last a century. In the new age the United States Navy sought command of the sea through engagements between opposing fleets of capital ships. This was Mahan's idea, borrowed from the British, but it was shared by many men in high places.

=====

No politician in American life personified the new order more perfectly than Theodore Roosevelt, the first assistant secretary of the navy in the administration of William McKinley. Brilliant, brash, and pugnacious, he overshadowed the meticulous and pensive secretary, John D. Long, an older man. Both were Republican reformers, and each was deeply dedicated to public service; but in age, temperament, and philosophy they were poles apart. For the fifty-nine-year-old Long, the Navy Department represented the capstone of a distinguished career; for the thirty-nine-year-old Roosevelt it constituted a stepping stone to national renown. Long had made American politics his lifelong study; Roosevelt, the nephew of the Confederate naval agent James D. Bulloch, had studied the navy and had published in 1882 what may still be the definitive naval history of the War of 1812. Long loathed war and avoided military duty in the Civil War;

Roosevelt loved combat as a test of manly and civic virtue and welcomed the chance to prove himself in the looming contest with Spain. All of this the older man fully understood. As he confided to his diary in February 1898, Roosevelt "is full of suggestions, many of which are of great value to me, and his spirited and forceful habit is a good tonic for one who is disposed to be as conservative and careful as I am." The combination of these two disparate personalities enabled the young assistant to leave an imprint on strategy during the crucial months between the McKinley inauguration of 4 March 1897 and the declaration of war against Spain on 25 April 1898.

Roosevelt was Mahan distilled. "It is certain that we need a first-class navy, not merely a navy for defense," he lectured the officers of the Naval War College in June 1897. That meant battleships in large number, an isthmian canal, and possession of Hawaii. In those goals he was echoing and propagating Mahan, who was now retired and earning a comfortable living popularizing his ideas in leading journals. At the moment, in the summer of 1897, the two naval imperialists were agitated by the threat and opportunity promised by Tokyo's concern over the all-white Hawaiian government's prohibition of further Japanese immigration to the islands.

Roosevelt wanted a preemptive strike, as he made clear to Mahan in May:

> If I had my way, we would annex those islands tomorrow. . . . I believe we should build the Nicaraguan canal at once, and . . . build a dozen new battleships, half of them on the Pacific Coast; . . . I am fully alive to the danger from Japan. . . . My own belief is that we should act instantly before the new Japanese warships leave England.

Roosevelt was worried about the Japanese sister ships *Fuji* and *Yashima*, nearing completion in Great Britain. Each was designed to displace 12,300 tons, mount four 12-inch guns, and reach a speed of 15 knots. The U.S. Navy's heaviest type in commission was still the 10,000-ton *Indiana* class, represented on the West Coast by the *Oregon*.

Even the phlegmatic Long sensed a crisis, and as it peaked in July he took precautionary measures. He authorized the squadron commander in Hawaii to proclaim a protectorate if relations with the Japanese residents of Honolulu deteriorated markedly; he directed the naval attaché in Yokohama to advise the department of significant Japanese naval movements; and he ordered the commanding officer of the battleship *Oregon* to be ready to steam to Hawaii from Puget Sound at any time. This saber-rattling by the Navy Department and firmly aggressive diplomacy by the State Department induced Japan to confine its intervention on behalf of its nationals in Hawaii to diplomatic protests.

The Hawaii–Japan episode of 1897 revealed with remarkable clarity the territorial grasp of the most influential big-navy man in the McKinley administration, the depth Roosevelt's animosity toward Japan, and the wholly new global element of American strategic planning in the battleship era. With characteristic acumen and succinctness, Roosevelt encapsulated the last point in a "special problem" he ordered the Naval War College to study in June 1897:

> Japan makes demands on Hawaiian Islands. This country intervenes. What force will be required to uphold intervention? Keep in mind possible complications with another power in the Atlantic.

The Atlantic power Theodore Roosevelt had most in mind was Spain, whose brutal attacks on Cuban nationalists had become the prime object of American popular and naval attention by the end of the summer of 1897.

At that time Secretary of the Navy John D. Long did what his Democratic predecessor had done: He convened an advisory panel, the Naval War Board, which met in June 1897 to plan operations against Spain. The holdover member was Richard Wainwright, director of the Office of Naval Intelligence when it developed the war plan calling for a blockade of Cuba and an attack on the Philippines. Wainwright was close to Assistant Secretary Roosevelt, who later recalled, "I leaned a little more on you than on anyone else." The other "natural allies" to whom Roosevelt turned for ideas on how to fight Spain included Mahan, Senator Henry Cabot Lodge, and such active naval officers as the aggressive Robley D. Evans of the *Baltimore* affair and William T. Sampson, chief of the Bureau of Ordnance. Those and a handful of other like-minded men with access to the department shaped a two-part strategy. They decided to attack the Spanish fleet in the Philippine Islands, an echo of proposals made by senior naval officers in 1855 and 1873. Their second decision was to insist that the North Atlantic Squadron make the destruction of Spain's fleet in the Western Hemisphere its highest priority. The net results of this strategy would be the creation of an American empire in the Philippines and the apparent confirmation of the battleship theory of naval warfare.

The Wainwright–Office of Naval Intelligence plan to "capture and reduce Manila at the earliest possible date" had reached the secretary of the navy in June 1896. In 1897, at one of the meetings of Roosevelt's group, Mahan recommended attacking Manila as a sure way to defeat the mother country, an inspiration he derived from studying British empire-building in the seventeenth century. Secretary Long gave his grudging consent in October.

Roosevelt's candidate to command the Asiatic Squadron, Commodore George Dewey, was chosen more because of his social and political connections than for his naval reputation. He had graduated first in his class at the Naval Academy and had served ably under David G. Farragut in the Civil War, but his record for the intervening thirty years lacked distinction. Since 1889 he had lived in Washington, D.C., first as chief of the Bureau of Equipment and later as president of the Board of Inspection and Survey. Both jobs put Dewey near the navy's center, but neither was onerous, so the commodore filled some of his ample free time dining at Washington's prestigious Metropolitan Club and horseback riding in Rock Creek Park with fellow member Theodore Roosevelt. It was Roosevelt who enlisted an old friend of the Dewey family, Senator Redfield Proctor, to place Dewey's candidacy directly before President McKinley. On 21 October 1897 he was ordered to assume command of the Asiatic Squadron.

While the well-briefed Dewey prepared to lead his squadron against the Spanish forces in the Philippines, the McKinley administration stumbled blindly toward war with Spain. The president genuinely opposed war so long as Spain continued to move as fast as possible toward granting Cuba autonomy within the empire. But three perfectly reasonable American decisions led to an unforeseeable disaster with uncontrollable consequences. In early January the president authorized Secretary Long to move the North Atlantic Squadron to the naval base at Key West for winter maneuvers off the west coast of Florida, suspended for the last two years out of deference to Spain. Then, in mid-January, McKinley took alarm at reports from Consul-General Fitzhugh Lee about the dangers rioting mobs posed to Americans living in Havana. He authorized Long to redeploy the European Squadron—the former Mediterranean Squadron—from the Mediterranean Sea to Lisbon, Portugal, where it could observe and possibly intercept Spanish naval or military reinforcements headed toward Cuba. Finally, in response to a suggestion from Long, McKinley on 24 January decided to send a warship from Key West to Havana to protect Americans in the colonial capital. The visit was to be masked as a courtesy call.

The warship selected was already at Key West and under the telegraphic control of Consul-General Lee. An armored cruiser or light battleship authorized by Congress in 1886, the *Maine* was not the most imposing ship in the North Atlantic Squadron, which included the newer and much heavier battleships *Indiana, Massachusetts*, and *Iowa*. She therefore seemed to the Navy Department a perfect vessel for a touch of old-style "gunboat diplomacy." But the wife of the ship's executive officer expressed the crew's more accurate foreboding: "You might as well send a lighted candle on a visit to an open cask of gunpowder!" Mrs. Richard Wainwright's prophecy was borne out, resulting in death for 253 men of the *Maine* on 15 February 1898.

The explosion that tore open the *Maine*'s forecastle at 9:40 P.M. that Tuesday evening handed the yellow journalists and jingoists the *casus belli* they had been seeking, even though cooler heads cautioned circumspection. The doomed ship's skipper, Captain Charles D. Sigsbee, sent a message to Secretary Long pleading for temperance: "*Maine* blown up . . . and destroyed. . . . Public opinion should be suspended until further report." Richard Wainwright, who survived and remained in Havana as custodian of the sunken hull, ignored that recommendation and prematurely decided that an external mine had blown up his ship. The naval court of inquiry in Havana, headed by Captains William T. Sampson and French E. Chadwick, similarly concluded that "the *Maine* was destroyed by a submarine mine, which caused the explosion of two or more magazines."

Sampson's prestige as an ordnance expert enhanced the credibility of his findings, but there were dissenting opinions. The Spanish board of inquiry blamed an accidental internal explosion in one of the forward powder magazines, an opinion shared by a distinguished American naval engineer, Commodore George W. Melville, chief of the Bureau of Steam Engineering in 1898. Much later, after an exhaustive analysis incorporating modern computer technology, Admiral Hyman G. Rickover published a book sustaining the dissenters. But at the time the doubters in uniform were intimidated by such popular bloodlust as the New York *Journal*'s offer of a $50,000 reward "for the conviction of the criminals who sent 258 [sic] American sailors to their death."

A cry for vengeance shook the land in the month between the explosion and the submission of Sampson's report on the *Maine* on 21

March. On 8 March the House unanimously approved an "emergency bill appropriating $50,000,000 for national defense." It authorized construction of three new battleships, sixteen destroyers, fourteen torpedo boats, and four monitors. This was the beginning of a total naval appropriation of $57 million for 1898 and the first step in adding 128 vessels to the navy that year. On 17 March Senator Redfield Proctor, considered a moderate but fully informed of the navy's planning, eloquently moved the nation closer to war with a Senate speech depicting the horrors of the Spanish concentration camps in Cuba. Within his own administration the president faced determined and restless warmongers.

The assistant secretary of the navy led the pack. From the moment he learned of the explosion, Theodore Roosevelt prayed that "President McKinley would order the fleet to Havana tomorrow. . . . The *Maine* was sunk by an act of dirty treachery on the part of the Spaniards, *I* believe." Roosevelt found McKinley's patience despicable. The president had "no more backbone than a chocolate éclair." The secretary of the navy, to whom Roosevelt remained overtly loyal, was also an obstacle to circumvent.

Roosevelt's moment came on Friday, 25 February, when an exhausted Long took the afternoon off, leaving Roosevelt in the department as acting secretary despite a "lack of confidence in his good judgment and discretion." Temporarily empowered, Roosevelt sent out a batch of orders, the most famous of which was a cable to Commodore Dewey ordering the Asiatic Squadron to Hong Kong to fill its bunkers with coal. "In the event [of a] declaration of war with Spain, your duty will be to see that the Spanish squadron does not leave the Asiatic coast and then [to take] offensive operations in the Philippines." This very energetic man somehow found time that same afternoon to write a personal letter, apparently intended for the governor of New York, proclaiming that in event of war, "I want to go" with the army.

Long broke protocol by returning to work on Saturday "because, during my short absence, I find that Roosevelt, in his precipitate way, has come very near causing more of an explosion than happened to the *Maine*." But as annoyed as he may have been, he did not countermand the orders to Dewey. The reason is quite simple: Since October 1897 the navy had planned to fight the Pacific war by demolishing the Spanish squadron and capturing Manila. Dewey had known that before he left Washington, and Long knew it. The Roosevelt cable merely confirmed standing orders.

Long did not believe Spain was responsible for the *Maine* disaster, and he still hoped for peace, but from this point forward he was fully enmeshed in all of the preparations for war. On 26 February he cabled Dewey and the other squadron commanders—the Pacific, North Atlantic, and European—to "Keep full of coal, the best that can be had." In March he began regular consultations with the chairmen of the House and Senate naval committees, meeting with both men three days before the House approval of the emergency appropriation. On 7 March he telegraphed the captain of the *Oregon*, then at Bremerton, Washington, to "go to San Francisco as soon as possible and get ammunition." Twelve days later the noble ship left the Golden Gate on her historic sixty-seven-day, 14,700-mile run around Cape Horn, averaging an unprecedented 12 knots. She arrived battle-ready at Jupiter Inlet, Florida, on 24 May. Her dramatic feat helped crystallize opinion about the value of battleships, which had come into question as a result of the destruction of the *Maine*.

Roosevelt again succinctly summarized the issue. He worried that "shortsighted" men would want to stop building battleships because one had blown up, "and we shall have to meet a great revival of the cry for coast defense monitors, cruisers and torpedo boats—all of them very good in their way, but none of them substitutes for battleships." Secretary Long shared Roosevelt's appreciation of the tentativeness of the national commitment to capital ships: "Our great battleships are experiments which have never yet been tried and in the friction of a fight have almost as much to fear from some disarrangement of their own delicate machinery or some explosion of their own tremendous ammunition as from the foe." The final confirmation of the battleship as the backbone of the new American navy—and the corollary strategy of sea control through victorious fleet engagements—would come only with the ship's success in the coming war with Spain.

Long and Roosevelt orchestrated the combat experiment to ensure a positive result through their direct orders to William T. Sampson, who assumed command of the prestigious North Atlantic Squadron on 24 March 1898, two days before the badgered president dispatched an ultimatum to Spain strongly implying a demand for the independence of Cuba. A relatively junior captain abruptly promoted to rear admiral, Sampson took over a powerful but diluted force.

Political pressure for visible protection of the Atlantic Seaboard induced Long to create a "Flying Squadron" by detaching the heavy battleship *Massachusetts*, the *Texas*—sister ship of the *Maine*—and the armored cruiser *Brooklyn* from Sampson's forces at Key West. Sampson retained nominal command over the new squadron, but Commodore Winfield Scott Schley was the immediate commander charged with patrolling the American coastline from Hampton Roads, Virginia, to Florida. The more northern seaboard cities fearing bombardment by Spanish ships had to rely on the three protected cruisers of the Northern Patrol Squadron and an Auxiliary Naval Force, or "mosquito flotilla," of unseaworthy monitors, yachts, and tugs. In a letter of 14 March Theodore Roosevelt explained the department's reasoning to Mahan: Only Newport News, Virginia, where the new battleships were under construction, warranted serious protection. With Newport to his back, Schley was to search for Spanish raiders and reinforcements heading west from the Cape Verde Islands while Sampson prepared the main body for action off Cuba.

Leaving nothing to chance, Long and Roosevelt supervised the development of a departmental war plan. Roosevelt himself headed a new Naval War Board, where his principal agent was a Mahan protégé, Captain Caspar F. Goodrich, the current president of the Naval War College. Roosevelt sent the board's plan to Mahan, who was in New York packing for a vacation in Europe. A resulting memorandum, "based largely on certain suggestions made by Captain Mahan," became the department's guidance for the North Atlantic Squadron. It stipulated a three-ring blockade of the Cuban ports of Matanzas and Havana, with torpedo boats furthest in, cruisers in the middle ring, and the battleships keeping the sea as far as 25 miles offshore. The memorandum assumed a prey worthy of blockading, and the blockade itself was preparatory to the major move of the squadron, which was to "concentrate the fleet and strike a telling blow at the Spanish fleet." The deployment pattern and goal of a fleet engagement resembled Horatio Nelson's 1805 blockade off Cadiz preceding the Battle of Trafalgar.

On station, Captain French E. Chadwick, the skipper of the flagship *New York*, oozed optimism: "This squadron as it stands," he advised Roosevelt, "could wipe up everything Spain has in twenty minutes. Our losses would be nothing. We could no doubt take Havana by assault. But what's the use?" In hourly contact with each other, Chadwick and Rear Admiral Sampson began to devise a plan of operations quite different from the one favored in Washington. On the basis of detailed observations he had made in Havana while investigating the *Maine* explosion, Sampson concluded that naval bombardment could force the Spanish forces in the colonial capital to capitulate at the very beginning of the hostilities.

Sampson proposed combining heavy ships and two monitors—the *Puritan* and *Amphitrite*—to destroy the unfortified guns on the western approaches to the city. "Having silenced the western batteries, it would be quite practicable to shell the city, which I would do only after warning given twenty-four hours in advance." He understood that "we would have no troops to occupy the city if it did surrender, yet, Mr. Secretary, it will be very unfortunate, besides a great loss of time, if we must delay until the rainy season is over." His plan of operations was reminiscent of the Union navy's attacks on Confederate cities in the Civil War; his concern for human suffering went back to an even earlier age, to General Winfield Scott's campaign against Mexico. The admiral was seconded by the captains of his major combatants: French E. Chadwick, Henry C. Taylor, and Robley D. Evans.

With Roosevelt at his side, Long rejected the plan of his senior on-scene commanders. There was no drydock large enough for a battleship in the Gulf of Mexico, so to expose battleships to heavy shore fire was, as the Roosevelt protégé Rear Admiral John G. Walker noted, "suicidal." It was absolutely essential to destroy the Spanish squadron en route from Cape Verde before risking the navy's heaviest and best ships in coastal bombardment. Moreover, as Secretary Long ruefully contended, the U.S. Army was unprepared for assault or occupation; it was "ready for nothing at all." On 6 April 1898 the secretary therefore categorically instructed Sampson:

> The Department does not wish the vessels of your squadron to be exposed to the fire of the batteries at Havana, Santiago de Cuba, or other strongly fortified ports in Cuba, unless the more formidable Spanish vessels should take refuge within those harbors. Even in this case the Department would suggest that a rigid blockade and employment of our torpedo boats might accomplish the desired object, viz., the destruction of the enemy's vessels, without subjecting unnecessarily our own men-of-war to the fire of the land batteries.

This directive remained in force as the navy went to war in late April. Long's cable to Sampson of 21 April—four days before the congressional declaration of war—ordered him to "blockade [the] coast of Cuba immediately. . . . Do not bombard, according to terms of my letter of April 6." The orders were repeated one more time in a confidential letter on 6 May 1898, the day Theodore Roosevelt resigned as assistant secretary of the navy to become a "lieutenant colonel of a regiment of mounted riflemen."

Roosevelt had done a great deal before going off to war. He had lobbied, albeit unsuccessfully, for creation of a position of uniformed chief of staff, to which he hoped to appoint Rear Admiral John G. Walker, "a first-class man." He had dragged the retired Mahan home from vacation in Europe to dominate a Naval War Board whose other members lacked national stature now that Roosevelt was removed. He had, perhaps without malice, helped prevent Sampson from making a reasonable effort to end the war before the army was mobilized. All the while he was negotiating a commission for himself in the army. Ironically, in his insistence that Sampson not bombard Havana before the enemy's fleet was found and destroyed, he helped initiate a blockade in which his favorite ship, the battleship, functioned in a way he himself found unsatisfying.

In a letter to Robley Evans, whom he greatly admired and who had baffled him by endorsing Sampson's plan, Roosevelt exposed the inconsistency of his own thinking and the superfluousness of battleships in the war against Spain:

> As you know, I have been a heretic about the bombardment until we destroy or cripple the Spanish fleet. I think we could probably whip the dagoes even with crippled battleships, but I don't want to try; and 10 and 12-inch guns even in the hands of the Spaniards might knock out one or two of our ships. If only the Army were one-tenth as ready as the Navy we would fix the whole business in six weeks. . . . You are quite right about not using battleships for blockading purposes, and I hope that we can speedily put them to better use.

The "better use" was never found.

As late as 21 April, the department's planning had concentrated almost exclusively on the Atlantic theater. When Sampson was ordered on that date to initiate a blockade of Cuba, an act the secretary of the navy correctly interpreted as "the beginning of the war," no corresponding orders went out to Commodore Dewey in the Far East, because President McKinley noted that the joint resolution of Congress recognizing the independence of Cuba dealt only with that one colony. This legalistic nicety, combined with distance and the difficulty of direct communication, left Dewey pretty much to his own devices, as he had been since hoisting his pennant in January 1898. He was planning, in fact, to do precisely what the department forbade Sampson to do: attack the capital of the nearest Spanish colony, the city of Manila in the Philippine Islands.

On 24 April 1898, two days before the president signed the declaration of war against Spain, Long initiated the action in the Pacific with a cable to Dewey: "War has commenced between the United States and Spain. Proceed at once to the Philippine Islands. Commence operations at once, particularly against the Spanish fleet." Dewey had already been ordered out of neutral Hong Kong by the British governor, whose affectionate postscript bespeaks the depth of Anglo-American sympathy on the eve of the war: "God knows, my dear commodore, it breaks my heart to send you this notification." The Englishman, like many Americans, doubted the Asiatic Squadron's superiority over the Spanish fleet of Admiral Patricio Montojo, but Dewey was confident that his force was "far superior to the Spanish." On 31 March he had written his son, "My squadron is all ready for war and would make short work of the defenses of Manila."

Disdaining China's neutrality, Commodore Dewey anchored in Mirs Bay (Dapeng Wan), a secluded anchorage 30 miles northeast of Hong Kong Island. As soon as the refugee American consul in Manila, Oscar F. Williams, came aboard the flagship *Olympia* with the latest news, Dewey steamed for the Philippines. Looking for the Spanish squadron, Dewey poked into Subic Bay. It was empty. "Now we have them!" Dewey exclaimed, correctly concluding that Montojo was hiding in Manila.

About midnight on 30 April 1898 the Asiatic Squadron entered the mouth of Manila Bay, 30 miles from the colonial capital. The flagship *Olympia* was in the van. To the suggestion that one of the supply ships take the lead to detonate any mines in the channel, Dewey curtly replied, "I have waited sixty years for this opportunity. Mines or no mines, I am leading the squadron in myself." His words echoed Farragut's at Mobile Bay and the parallel was self-conscious. "I confess," Dewey later wrote, "I was thinking of him the night we entered Manila Bay and with the conviction that I was doing precisely what he would have done." He did it so well that in the short run, at least, his fame far surpassed his mentor's.

As Dewey had anticipated, his ships struck no operable mines on the way in. By 3:00 A.M. he could see the lights of Manila. The city's heavy guns could have posed a serious danger to Dewey's thinly hulled cruisers, but to save the inhabitants from bombardment by the Americans Admiral Montojo had anchored his seven obsolescent ships well below Manila, in shallow water off the Cavite arsenal. Montojo's flagship, the *Reina Christina*, displaced 3,520 tons and mounted six 6.2-inch guns. The other Spanish ships were much lighter and mostly wooden-hulled. They were no match for Dewey's principal warriors, the cruisers *Olympia, Baltimore,* and *Boston,* all of which carried main batteries of 8-inch guns. The battle was over before it began.

At 5:40 A.M., nattily dressed in a white uniform and golf cap, Dewey leaned over the rail of the pilot house and shouted to the *Olympia*'s skipper, Captain Charles V. Gridley, "You may fire when you are ready, Gridley." For six hours, with a pause to count irreplaceable ammunition, Dewey's ships paraded in column before the anchored Spaniards, blasting them into bloody submission. By a little past noon Montojo had lost his seven warships and approximately four hundred men killed or wounded. The white flag went up over Cavite arsenal. The American ships had experienced limited superficial damage, and seven sailors were wounded. No American died in the battle that had eliminated Spanish naval power in the Pacific, an ignominious end for a proud people whose great explorer, Ferdinand Magellan, commanded the first European ship to reach the Philippines in 1521.

Dewey's work was not done. Manila's impudent shore batteries continued sniping at him until he silenced them with the threat of a bombardment. Then, when the Spanish governor general refused to let him use the cable to notify Washington of his victory, Dewey cut the underwater link with the rest of the world. His messages, carried by a dispatch boat to Hong Kong and then cabled to Europe and the United States, did not reach Washington until 7 May. In the meantime, the rumors flew thick and furious that the Spanish had inflicted heavy damage on his squadron.

The gloom settling over the Potomac was dispersed as if by sunburst with the news of the decisive outcome in Manila Bay. Dewey hats, cigarettes, canes, spoons, candlesticks, and paperweights appeared in every souvenir shop. Theodore Roosevelt notified Dewey: "Every American is in your debt." Senator Henry Cabot Lodge introduced a resolution authorizing bronze medals for all the men who fought at Manila and a jeweled sword from Tiffany's in New York for the newly promoted rear admiral. An anonymous poet set Dewey squarely in the American naval pantheon:

Dewey! Dewey! Dewey!
Is the hero of the Day
And the *Maine* has been remembered
In the good old-fashioned way—
The way of Hull and Perry,
Decatur and the rest
When old Europe felt the clutches
Of the Eagle of the West;
That's how Dewey smashed the Spaniard
In Manila's crooked bay,
And the *Maine* has been remembered
In the good old-fashioned way.

In the faroff "crooked bay" the newly minted hero wondered if this fame would last: "There must follow other battles in the Atlantic and the glory of triumph in them may surpass that which has come to me."

Meanwhile, he had to consolidate the American position in the Philippines. At any time he could force the Spanish to surrender Manila, but he lacked an occupying force. He therefore established a blockade of Manila while awaiting the arrival of the U.S. Army, en route from San Francisco. He was kept busy monitoring ships of the British, German, and Japanese navies, which had arrived to observe the siege and to be ready if a true power vacuum were created by a sudden American departure. Most troublesome to the commodore was the German Vice Admiral Otto von Diederichs, whose squadron for a time was stronger than Dewey's. The American overreached himself, insisting on a nonexistent right to board and inspect German warships entering the bay, and before the two flag officers reached a procedural accommodation Dewey's latent anti-Germanism had solidified into a paranoia that would affect his policy recommendations for the rest of his life.

Dewey also had to worry about an enemy squadron on its way to Manila from Spain, via the Mediterranean and Suez. The Navy Department reinforced him with two monitors and promises of more modern warships, but the Spanish squadron of Admiral Manuel de la Cámara was on paper superior to Dewey's in weight of armor and caliber of gun. This threat evaporated on 9 July with the Spanish government's decision to recall Cámara. American preparations for an attack on the Spanish coast by battleships of the now victorious North Atlantic Squadron had sobered Madrid and saved Dewey from embarrassment. Although Cámara had reached the Red Sea, Dewey had not developed a plan of operations. It is uncertain whether he intended temporarily to abandon Manila Bay to Cámara while rendezvousing with reinforcements coming from San Francisco or to steam south from Manila to intercept Cámara while the Spaniard was still encumbered with supply ships.

Once Cámara turned back and Dewey reached a modus vivendi with von Diederichs, the commodore had only three competing groups on his hands: the Spanish in Manila, the Filipino insurgents led by Emilio Aguinaldo, and an American army of ten thousand men commanded by General Wesley Merritt. On 4 August Dewey's bluewater force was augmented by the monitor *Monterey*, a heavily armored low-profile, light-draft weapons platform ideal for attacking large shore batteries from a variety of angles in the shallow waters around Manila. Two days later he gave the Spanish notice of imminent attack. He and General Merritt negotiated a complicated plan with the Spanish to permit occupation of Manila after nominal face-saving mutual artillery fire and without loss of life, but the arrangement miscarried and two American soldiers were killed approaching the city. Dewey inconsiderately blamed his sister service: "The Spanish carried out their part to the letter. So did my ships; but, as I said before, the army was too brash and rushed in too soon."

With the city successfully occupied by the army on 13 August, Dewey washed his hands of the difficult problem posed by the Filipino insurgents, who understandably thought they had a right to joint occupation of Manila and who distrusted the Americans. Like any American naval officer, he took pride in thinking himself apolitical. Moreover, he was ambivalent about the insurgents' capacity for self-rule. In September an army general reported to the secretary of state that "Admiral Dewey fully concurs" in the view that Aguinaldo and his followers "cannot maintain independence without the help of some strong nation." As an open rupture between the U.S. Army and the insurgents appeared increasingly likely, Dewey became apprehensive. "We don't want a war with them if we can help it and perhaps it would be better to give up the islands rather than have one." It was too late.

In December President McKinley's delegates at Paris negotiated Spanish cession of the entire Philippine archipelago to the United States. The Filipino nationalists were dismayed, and by early February 1899 a war between the former insurgents and the United States was in full bloom. In failing to make a precise recommendation about the future of the Philippine Islands at the height of his fame in late 1898 Dewey had missed a historic opportunity to defer the onset of overseas American imperialism.

While Dewey fretted about the deleterious effect that a decisive naval battle in the Atlantic might have on his own immortality, Rear Admiral William T. Sampson chafed under the department's restrictive orders relayed to him by telegraph to Key West and from there by dispatch boat to his flagship, wherever it might be in the Caribbean or West Indies. He was a commander in name only; in fact all the shots were called by Washington. As late as 21 April Assistant Secretary Roosevelt had assured the father of the battleship navy, former Secretary Benjamin F. Tracy, "I am of course utterly against bombarding Havana or any other port where there is any risk of damage to our ships until the Spanish fleet is disposed of." There could be no Farragut or Dewey in Cuba.

Outward bound from the Cape Verde Islands, Admiral Pascual Cervera y Topete anticipated a quick defeat at the hands of the North Atlantic Squadron. His heaviest ships were four cruisers, one of which, the *Cristóbal Colón*, steamed from Spain minus her main battery. None of them matched the American battleships in thickness of armor or caliber of rifle. He would run for Cuba, tuck into a protected port, and await the summons to sacrifice himself for Spanish honor. Cervera's appreciation of the qualitative inferiority of his own squadron made an ironic counterpoint to the debilitating sense of insecurity felt by the American public, which had led to the formation of the Mosquito Flotilla and the Flying Squadron under Commodore Schley.

The most optimistic American was the one farthest removed from the collective anxiety settling over the East Coast: Captain Charles E. Clark, skipper of the magnificent *Oregon*, racing from San Francisco to intercept Cervera and hoping to defeat the Spaniard's four cruisers single-handedly. Clark planned to capitalize on the high speed of his ship in running from them until they became strung out like beads on a necklace; then he would turn upon them with his 13-inch guns and destroy them one by one. Such audacity worried a Navy Department jealous of its new battleships, but Long could do nothing to control a bold man far at sea. The relief in Washington therefore was almost audible when Clark cabled his arrival at Jupiter Inlet, Florida, on 24 May. Five days earlier Cervera had slipped into Santiago de Cuba, where he sulked as yet undetected by Sampson or Schley.

The Navy Department had retained Schley's Flying Squadron at

Hampton Roads until it was conclusively learned that Cervera was in the Caribbean, headed for Cuba. At that point Schley was ordered to Key West. He rejoined Sampson, who had sortied to Puerto Rico, which he bombarded in frustration after a fruitless search for the Spanish fleet. Still hoping to intercept Cervera and engage him in a sea battle before he reached a sanctuary, Sampson detached Schley to blockade the southern Cuban port of Cienfuegos while he headed for Havana on the north coast.

By 23 May Sampson believed the "Spanish squadron [was] probably at Santiago" and ordered Schley to that south coast port "if you are satisfied that they are not at Cienfuegos." Schley tarried for another day, then steamed slowly toward Santiago and when only 20 miles from Cervera's nest turned back toward Key West for coal. On 27 May a dispatch boat brought him a direct command from the Navy Department to determine for certain whether Cervera was at Santiago, but Schley "regretted" that he could "not obey [the] orders of the department." After the battleship *Texas* replenished from an under way collier, he again reversed himself and headed back to Santiago. He finally spotted the anchored Cervera on 28 May. Four days later Sampson arrived with the rest of the battlefleet to take command of the entire operation. For a month there would be a tactical stalemate: Sampson could not enter the narrow channel snaking into Santiago without facing mines and powerful shore batteries; Cervera could not come out without encountering the vastly superior American fleet.

In the interim, a 17,000-man expeditionary force commanded by Major General William R. Shafter arrived from Tampa, Florida, and was landed at Daiquirí beach, 16 miles east of Santiago. Shafter and Sampson conferred on 20 June, each concluding that the primary objective was the one most congenial to the reputation of his service. Sampson thought they had agreed to concentrate on the batteries protecting the channel into the harbor; Shafter believed the city itself was the immediate goal. Heavy casualties suffered by the army on 1 July at El Caney and San Juan Hill—where "Rough Rider" Theodore Roosevelt propelled himself toward the presidency—frightened Shafter, and another army–navy conference was scheduled for 3 July. Early that day, as the armored cruiser *New York* pulled away from the blockade to take Sampson to the rendezvous with Shafter, the reluctant Cervera, under orders from the Spanish governor general to sortie before the city fell to the American army, began his doomed flight from Santiago.

The Americans could not lose. Their three battleships—the *Indiana, Iowa,* and *Oregon*—were themselves sufficient to demolish a few obsolete cruisers scurrying along the coast. The *Oregon*—"the bulldog of the fleet"—almost sufficed by herself. She alone of the blockading ships had all her boilers lit and was fully ready for action when Cervera began his egress. Her reward was a long stern chase in pursuit of the swift *Cristóbal Colón.* It terminated about 1:10 P.M., when a 13-inch shell fired at maximum elevation from the *Oregon's* forward turret splashed so close beside the *Colón* that the Spanish skipper wisely ran his ship aground. By then the rest of Cervera's fleet had been destroyed or beached. In the brief morning's action more than three hundred Spanish sailors died and 150 more were wounded. The American navy suffered one fatality and one sailor seriously wounded. Sampson's victory message to the Navy Department savored the moment: "The fleet under my command offers the nation as a Fourth of July present the whole of Cervera's fleet."

Harmony did not long reign among the victors. At the very opening of the engagement, as Cervera's flagship, the *Infante Maria Teresa,* poked its bow into open water, Schley's flagship, the armored cruiser *Brooklyn,* turned sharply to starboard away from the *Teresa* and across the bow of the *Texas,* which had to back all engines to avoid a collision. Schley's reputation as a tactician was shot. He later claimed a fathomless brilliance for the maneuver, saying it was "proper" and had "saved the day beyond any doubt." But no one believed him after he became embroiled in a bitter public dispute with Sampson, who had sped back from the aborted conference with Shafter in time to assume tactical command at the last stages of the battle.

The issue was whether Sampson or Schley deserved credit for winning the Battle of Santiago. In the opinion of Secretary of the Navy John D. Long, a keen judge of men, the "whole thing" was "as plain as a pikestaff." Schley was "one of the pleasantest fellows in the world," but whenever he encountered "any great exigency or emergency" he sought "not to meet and overcome it directly, but to swerve and get around it. This is the reason why, when he approached Santiago and the winds blew and the sea rose, and there was a question of coal supply . . . he flinched and started back to Key West." During the battle, when he turned away from the enemy and into the path of the *Texas,* Schley unhappily had "displayed the same quality." Sampson was an altogether different animal. "He conducted a campaign of great scope and enormous responsibilities to a successful and brilliant close, which terminated the war by the destruction of . . . Spanish sea-power." Long's private judgment was officially sustained by a court of inquiry chaired by Admiral George Dewey, but even then the sniping dragged on until Theodore Roosevelt, by then president, ordered an end to "this unhappy controversy."

From a naval officer's viewpoint a great deal was at stake. The sacrosanct tradition of seniority had been breached, first by the appointment of Sampson over Schley as commander of the North Atlantic Squadron, and after Manila Bay by the meteoric ascension of Dewey from commodore to full—that is, four-star—admiral, a rank previously held only by David G. Farragut and David Dixon Porter. In addition to the elevated rank, Congress authorized Dewey to remain on active duty at full pay for life, and he was appointed head of the new General Board of the Navy. That did not make him the navy's chief of staff, a position for which officers had intermittently lobbied throughout the nineteenth century, but by placing him at the elbow of the secretary of the navy it permitted him to direct the formulation of strategy in the crucial first decade of the new era.

It is no wonder that Sampson was maddened by the professional fallout of the war he had waited for all his life. Selected by the secretary of the navy for the war's crucial command, he had proposed a plan for a quick and almost bloodless victory, a plan his highly competent ships' commanders appraised in the aftermath as thoroughly feasible. Now Sampson was displaced within the navy and in history by a man who had gone into battle at the very moment that Sampson was being reined in by a Navy Department that feared risking battleships in attacking an enemy's coastal city.

Sampson's approach was the one the United States traditionally employed against weaker powers. Its antecedents can be found in the campaigns of Edward Preble off North Africa, Matthew C. Perry in the Gulf of Mexico, and David G. Farragut at New Orleans and Mobile Bay. It belonged to the limited-purpose nineteenth-century American navy more than to the twentieth-century United States Navy of battlefleet engagements and command of the seas.

———

The war and its consequences seemed to validate the theories of Alfred Thayer Mahan, whose published writings and correspondence influenced the shapers of strategy. It was Mahan's war in that it permanently wedded the United States Navy to his preferred strategy of capital-ship warfare, the goal of which was command of the seas achieved through decisive engagements between battlefleets. Trafalgar was always his model, as anachronistic as this may have been in 1898.

At the same time that the Spanish–American War permanently transformed the strategy of the United States Navy it also fundamentally altered the geopolitical relationship between the United States and the rest of the world. With Spain's permanent cession of Guam and the Philippine Islands, the forwardmost American naval base in the Pacific was to be in the Philippines, at either Manila Bay or the more defensible Subic Bay. To secure its lines of communications to this island bastion, the United States Navy soon built bases in Hawaii and on Guam. One great question of the coming century would be whether this thin line could be protected against the other new sea power of the Pacific—Imperial Japan.

In the Caribbean, Cuba achieved nominal independence because Congress had appended the Teller Amendment prohibiting American acquisition of the island to the declaration of war. But the United States soon forced Cuba into semiprotectorate status by means of the Platt Amendment to the army appropriations bill of 1901. That device authorized the U.S. Army to maintain order on the island at the same time that the navy was guaranteed a permanent base at Guantánamo Bay. With another naval base in Puerto Rico and a quickening national interest in building a transisthmian canal, the United States was rapidly making the Caribbean an American lake, which the new Mahanian navy would soon have to defend against yet another rising sea power—Imperial Germany.

8

"Incomparably the Greatest Navy in the World"

1898 – 1918

THE turn-of-the-century transformation of American naval strategy was profound. As a direct result of the victories of 1898, the United States Navy abandoned its historic strategies of commerce raiding and coastal defense in wars against stronger powers and commerce raiding and offensive coastal operations in wars against weaker enemies. That strategy had consistently helped preserve the nation from defeat by the world's greatest sea power, Great Britain, and had persuaded France to terminate the Quasi War on terms acceptable to the United States. It had led to outright victory in the Mexican War. In the Civil War, an extension of the techniques learned in the Mexican War helped to strangle and partition the Confederacy. Looked at from the other side's vantage point, Confederate commerce raiding crippled the enemy's merchant marine, even though the Union's proximity and overwhelming material advantages nullified every effort by the Confederacy to defend the seaboard.

Now the United States Navy was turning its back on a history of great virtue. To the extent that the navy was abandoning a strategy followed instinctively by weaker powers, the revolution made sense. But the navy was also abandoning a strategy universally subscribed to by continental powers great and small—Russia and France, Sweden and Belgium—and in this regard it was dismissing as irrelevant the continental essence of the United States in favor of an insular model—

that of Great Britain—which by any geographical measure bore no resemblance to the North American colossus.

By adopting the Mahanian precepts of capital ships, fleet engagements, and command of the seas, the United States Navy was joining a league long dominated by Great Britain. More recently two other rising powers had entered the competition for command of the sea: Germany and Japan. Thus, by 1900, there were four competitors for the title of the world's greatest sea power. Forty-five years later, there was only the United States Navy. The epic story of the first half of the twentieth century is the systematic American elimination of its three great naval rivals.

John D. Long remained at the helm of the Navy Department in McKinley's last years. He was the perfect example of a reluctant imperialist. His "instincts and prejudices" repudiated annexation of the Philippines, but he convinced himself it was wise "to Americanize and civilize" the Filipinos and give them "a chance for independence, if they prefer it." American naval logistics became more important to Long than the historic American tradition of refraining from overseas territorial expansion. By December 1898 he had concluded, "We must establish naval stations at Porto Rico, Cuba, Guam, and Manila."

Within two months American troops were fighting Emilio Aquinaldo's Filipino nationalists outside Manila and Cavite, and Long became a wartime secretary once again. In three years of awful savagery on both sides, the navy was crucial to American offensive operations. Ships of the Asiatic Squadron conveyed soldiers to battle throughout the archipelago and softened up landing areas with bombardments. Marines and bluejackets landed to assault forts and to fight ashore. Offshore, the navy struggled to interdict shipments of guns and ammunition to the insurgents.

Secretary Long quickly discovered that deep-draft ships were less effective than smaller vessels for coastal interdiction, landings, and riverine operations. The gunboats *Petrel* and *Princeton* and the monitors *Monadnock* and *Monterey* proved themselves indispensable everywhere, whereas the cruisers *Baltimore* and *Charleston* were intimidating only in deep-water bays like Manila and Subic. Battleships were nowhere to be found in Philippine waters; Long kept most of them in the Atlantic as a hedge against Germany and Britain. The Philippine Insurrection therefore was the twentieth century's first brown-water war. Ugly in the field and unpopular at home, it demonstrated the limited utility of capital ships in the kind of conflict that would characterize many American naval operations of the twentieth century. But it taught lessons the U.S. Navy did not want to learn.

American imperialists valued the Philippines primarily as "pickets of the Pacific, standing guard at the entrances to trade with the millions of [people in] China and Korea, French Indo-China, the Malay Peninsula, and the islands of Indonesia." Pivotal China was in mortal danger of dismemberment. Russia, Japan, Germany, and France were nibbling at its ports and apparently waiting an opportune moment to divide and devour it. Only Great Britain and the United States saw future profit in continued access to open markets and investment opportunities under the enfeebled Manchu dynasty.

Very suddenly, on 6 September 1899, Secretary of State John Hay took a formal stand in favor of the "open door" of China. He sent identical notes to the major powers asking respect for equal trading opportunities within their spheres of special interest in China. That was the first of two sets of notes by which Hay enunciated a policy toward China that the United States lacked both the material and moral power to enforce in the long run. The second and politically more ambitious set called for China's "territorial and administrative entity." It went out on 3 July 1900 as a direct result of the Boxer Rebellion.

The "Boxers" were a secret society of militant Chinese nationalists who in 1900 went on a bloody antiforeign rampage culminating in a siege of the foreign legations in Peking (Beijing). The European powers and Japan landed a multinational relief expedition at the seaport of Tientsin (Tianjin), and the United States joined in. The ostensible American goal was to help save endangered Americans in Peking; the equally compelling motive was to keep an eye on the other interventionists and discourage permanent occupation and vengeful partition of China. The exercise gave John Long a second imperial skirmish to fight simultaneously with the Philippine Insurrection.

The Western intervention in China coincided with the Republican National Convention, which drew Long from Washington for several weeks while he was a candidate for the vice presidential nomination, which went eventually to Governor Theodore Roosevelt of New York. Still, the secretary found time personally to bid farewell to a contingent of marines departing from Washington, D.C., for China. The moment etched itself into a mind tutored in the classics:

There is something very pathetic and, at the same time, very stirring, in such scenes. Yesterday, I took my translation of [the] *Aeneid* and read the scene where King Evander sends troops, under the command of his son, Pallas, to fight the battles of Aeneas. After all, it was the same scene over again; the same tears of parting, the same high spirit of the boys that were going to the front. The same parade, in marching and glistening of arms; the same love and sorrow of mothers, wives and sisters.

This gentle man from Massachusetts had drunk from the bitter cup of imperial warfare. Now he was being retired by a party and country that found the warrior ethic of Theodore Roosevelt more consistent with the mood of the new century.

In the hot summer of transition Long ordered the deputy commander of the Asiatic station, Rear Admiral Louis Kempff on the cruiser *Newark,* to cooperate with the European squadrons off the Taku (Daqu) forts shielding Tientsin—the same waters where Flag Officer Josiah Tattnall in 1859 had joined a British assault against the Chinese in the metaphoric belief that "blood is thicker than water." But Long was as wary of European intentions as anyone in the Mc-Kinley administration. As early as December 1898 he had instructed Commodore Dewey to scan the China coast for a place where the United States might extract "the same concessions in some Chinese port, for the benefit of our ships, and the extension of our commerce, as are enjoyed by some other nations." During the crusade against the Boxers he persuaded Secretary of State Hay to extort a base from China in Sansha Bay, on the China coast above Foochow (Fuzhou) at the northern entrance to the Formosa Straits. Japan, the predominant non-Chinese power in the region, blocked the ploy by pointing out to Hay that he had contravened his own principle of maintaining China's political integrity.

To match the Europeans' firepower during the intervention, Long temporarily reinforced the northern element of the Asiatic Squadron with the 11,500-ton battleship *Kentucky.* As the crisis peaked in the late summer of 1900, the squadron numbered forty-two ships, compared to the North Atlantic's six. Most of those were soon withdrawn to reestablish the European Squadron—shut down as a war measure in 1898—or to patrol the Caribbean, where new naval bases at Guantánamo Bay, Cuba, and in Puerto Rico were encouraging the United States to become a regional policeman.

The postwar deployment of John D. Long's ships followed the familiar nineteenth-century pattern of global distribution among the overseas cruising stations, but several of his administrative reforms broke new ground. To end a half-century of professional rivalry, he forced an amalgamation of the line officers and engineer corps and insisted that future line officers master the rudiments of steam engineering as midshipmen at the Naval Academy. No longer would there be a body of second-class officers who manipulated the engines but were forbidden to con the powerful new steamers coming on line in steady annual accretions. To streamline the design and construction of new ships, Long tried to consolidate the governing bureaus of the navy, but the bureau chiefs, the "little princes of equal power," blocked him.

Congress could have curtailed the autonomy of the bureau chiefs by creating a naval chief of staff, a measure favored by older reformers like Rear Admiral Stephen B. Luce and younger ones like Bradley A. Fiske and William S. Sims. Long's rejection of that step as detrimental to civilian control over the navy left him in desperate need of administrative coherence among the navy's most senior officers at the department in Washington. His solution was the General Board of the Navy. Created by his edict on 13 March 1900, it could be eliminated at a stroke of the secretary's pen. His appointment of Admiral George Dewey as the board's first president was an inspired containment of power: Dewey would advise the secretary on strategy, war plans, and ship design; he would not command a single operating unit.

If the "bottom line" of a navy is its ships, John D. Long should rank as a great secretary. By 1900 the United States stood sixth among the world's naval powers in battleships commissioned or under construction. In the summer of 1901 a total of sixty ships of all classes were under construction, and the $78 million appropriation bill passed that fall was the largest in American peacetime history. In addition to battleships, this balanced fleet included cruisers, destroyers, monitors, gunboats, and six true harbingers of the future: the *Holland*-class submarines. When Long retired in April 1902 the navy was rated fourth in the world, after Great Britain, France, and Russia. That standing reflected more than the work of a caretaker. It was a generous bequest to Long's former assistant secretary, Theodore Roosevelt, who became president—and in effect his own secretary of the navy—upon the assassination of William McKinley in September 1901.

From the outset of the Roosevelt administration, the four great Mahanian sea powers of the twentieth century—Great Britain, the

United States, Germany, and Japan—choreographed a complex strategic ballet. Threatened in home waters by the expanding German battlefleet and desirous of concentrating more of its own heavy ships in the English Channel, Britain made two adjustments of force that directly affected the United States. In 1902 the Foreign Office negotiated an Anglo-Japanese alliance directed in large measure against Russian expansion in the Far East but subject to American interpretation as an erosion of the already tenuous security of the Philippine Islands. In 1906 the Royal Navy closed its base at Jamaica, leaving the United States Navy as the unquestioned master of the Caribbean and the West Indies. Admiral John Fisher was confident that in those waters "the protection of British interests was very properly entrusted to the United States Navy, as we are at any time ready to protect theirs in any part of the world where our ships have to be present and theirs have not."

The Royal Navy's virtual withdrawal from the Caribbean and the West Indies eliminated Great Britain as a possible naval threat in the Western Hemisphere. By the same token German aggression was unlikely. Germany lacked bases in the Western Hemisphere, and in Europe Berlin faced potential enemy armies on two fronts. Additionally, the Royal Navy stood between Germany and the United States. As the historians Harold and Margaret Sprout have observed, Roosevelt and his naval strategists "might reasonably have taken a highly optimistic view of the politico-strategic outlook in the Western Atlantic." Instead, Roosevelt formed an "obsession" about German intentions and capabilities. "The specter of German aggression in the Caribbean or elsewhere in Latin America, became a veritable nightmare with him." This "pathological suspicion" of the kaiser and Germany was widely held in the Roosevelt coterie, and it precluded stationing the "main fighting fleet in the Pacific where, after 1900, it was more urgently needed than in the Atlantic."

The United States Navy had historically divided the Pacific Ocean into two operating zones, with a squadron for each. For purposes of strategic planning in the capital ship era, an east–west division of the Pacific still made sense. The only potential major enemy in the eastern Pacific was now Japan, which accepted the Mahanian premise that the most important objective of naval warfare was the destruction of the enemy's fighting fleet. But to invade the West Coast of the United States, Japan's battlefleet would have to include a large number of auxiliary vessels for resupply and repair in a hostile environment. The escort of those auxiliaries in turn would severely tax the invading fleet. The strategic and tactical advantage therefore would lie with the defending American battlefleet, which could choose when and where to fight.

The Sprouts have emphasized "the remarkable security which the United States had come to enjoy, as a result of geographical isolation, of its own naval development, and of the increasing complexites of naval technology." Ostensibly Theodore Roosevelt "understood these facts more clearly" than anyone else, and the inherent superiority of continental American defense over an offensive Japanese seaborne assault should have called into question the entire Mahanian formula. But during the 1907–1908 crisis with Japan over racism in California, the president "displayed astonishing alarm lest the distinctly inferior Japanese Navy launch an attack in force on our Pacific seaboard." Rationality did not necessarily dominate Roosevelt's strategy.

The president was on sounder ground in depicting the Philippines as the American "heel of Achilles" in 1907. Acquisition of Guam and the Philippines gave the United States sites for bases which could support large-scale naval operations in the western Pacific. But the bases were undeveloped, and the fleet was not strong enough to defend them with certainty against attack by a major naval power, that is, Japan. The new island possessions therefore were as much liabilities as assets, a fact recognized at the time by John D. Long. The dilemma defied solution so long as the United States retained sovereignty over the Philippines, as the Sprouts observed cogently:

> An American fleet, strong enough to guarantee security to the Philippines, could destroy the Japanese Navy and blockade Japan. On the other hand, a fleet that could defend the Japanese homeland against the United States, would constitute a standing menace to the security of the Philippines. Any aggressive movement on the part of either Power to strengthen its navy would quickly arouse anxiety in the other country. While the United States was potentially the stronger, it was not then certain that the American people would support their government to the bitter end in a naval race with Japan.

The strategic picture in the Far East was darkened further by the Anglo-Japanese Alliance of 1902, the terms of which assured Tokyo of Britain's neutrality in the event of a war between Japan and one other power. If Japan fought two other powers, the English were obliged to join the Japanese as cobelligerents. Washington therefore would be denied even benevolent neutrality from London in the event of a Japanese–American war.

Despite this diplomatic isolation, President Roosevelt at first identified Russia as America's principal Far Eastern rival. Russia's aspirations for economic hegemony in Manchuria, a 400,000-square-mile province in northeastern China, competed with those of well-placed American entrepreneurs. Japan also saw a threat from Russia, both to its desire for a naval base at Port Arthur in Manchuria and to its aspirations for a free hand in Korea. In a surprise attack on 8 February 1904, ten Japanese destroyers slipped into the naval base at Port Arthur and struck Russia's anchored battleship-cruiser force. The blow crippled Russia's Far East fleet, and Roosevelt cheered, "for Japan is playing our game." By the time Port Arthur surrendered in January 1905, the entire Russian Asiatic fleet was destroyed, and Roosevelt was changing his mind.

In late May 1905, at the Battle of Tsushima Straits, the Russian Baltic fleet went to the bottom in a Trafalgar-like encounter with the rampaging Japanese. Roosevelt was now alarmed. He offered mediation and hosted negotiations near the naval base at Portsmouth, New Hampshire. In the peace signed on 29 August 1905, Japan achieved preponderance in Manchuria and Korea but was irritated by Roosevelt's inability to extract the traditional cash indemnity from a vanquished power.

The seeds of conflict were germinating. By defeating historic empires, emergent Japan and the United States had won principal roles for themselves in East Asia. They now faced each other. Japan had covered its strategic flank by an alliance with Great Britain. A less formal rapprochement between London and Washington permitted Theodore Roosevelt to meet the Far Eastern threat in a more typically American way: through industrial output and technological grandeur.

One key to Roosevelt's naval strategy was the Panana Canal. It would cut the maritime distance between Cuba and San Francisco from about 14,000 to 5,200 miles, greatly facilitating the transfer of battleships from the Atlantic to the Pacific. In future crises with Germany or Japan, ships would be spared the taxing high-speed runs around treacherous Cape Horn such as the *Oregon* had had to make from the West Coast to Florida. A canal would give the United States a two-ocean navy at much less than twice the cost of a single-ocean fleet. It was now possible to build and fortify a canal unilaterally, because Britain had conceded that right to the United States as the core of the Anglo-American rapprochement in the Hay–Pauncefote Treaty of November, 1901.

The opportunity came in 1903, when a group of U.S.-inspired Panamanians revolted against Colombia. Alerted to the impending uprising, the acting secretary of state on 3 November 1903 cabled instructions for the commanding officer of the unarmored 1,300-ton gunboat *Nashville*, moored at the Panamanian harbor of Colón: "In the interests of peace make every effort to prevent [Colombian] Government troops at Colón from proceeding to Panama [City]." On 4 November Commander John Hubbard landed a small force. The *Nashville*'s sailors kept the Colombian soldiers off the American-owned railroad until a battalion of marines arrived the next day. Secretary of State John Hay immediately recognized the revolutionary government. In less than two weeks he negotiated the Hay–Bunau–Varilla Treaty granting the United States sovereignty over a 10-mile-wide zone. Construction of the canal began on 4 May 1904; it took ten years to complete.

The intervention in the 1903 Panamanian revolution against Colombia dramatically exposed the Roosevelt administration's ruthless determination to control the Caribbean and the West Indies through the threat and use of naval force. In January of the same year the German navy bombarded two Venezuelan forts as part of an Anglo-German scheme of intimidation intended to force Venezuela to repay part of its debt to European investors. Theodore Roosevelt brooded, "The only power which may be a menace to us in anything like the immediate future is Germany." A year later the chronic instability and insolvency of the Dominican Republic intensified his concern for the viability of the Monroe Doctrine. On 6 December 1904 he advised Europe generally, and Germany in particular, not to intervene in the Western Hemisphere. The United States, as a "civilized nation," would serve as the "international police power."

President Roosevelt and his successors through Herbert Hoover (1929–1933) molded this "corollary" to the Monroe Doctrine into a rhetorical umbrella to cover American naval and Marine Corps intervention throughout the Caribbean. The list of countries affected included Nicaragua, Honduras, Mexico, Cuba, Haiti, and the Dominican Republic. Roosevelt's second secretary of state, the corporate lawyer Elihu Root, saw this as a natural progression in the line of duty: The "inevitable effect of our building the Canal must be to require us to police the surrounding premises." Some of the occupations were quite protracted, and all of them had the objective of altering the political and social structure of the occupied country. In this regard the new naval imperialism differed fundamentally from the "gunboat diplomacy" of the nineteenth century, the object of which had been confined to winning favorable treatment for Americans imperiled in alien societies.

Within the navy, the agency charged with planning for American hegemony in the Caribbean was the General Board. Headed by Admiral George Dewey, it consisted principally of the director of the Office of Naval Intelligence, Captain Charles D. Sigsbee, and the president of the Naval War College, Captain French E. Chadwick. The brightest junior officers of the day were assigned as "staff assistants." Several members of the board had served with Dewey in the Philippines, and all had heard the stories of his encounters with the German fleet in Manila Bay. Sigsbee and Chadwick were typical in their conviction that Germany harbored imperial ambitions regarding Brazil, Cuba, Santo Domingo, the Danish West Indies, Venezuela, and Haiti. They needed little prodding to develop a plan for war against Germany.

Their working assumption was summarized in a 1904 War College report: When "Germany's accelerated [shipbuilding] program is completed, she will still be unable to meet England successfully but will surpass us in naval strength. Germany will then be ready to take issue with us over the Monroe Doctrine." In Plan Black they concluded that Germany would first try to seize Puerto Rico and the offshore island of Culebra as preparation for landings in Cuba and hit-and-run strikes along the Gulf Coast of the United States. To counter that, they planned to intercept and destroy the attacking German battlefleet with a preemptive capital-ship reinforcement of Puerto Rico and a sweeping search of the approaches to the island by lighter vessels. The navy had tested the concept at the time of the 1902–1903 crisis over Germany's blockade and bombardment of Venezuela. Admiral Dewey himself had directed an exercise combining fifty-four ships of the North Atlantic, European, and South Atlantic Squadrons. The mock "raiding" force easily eluded the screen of defenders and slipped into Puerto Rico, as the War College had soberly predicted.

Dewey reached the naïve and unwarranted conclusion that the exercise had been a hugely successful "object lesson to the Kaiser." His General Board doggedly persevered with Plan Black, a curiously prescient mirror of the secretly evolving German *Operationsplan III*. The admiral and his coterie decided that the United States ought to outbuild the Germans, whose Fleet Law of 1900 aimed at thirty-eight first-line battleships by 1920. The proportionate counterweight in American battleships, in the opinion of two influential members of the General Board, was "one for each state in the union." This romantic gambit curiously discounted the historic role of the Royal Navy as a check on European naval penetration of the Western Hemisphere, and it certainly did not stampede the Congress. Sadly, by focusing on the German battlefleet, the navy's top planners missed the point: The German threat to American maritime interests would come from the fragile new submarine, not from the glamorous battleships that attracted all of the attention.

Dewey's gifted aide during the Caribbean fleet exercise, Commander Nathan Sargent, drew a tactical conclusion vaguely reminiscent of the *mea culpas* sounded after the fleet mobilization following the *Virginius* crisis of 1873: The "formations, both in line and in column, were ragged, distance and guide being badly kept, speed not well regulated and turns unskillfully executed." The Navy Department made the bureaucratic response to Nathan's observations: It withdrew the battleships from the Atlantic and Mediterranean cruising squadrons and combined them into a single battleship force in the North Atlantic Fleet. By operating together as a unit throughout the year, they would maneuver more smartly during future exercises, and by being clustered into a single unit they met the Mahanian strategic dictate for concentration of force. The redeployment was historic and lasting. Despite the growing menace of Japan, the navy would not create a comparable Pacific battlefleet until after the defeat of Germany in World War I.

═══

The Anglo-Japanese Alliance, Japan's conclusive victories over a major European power at Port Arthur and Tsushima, the inability of the U.S. Army and Navy to agree on a plan of fortifications for the Philippines, and vicious anti-Japanese eruptions in California combined to set the navy's teeth on edge by the middle of the second Roosevelt administration. In the summer of 1907, as riots in San Francisco elicited war cries in Japan, the president asked for contingency plans. Under Admiral Dewey's chairmanship the Joint Army-Navy Board, created in 1903 to harmonize interservice planning, agreed in principle on how to fight Japan. The Joint Board called for a spirited defense of a base in the Philippines by army troops and by the navy's Asiatic gunboats, monitors, and torpedo boats. The larger warships would withdraw to Pearl Harbor to rendezvous with the

Atlantic Fleet. The combined battle force then would thrust back across the central Pacific to relieve the defenders and reclaim the Philippines preparatory to isolation of the Japanese home islands. This scenario, formalized as Plan Orange in 1911, anticipated Admiral Chester Nimitz's central Pacific campaign of World War II.

A paralyzing disagreement remained over whether to fortify Subic Bay, as Dewey wished, or Manila, as the army preferred. In the opinion of a furious President Roosevelt, the "vacillation" of the Joint Board on this question did "grave harm" to both services. It did more than that. A national consensus on how to defend the Philippines was never reached, and as a result a major fortified naval base was never constructed west of Hawaii. Japan reaped the rewards of that interservice rivalry in 1941–1942.

The one positive result of the deliberations of mid-1907 was a recommendation for a Pacific Ocean practice cruise of the battlefleet as a means of impressing Japan with American naval might. The idea was conveyed by Captain Richard Wainwright to President Roosevelt on 27 June. It was attractive because the exercise would neither violate the doctrine of concentration of force by dividing the battlefleet nor alarm the politically sensitive and powerful East Coast by transferring the battleships to the Pacific.

Roosevelt selected his favorite war horse, "Fighting Bob" Evans, now a rear admiral, to command sixteen battleships plus auxiliaries in an unprecedented world cruise. Steaming out of Hampton Roads, Virginia, on 16 December 1907, the "Great White Fleet" rounded Cape Horn; touched at San Francisco; visited New Zealand, Australia, the Philippines, and Japan; and cut through the Indian Ocean, the Suez Canal, the Mediterranean. It covered 46,000 miles without a serious breakdown. On 22 February 1909 Roosevelt and his naval aide, William S. Sims, boarded the presidential yacht *Mayflower* to welcome it home. Eighty years later the cruise remained synonymous with Teddy Roosevelt's naval policy.

On 3 March 1909, in a letter to his chosen heir, William Howard Taft, Roosevelt accurately summed up as his naval "legacy" the strategic doctrine that had guided him as president:

> Under no circumstances divide the battleship fleet between the Atlantic and Pacific Oceans prior to the finishing of the Panama Canal. . . . It is nearly four years since the Russian–Japanese War. There were various factors that brought Russia's defeat; but the most important by all odds was her having divided her fleet into three utterly

unequal divisions. The entire Japanese force was always used to smash some fraction of the Russian force.

He sent a similar credo to Captain Mahan the same day.

Roosevelt's real monument was the growing strength of the navy, which ranked second or third in the world when he left office. Britain stood first, and Germany was second in overall tonnage; but in the category of capital ships only the Royal Navy outnumbered the United States Navy. In the decade since the Spanish–American War a consistent building program had added an average of more than one battleship to the fleet annually. Early in the presidential election year of 1908 three more were commissioned: the *Mississippi, New Hampshire* and *Idaho*. These were the last of the "pre-dreadnoughts."

Dewey and the General Board, abetted by the brilliant gunnery officer William S. Sims, had pressed President Roosevelt and Congress to authorize construction of dreadnoughts—the superships of the day. The opposition had been formidable; no less an authority than Alfred Thayer Mahan publicly espoused the traditional battleship bristling with guns of various sizes. But in 1906 Sims bested the old prophet in a journal article that must rank as the most seminal one ever published on the arcane subject of naval gunnery. Sims was lobbying for an "all-big gun" battleship of great speed and displacement in the same year that King Edward VII secretly christened H.M.S. *Dreadnought*. Persuaded by Sims and by reports on the Russo-Japanese War written by the trusted Nathan Sargent, Dewey induced the House Naval Affairs Committee to fund American dreadnoughts.

The first one, the *Michigan*, was commissioned in 1910. The *Nevada* and *Oklahoma* were authorized a year later. They marked the transition from coal-burning to oil-fired boilers and a 40-percent increase in the operating range of capital ships. The *Nevada* embodied everything that William S. Sims and the reformers had sought in battleship design: enormous offensive and defensive power. One sagacious observer concludes, "For the first time since the monitors of the Civil War, our navy had ships of the battle line that could take it as well as dish it out." Sims's reward was to be named the *Nevada*'s first commanding officer in 1914.

William Howard Taft had inherited a world-class capital-ship navy, and he intended to keep it that way. The policy of building two dreadnoughts a year, he said, was "one Roosevelt policy about which there should not be the slightest question." There were two others:

"the union of all the fighting material at one point" and completion of the Panama Canal. Taft would concentrate the battlefleet in the Atlantic and "when we need it in the [Far] East we will send it all there." Congress in 1911 and 1912 ensured the fleet's unhampered access to the canal with a $5 million appropriation for fortifications, a step the General Board regarded as "not only a right, but a duty." The navy also pressed ahead with dredging the channel into Pearl Harbor, Hawaii, the fulcrum of defensive and offensive operations in the Pacific, and on 14 December 1911 the armored cruiser *California* became the first heavy warship to thread its way through the coral.

The Taft administration strengthened the foundations of American naval power in the eastern Pacific but refused to expand the Asiatic Fleet, which by 1910 had dwindled to three cruisers and an assortment of smaller vessels, including a half-dozen gunboats patrolling China's Yangtze River (Chang Jiang). Simultaneously, Taft espoused "dollar diplomacy" and an activist "open door" policy in China without calculating the possible impact that an economically aggressive and morally righteous but militarily weak China policy might have on expansionistic Japan. In 1912 the American minister to China, William J. Calhoun, bemoaned the American condition:

> If we had a fleet of battleships ploughing the Pacific; if we had a foreign policy, persistent and consistent in its nature, and supported by the "big stick"; if the necessity of market conditions once came home to the American people in such a way as to make them support a national policy in the Far East that insured the "open door" and equal opportunities, the attitude of the nations towards us might be very different. As it is, we are comparatively helpless. Diplomacy, however astute, however beneficent and altruistic, it may be, if it is not supported by the force that not only commands but demands respect and consideration, it will avail of but little.

Calhoun's lament anticipated the critique of American Far Eastern policy that has been sounded by "realists" ever since.

Taft's challenge to Japanese hegemony in Manchuria coincided with Washington's refusal to tolerate a Japanese naval toehold in Mexico's Magdalena Bay, an acquisition that seemed likely in 1912. Republican Senator Henry Cabot Lodge was the instrument of exclusion. He sponsored a Senate resolution warning that the United States would view with "grave concern" Japan's acquiring a Mexican harbor "for naval or military purposes." This so-called Lodge Corollary to the Monroe Doctrine was a legislative expression of the General Board's proscriptive attitude toward any naval expansion into the Western Hemisphere by Japan or Old World powers.

Germany, the General Board's European hobgoblin, was the Taft navy's chosen yardstick for measuring its own potency. In 1911 Germany operated thirty-six battleships, the United States thirty-seven; but the Germans had two more armored cruisers than the Americans. It was a tight and expensive naval race; each battleship demanded a screen of cruisers and destroyers, and all of those required crews, maintenance, and overhaul. The East Coast was the economic beneficiary. The dreadnoughts and all battleships less than ten years old—a total of twenty-one—were assigned to the active battlefleet based at the four principal Atlantic navy yards: Boston, New York, Philadelphia, and Norfolk.

Secretary of the Navy George von Lengerke Meyer in November 1911 advised Congress that in order to ensure a "balanced fleet" stronger than Germany's in the future it would be necessary to build seven battleships, eight battle cruisers, thirty-three protected cruisers, 132 destroyers, thirty-eight submarines, and assorted support vessels. But by 1911 a divided Republican party had surrendered chairmanship of the House Naval Affairs Committee to the Democrats, and an appropriation of this magnitude was out of the question. The German shipbuilding program would continue to outweigh the American by 963,845 tons to 824,162. So even though Congress authorized $60 million more for the navy during the Taft presidency than in the four years of the second Roosevelt administration, the United States Navy was losing its capital ship race with Germany.

It was an ill-conceived race in the first place. In the 1895 dispute with Great Britain over the Venezuela boundary, Secretary of State Richard Olney had demonstrated that a verbal "twenty-inch gun" was more effective than naval ordnance in deflecting great power challenges to the Monroe Doctrine. Since that time Anglo-American relations had been amicable, and in the General Board's estimation they were "particularly cordial" by 1910. This meant that despite British cooperation with Germany's intimidation of Venezuela in 1902, the Royal Navy still barricaded the Atlantic against continental European penetration of the Western Hemisphere. Moreover, the Anglo-German naval race was in full swing by 1911, and there was no chance that Germany would lower its home guard to fight a numerically equal United States Navy in America's maritime backyard.

A solitary senior American naval officer had grasped the impli-

John Paul Jones, one of the most illustrious officers of the Revolutionary War navy, serving a quarterback gun aboard the *Bonhomme Richard*. He directed the aiming and firing of the smoothbore muzzle-loading guns while members of the crew stood by to reload and marines in the rigging offered some protection with rifles or muskets. (Beverley R. Robinson Collection, U.S. Naval Academy Museum)

Stephen Decatur, Jr., in dress uniform on the deck of a warship of the sailing navy. The breeches of two muzzle-loading smoothbores are visible on the right. Behind Decatur is a capstan used to raise and lower sails and hoist the anchors. (Beverley R. Robinson Collection, U.S. Naval Academy Museum)

The 44-gun frigate *Constitution* dismasting and capturing the British frigate *Guerrière* on 19 August 1812. In this engraving the *Constitution* has outmanuevered her opponent and "crossed the T" enabling her to "rake" the *Guerrière*'s deck with deadly and disabling fire from her broadsides. (Beverley R. Robinson Collection, U.S. Naval Academy Museum)

Oliver H. Perry being rowed from the 20-gun brig *Lawrence* to the *Niagara* during the Battle of Lake Erie on 10 September 1813. The American naval campaigns on Erie, Ontario, and Champlain were more decisive to the outcome of the War of 1812 than the more glamorous and famous frigate actions on the oceans. (Beverley R. Robinson Collection, U.S. Naval Academy Museum)

The U.S. steam frigate *Merrimack*. This engraving shows the hybrid nature of the ship, with sails flying and funnel spewing smoke. Commissioned in 1855, displacing 3,200 tons and mounting forty guns, the *Merrimack* was the leader of a class of ships that marked the end of the free-roving sailing frigates and the beginning of the American dependence on overseas supplies of coal and machine parts. (Beverley R. Robinson Collection, U.S. Naval Academy Museum)

The 12,000-man U.S. Army landing force of General Winfield Scott leaving the ships of the Gulf Squadron on 9 March 1847 and rowing in surf boats to attack Veracruz, Mexico. The mixed composition of the squadron is evident in this lithograph. (Beverley R. Robinson Collection, U.S. Naval Academy Museum)

The U.S. frigate *Cumberland* being attacked and sunk by the C.S.S. *Virginia*—formerly the U.S.S. *Merrimack*—at Hampton Roads, Virginia, on 8 March 1862. This engagement dramatically underscored the vulnerability of wooden-hulled ships when attacked by armored, steam-driven rams. (Beverley R. Robinson Collection, U.S. Naval Academy Museum)

The immortal duel between the C.S.S. *Virginia* and the *Monitor* at Hampton Roads, Virginia, on 9 March 1862, with an assortment of warships observing. Tactically and strategically this encounter was a draw, but it inspired the Union to build many more monitors for blockade duty in the shallow coastal waters of the South. (Beverley R. Robinson Collection, U.S. Naval Academy Museum)

Shallow-draft Union gunboats attacking Fort Henry, which commanded the Tennessee River, in February 1862. The effective fire of the gunboats silenced the fort's batteries, permitting its capture by the army. This sort of riverine operation would inspire the naval high command a century later, during the Vietnam War. (Beverley R. Robinson Collection, U.S. Naval Academy Museum)

Rear Admiral David G. Farragut observing the action from the rigging of the screw sloop *Hartford* during the attack on Mobile Bay, Alabama, on 5 August 1864. The crew in the foreground is loading a smoothbore gun to fire at the Confederate ironclad ram *Tennessee* close alongside on the right. (Beverley R. Robinson Collection, U.S. Naval Academy Museum)

The C.S.S. *Alabama*, history's most famous American commerce raider. Under the command of Raphael Semmes, she took sixty Union merchant vessels in a rampage that helped to permanently weaken the U.S. merchant marine. (U.S. Naval Institute)

The protected cruiser *Atlanta*, launched in October 1884. She and the other two "*ABC*" cruisers—the *Boston* and *Chicago*—marked the advent of the new navy of steam propulsion and steel hulls. The transitional nature of the three ships is shown in this picture, where the sailors are manning the *Atlanta*'s yardarms, which carried sails for cruising. (U.S. Naval Institute)

Rear Admiral Stephen B. Luce (1827–1917), the officer who inspired the creation of the U.S. Naval War College and became its first president in 1884. He was responsible for the assignment of Captain Alfred Thayer Mahan to the War College faculty in 1885. (U.S. Naval Institute)

Alfred Thayer Mahan (1840–1914), the naval officer who popularized the idea of battlefleets in his lectures at the War College and in his numerous books, especially *The Influence of Sea Power upon History, 1660–1783*, published in 1890. (U.S. Naval Institute)

This "bows on" shot of the battleship *Connecticut* shows the formidable power and majesty that made battleships so popular with naval leaders beginning about 1890. Displacing 16,000 tons, she is shown here on a trial run shortly after her launching in September 1904. (U.S. Naval Institute)

Battleships *Ohio* (*l.*) and *Missouri* (*r.*) passing through the locks of the newly opened Panama Canal on 16 July 1915. The war in Europe was on, but the United States remained neutral. This symbolic passage of two battleships expressed the navy's willingness to fight with equal commitment in the Pacific or Atlantic, depending on where the challenge to national interests was greater. (U.S. Naval Institute)

Secretary of the Navy Josephus Daniels and Chief of Naval Operations William S. Benson. These two men, abetted by Assistant Secretary of the Navy Franklin Delano Roosevelt, directed the navy's strategy from Washington, D.C., during World War I. (U.S. Naval Institute)

Submarine chasers in the Brooklyn Navy Yard, 1918. These were among the vessels designed to defeat the U-boat and protect transatlantic shipping in a strategy advocated by William S. Sims which challenged the prevalent Mahanian doctrine. (Photograph by Burnell Poole, courtesy of the family of Burnell Poole)

The navy's first aircraft carrier, the U.S.S. *Langley*, was a converted collier recommissioned in 1920 to conduct experiments in launching and recovering aircraft from her flush right deck. (U.S. Naval Institute)

Within twenty years of the *Langley*'s commissioning, carrier-borne naval aviation had become a major feature of fleet operations. This 1940 photograph shows the fleet air arm flying over the battle line. Even though aircraft carriers and their air groups were now included in the fleets, the battleship remained at the center of plans and operations. (U.S. Naval Institute)

Pearl Harbor, Hawaii, from the air on 30 October 1941. Ford Island lies in the center of the photograph, and "battleship row" is to the left of Ford Island. On 7 December 1941 Japanese carrier-based aircraft swept down on this tranquil scene, destroying once and for all the primacy of the battleship in naval warfare. (U.S. Naval Institute)

President Franklin Roosevelt conferring with his two senior Pacific commanders, General Douglas MacArthur (*l.*) and Admiral Chester W. Nimitz (*r.*), on a cruiser at Pearl Harbor in 1944. (U.S. Naval Institute)

A boarding party from the escort carrier *Guadalcanal*, commanded by Captain Daniel V. Gallery, capturing the German U-505 in a hunter-killer antisubmarine action on 4 June 1944. This was perhaps the most dramatic episode in the Atlantic war against the U-boat. Gallery was from Chicago, where U-505 is now on exhibit. (U.S. Naval Institute)

A crowded Normandy beachhead shortly after the landing of 6 June 1944. The greatest amphibious assault in history was in many ways the end of the Atlantic war for the navy. (U.S. Naval Institute)

The carriers *Wasp, Yorktown, Hornet, Hancock, Ticonderoga,* and *Lexington* at Ulithi Atoll in the Pacific, 8 December 1944. This assembled naval power stretching to the horizon epitomizes the popular image of carrier aviation as the principal ingredient of the victory over Japan in World War II. (U.S. Naval Institute)

One of the technological secrets to prolonged operations by American aircraft carriers is the ability to replenish while underway ("unrep"). This photograph documents the technique as practiced during the Korean War. The carrier *Antietam* and the destroyer *Shelton* take on fuel simultaneously from the oil tanker *Tolovana* while the carrier *Essex* and her destroyer escort wait their turn. (U.S. Naval Institute)

U.S.S. *Nautilus*, the world's first atomic-powered submarine, signaled "under-way on nuclear power" on 17 January 1955. The fruit of Hyman Rickover's labors, she was the necessary predecessor to all subsequent attack and missile-launching nuclear-powered submarines. (U.S. Naval Institute)

The navy's first nuclear surface task force which began a circumnavigation of the globe in July 1964. The task group did not refuel during a voyage of 30,000 miles. From the bottom, the ships are the carrier *Enterprise*, the missile cruiser *Long Beach*, and the missile frigate *Bainbridge*. This assembly eloquently bespeaks the navy's confidence in the supercarrier, especially nuclear-powered ones. (U.S. Naval Institute)

Three PBR's (Patrol Boat, River) of "Operation Game Warden" during the riverine warfare in Vietnam, 1967–1969. Game Warden was initiated in 1966 primarily to harass the Viet Cong, who were using sampans plying the intricate waterways of the Mekong Delta to resupply themselves with men and matériel. (U.S. Naval Institute)

A port bow view of the *Wisconsin*, an *Iowa*-class battleship. First launched in 1943 and placed in "mothballs" after World War II, she was recommissioned in October 1988. The 16-inch guns are now of limited value in surface combat, but the navy contends that they remain useful for offshore bombardment. The impressiveness of the ship gives her a role in maintaining a "presence" overseas as an instrument of modern "gunboat diplomacy." (U.S. Naval Institute)

Admiral Elmo R. Zumwalt, Jr., the senior naval commander in Vietnam from September 1968 until June 1970 and the chief of naval operations from July 1970 to June 1974, was an ardent advocate of the "surface navy." (U.S. Naval Institute)

John F. Lehman, Jr., was President Ronald Reagan's secretary of the navy from 1981 to April 1987. He emphasized aircraft carriers and aimed for a "600-ship navy." (U.S. Naval Institute)

The guided missile frigate *Gary* (FFG-51), which saw service in the Persian Gulf in 1988 and 1989–1990 is 453 feet long, displaces 4,100 tons, and is armed with two helicopters. A small workhorse capable of surface, anti-aircraft, and antisubmarine warfare, she is the kind of ship advocated by critics of the large capital ships that have dominated the American navy arsenal for much of the twentieth century. (U.S. Naval Institute) cations of the European alliance system for American security from the outset. In 1903 the godfather of modern American naval strategy, Rear Admiral Stephen B. Luce, incisively wrote, "It is not easy to see how the balance of power on this side of the world can be disturbed. . . . I do not share the common apprehension of Germany."

But the pervasive anxiety over German intentions was fueled by a powerful group of naval Anglophiles including Admiral Caspar F. Goodrich and Commander William S. Sims. In 1910 Sims promised a London audience a total American naval commitment if the British Empire was attacked by a foreign enemy. The previous year Goodrich, a Mahan protégé, had publicly proposed an Anglo-American division of responsibility for the defense of the Atlantic and Pacific. The persistent agitation for a capital ship navy superior to Germany's must therefore be attributed as much to political bias as to geopolitical realism.

The Taft administration showed similar disdain for dispassionate strategic calculations in its consistent intervention in Nicaragua. Theodore Roosevelt had lost interest in that politically turbulent Central American state once he had acquired Panama as the site for his transisthmian canal. But Taft's secretary of state, Philander C. Knox, found Nicaragua's dictator, José Santo Zelaya, so morally repugnant that he supported and sustained the revolution of Adolfo Díaz.

In May 1910 the Panama battalion of 354 marines, under the colorful Major Smedley D. Butler, was sent ashore from the 1,000-ton gunboat *Dubuque* to establish a neutral zone favorable to the rebels. Díaz was in power within three months. For the next two years Díaz was bolstered by Butler's battalion, a regiment under the command of Colonel Joseph H. Pendleton, and an assortment of sailors from American cruisers and gunboats. His survival was in doubt until the marines defeated two rebel armies in the fall of 1912. In November, the very month in which Taft lost the presidential election at home, the American combat units were withdrawn from Nicaragua.

The new Democratic president, Woodrow Wilson, had given little attention to foreign or naval policy prior to his election. His interests lay in domestic political and social reforms, and his cabinet appointments were made to consolidate his following and to repay partisan debts. He appointed the Midwestern agrarian populist and pacifist William Jennings Bryan as secretary of state. He picked an equally radical Southerner, Josephus Daniels, to be secretary of the navy. For sectional and temperamental balance within the department he named a New Yorker, Franklin Delano Roosevelt, to the number two position of assistant secretary of the navy.

Daniels was an odd mixture for a secretary of the navy: a Southern populist running a highly elitist institution; a prohibitionist who broke hallowed naval tradition by banishing wine from shipboard officers' wardrooms; an advocate of disarmament who referred to the members of the General Board as "statesmen." At meetings of the General Board he sat beside Dewey rather than in the presiding officer's chair, but the deference was a mark of courtesy and not a sign of concurrence with the board's recommendations. Dewey's men asked for four battleships in 1913 in order to achieve "a Fleet in 1920 of measurable equality with the Fleets of Germany and Japan." Daniels more modestly wanted "a well proportioned Navy" with "a capable and creditable fleet in both the Pacific and the Atlantic Oceans" so he cut the board's request in half. His "golden mean" matched the mood of the Congress in the spring of 1914. The two-battleship program sailed through the House, and the Senate added a third.

Daniels toyed with a concept of "parity" in battleship distribution between the Atlantic and Pacific coasts. The Panama Canal was nearly finished, and soon the full battlefleet could be expeditiously reunited in either ocean if war with Germany or Japan became imminent. But dividing the battleships was heresy to Daniels's young assistant secretary. Adhering to his distant cousin's dictum of strategic concentration, Franklin asked Theodore and Alfred Thayer Mahan to denounce publicly any division of the battlefleet, and they complied with articles in *The Outlook* and the *North American Review*. This early resort to public pressure by the navy's number two man was an omen of serious divisions at the top of the Navy Department.

The sometimes strained relationship between Franklin Roosevelt and his chief recalled "Uncle Ted's" experience with John D. Long. In both instances the senior man, a seasoned politician, was slow-moving and deliberate, whereas the younger was inexperienced and brash. Long and Daniels abhorred war. Neither Roosevelt flinched from it, and Franklin consistently took a more militant stand in international crises than his pacifist-minded boss. Both older men marveled at the presidential potential in their assistants, who came to Washington as navy buffs prepared to study and master the service while grooming themselves for higher office. Franklin particularly benefited from his seven and a half years as the secretary of the navy's senior deputy. It was, in the words of his biographer Nathan Miller, "the most thorough training conceivable for his later service as a war President."

The apprenticeship began immediately. Less than a month after assuming power in March 1913, the Wilson administration encountered a sharp international crisis precipitated by a California bill denying Japanese and other Orientals "ineligible to citizenship" the right to own land. Tokyo erupted in mass protests, and a genuine war scare followed passage of the act on 15 April. Throughout a two-month period of tension, President Wilson, Secretary of State Bryan, and Secretary of the Navy Daniels strove to avoid any provocative military or naval move that would further exacerbate relations. In their restraint they were not seconded by Assistant Secretary of the Navy Roosevelt, and they were deviously undercut by two of the most powerful men in uniform, the army's General Leonard Wood and the navy's Rear Admiral Bradley A. Fiske.

Much as Theodore had done in 1898, the younger Roosevelt in 1913 capitalized on a stint as acting secretary of the navy to stir up war sentiment. He carried an advisory to the president from Admiral Dewey's General Board declaring Japan's resentment toward the California measure "sufficiently serious to demand . . . preparation for possible war." He fired off "Secret and Confidential" telegrams to naval commanders detailing plans for operations "in the event of war." "You remember what happened the last time a Roosevelt occupied a similar position," he warned. But unlike 1898, there was no tangible *casus belli*, and the United States Navy was relatively weak in the prospective theater of operations. Wilson was not McKinley; he and Daniels squelched Roosevelt, Fiske, and the hawks on the Joint Board. Restrained diplomacy dissipated the crisis, but in its short duration it had exposed severe differences of opinion on naval strategy within the department.

Roosevelt's bellicosity surfaced again in April 1914. Woodrow Wilson had substituted a moralistic standard for the "big stick" and "dollar diplomacy," but his Latin American interventionism was no less political in purpose than that of his two Republican predecessors. He was determined to unseat the "government of butchers" in Mexico personified by General Victoriano Huerta, whom he described as a "diverting brute! . . . seldom sober and always impossible." He authorized arms shipments to the "Constitutionalist" rebel, Venustiano Carranza, and posted warships off the Mexican Gulf ports of Veracruz and Tampico.

On 9 April Huerta's troops arrested eight American sailors who were loading supplies on a whaleboat at Tampico. The local commander quickly apologized, but he refused to fire a twenty-one-gun salute to the American flag, as demanded by Rear Admiral Henry T. Mayo. Wilson backed the admiral's ultimatum, telling reporters that "the salute will be fired." He requested congressional authorization to intervene in force. Franklin Roosevelt was called home from a tour of Pacific Coast installations and on the way told a reporter the crisis meant, "War! And we're ready." Josephus Daniels muzzled his assistant, who, he said later, "was young then and made some mistakes."

Roosevelt nonetheless got the action he sought, and without the inconvenience of a declaration of war. The arrival at Veracruz of a German steamer loaded with machine guns and ammunition destined for Huerta provoked the administration to order the navy to interdict the shipment by seizing the customs house. On 21–22 April an assembled fleet including six battleships landed 4,000 sailors and marines. They were engaged by desperate street fighters, and before the city was captured seventeen Americans and at least 126 Mexicans died. The bloodshed temporarily united Mexico behind Huerta and cooled Wilson's ardor. No Mexican salute was ever fired. Huerta gave way to Carranza, and Carranza in turn was attacked by Francisco (Pancho) Villa. The navy was withdrawn from Veracruz in November, as the problems of American neutrality during a major European war finally drew the Navy Department's attention to the Atlantic.

The early months of World War I witnessed great excitement within the department. On 1 August 1914, the day Germany declared war on Russia, Roosevelt predicted, "It will be the greatest war in the world's history." Eager for action, he rushed to the department and was shocked to find that "everyone was asleep and apparently oblivious to the fact that the most terrible drama in history was about to be enacted." He decried the passive Daniels's excessive "faith in human nature and similar idealistic nonsense" and set to work "alone to get things ready . . . for what *ought* to be done by the Navy." He correctly identified the salient maritime issues as "Questions of refugees, of neutrality, of commerce." These were the historic problems that had bedeviled Presidents Washington, Adams, Jefferson, and Madison a century earlier, the last time the largest European continental power—France then, Germany now—had fought the leading European sea power—Britain, always.

Following the example set by George Washington in 1793,

Woodrow Wilson on 4 August 1914 issued the first of a series of neutrality proclamations. Two weeks later he begged every American to be "impartial in thought as well as in action." So far so good, but the American posture vis-à-vis Europe had altered profoundly in the century since the last Anglo-European war. Jefferson's idealized agrarian republic had matured into a transcontinental industrial giant exporting arms as well as foodstuffs. In the time of Washington and Jefferson the West Indies were a cockpit of European mercantile rivalry, attracting only those American merchantmen bold enough to risk seizure and confiscation as the price of doing business. In 1914 the United States dominated the Caribbean.

The opening of the Panama Canal in the same month that Europe went to war blended two American coasts into one, making secure control of the Caribbean and West Indies absolutely vital to the defense of the United States. The navy charged with that defense bore no resemblance to the scattered force of six frigates and a couple of hundred gunboats with which Madison bravely faced the Mistress of the Seas in 1812. Wilson's navy was first-class by any standard; its dreadnoughts were the spine of a fleet intended to fight for command of the sea, although it would justify the contest as a means of driving Old World attackers back before they could invade the Western Hemisphere. Roosevelt, who had grasped the maritime issues of 1914 immediately, also understood the new strategy—"we should unquestionably gather our fleet together and get it into the highest state of efficiency."

The gathering of forces Roosevelt wanted finally began with the withdrawal of all units from Veracruz in November 1914. During the concentration, while the navy prepared to defend the coastline with offshore fleets of capital ships, there was a six-month period in which the Wilson administration attempted to apply the traditional American standards of neutrality to a world at war. The goal as always was to maximize trade with all belligerents. As in the Anglo-French wars a century before, Great Britain sought to restrict continental European imports of materials useful to the war effort. By September 1914 the British list of contraband included unwrought copper, iron ore, rubber, and petroleum. The Royal Navy was prepared to interdict American transports carrying such goods to Europe, and the Wilson administration began to file protests, as had Jefferson and Madison in the early years of the nineteenth century.

The problem of neutrality was complicated in 1914–1915 by the need of France and England to finance the purchase of American materials with loans or "credits" underwritten by American banks. Secretary of State Bryan believed "money is the worst of all contrabands because it commands everything else," and he briefly blocked the extension of credit to France and England; but the demand and potential for profits were too great. In October Wilson approved "credits" to foreign belligerents by private American banks. The genie was out of the bottle; in 1915 Great Britain purchased more than $200 million in ammunition from the American Locomotive Company and Bethlehem Steel alone. The British government had tied the American economy to Anglo-French success in arms at the same time that the Royal Navy blocked American shipments to Germany and Austria-Hungary.

But the gravest peril to American neutrality came from a totally unexpected source: the German commerce-raiding submarine. Frustrated by the Royal Navy's virtual blockade of the Continent and the bottling up of the High Seas Fleet in the North Sea, the German naval high command in February 1915 persuaded the kaiser to declare a war zone around Great Britain. In those waters submarines were ordered to sink enemy merchant ships without warning, "even if it may not be possible always to save their crews and passengers." Neutral ships—that is, those of the United States—were "exposed to danger" because Britain had used neutral flags to mask the identity of British merchantmen. The Germans would put an end to this deception by attacking suspicious vessels flying nonbelligerent flags.

The technology of the day made German ruthlessness inevitable. The small submarines of World War I had thin hulls and very light armament. When surfaced, as they had to be if warning a target, they were highly vulnerable. An unarmed merchant vessel could ram and sink one; an armed merchant vessel—and the British practice of mounting guns on merchant vessels was as old as naval warfare—could blast one out of the water. To survive, the U-boat had to fire its torpedoes before being spotted.

Woodrow Wilson was appalled. The German proclamation was "so unprecedented in naval warfare" that he could not believe Berlin "contemplates it as possible." He was dead wrong. The genteel days of commerce raiding à la Raphael Semmes and the *Alabama* were gone forever.

The *Kriegsmarine* bared its fangs on 1 May 1915. Without warning, a German submarine torpedoed and sank an American oil tanker, the *Gulflight*, off the southwestern coast of England. Three Americans died. Neutral ships were no longer safe in the German-declared war zone. A week later the German submarine U-20 fired a single torpedo into the British Cunard passenger liner *Lusitania*, which Germany believed was carrying arms and ammunition. She sank in eighteen minutes, taking to the bottom a contraband cargo of 4.2 million rounds of rifle ammunition. Of the 1,959 people aboard, 1,198 died, including 128 Americans.

The nation was stunned. Former President Theodore Roosevelt decried an act of "piracy on a vaster scale of murder than old-time pirates ever practiced." But Secretary of State Bryan correctly argued, "ships carrying contraband should be prohibited from carrying passengers. . . . Germany has a right to prevent contraband going to the Allies and a ship carrying contraband should not rely upon passengers to protect her from attack—it would be like putting women and children in front of an army." Wilson, however, insisted on the alleged right of Americans to make such dubious voyages. He protested strongly to Germany and refused to lodge a commensurate objection to Britain's abuse of well-established American maritime rights. Secretary of State Bryan accused him of being pro-British and resigned. Bryan was replaced by Robert Lansing, a man who favored close economic ties with England and France.

The sinking of the *Lusitania* on 7 May 1915 marked the beginning of the U.S. Navy's serious preparation for war in the Atlantic. Insisting that Germany must follow the rules of cruiser warfare, which included giving fair warning before destroying a merchantman, Wilson ordered the War and Navy departments to prepare bills for increased appropriations to be presented to Congress when it reconvened in November. Assistant Secretary of the Navy Franklin Roosevelt was elated. On the stump and in magazine articles he had already been campaigning for a stronger navy. One of his public supplications foreshadowed his own hemispheric defense and convoy policies of 1939–1941. "Our national defense must extend all over the western hemisphere, must go out a thousand miles into the sea," he thundered. "We must create a Navy not only to protect our shores and our possessions, but our merchant ships in time of war, no matter where they may go."

The General Board obliged with a $285-million package for the coming year. It was centered on four new battleships and four battle cruisers. This was part of a long-range proposal envisioning a two-ocean war fought by the United States without allies. It did not contemplate involvement in the current European war. In the judgment of William R. Braisted, the most careful student of America's naval policy in the Progressive Era, "it is difficult to avoid the conclusion that the board conceived the most ambitious program feasible within the limitations of American shipbuilding facilities and then methodically assembled threats to justify its requests."

Before this visionary request could be submitted to Congress, Wilson's stringent diplomacy extracted from Germany a promise— the so-called *Arabic* pledge of 1 September 1915—that passenger ships would be sunk "only after warning and saving of lives provided they do not flee or resist." That concession and the entrenched progressive-pacifist aversion to war blocked naval expansion for the rest of 1915.

While the nation held its breath over the possibility of joining an international war, the navy became the arena for a contest over civilian control of the military. A group of talented and outspoken naval officers agitated privately and publicly for the creation of a naval general staff system. In Secretary Daniels's disapproving words, it would "be organized according to the German idea of bureaus reporting to and acting under the direction of the Chief of Operations."

Rear Admiral Bradley A. Fiske and Captain William S. Sims spearheaded the insurgents. In 1915 Fiske was the naval aide for operations, one of the four advisory and coordinating positions created by George von Lengerke Meyer in 1909 to advise the secretary and coordinate the technical bureaus that since 1842 had controlled the daily functioning of the installations supporting the navy's ships. As the senior uniformed adviser to the secretary of the navy, Fiske regarded himself as the likely head of a new naval staff system in which the secretary became a figurehead and an officer serving as chief of staff directed the operating forces. Fiske had friends in Congress, including Representatives Richmond P. Hobson, an Alabama Democrat who had fought bravely with Sampson at Santiago, and Augustus P. Gardner of Massachusetts, son-in-law of Republican Senator Henry Cabot Lodge.

Daniels saw the proposal for what it was, a challenge to civilian control over the navy. The secretary's allies in Congress watered down the Fiske-Hobson measure so that the act of 3 March 1915 permitted the chief of naval operations to govern "the operations of the fleet," but only "under the direction of the Secretary of the Navy." The wily Daniels then bypassed twenty-six rear admirals, five senior captains, and all the insurgents to appoint Captain William S. Benson as the first chief of naval operations (CNO). A relatively junior officer, Benson had used his position as commandant of the Philadelphia

Navy Yard to ingratiate himself with Daniels by speeding up construction on ships of special interest to the secretary and by praising Daniels's emphasis on naval education and his tough policies on labor practices in the yards. Daniels thanked him for accepting the post: "Your coming here in this important position makes me happy. We will have real team work . . . for steady improvement of the service."

The irate Fiske retired from the navy immediately. Two years later the Anglophile Sims, now a rear admiral, was posted to London as the navy's direct liaison with the British Admiralty. From that vantage point he would restructure American naval strategy over Benson's objections. From the beginning, therefore, the power of the chief of naval operations was circumscribed by secretarial intent and professional jealousy. By checking the reformist officers, Josephus Daniels had ensured the survival of civilian supremacy within the Navy Department. His vigilance preserved a cherished American constitutional principle.

Benson's arrival in Washington and his organization of the new central office coincided with the growing sentiment in favor of greater preparedness that the Wilson administration gradually nurtured into the unprecedented Naval Appropriation Act of 1916. The president was converted to military and naval expansion by hawkish advisers, principally the new secretary of state. Robert Lansing darkly imagined a coalition of three enemies of democracy—Germany, Russia, and Japan—setting out to partition the world at the expense of the United States. Other advisers fretted about the obligations Britain was incurring to its ally Japan as a result of the Japanese war on German possessions in the Pacific. Great Britain was not exempt from inclusion on the list of possible antagonists, and the Anglo-Japanese alliance of 1902 appeared increasingly dangerous to the United States after Japan challenged the open door policy with the infamous "Twenty-One Demands" on China.

In considering several scenarios, the General Board, still nominally headed by the aged hero of Manila Bay, concentrated on meeting a German–Japanese ("Black–Orange") coalition in both oceans. Rear Admiral Austin M. Knight, the president of the Naval War College, thought the United States certainly faced a war in which Japan would be joined by either Germany or Britain, depending on which country was victorious in Europe. But regardless of the precise composition of the opposing confederation, the navy's top uniformed leadership, Admiral Benson and the General Board, concurred that the battleship must remain at the heart of an American navy that would become "equal to the most powerful . . . by not later than 1925." In response to a directive from Secretary Daniels, the General Board in October 1915 recommended an immediate active fleet goal of ten battleships, six battle cruisers, fifty destroyers, and numerous small vessels. Daniels emphatically agreed with the board that by 1921 the United States Navy should have fifty-two battleships and six battle cruisers to face Britain, Germany, Austria, and Japan individually or in some combination. He requested that Congress authorize two battleships and two battle cruisers in 1916, the first installment of a five-year building program costing $100 million annually.

Election-year politics stalled the five-year plan on Capitol Hill, and Wilson was forced to stump for his program of military and naval expansion. In a February speech at St. Louis, Missouri, he pleaded for "incomparably the greatest navy in the world." He had foolishly let the cat out of the bag, and even that most ardent of naval expansionists, Theodore Roosevelt, criticized the president's political imprudence in challenging the primacy of the Royal Navy. Wilson's Senate ally, the chairman of the Naval Affairs Committee, limited his support to "the *second* greatest Navy afloat." Wilson and Daniels backed off, but in testimony before the House Naval Affairs Committee Admiral Benson remained determined "to meet the biggest navy . . . in the world" (the British) plus "a combination of the two smaller navies" (the German and the Japanese). The navy's senior admiral was laying the foundation for the American assault on British sea power that would be launched in full force immediately after World War I.

Exhortations by Benson and other admirals failed to elicit a definite naval appropriations decision from Congress until three distinct developments converged in the early summer of 1916. One was the conclusion of a Russo-Japanese alliance, which some opinionmakers interpreted as inimical to American interests in China. Second, a war with Mexico became not unlikely following a clash between Mexican troops and the American punitive expedition pursuing Pancho Villa deep inside Mexico. The *Army and Navy Register* reported that some congressmen were persuaded to vote for massive naval expansion by the fear that Japan would exploit a Mexican–American war to settle old scores with the United States. But the big jolt came from across the Atlantic.

On 3 June 1916 Washington learned of the Battle of Jutland, the one colossal battlefleet engagement of the entire war. The consequence of an Anglo-German search for the decisive battle at sea,

Jutland demonstrated the awesome firepower of dreadnoughts and the pitiful vulnerability of any thinly armored warship caught in the line of fire of their 12-inch guns. But the battle left the naval balance in the North Sea where it had been: with the Royal Navy in blockade far offshore and the German High Seas Fleet tucked into protected harbors. In the interwar years, the U.S. Naval War College would overlook Jutland's strategic inconclusiveness and replay it in endless war games, as if it somehow sustained Mahanian theory.

Jutland's immediate impact on the U.S. Navy was to permit two big-navy senators, Republican Henry Cabot Lodge and Democrat Claude A. Swanson, to revise the administration's naval bill upward. They persuaded the Congress to compress the General Board's five-year plan into a three-year span and to begin in 1916 with four battleships and four battle cruisers—eight capital ships in all. The Senate vote for the largest American naval expansion in history was overwhelming: 71 to 8, plus abstentions.

The 1916 act had little to do with the possibility of fighting in the European war. As William R. Braisted has written, "It was primarily designed to prepare the nation for a later contest in which the United States might face a coalition attacking in both oceans." As such, it was directed with fine impartiality against Germany, Japan, and Great Britain. When informed that Britain disapproved of the American bid for equality in capital ships, the president curtly retorted, "Let us build a navy bigger than hers and do what we please."

The ships' sizes as well as their numbers were growing exponentially. Testimony in support of the appropriation bill of March 1917 revealed that the navy had plans for battleships displacing more than 40,000 tons, a 25 percent increase over the largest American battleship then under construction. Ostensibly a reply to planned Japanese ships, the new Goliaths would mount twelve 16-inch guns. Their irrelevance to American national security was demonstrated within a month.

Germany had resumed unrestricted submarine warfare against allied and neutral maritime commerce on 1 February, and by early April Woodrow Wilson was driven to ask Congress for a declaration of war. The Germans knew that by resuming unrestricted submarine warfare they would force the United States to declare war, but Berlin calculated that in the interval between the American declaration and full mobilization the U-boat blockade would starve Britain into submission. In strategic terms, therefore, Germany's decision to sink without warning all ships entering a prohibited zone around the British Isles was the essence of rationality. It was a perfect calculus based on a faulty premise. Germany underestimated the American industrial and social capacity to continue supplying matériel to Britain and France while mobilizing an army.

For the American navy, Germany's decision and Wilson's response meant a complete reorientation of strategy from long-range planning to immediate war-fighting. As late as January 1917 the General Board had remained committed to planning "for American naval domination of the western Pacific" at Japan's expense, a preoccupation that again would characterize naval planners in the decades between the two world wars. In April 1917, however, the overriding problem was not Japan and its battlefleet; the enemy was Germany and the modern commerce raider, the *Unterseeboot* or "U-boat."

Prewar German naval planners had believed that the battleship was the ultimate naval weapons system and that *guerre de course* was an obsolete strategy. They had concentrated on building a battlefleet and had laid down fewer than fifty U-boats, but during the war the impasse at Jutland and the ravages their submarines inflicted on merchant shipping bound for Britain forced the German naval strategists to reorient their strategy from *guerre d'escadre* to *guerre de course*.

Every major maritime nation had conveniently underrated the lethal power of the submarine at the onset of World War I. The British especially, but also their naval disciples, the Americans, had anticipated "a new Battle of Trafalgar which would destroy German sea power as decisively as Nelson had destroyed French and Spanish sea power." The stalemate at Jutland had given the lie to this easy solution, but American naval planners remained unrepentant. On 5 April, the day before Congress declared war, the General Board recommended to Secretary Daniels that he "steadily increase the strength of the fighting line" of battleships, because of "the possibility of the United States being in the not too distant future compelled to conduct a war single handed against some of the present belligerents." Almost immediately following the American declaration of war, the navy was forced to challenge those cherished assumptions and prepare to defend against the *guerre de course* which Mahan had proclaimed trivial in the age of steam and steel.

In April 1917 the Mahanian preoccupation with decisive battlefleet engagements continued to dominate British thinking as well. When advised that the German submarine offensive would very soon lead to the defeat of Britain, Admiral Sir John Jellicoe, who had commanded the fleet at Jutland, concluded that the Admiralty had no strategic solution whatsoever to the U-boat menace. The first sea lord could not conceive of drawing destroyers from the blockade of the German High Seas Fleet to convoy cargo vessels past the submarines.

The officer who would redirect both British and American naval strategy away from the stalemate of the battlefleets toward defeat of Germany's modernized *guerre de course* was Rear Admiral William S. Sims. Ordered to London in April 1917 as the direct link with the British Admiralty, the Canadian-born Sims was notoriously pro-British. He focused on the immediate naval menace, the U-boat, rather than on the postwar anti-American coalition of Germany, Austria, and Japan hypothesized by planners in Admiral Benson's office. The chief of naval operations himself was extremely distrustful of the British throughout the war, and Sims later recalled that the CNO's parting advice had been, "Don't let the British pull the wool over your eyes. It is none of our business pulling their chestnuts out of the fire. We would as soon fight the British as the Germans."

Benson was not Sims's only obstacle to a successful campaign against the U-boat. He also had to overcome Jellicoe's fixation on *guerre d'escadre*. This he did by appealing directly to Prime Minister David Lloyd George, who became convinced that convoy escorts held the key to victory at sea. Lloyd George intervened directly with the Admiralty, permitting Sims to form a working alliance with some of the less senior British naval officers who shared his views. By early May the British were diverting ships from the Grand Fleet to escort convoys of merchantmen.

In convincing his own Navy Department of the validity of his strategy, Sims was helped immeasurably by Captain William V. Pratt. Perhaps the shrewdest officer on Benson's staff, and regarding himself as "straight Anglo-Saxon to the bone," this close friend of Sims gradually overcame the Navy Department's dual fear of Japanese aggression and a German naval breakout into the Atlantic. He concurred with Sims's war-winning formula for scores of destroyers to convoy hundreds of ships—cargo vessels and troop ships—to England through U-boat-infested waters. That became the navy's policy on 21 July 1917, when Secretary Daniels approved a building program that would bring the navy's destroyer total to 273. Public and private shipyards would be employed exclusively to build antisubmarine craft and transports, except where capital ships had actually been laid down. The end result was the commissioning of a grand total of 406 submarine chasers of all classes in 1917 and 1918, of which at least 235 crossed the Atlantic.

As Rear Admiral Sims had predicted a few days before Daniels made his decision, "the convoy system . . . will be the solution to the submarine question. That is, . . . it will reduce the losses [of transports] considerably below the rate of the building, and this will mean that the submarine campaign will be defeated." And so it was. The institution of a systematic Anglo-American convoy system dramatically reduced the allies' shipping losses to U-boats, while the number of U-boats sunk increased steadily. "By mid-1918," concludes the historian Elmer B. Potter, "the U-boat had ceased to be a serious menace except to the vessels that continued to sail independently." It was the elimination of the U-boat threat that permitted the American Expeditionary Force to cross the Atlantic. As Paolo E. Coletta has noted, "during the summer of 1918 the United States was landing seven soldiers and their equipment in Europe every minute of every day and night." Of a total of 450 transports used by the United States during the war, only eight were lost to enemy action.

Germany's revival of *guerre de course* had failed because the United States Navy, with great reluctance, temporarily abandoned its capital ship construction program to send to sea an overwhelming number of transports and escorting submarine destroyers, which were hardly less fragile or more seaworthy than their underwater prey.

The American navy that defeated the U-boat had its roots in the European *guerre de course* of the eighteenth century as absorbed by the great American commerce raiders of the early national period. The tradition of commerce raiding had vigorously reasserted itself in the post–Civil War postulations of the *Alabama* as a prototype for future American naval warfare. World War I had now shown how lethal commerce raiding could be when wedded to the new submarine technology. The next world war would witness another defensive American antisubmarine campaign in the Atlantic and expose a new American mastery of offensive, unrestricted submarine warfare against Japan. *Guerre de course* was alive and well.

========

For the most part, the pride of the American battlefleet sat comfortably in Atlantic Coast ports throughout the war. Keeping the battleships concentrated at home was part of Admiral Benson's plan to be ready for anticoalition warfare following World War I. Also, by hugging the Atlantic ports, the battlefleet could interdict German surface raiders in the unlikely event that any broke through the British blockade. Such a role of coastal defense was anathema to most offensive-minded battlefleet enthusiasts, although it had been suggested as a dubious justification for battleships in Secretary Tracy's 1889 report calling for a fleet to "beat off the enemy's fleet on its approach."

The upshot of the conservative deployment of the American battlefleet was that the Navy Department procrastinated in meeting the British request for a division of battleships to relieve a group of British pre-dreadnoughts whose crews were needed on antisubmarine patrols. The decision to attach five American dreadnoughts to the British Grand Fleet as a battle squadron under Rear Admiral Hugh Rodman came only in November 1917, when the Lansing–Ishii Agreement temporarily calmed the administration's apprehension that Japanese aggrandizement in China might lead to a Pacific war that could be fought only by long-legged capital ships.

The British government not surprisingly discouraged the residual American sentiment in favor of renewed capital ship construction. In the spring and summer of 1917 Britain's foreign secretary, Arthur James Balfour, promised the United States "some sort of call upon Allied capital ships" in exchange for a shift in American naval construction "from capital ships to . . . vessels suitable for antisubmarine warfare." The British purported to believe that the Americans were wasting their resources in building heavy ships, since they already enjoyed a "considerable preponderance" over Japan in battleships. In truth, of course, London feared postwar competition with the United States in the class of warship universally acknowledged at the time as the only meaningful standard of world-class navies.

The competition would be fueled by the resentment felt in Washington toward Britain for the Anglo-Japanese Alliance and by American apprehension that the British would further strengthen America's major transpacific sea power rival by permitting Tokyo to acquire some of the German-held islands as a reward for Japanese participation in the war. By the summer of 1918, therefore, Secretary Daniels and the General Board were taking the first steps toward construction of two 40,000-ton battleships, and First Lord of the Admiralty Sir Eric Geddes invited himself to the United States for a preemptive plea. Secretary Daniels advised Wilson that Geddes's public opposition to renewed American capital ship construction was an attempt to perpetuate British naval supremacy after the war. The president fumed: "I don't like it a bit." He was barely civil to Geddes, and on 15 October, two days after the first lord departed for England, he approved a new three-year naval construction program replicating the 1916 act. He would ask Congress for $600 million to build ten battleships, six battle cruisers, and 140 smaller vessels.

The revival of American capital ship construction in 1918 had nothing whatever to do with the defeat of the *Kriegsmarine*. Geddes's arrival in Washington had coincided precisely with a German overture to Wilson looking toward a peace based on the American president's Fourteen Points; the Briton's departure occurred just as Admiral Benson was sailing for Paris, where he would supplant Sims as the senior American naval officer on the Allied Naval Council.

William S. Sims had correctly sensed the essence of twentieth-century naval warfare, even though in doing so he perhaps willingly served the long-term British goal of maintaining the Royal Navy's international lead in capital ships. By contrast, in doggedly focusing on that long-range challenge at the beginning of the war, Admiral Benson had missed a paradigmatic moment in naval history. At war's end he was about to repeat his mistake. He and his colleagues remained mesmerized by the largest capital ship navy in the world: "With Germany disarmed," his planners in London reminded the chief of naval operations, "there is no occasion for Great Britain to possess a Fleet greater than her present Fleet, unless the power of the Fleet is designed to restrain us." The battle with Germany was over; the battle with Britain and Japan was about to begin.

9

Facing the Island Empires

1919 – 1933

Wₕₑₙ the Allied Naval Council convened in Paris
in late October 1918, Admiral Benson sent Admiral Sims back to
London so that he would be the unquestioned head of the American
naval delegation. Benson was then free to pursue a two-tiered approach of hewing to the policies of the civilian leadership of the
administration and articulating an anti-British position within the Naval Council. The American naval planners in Paris saw the Anglo-
Japanese Alliance as a great danger to the United States. They
recalled that during the war Great Britain seemingly had promised to
transfer five dreadnoughts to Japan at the end of hostilities. Distribution of the surrendered capital ships of Germany and the Central
Powers would give the Anglo-Japanese navies a ratio of sixty-seven
heavies to the Americans' seventeen. Britain historically had fought
and defeated its strongest commercial-maritime rivals: Spain, Holland, France, and Germany. It now faced "the greatest one yet" and
would undoubtedly resist this new challenge to its maritime and naval
supremacy. To be ready, Benson and Admiral Henry T. Mayo, the
commander-in-chief of the Atlantic Fleet, wanted a new American
class of fast battleships concentrated in "a homogeneous force far
more powerful in offense and defense than anything now contemplated by any naval power."

This Anglophobic posture was not difficult for Benson to maintain, because the administration's naval policy was increasingly anti-

British. On 28 October the president transmitted his naval terms to Benson and the senior American representative in Europe, Colonel Edward M. House. Wilson wanted to prevent the resumption of naval warfare, but he did not want to mortify Germany, which could serve as a check on England in Europe. He insisted that his conception of freedom of the seas—one of his Fourteen Points—be established by international covenant and guaranteed by his new league of nations. He did not require that the entire German fleet be surrendered as a prelude to an armistice. The British accurately analyzed Wilson's insistence on freedom of the seas as a resentment that "seaborne trade and maritime development proceeded only with the permission and under the shadow of the British Navy."

British interference with neutral shipping in wartime was as old as the Republic. It lay at the root of the War of 1812, and many of Wilson's predecessors in the White House had tried to regulate it through diplomacy. They had failed, just as he would fail. Even by tentatively threatening a separate peace with the Central Powers, Edward House could not budge the English. British Prime Minister David Lloyd George told Colonel House, "We could not give up the blockade, the power which enabled us to live . . . we will fight on." Georges Clemenceau, the French premier, concurred, "Yes, war would not be war if there was freedom of the seas." So Wilson was checked well before he sailed for the peace talks, soon to be the scene of the so-called naval battle of Paris.

When Wilson departed for Paris on 4 December 1918, the administration's naval program was in deep and highly public trouble. The people had voted Republican majorities for both houses of Congress at the November elections, and the lame duck leadership failed to ram through the three-year naval construction bill prior to expiration of the Democratic Congress on 4 March 1919. Senator Henry Cabot Lodge contributed to the legislative impasse, partly for partisan reasons; but he and former President Theodore Roosevelt also objected to the anti-British aspect of Wilson's naval policy. The two Republican elders attacked the administration in letters to the British prime minister and foreign secretary. Roosevelt did not "understand . . . Mr. Wilson's interpretation of 'freedom of the sea'. . . . We feel that the British Navy from the necessities of the British Empire should be the most powerful in the world, and we have no intention of rivaling it." From London the former president's naval sidekick, William S. Sims, joined the chorus. Wilson thought Sims should start wearing a British uniform.

The president's principal goal at Paris was to win French and British acceptance of a league of nations to enforce the peace. All other matters were secondary at best, including freedom of the seas, a concept Wilson had purposely left vague to facilitate compromise. Wilson's naval advisers at Paris had already been stung by Britain's repudiation of freedom of the seas, and in the first four months of 1919 they concentrated on two other issues: preventing the distribution of the captured German fleet among the victorious powers and guaranteeing Germany the right to rebuild its navy when economically feasible. Redistribution of the captured ships was objectionable, because it would proportionately strengthen the Royal Navy far more than the American. A future reconstruction of the German navy was desirable as a means of distracting Britain from its incipient naval rivalry with the United States.

Benson and his staff were backed to some extent by Colonel House and more firmly by Secretary Daniels, who arrived in Paris on 25 March. But Lloyd George had rather direct access to Wilson, and he brought out his big guns from the admiralty—the first lord and the first sea lord—to challenge Benson personally in meetings with Daniels. The maximum British goal was to persuade the Americans to abandon construction of the sixteen heavy ships authorized by the 1916 act and currently under construction. The ultimate ploy was periodically to threaten nonadherence to Wilson's league.

The upshot of four months of interplay between statesmen and navalists was omission of any mention of the fate of the German navy in the treaty of peace and continued American construction under the 1916 law. On 21 June 1919 the German naval officers and men resolved the former issue by scuttling their interned fleet at Scapa Flow, an embarrassing episode that Colonel House noted with some glee: "Everyone is laughing at the British Admiralty. It is all to the liking of Benson and myself who wanted the boats sunk."

The Anglo-American naval race had defied an easy solution at Paris in 1919. In a way it was diverted to the Washington Conference on the Limitation of Armaments of 1921–1922. In another way, historian William R. Braisted has concluded,

> the engagement of 1919 was as significant a turning point in the history of world sea power as the defeat of the Spanish Armada in 1588 or the battles of Trafalgar, Tsushima, and Midway [1942]. In 1919 British statesmen and naval men fought to retain acknowledged first place for the Royal Navy, but they failed because the exhausted island kingdom

was unable to match the great resources of [the] continental United States.

The trident would finally pass peacefully from Britain to the United States at the Washington Conference, but already in 1919 the navy's position had been sketched by Captain Frank H. Schofield, next to Benson the officer who contributed most of the memoranda written in Paris. Schofield would mold the position of the General Board on the eve of the Washington Conference, but he and Benson articulated the navy's underlying assumptions in a memorandum of 13 March 1919:

> There are in the world two great powers whose existence depends on naval strength. These are Great Britain and Japan. In the past Great Britain built with the exclusive idea of keeping a safe superiority over the German fleet. In the future her sole naval rival will be the United States, and every ship built or acquired by Great Britain can have in mind only the American fleet.
>
> Japan has no rival in the Pacific except America. Every ship built or acquired by Japan can have in mind only opposition to American naval strength in the Pacific.

The navy was internally divided about whether Japan or Great Britain posed the greater menace to American security. Rear Admiral Josiah S. McKean, the acting chief of naval operations during Benson's absence in Europe, echoed his boss in objecting to "having the American Eagle second to the British Lion under any conditions . . . at any time, in any place in the world." But in the planning section of the CNO's office Captains Thomas C. Hart and Harry E. Yarnell viewed Japan as "the most probable enemy." However, since the postwar budget-cutting environment did not permit the navy to sell Congress a policy of challenging two major enemies at once, the appropriations for fiscal year 1920—the largest in peacetime history— merely continued the 1916 building program without adding new capital ships.

As it had been since 1890, the battleship was the weapons system of choice for the vast majority of officers. Alfred Thayer Mahan's writings had popularized it, and the Battle of Santiago had elevated it to unquestioned first place in the American navy's arsenal. Jutland's ambiguous outcome notwithstanding, it continued to set the standard of relative strength for the world's great navies. By 1921 the "gun club" of battleship admirals and captains ran the United States Navy. They were united in their preference for battleships; they differed only on whether to trade caliber of gun and weight of armor for added speed in the next generation of capital ships, a disagreement contributing to the congressional refusal to fund new construction in fiscal 1920.

With Germany removed from the international naval equation after Scapa Flow, it seemed fatuous to keep all of the battleships in the Atlantic, so Secretary of the Navy Daniels divided the battlefleet between the two oceans. On 12 July 1920 he reorganized the forces afloat into three fleets, the Atlantic, Pacific, and Asiatic, each commanded by a four-star admiral. By stationing the largest number of the heaviest 14-inch-gun ships in the Pacific Fleet, he indicated who he thought the most likely enemy was and which coast of the United States was most exposed to attack. For that definitive step he was of course criticized. Admiral William S. Sims, by now president of the Naval War College, publicly stressed "the urgency of one grand fleet" trained to fight as a unit "rather than divided into two fleets—which are not grand at all." But that Mahanian doctrine of concentration, however tactically sound it might be in theory, ignored the political advantage Daniels derived from at last stationing some of the heavies within sight of the Pacific Coast populace, which had helped pay for the battleship navy.

The 1916 American building program had outraged British navalists from the outset. At the time of the armistice, former First Lord of the Admiralty Winston Churchill had blustered in the House of Commons, "Nothing in the world . . . must lead you to abandon that naval supremacy on which the life of our country depends." But postwar Britain, deeply in debt to the United States for the war loans that had financed its defense, could not keep up with even the relatively modest naval construction authorized by Congress in 1916. In September 1921 the General Board reported that Britain had just begun four capital ships, for a total of 172,000 tons, as against the fifteen the United States had laid down for an aggregate of 618,000 tons. The unwinnable naval race compelled the Admiralty to seek a negotiated parity with the United States Navy in capital ship tonnage.

To complicate the picture further, the Anglo-Japanese Alliance, renewed in 1911 for ten years, would soon expire. It was a dangerous partnership, because it could force the British into what a Foreign Office memorandum called a "pro-Japanese intervention, in spite of the fact that our national sympathies would be on the American side."

The English diplomats reasoned that in war the United States would fight much as Britain traditionally fought: with arbitrary visit and search of neutral vessels and destruction of arms-carrying ships. Those practices would prove as outrageous to a neutral Britain as they historically had proved to the United States when Europe was at war.

Nor could the Foreign Office tolerate a belligerent United States "reducing Japan to complete bankruptcy." Perhaps Japan could be sustained and prodded to expand in the direction of Manchuria rather than to the south, toward Shanghai, Hong Kong, and Singapore. But that tack was treacherous, for it flew in the face of the American open door policy. London therefore would somehow have to disengage from Japan without driving an irate Tokyo to pounce on the distant outposts of the British Empire. The solution lay in an international conference of the three major Pacific powers, Great Britain, Japan, and the United States.

On 8 July 1921 Secretary of State Charles Evans Hughes proposed "a conference on limitation of armament . . . to be held in Washington at a mutually convenient time." He initially invited Britain, Japan, France, and Italy. China, Belgium, the Netherlands, and Portugal were added later. Hughes approached the Navy Department for a "yard stick" of naval armaments and a standard for reductions. The General Board wanted to complete the remaining fifteen capital ships of the 1916 act. Hughes and Assistant Secretary of the Navy Theodore Roosevelt, Jr., insisted on a "stop now" formula to end immediately the costly naval race among the United States, Britain, and Japan. Roosevelt entrusted Captain William V. Pratt with personally drafting and typing the secret plan Hughes would present at the opening session of the conference.

Pratt's sense of kinship with the English was counterbalanced by his distaste for the Japanese. He deplored the Anglo-Japanese alliance and sought a "wise administration of sea power in the hands of an undivided Anglo-Saxon race." A Sims protégé and a classical Mahanian, Pratt measured naval strength in terms of capital ships—battleships and battle cruisers. Aware that Great Britain was groping to retain parity with the United States, he proposed a tonnage ratio in capital ships to satisfy the Admiralty and give the United States a nearly two-to-one advantage over Japan. The formula for the United States, Britain, and Japan became 5:5:3.

The Navy Department's prerequisite for discontinuing construction of capital ships was the abrogation of the Anglo-Japanese alliance. It also insisted that the State Department seek a modus vivendi with

Japan regarding the open door in China and the Pacific Islands mandated to Tokyo at the Paris peace conference. As a League of Nations trustee, Tokyo had acquired three former German archipelagos: the Marianas, Caroline, and Marshall islands. Those put Japan athwart the American line of communications running from Hawaii through Wake and Guam to the Philippines, although under the League of Nations mandate the acquired island groups were to remain unfortified. Japan could, however, legally fortify its other insular possessions lying roughly midway between Guam and the Philippines to the south and the home islands to the north: the Bonins, the Ryukyus, Formosa, and the Pescadores.

America's strategic Pacific outposts had become surrounded targets. Admiral Clarence S. Williams, head of the navy's War Plans Division, concluded that implementation of the island-hopping campaign contemplated in the 1911 Plan Orange might already have become "pratically impossible" and certainly would be if the Japanese fortified their insular possessions. A preclusive agreement was essential to the defense of the American empire in the Pacific.

On 12 November 1921, at the first plenary session of the Washington Conference on the Limitation of Armaments, Secretary Hughes startled everyone with a concrete proposal to scrap a large number of pre-dreadnoughts and to terminate construction of all capital ships now on the ways. He sought an immediate tonnage ratio in capital ships of 525,000 tons each for Great Britain and the United States and 315,000 tons for Japan, the 5:5:3 formula. The American public reacted euphorically to the "sinking" of sixty-six battleships, but the naval experts of every country dug in their heels to fight for their own national naval priorities. Japan wanted a larger capital ship fleet. Great Britain would exempt light cruisers from tonnage ratios, because they were the modern equivalent of the frigate, the historic policeman of the far-flung British Empire. London wanted also to abolish submarines, because World War I had shown that in the hands of unscrupulous lesser powers they were lethal to the supply lines of the British Isles. France and Italy were miffed at Hughes's cavalier attitude toward their naval significance. As industrially weaker continental powers they had special interests in cruisers, destroyers, and submarines, the contemporary instruments of *guerre de course* and coastal defense.

Theodore Roosevelt, Jr., the thirty-four-year-old assistant secretary of the navy, chaired the explosive committee of experts. When impasses developed, the senior civilian delegates struck compromises. But only one important on-the-spot agreement extended much beyond the capital ship and Far Eastern solutions already worked out within the American government, where it was clearly understood that on those particular issues London and Washington agreed.

After three months of intense negotiations, the diplomats reassembled in plenary session. On 6 February 1922 they signed three separate pacts, the Five-, Four-, and Nine-Power treaties. The first of those established a tonnage ratio in capital ships for the navies of the five greatest powers: the United States, Great Britain, Japan, France, and Italy. This was Captain Pratt's formula with two countries added, making the final ratio 5:5:3:1.75:1.75. To win Tokyo's adherence to a less favorable ratio of capital ships, the United States and Britain agreed in the Five-Power Treaty not to fortify further their military and naval installations in the western Pacific within striking distance of the Japanese. Although the British renounced the right to fortify their possessions in a large quadrangle of the Pacific, Singapore was not covered by the treaties. For the United States the agreement meant the nonfortification of all possessions west of Hawaii and west of the Aleutian chain in Alaska. The Japanese reciprocally bound themselves not to fortify the Bonins, the Ryukyus, Formosa, or the Pescadores.

The novel American concession on fortifications originated with Secretary of State Hughes at the conference and had not been anticipated in the navy's planning. Naval officers forever after criticized it as a sellout, but at the time Assistant Secretary of the Navy Roosevelt described it with a statesman's historically sensitive appreciation for America's inevitable postwar congressional parsimony:

> In general it leaves us, in my opinion, in a slightly better position than Japan. We trade certain fortifications, which we would never have completed, for fortifications which they would unquestionably have completed. We retain one outpost in the Pacific of great importance [Hawaii], and they give up all but their mainland.

William Pratt, Roosevelt's loyal amanuensis, defended his own handiwork in similarly realistic terms: "Guam and the Philippines never were, and never would be adequately fortified by us in peace, as they might be by a more military government."

Two other accords negotiated at Washington further diminished Japanese autonomy in East Asia and the western Pacific. Inspired by the British delegate, Arthur James Balfour, and signed by Britain, the

United States, Japan, and France, the Four-Power Treaty terminated
the Anglo-Japanese Alliance, a *sine qua non* for the American naval
staff's acquiescence. In the new nonaggression pact Japan promised
to respect American sovereignty over the Philippines and Guam. As
William R. Braisted notes, "It was in the tradition of the Root–
Takahira Agreement, which [President] Theodore Roosevelt and
[Secretary of State Elihu] Root had concluded in 1908 when the
American battle fleet was held in the Atlantic for protection against
Germany."

Equally traditional was the toothless Nine-Power Treaty.
Drafted at Washington by the same Elihu Root, seventy-six years old
in 1921, it bound its signatories to promote the open door in China
and to respect China's political integrity. It had no provision for
verification, let alone enforcement.

The navy was unhappy. Rear Admiral William L. Rodgers in
March 1922 expressed the opinion of the General Board to the secretary of the navy:

> [T]he naval situation of the United States in the Pacific, both as to ships
> and as to bases, resulting from the Treaty . . . will be such as greatly
> to lessen the power of the United States . . . to defend its interests or
> . . . enforce its policies in the Western Pacific, should these be seri-
> ously threatened.

A former commander of the Asiatic Fleet, Rodgers distrusted
Japan. In a letter to the secretary of the navy he once characterized
the Japanese as "the Germans of the East . . . whose Asiatic version
of the Monroe Doctrine is that Japan only is to rule in Eastern Asia."
Perhaps so, but Rodgers's geopolitical analysis was heavily shaded by
the racist baggage carried by many Americans of his time. His main
contribution to the China question during the Washington Conference was a letter forwarded to Secretary Hughes declaring, "If the
great white nations stand for the 'open door' . . . militaristic Japan
will scarcely be able to maintain her stand of selfish exploitation of
China." From his perspective, the "white nations" had knuckled under at the Washington Conference.

Rodgers's internal criticism of the treaties was matched publicly
by Dudley W. Knox, who retired as a captain to become the naval
editor of the *Army and Navy Journal*. Knox contended that the tonnage limitation on capital ships and the prohibition on fortifying Guam
and the Philippines "virtually doubled Japan's defensive strength and

her offensive power in the Orient, bringing her ratio for these purposes up to at least 10 to America's 5." His thin polemic, *The Eclipse of American Naval Power*, became the bible for uniformed critics of naval limitations.

Knox was a key member of the navy's interwar strategy-shaping intelligentsia. As a nominally retired officer, he directed the Office of Naval Records and Library, a division of the Office of Naval Intelligence. In that capacity he collated the nineteenth-century records of the navy, but more important, in 1936 he published a book-length Mahanian espistle on sea power, *A History of the United States Navy*, for which then Vice Admiral William L. Rodgers wrote an appreciative introduction. The book was part of a broadly based propaganda campaign undertaken at the time of the international collapse of the Washington agreements to alert the nation to the importance of naval rearmament. It represented the final chapter of the naval dissidents' commentary on the treaties.

The officers who criticized the treaties shared two vital assumptions with those, such as William S. Sims and William Pratt, now a rear admiral, who championed it. They all accepted without question the right of the civilian leadership to dictate diplomacy and policy; at the same time they were determined to build "a Navy second to none in conformity with the ratios for capital ships established by the treaty for limitation of naval armaments." That meant a battleship navy directed against Japan.

Imperial Japan was the only worthy opponent of the 1920s. Germany, the useful "threat" of Plan Black, was defeated and disarmed, its battlefleet scuttled at Scapa Flow. Great Britain, the other viable European antagonist as late as 1916, was on the ropes. The historian Paul Kennedy observes the effect of World War I on the English naval-industrial complex:

> [T]here had been no real victory for Britain: she had suffered grievous losses in manpower and shipping, strained her industrial and fiscal system, declined further in world commerce, lost her hitherto unchallenged financial predominance and—as a result of all this—was now in no position to maintain maritime supremacy against the United States; naval equality, and that on the basis of an uneasy truce, was all that could be hoped for.

A humbled England acting as a junior partner seemed even more attractive to the Anglophiles in the navy who were rising to positions of high seniority. William S. Sims had become president of the Naval War College in 1919. William V. Pratt, already marked for the highest commands, passed through Newport as the war college's president in 1925–1927 before becoming commander-in-chief of the U.S. Fleet and ultimately chief of naval operations in 1930–1933. Both of them thought of the Anglo-Americans as guardians of world peace. For men of their persuasion, Japan was the only great naval power left to challenge the United States.

The emergence of Japan as the navy's bête noire and the recent completion of the Panama Canal had led Secretary of the Navy Daniels to attach about half of the navy's battleships to the Pacific Fleet in 1919. At the time of the Washington Conference, Daniels's Republican successor, Edwin Denby, concluded it was time more American battleship "keels become acquainted with the western ocean and our navy yards and bases on the west coast receive their crucial test." On 6 December 1922 he reorganized the navy so that the bulk of the battlefleet was stationed in the Pacific. The nominal operational commander of the navy afloat, the "commander-in-chief United States Fleet" (CINCUS), remained in the Atlantic, directly supervising the "Scouting Fleet" of the six oldest and slowest battleships. "Everyone knew that these old ships were useless for scouting," one historian has caustically observed, "but their repair and overhaul provided a significant amount of employment for the Atlantic Coast Navy yards." The navy's real striking power lay at San Pedro, near Los Angeles, with the twelve best battleships commanded by the four-star "commander, Battle Fleet." Upon commissioning, the heavy carriers *Lexington* and *Saratoga* also fell under his command.

Reorientation toward a Pacific strategy accentuated the inadequacy of the drydock and repair facilities on the West Coast. Throughout the 1920s the navy beseeched Congress for funds to create large-capacity support bases in Hawaii, San Francisco, and Puget Sound. Congressmen whose districts would benefit economically from naval base construction and expansion obligingly depicted Japan as "the great trouble of this world," but the majority in Congress preferred to trim naval expenditures in the postwar Republican spirit of laissez-faire economics and political normalcy. As late as 1928 the chief of naval operations, Admiral Charles F. Hughes, was vainly reminding a congressional subcommittee that "even as nearly self-sustaining as the fleet may be, it must have shore bases. We have not the facilities on the Pacific to base them all." The battlefleet would remain divided regardless of strategic doctrine and the menace of Japan.

The navy's principal scheme for meeting Japanese aggression remained Plan Orange. First formalized in 1911, Orange was revised in the 1920s to take cognizance of the "5–3 ratio with Japan in all classes of fighting ships and personnel." But the underlying premise of the plan never changed. The Philippine Islands, as the Joint Army–Navy Board would later note, must be defended "as an *entrepôt* to the markets of the adjacent islands and the Asian mainland. . . . The United States has always supported . . . the open door Policy."

Plan Orange still called for the "reinforcement of Manila Bay, recapture of Manila Bay, [and] occupation or control of all naval positions in the . . . Philippines." It was the army's thankless mission to hold out in Manila Bay until the navy could lift a Japanese siege and launch a final "close military and commercial blockade of Japan." The General Board exposed the immensity of the task by listing three nonexistent prerequisites: "mobile upkeep, docking and repair equipment" to accompany the battlefleet; a ready "expeditionary force" of marines; and "good relations with possible benevolent neutrals such as Holland, Russia, or China."

Soviet Russia was not even recognized by the United States until 1933, and chaotic China descended into two decades of revolution in 1927. They were hardly valuable as potentially benevolent neutrals.

The Netherlands was a different case. The Dutch East Indies held incalculable oil reserves attractive to resource-poor Japan, but the Dutch navy was at best a third-class force. For mutual defense against Japan, the Dutch and the British therefore turned informally toward each other. Nicholas Roosevelt, a correspondent for the New York *Times*, explained the geopolitics: "[I]f the Japanese decide to take the Dutch East Indies, they would have to occupy Singapore, and if they wanted Singapore they would have to take the Indies."

The American navy of the 1920s and 1930s approved of the informal Anglo-Dutch entente. British construction of the great naval base at Singapore in the 1920s was welcomed as vital to the defense of the East Indies, which in turn could house the United States Navy if it were evicted from the Philippines by Japan. The French, who owned Indochina, the vulnerable way station on the Japanese road to Singapore, put the American connection best in an editorial in *Le Figaro* of July 1923:

One would readily understand that, as an experiment, the same [United States] government which for a century found certain advantages in reconciling the Monroe Doctrine with the existence of an immense English fleet might find it profitable and perhaps convenient to tolerate temporarily at Singapore, opposite eternal Japan and the Philippines, which are little fortified, *a [British] fleet in being*, capable of doing police duty in those distant waters.

In the spring of 1922, during deliberations over a "naval policy" statement requested by Secretary of the Navy Edwin Denby, Admiral Rodgers's General Board made it quite clear that the U.S. Navy would meet "eternal Japan" primarily with battleships. The secretary's advisers settled on a fleet of eighteen battleships and about 95,000 enlisted men, at an annual expenditure approximately 25 percent less than the one for 1921. For its "Peace Strategy of the Pacific" in the 1920s the board wanted all battleships "built to operate trans-Pacifically." This required a displacement of at least 35,000 tons each, an extended operating radius, and a speed of 21 knots. Only oil-burning ships could meet those standards, so the old coal-burners had to be converted. Antiship bombing tests beginning in 1921 showed that land-based aircraft could sink ships, so the battleships of the "treaty navy" would need anti-aircraft gun batteries and thick steel decks in addition to armored hulls.

The rationale for battleships dated back to Alfred Thayer Mahan and through him to the Swiss commentator on Napoleon Bonaparte's warfare, Antoine Henri, Baron de Jomini. Assistant Secretary of the Navy Theodore Roosevelt, Jr.'s 1922 justification of the capital ship shows that the Napoleonic roots of the idea nurtured strategists in high places:

> The capital ship forms the body of the Navy in the same way that the Infantry forms the body of the Army. . . . [A]nd in the final analysis, the old maxim about the Infantry that I think was put forward by Napoleon and other numerous gentlemen in the past, holds true of the capital ship . . . "The Infantry is the Army—when the Infantry is defeated the Army is defeated!" . . . That, in my opinion, holds good of the capital ship in the navy.

Roosevelt did not—because he could not—explain how large numbers of lightly armed, fast-moving men could be equated with a very small number of extremely heavily armed, relatively slow ships.

Exclusive emphasis on battleships was a foregone conclusion given the makeup of the General Board in 1922–1923, but the result constituted a tragic commentary on the ingrained technological conservatism of the capital ship navy and on the inhibiting effect of a rigid seniority system on the evolution of naval weapons systems.

The three senior rear admirals on the board had graduated from the Naval Academy before 1890. In the opinion of the historian Gerald Wheeler, they "were unfamiliar with aircraft and Rodgers seemed unwilling to learn anything about them." They were operating in complete ignorance: "No member of the board had any direct experience with aviation." For those officers, as Captain Edward L. Beach has noted, "Psychologically, the ships of the line of naval battle *were* the navy, and had always been." The aviators on the staff of the board were too junior to command the attention of the members on matters of policy and strategy. Moreover, the chief of the new Bureau of Aeronautics, Rear Admiral William A. Moffett, a former battleship skipper, was as interested in seaplanes and dirigibles as in aircraft carriers.

The Washington Conference had classed aircraft carriers as experimental vessels displacing no more than 27,000 tons each, with a total tonnage quota of 135,000 tons for the United States and Great Britain, 81,000 for Japan, and 60,000 each for France and Italy—the only successful extension to auxiliary combatants of the 5:5:3:1.75:1.75 capital ship ratio. The door was open to accelerated research and development of the platform and air group that even then a handful of relatively junior officers sensed as the weapon of the future. The new breed of officer, the naval aviator, was asking what Captain Beach describes as the "pertinent question: What use was a battle line with weapons of twenty-mile range if aircraft carriers could send weapons with greater accuracy ten times as far? . . . Why was a twentieth-century navy still enamored of the eighteenth-century line of battle?"

But the navy did not want to hear the question. In the 1920s it limited its carrier program—after the transformed collier Langley was commissioned in 1922—to converting two battle cruisers into the carriers *Lexington* and *Saratoga*, commissioned in 1927. The conversions were a fiscally prudent evasion of congressional reluctance to authorize new ships, and in the case of the *Lexington* and *Saratoga* they made sense strategically. Both ships displaced about 33,000 tons, a special exemption permitted at the Washington Conference. Their greater size, range, and speed proved important in the western Pacific during World War II. On the other hand, because they ate up 66,000 of the 135,000 total carrier tons allowed the United States Navy, they forced construction of smaller new carriers. *Ranger*, the first American ship built as an aircraft carrier from the keel up, displaced a mere 14,500 tons when she joined the fleet in June 1934.

Moffett and his senior flying aide, Captain Henry C. Mustin, had wanted much more. In the 1922 hearings of the General Board Mustin argued for three 23,000-ton carriers to follow the *Lexington* and *Saratoga* and reach the 135,000-ton ceiling straightway. Bombers from those carriers could hit targets ten times farther inland than the 14- and 16-inch guns of the battleships could reach. But when Mustin described the carriers' offensive bombing role in a war against Japan, the board immediately forced him to deny the implications of his testimony.

Captain Luke McNamee, a future commander of the navy's "Battle Force," accused Mustin of "contemplating a carrier that will operate singly and not with the fleet." Mustin retreated: "No, sir. I have thought all along that if any carrier operations were made on the coast of Japan that the striking group would be composed of the five carriers, the eighteen battleships, and the ten light cruisers." Five bomber squadrons escorted by fifteen fighter squadrons would make the raids over Japan. That composition of the attacking fleet would necessitate "eight squadrons of fighting planes for protection of the battleships." Mustin's attacking force significantly included the entire battleship and carrier force planned by the navy for the 1920s. This meant that the United States would enter Japanese home waters with the 5:3 tonnage ratio in capital ships and carriers established at the Washington Conference. It is incontrovertible evidence that in 1922 American naval planners regarded Japan as the only potential major enemy.

Mustin did not have time to point out that the defense of the battleships diminished the fighter cover available to the bombers before Admiral Rodgers vented his suspicions: "Do you contemplate making all naval warfare in support of the air attack?" Again, Mustin disingenuously backed down. "No sir. Our whole aviation program is laid out on the basis that the battleship is the dominant factor in naval warfare, provided it is properly supported by aircraft."

The "treaty navy" of the 1920s grappled with another new technology of enormous but underestimated potential, the submarine. At the Washington Conference Secretary Hughes had sought tonnage ratios for all warships, but the French could not sharply limit auxiliary craft and submarines "without impairing the vital interests of the country and of its colonies and the safety of their naval life." England concluded that the French submarine force could be directed only against the Royal Navy and refused to sanction limits on cruisers and destroyers, the primary antisubmarine vessels. This cycle of suspicion would be repeated at subsequent naval conferences in the 1920s and 1930s.

Blocked by France and England, Elihu Root in 1922 had extracted a face-saving clause branding submarine skippers as pirates if they attacked merchantmen without warning and without providing for the safety of passengers and crew. Even that sop to the "man in the street" evaporated in 1926, when the British Admiralty warned that "if in a naval war we were forced to sink merchant ships as a reprisal we might have to suspend or abrogate this provision." The early demise of Root's attempt to prevent the resurrection of unrestricted submarine warfare gave the United States Navy both warning and opportunity, but the bitter memory of Imperial Germany's murderous commerce raiding was too strong to permit cold-blooded planning for a similar kind of American warfare. It would take Nazi Germany's deadly revival of the practice in the Atlantic in World War II and the public trauma over Japan's attack on Pearl Harbor to transform the Americans into practitioners of unrestricted submarine warfare in the Pacific.

Conditioned to think only in terms of decisive engagements between surface fleets of capital ships, and conveniently repelled by the brutal effectiveness of submarine *guerre de course*, American naval planners in the 1920s and 1930s made fundamental errors with submarines and their ordnance. One was in rehearsals. In annual war games submarines played two distinct roles: as scouts of the battlefleet and as attacking enemies. Like aircraft, they were welcomed as scouts with far-seeing eyes. But—again like aircraft—as attackers they were embarrassing omens of the dreadnoughts' vulnerability. "Enemy" submarine commanders who charged toward the battlefleet for a close-in attack were dismissed as "reckless" violators of tactical doctrine. They were "rated irresponsible and marked down in command ability." Highly conservative and orthodox submariners therefore succeeded to command in the interwar years, only to be displaced by a new breed of "unabashedly aggressive" skippers in the trial of Pacific warfare after 1941.

One of America's greatest submariners, Captain Edward L.

Beach, has explained the underlying cause of the stasis in American submarine policy in the 1920s and 1930s:

> The minds of the men in control were not attuned to the changes being wrought by advancing technology. Mahan's nearly mystical pronouncements had taken the place of reality for men who truly did not understand but were comfortable in not understanding.

Although the battleship men were disdainful of submarines and cool toward aircraft carriers, they had definite feelings about cruisers, a class of warship distinguished from battleships only by a thin line of tonnage and gun caliber. At American insistence, the Washington treaties of 1922 limited a cruiser's displacement to 10,000 tons and the diameter of its guns to 8 inches. But Washington had not limited the number of cruisers each nation could maintain, and as the 1920s wore on the attempt to restrict construction of this type of vessel came increasingly to occupy the attention of American naval planners. It was first pressed on them by President Calvin Coolidge, who told the nation in 1924, "I am opposed to any policy of competition in building and maintaining land or sea armaments." Coolidge pressed to extend naval limitations from capital ships to cruisers and other smaller vessels. He advocated a new international conference, to be held in Geneva, Switzerland, in the summer of 1927. The principal participants were the United States, Great Britain, and Japan.

The General Board's preparation for the conference reflected once again the predominance of Japan as the navy's most likely enemy. "The desire of Japan for security to her sea lines of communication is in conflict with the American desire for security of sea lines of communication to China and the Philippines," the board posited. The 5:3 ratio of the Washington Conference had undermined the navy, and to "further weaken our position" by establishing unfavorable ratios for cruisers and other lesser combatants "would not conduce to peace" with Japan. Nor could the navy contemplate greater restrictions on the reinforcement of friendly Pacific naval bases. The calculated exclusion of Singapore from the 1922 base limits had given the British a free hand to fortify that bastion, which *may well serve our interests there at some future time.*" The General Board also underscored the fact that the United States and Britain *are in accord on most of the great problems of that area.*" There was little likelihood of war between the British and the Americans, "provided an equality in naval strength between the two countries is maintained."

The emerging Anglo-American naval entente was sorely tested at Geneva when a serious breach developed between the naval delegations of the two powers. The American representative, Rear Admiral Hilary P. Jones, demanded the right to build a large number of 10,000-ton heavy cruisers with 8-inch guns and extended cruising ranges. This was the largest vessel classified as a subcapital ship or auxiliary combatant under the ratios of the Washington Conference. The navy claimed it was necessary for fleet operations in the western Pacific and to protect convoys against Japanese or other surface raiders. The British delegation, led by Admiral of the Fleet Earl Jellicoe, the victor of Jutland, wanted strict limits on 8-inch-gun cruisers but a high ceiling on light, 6-inch-gun ships, which could operate effectively with short legs from the innumerable overseas bases of the British Empire. Admiral Jones objected to a proliferation of those light raiders because they could attack unarmed American merchantmen throughout the Pacific. The disagreement scuttled Anglo-American naval harmony for the next two years.

Japan also was building 8-inch-gun cruisers and at Geneva demanded a higher ratio in auxiliary combatants than the 5:3 proportion in capital ships established at Washington in 1922. The United States Navy, already trailing Japan in all classes of cruisers by a count of eighteen to twenty-nine, could not countenance the Japanese demands. On these shoals the conference foundered, with the result that President Coolidge changed his mind about naval construction.

On 6 December 1927 the president described the results of the conference as "negative" and informed Congress that no naval limitations agreement could be reached without "a considerable building program on our part." He now wanted the kind of diplomatic leverage at future conferences that the United States had enjoyed at Washington but not at Geneva: a large potential or real fleet of the type of ships whose reduction was under discussion. He therefore backed a huge "71 Ship Bill," which appalled pacifists and economy-minded legislators. Even when the administration gingerly substituted a more modest "15 Cruiser Bill," Congress still did not act.

Overseas, Britain and France bilaterally agreed to limit the 10,000-ton, 8-inch-gun cruisers favored by the United States. Coolidge responded with an Anglophobic Armistice Day speech edited by the chief of naval operations and two other admirals. "Having few fueling stations," he lectured a gathering of the American Legion, "we require ships of large tonnage, and having scarcely any merchant vessels capable of mounting five- or six-inch guns [for self-defense], it is obvious that . . . we are entitled to a larger number of warships than a nation having these advantages."

Coolidge's naval bill finally cleared Congress on 13 February 1929, only a few days after the Senate voted 85–1 to approve the Kellogg–Briand Pact renouncing war "as an instrument of national policy." The popularity of that treaty explains a proviso in the naval act permitting the president to suspend construction of the fifteen cruisers and one aircraft carrier if another international conference for naval limitations were scheduled. Within two weeks, on 4 March 1929, Herbert Hoover became president. A Quaker who abhorred war, Hoover in his inaugural address declared, "Peace can be promoted by the limitation of arms." The navy was hemmed in on all sides.

———

Pacifism, fiscal conservatism, and isolationism had proved more deadly than enemy navies in a decade of prosperity. The inauguration of a Quaker Republican president in 1929 would be followed by a massive stock market "crash" and the onset of the Great Depression, making a bad situation much worse.

As president-elect, Herbert Hoover had endorsed the "15 Cruiser Bill" to keep peace in the Republican party, but once in office he focused on naval limitations through international conferences. Should that process fail, he favored the economical alternative of a navy adequate only for coastal defense. As the historian Gerald E. Wheeler observes, "protection of foreign possessions, overseas investments, and its foreign trade were luxuries not worth the maintenance of an expensive Navy." For secretary of the navy, he selected Charles Francis Adams III, a world-class yachtsman and distinguished scion of a family well acquainted with naval affairs, but Hoover rarely sought his advice.

In planning his first naval conference, Hoover bypassed Adams to work with Secretary of State Henry L. Stimson. Very much in control, Hoover in June 1929 sent Ambassador Charles G. Dawes to London to pave the way for talks on the limitation of auxiliary combatants, that is, cruisers, destroyers, and submarines. In August he suspended work on three of the five heavy cruisers authorized by Coolidge's naval act. That symbolic act helped persuade the British to participate, and Hoover then appointed Admiral William V. Pratt to head the U.S. Naval Technical Staff at the London Naval Conference of 1930.

Pratt, whom Hoover would soon name as chief of naval operations, was hardly the big-navy men's choice for the job. As the commander-in-chief, U.S. Fleet (CINCUS), he held the top operational command in the navy. But he also was an architect of the 1921–1922 limitations, and in 1930 from his position as CINCUS he took the highly unorthodox step of publishing and distributing fleet-wide a pamphlet defending his diplomatic handiwork. The Nine-Power Treaty, he wrote insightfully, "was a statesman's victory gained over conservative elements of the Navy." He thought the Washington treaty had created a "better understanding" with Japan, but most importantly, "It was the only method without war and without engendering lasting hatred whereby we could obtain parity in naval matters between the two great Anglo-Saxon speaking nations." In 1930 the Anglo-American naval entente was back on track.

Pratt's Anglophilia served the London Conference well. Convinced that Britain would side with the United States in any war with Japan, he saw no threat from the British quest for superiority in light cruisers and readily acquiesced to Britain's demand for a reduction in the General Board's minimal figure of twenty-one heavy American cruisers. By agreeing to a limit of eighteen 8-inch-gun ships, Pratt and his London naval staff allayed British suspicions and pacified the Japanese. An entire set of limits followed forthwith, the essential meaning of which was that the Washington 5:5:3 ratio was continued for capital ships and aircraft carriers but modified upward to the Japanese advantage of about 10:10:7 in cruisers and destroyers. In addition, Japan was granted parity with the English and Americans in submarine tonnage. France, worried by the Italian navy and desperate for a firm mutual security pact with England or the United States, refused to adhere to the cruiser and destroyer limits. The treaty therefore became essentially a three-power accord establishing a five-year holiday in capital ship construction and a regular schedule for replacement construction in the lesser categories of warships. It would expire in December 1936.

Admiral Pratt was well rewarded for his diplomacy. On his way back to the United States he received notice that in October he would become the chief of naval operations, the navy's top staff job. His service in Washington actually began in May 1930 with appearances before the Senate Foreign Relations Committee in defense of the London naval treaty. The administration needed him as the designated titular head of the navy, because the General Board objected to the treaty, calling it a State Department ploy that was "wholly impracticable, dangerous and impossible of execution."

Pratt's lack of enthusiasm for the 10,000-ton, 8-inch-gun cruiser, the General Board's favorite auxiliary combatant, contrasted with his defense of lighter cruisers for "fleet work" against destroyers. But the core of his case stressed the "definite program" of warship replacement and "a Navy which is not a creature of great ups and downs." The Senate bought Pratt's analysis. On 21 July 1930 it consented to ratification by a vote of 58 to 9. The navy would never forgive Pratt his apostasy, and he retired in July 1933 an isolated man.

For the remainder of the Hoover presidency the navy faced hard times. Despite a major crisis with Japan over Manchuria in 1931–1932, Hoover remained committed to reducing the navy. He sensibly hoped for American disengagement from the Far East through Philippine independence and gradual abandonment of the open door policy for China. In Europe he sought solace from the World Disarmament Conference, held in Geneva in 1932.

Once again, Admiral Pratt headed the naval delegation, this time choosing colleagues who also favored the 6-inch-gun cruiser over the 8-inch version. The General Board was not consulted in picking the slate, and Secretary Adams came near resignation in disgust at the president's consistent undermining of the navy. The muckraking columnist Drew Pearson caught the flavor of Hoover's Navy Department: "Charles Francis Adams is God's answer to the admiral's prayer. . . . For Charles Francis advocates as big a navy as any admiral, can sail a ship better than most of them, and has reputedly risked his Cabinet job for them."

Too loyal a public servant to resign, Adams stayed on as secretary until the inauguration of Franklin D. Roosevelt in March 1933. He watched the World Disarmament Conference of 1932 come to nothing, faced congressional outrage when he tried to pare the civilian work force in the navy yards, and ached at the deterioration of old equipment and officers' morale. But there were silver linings in Adams's navy. Ten heavy cruisers entered service during his stewardship; the new carrier *Ranger* was laid down in September 1931; additional air squadrons flying from the heavy carriers *Saratoga* and *Lexington* paved the way for *Ranger*'s easy incorporation into the operating fleet during the Franklin D. Roosevelt administration; and young men with high mechanical aptitude seeking refuge from the Depression raised the level of enlisted talent to an all-time high.

Because the statutory limit of 5,499 commissioned line officers remained fixed, the best enlisted men received the opportunity to become naval aviators. They joined graduates of the Naval Academy and naval reserve ensigns to form the new flying elite of the navy of the future, the carrier navy. This evolution could not have been foreseen by Adams. It would be bitterly resisted by the senior battleship admirals until the Japanese attack on Pearl Harbor demonstrated the obsolescence of battleships and left the navy without a battlefleet. But from the long historical perspective, nothing vital was lost through the moratorium in capital ship construction forced on the navy by Herbert Hoover at the London Naval Conference.

10

Guerre de Course
Once Again

1933 – 1945

THE inauguration of the Democrat Franklin Delano
Roosevelt as president on 4 March 1933 came as a relief to the navy.
The outgoing chief of naval operations, Admiral William V. Pratt,
expressed the uniformed hierarchy's satisfaction in a letter to his new
commander-in-chief. It was "a pleasure . . . to know that the fate of
the Navy lies in the hands of a man who loves it as you do."

The former assistant secretary of the navy knew the service
better than any previous president, with the possible exception of his
cousin Theodore. After six years as president he would boast to his
old boss, Josephus Daniels, "You know I am my own Secretary of the
Navy." But that was later. In 1933 devising a policy of recovery from
the nation's worst sustained economic depression took precedence
over toying with reconstruction of the fleet. The navy was therefore
fortunate that the Democratic victory in the congressional election of
1930 had resulted in the ascension of Carl Vinson to the chairmanship
of the House of Naval Affairs Committee.

A representative from rural inland Georgia whose district
boasted no naval installations, Vinson defied the facile stereotype that
equates support for a big navy with congressmen from the seaboard
who vote naval appropriations in order to employ and enrich their
constituents and win perpetual reelection for themselves. The New
York *Times* caught the irony that a "Navy which sees itself in danger

of pernicious anemia looks hopefully toward a Georgia country lawyer." As early as 1925, during the "Morrow Board" hearings over
Army Brigadier General William "Billy" Mitchell's allegations that
the navy was obsolete in the age of the strategic bomber, Vinson had
defended a large balanced navy composed of surface combatants,
aircraft carriers, and submarines. Forty-two years later, the retired
congressman boasted that the policies he outlined in 1925 remained
"substantially the policy used today." His twenty-five-year chairmanship of the Naval Affairs Committee was instrumental to that outcome, and the appreciative navy bestowed its highest accolade for a
lifetime of support. In 1982 it named its fourth nuclear carrier the
U.S.S. *Carl Vinson* (CVN-70).

The intermediary between Vinson and President Roosevelt was
Secretary of the Navy Claude A. Swanson of Virginia. A member of
both the House Foreign Relations and Naval Affairs committees during the Wilson administrations, Swanson had worked closely with
then Assistant Secretary of the Navy Roosevelt. An ardent and well-
informed big-navy man, he had shaped the construction bill of 1916.
In the 1920s his virulent anti-Japanese views reflected the prevalent
navy sentiment. Seventy years old at the time of his appointment in
1933, Swanson would cling to office until his death in July 1939.
Roosevelt backstopped him with a distant relative, Henry Latrobe
Roosevelt, who had attended the Naval Academy and had served in
the Marine Corps for twenty years. When Latrobe died in 1936,
Roosevelt picked Charles Edison, the son of the inventor, as assistant
secretary. The past again was prologue for the New Deal navy:
Charles Edison had assisted his father on the Navy Consulting Board
of World War I, a nepotistic post that brought him into regular contact with Josephus Daniels and Roosevelt.

The naval reconstructionists of Franklin Roosevelt's first administration (1933–1937) did not have a smooth path to follow. Defense
spending as a means of rebuilding and sustaining the national economy was unthinkable, in part because American policymakers had not
yet been converted to Keynesian economics. Moreover, the U.S.
Navy's would-be enemy, Japan, continued to abide by the Washington and London construction limits until 1936. Finally, a popular
American theory held that profit-seeking "munitions makers" had led
the United States into World War I, and it must not happen again.
Antiwar propaganda proliferated. In 1932 the nationally prominent
revisionist historian Charles A. Beard published the scathing anti-

navalist challenge, *The Navy: Defense or Portent?* Beard highlighted congressional testimony that no American battleship had fired a shot in anger during World War I, and he questioned the battleship's utility in any future conflict. The limited expansion of the navy in this milieu of Depression, isolationism, and pacifism testified to Franklin Roosevelt's political legerdemain.

The manipulative and somewhat disingenuous political pattern was set at the very beginning. Repeatedly frustrated in attempts to legislate a long-term naval construction program in the Hoover administration, Representative Vinson now helped persuade Franklin Roosevelt to allocate some of the funding of the "100 Days" emergency national recovery legislation to the navy. The National Industrial Recovery Act served as the cover. Congress passed this $3.3-billion appropriation for public works on 16 June 1933, and on the same day the president directed that $238 million of Public Works Administration funds be spent for construction of two aircraft carriers, four cruisers, twenty destroyers, four submarines, and two gunboats. That one-shot approach did not provide for continuous new construction or replacement of the aging battleships, but it did give the navy the carriers *Yorktown* and *Enterprise,* the saviors of the Pacific in 1941–1942.

Vinson meanwhile worked painstakingly on the Hill to systematize naval reconstruction. He was deeply concerned that the United States was not building the number of cruisers, destroyers, and submarines permitted by the Anglo-American-Japanese agreement reached at the London Conference. He introduced a bill to authorize construction in those classes over the next several years, arguing that steady building would "contribute to better designs, better workmanship, less disruption of industry," and a more reliable navy than existed "under old wasteful methods of bulding a navy by alternate spasms of intense activity and practically complete idleness." He encountered stiff popular opposition, perhaps best summarized in a letter from the ministers of forty-five churches in Buffalo, New York. Vinson's naval bill, they intoned,

> would launch the most gigantic battle-ship building program in history, precipitate a dangerous armament race between nations, destroy good will and foment suspicion especially in the nervous Pacific and play directly into the hands of the meddlesome munitions-makers and eventuate ultimately in war.

A representative and fair prediction, but no deterrent to Vinson.

In early 1934 Vinson successfully pushed his bill through the Naval Affairs Committee and floor-managed it to passage in the House. The Democratic Senator Alexander Trammel of Florida guided it through the upper chamber, and on 27 March 1934 President Roosevelt signed what became known as the Vinson–Trammel Act. The measure was a beacon for the future, but as Roosevelt explained to the press it was an authorization, not an appropriation of funds. Congress still had to vote the money to pay for the seventy new warships and 730 additional naval aircraft now authorized to be built between fiscal year 1935 and fiscal 1939. Before that could happen, a series of international developments threw into question the fundamental post–World War I naval premise that Japan was the only likely enemy of United States Navy.

Anglo-American-Japanese talks were held throughout 1934 in anticipation of a London naval limitation conference scheduled for the next year. The preparatory exchanges revealed irreconcilable differences. Roosevelt's naval men sought to maintain or even lower current limitations. Great Britain, as before, wanted increased allowances for light cruisers. Japan demanded the inadmissible: naval parity with the Anglo-Saxons. Facing an impasse, Tokyo gave the requisite two-year notice that after 31 December 1936 Japan would no longer be bound by the Washington treaty limits. Six months later, on 18 June 1935, London and Berlin concluded a naval agreement stipulating that Adolf Hitler's government would not build a navy beyond 35 percent of the Royal Navy. The pact sanctioned the rebirth of the defunct German navy, signified Britain's growing sense of insecurity and preoccupation with Europe, and for the first time raised the specter of a "two-ocean war" for the United States.

Congress in August 1935 reacted to the naval rearmament and continental revanche of Germany with the first of a series of neutrality acts designed to preclude American entry into a European war. The measure compelled the president to embargo the shipment of arms to any country he designated as a belligerent. Two more acts followed in 1936 and 1937. The act of February 1936 forbade making loans to belligerents, a vain attempt to prevent the kind of economic entanglement with Britain and France that had characterized the years immediately preceding the American entry into World War I. Still, the lure of profits was strong, and in 1937 Congress passed a third neutrality act permitting belligerents to purchase American arms on a "cash and carry" basis.

The second of the three acts was passed about a month after Japan's withdrawal from the London conference. The Japanese departure had been orchestrated by Roosevelt, who wanted to appear as a champion of disarmament and to place the onus for a breakdown on Japan. His November reelection by the biggest electoral majority since Monroe's in 1820 gave further evidence of his political acumen, but it did not reduce the strength of neutrality sentiment in Congress or loosen the congressional purse strings for the navy. Nor did it slow down the Japanese advance.

Two months after passage of the third Neutrality Act an incident involving Chinese and Japanese troops at the Marco Polo Bridge near Peking (Beijing) led to a full-scale Sino-Japanese war. Japan proclaimed a blockade of the China coast and bombed Shanghai in August, the first example of classic World War II "strategic" bombing of a civilian population. On 5 October Roosevelt tested isolationist sentiment with a speech in Chicago proposing somehow to "quarantine" the "epidemic of world lawlessness" fostered by the dictatorships in East Asia and Europe. The popular and editorial reaction appeared negative to Roosevelt and his secretary of state, Cordell Hull, so the speech led to nothing but an endless debate over what Roosevelt really meant.

The commander-in-chief of the small Asiatic Fleet offered his own spicy interpretation in a recommendation to the chief of naval operations on 15 October. Rear Admiral Harry E. Yarnell proposed a "naval war of strangulation" against Japan in coalition with Great Britain, France, the Netherlands, and Soviet Russia. By using bases stretching from Alaska through Hawaii, Guam, the Philippines, and Java to Singapore, the allies could isolate resource-poor Japan from the rest of the world. Japan's interference with Western dominance of China's large rivers could be handled with even greater simplicity. From the Yangtze (Chang Jiang), Yarnell wrote that "a few squadrons of our carrier planes would clear this river of Japs in 24 hours."

The assertion that no fleet action would be necessary to constrict the Japanese empire was heresy in the United States Navy. Regardless of the popular isolationist sentiment at home, Yarnell's proposals had no chance of endorsement by a naval leadership that had rejected *guerre de course* a half-century earlier and had been planning for a fleet action with Japan since before World War I.

The "Japs" soon perversely validated Yarnell's thesis that limited use of air power could determine the control of China's rivers. On 12 December 1937 Japanese airplanes bombed, strafed, and destroyed the United States gunboat *Panay*, which was convoying three Standard Oil Company tankers on the Yangtze River. Two American sailors died and thirty were wounded. The popular American outcry faded quickly, and Hull on 24 December accepted a Japanese explanation and apology he did not believe. He and the president understood the danger in the Pacific, but they saw a greater one across the Atlantic.

On the same day that Hull bowed to Japan, the president dispatched Captain Royal E. Ingersoll to London to begin staff talks with the Royal Navy. As Ingersoll later explained his assignment, "We had to make preliminary arrangements to explore what could be done—for communicating with each other, for establishing liaison, intelligence, and other things, so if war did come we would not be floundering around for months until we got together." It was the William S. Sims mission redivivus. Almost exactly twenty years earlier Woodrow Wilson had sent an American admiral to London to coordinate planning for an Anglo-American naval war against a German *guerre de course;* now his protégé and political heir was doing the same thing.

On 28 January 1938, a month after he sent Ingersoll to England, President Roosevelt asked Congress to vote a 20 percent increase in fighting tonnage. The chief of naval operations, Admiral William D. Leahy, explained to the sympathetic Naval Affairs Committee that Roosevelt wanted three new battleships, two carriers, nine light cruisers, twenty-three destroyers, nine submarines, and 950 naval aircraft. Leahy's original proposal to Roosevelt had not contemplated carriers, "in consideration of the increasing efficiency in both offense and defense of flying boats as compared with carrier based planes." The subsidiary and tentative role of aircraft carriers in the United States Navy obviously had not changed in the interwar years; they remained useful as long-range eyes of the fleet and perhaps as platforms for launching limited raids such as that recommended by Rear Admiral Yarnell against Japanese riverine gunboats. But the CNO held to the idea that the real work of defeating a major enemy at sea still must be done by the battle wagons. After hearing that testimony, Carl Vinson's committee added a few dollars to the $1.1 billion requested by Roosevelt and whisked the administration measure to the full House, where the Georgia Democrat drove it through to passage. On 7 May 1938 the president signed into law the so-called Second Vinson Act.

While the U.S. Navy was rebuilding, Adolf Hilter was swallowing Czechoslovakia. The Munich Conference of September 1938, which sanctioned his seizure of the Sudetenland, seemed to satiate him for a few months, but in March 1939 the German army occupied Prague and the remainder of the country. The world waited, and so did the American navy. With Britain and France committed to war if Hitler moved against Poland, the American naval planners now had to contemplate a two-front war without strong allies in the Pacific. The basic planning documents now assumed that Japan would try to "damage Major Fleet Units without warning, or possibly . . . block the Fleet in Pearl Harbor." America could respond with the long-planned transpacific offensive of Plan Orange, but unless the pivotal island of Guam was immediately reinforced its recapture alone "would require an expeditionary force of not less than 50,000 men . . . and would entail unwelcome losses." Congressional refusal to strengthen Guam therefore might force the adoption of a purely defensive policy in the Pacific.

Regardless of the response chosen for the Pacific, the two most crucial geographic areas now were the Caribbean and the approaches to the Panama Canal. For their protection, a "fundamental reliance" had to be placed on the navy, and the Latin American nations somehow must be discouraged from granting the Axis powers access to air bases within striking distance of the canal or to naval bases that could support attacks on American maritime commerce in the Atlantic. The threat of Axis interdiction of the American supply lines to Europe would have to be met by a much enlarged American antisubmarine force of aircraft carriers, escorts, and patrol vessels. This full menu was accepted by the House Naval Affairs Committee chairman as justification for yet another Vinson authorization bill.

Naval planners and the administration seemed to be moving in all directions when war finally broke out in Europe on 1 September 1939. The president at once unambiguously defined the Atlantic as the primary and active theater of naval operations. On 6 September 1939 he organized the Atlantic "neutrality patrol," a far more belligerent undertaking than anything permitted in the Pacific prior to the Pearl Harbor attack two years later. The Atlantic war of "Mr. Roosevelt's Navy" also marked a radical departure from the Wilson policy of neutrality "in thought and deed" followed in 1915 and 1916.

In the winter of 1938–1939 Roosevelt's evolving Atlantic-first naval strategy included the staging of the annual fleet exercise in the Caribbean rather than in the Pacific and a scheduled visit of the Pacific-based U.S. Fleet to the New York World's Fair. But the more telling evidence of a shift away from the Pacific came with the creation of the Atlantic Squadron and the assignment to it of fourteen new ships, the first time since 1932 that new combatants had not gone directly to the Pacific. To mollify a disgruntled cruiser commander who equated an Atlantic assignment with the backstage, the rear admiral directing ships' movements explained that "the function of the Atlantic Squadron . . . is evidently a gesture aimed at political conditions abroad. The President personally directed the formation of the Squadron." Roosevelt also effectively commanded it through a direct telephone line to the director of the Ship Movements Division in the office of the chief of naval operations. A wall chart in his White House office plotted the squadron's whereabouts for this very modern commander-in-chief.

The operating arc of Roosevelt's Atlantic cruiser and destroyer force stretched from the mouth of the St. Lawrence River in the North Atlantic to Veracruz in the western Gulf of Mexico. It reached about as far into the open sea as the president on a given day might delineate with a sweep of a pencil across his chart. Roosevelt once dumfounded his old friend, the chief of naval operations, Admiral Harold R. Stark, by sketching a line from Newfoundland to British Guiana running 1,000 miles east of Charleston, South Carolina, and asking, "How would the Navy like to patrol such a neutrality zone?" Hampered by a shortage of ships, aircraft, and trained crews, the navy answered with a tight watch over chokepoints, especially ones where German merchantmen and liners cowered in Mexico's Gulf ports, but this close-in surveillance did not preclude random interceptions of suspicious vessels far at sea.

British warship skippers occasionally resented an American's demand for self-identification, but they often benefited from the American tagging and fixing in plain-language radio transmission of German transports dashing back to Europe. A classic six-day pursuit took place in December 1939. Several American destroyers and a cruiser trailed the 32,000-ton German vessel *Columbus* from safety in Veracruz to her destruction at the hands of the British destroyer *Hyperion* 400 miles off Cape May. The navy took the official position that the cruiser *Tuscaloosa* had happened on the scene by chance, just in time to save lives. The truth was that she had dogged the *Columbus* until the Briton arrived and then had fallen off to watch the action. But as Admiral Stark noted, "we do not desire you to make public the details of the work of our . . . patrol."

Assisting in the destruction of merchant vessels was not really what Roosevelt had in mind when he first conceived the undeclared naval war against German shipping. In April 1939 he had informed the cabinet that he wanted to establish "a patrol from Newfoundland down to South America and if some submarines are laying [sic] there and try to interrupt an American flag and our Navy sinks them it's just too bad." He must have been piqued that Hitler wisely restrained his U-boat commanders from operating in the western Atlantic prior to the fall of France in June 1940.

"The Battle of France is over, the Battle of Britain is about to begin," Prime Minister Winston S. Churchill dourly proclaimed. France's surrender on 22 June 1940 gave Hitler control over almost the same geographical area of Western Europe as Napoleon had exercised at his peak. Once again England stood alone offshore. Unlike the early nineteenth century, however, Britain this time enjoyed the unswerving loyalty and support of the president of the United States.

Roosevelt was running for an unprecedented third term, and many Americans remained staunchly isolationist, favoring at most the erection of a "fortress America" to deter translatlantic aggression by Hitler. Their resistance compelled the president to mask the operational patrols of the navy in the rhetoric of hemispheric defense and to arrange naval aid to Britain as an ostensible exchange for bases essential to defend the Caribbean and the avenues to the Panama Canal.

Hemispheric defense was the rubric the president used in September, when by executive order he transferred fifty "over-age" destroyers to Britain in exchange for ninety-nine-year leases on bases in the Bahamas, Jamaica, Antigua, Saint Lucia, Trinidad, and British Guiana. Britain tossed in as outright gifts additional bases in Newfoundland and Bermuda. Churchill knew the swap was "decidedly unneutral," but Roosevelt grandiosely labeled it "the most important action in the reinforcement of our national defense . . . since the Louisiana Purchase." Fifty years later the U.S. Navy was flying antisubmarine patrols against the Soviet navy from some of those sites.

Popular support for self-defense also could be turned to the navy's advantage in seeking appropriations from an isolationist Congress. Three days after the German army entered Paris, the politically ingenious Roosevelt sent his companion-in-arms, Admiral Stark, to Capitol Hill to plead the case for a $4 billion "two-ocean" navy bill. The chief of naval operations asked for a 70 percent increase in the navy, or 257 more ships. He envisioned the construction of additional battleships of the new 45,000-ton *Iowa* class and some of an even newer class, the 53,000-ton *Montana* "super dreadnoughts." In addition, he wanted fleet carriers. These were the *Essex* class, destined in the words of a British analyst to "carry the U.S. Navy to victory in the Pacific War." The final authorization of 19 July 1940 provided for thirteen battleships, six carriers, thirty-two cruisers, 101 destroyers, and thirty-nine submarines. The bold request had been made within days of congressional approval of an 11 percent increase in warships, and its quick passage demonstrates the alarm felt in Washington at the collapse of France and the isolation of Great Britain.

The history of the modern American aircraft carrier as the backbone of American naval strategy began in the summer of 1940, but the sharp increase in aircraft carrier production was not at the time intended to place the carrier at the core of the American fleet. In hearings before the House Committee on Naval Affairs, Chairman Vinson plaintively sought reassurance from Admiral Stark: "The Navy still adheres to the belief that the backbone of the fleet is the battleship, just as the infantry is the backbone of the Army?" Three times in succession Stark answered affirmatively. The chief of naval operations and the navy's best friend in Congress understood that in the United States Navy of 1940 the battleship conceptually sat at the center of a battle group. It was surrounded by a protective screen of destroyers for defense against submarine attack, cruisers for protection from enemy destroyers, and carrier-based fighter aircraft to reinforce the anti-aircraft fire of the surface units. In other words, U.S. naval strategic planning still based itself upon a concept of the line of battle dating back to the age of Admiral Horatio Nelson, the hero of Trafalgar.

With a major war on the horizon, academic and popular writers were enlisted to make the case for battlefleets. In the spring of 1939 Harold and Margaret Sprout of Princeton University had published their avowedly Mahanian history of the U.S. Navy, *The Rise of American Naval Power, 1776–1918*, a rebuttal to the attacks of Charles A. Beard and other critics of a capital ship naval policy. As late as March 1941 a leading American naval strategist wrote in a book aimed at educating the layman about an arcane subject, "The relative strengths of the opposing battle lines have been the determining factor in naval campaigns of the nineteenth and twentieth centuries. . . . The power of aviation is increasing, but events of the current war indicate that the strength of the battle line is still the decisive naval factor."

Despite Roosevelt's emphasis on antisubmarine warfare when establishing the neutrality patrols, the United States Navy in 1940 and 1941 continued to disdain a strategy of commerce raiding and commerce protection, historically associated with weaker powers. It preferred instead to emulate the Royal Navy, with its grand tradition of driving enemy battlefleets from the high seas.

But despite all its naval might, Britain in the summer and fall of 1940 was in danger of being mortally bombed, starved, or occupied. The British army had been driven into the sea at Dunkirk. Hitler had captured France's Atlantic ports, expanding the operational radius of German submarines by over 20 percent. Coastal U-boat warfare was transformed into a midocean nightmare for British convoys chugging from North America to England. This was the "Golden Age" or "Happy Time" for U-boat skippers. Between June and October 1940 they sank 274 merchant ships, a total of 1,392,298 tons. All of this death and destruction was achieved with no more than twenty-five boats operational in any given month and only six or eight actually out on patrol at one time—*guerre de course* reborn with modern technology and ruthlessness.

Roosevelt promised to send Britain "all aid short of war," and the destroyers-for-bases "deal" of September 1940 fitted into this category. But presidential rhetoric necessarily exceeded performance at a time when the public and many in Congress remained opposed to American participation in another European war.

The appointment of two leading Republicans to a coalition cabinet in mid-1940 would bridge the gap somewhat. Henry L. Stimson, Hoover's secretary of state, became secretary of war, and the 1936 Republican vice presidential candidate, an old "Rough Rider" who had campaigned in Cuba with cousin Theodore, became the navy secretary. Frank Knox had to dissemble in his confirmation hearings, promising the isolationist Senator David I. Walsh that he was "not advocating aid to the allies short of war because of my love or regard for Great Britain, but wholly out of my concern for American safety." Privately, he was an Anglophile who included American convoy escorts on his personal list of appropriate aid for the beleaguered island people.

So long as Britain's survival was uncertain and until Roosevelt won reelection, the American naval commitment to England remained somewhat tentative. Prime Minister Churchill frequently asked Roosevelt to send ships of the Pacific fleet to Singapore "to keep the Japanese quiet," but the president would send them no farther west than Hawaii, where beginning in May 1940 he permanently stationed the U.S. Fleet, battleships and all. The chief of naval operations explained to the fleet's commander-in-chief, Admiral

James O. Richardson, "You are there because of the deterrent effect which it is thought your presence may have on the Japs going into the [Dutch] East Indies."

Richardson felt dangerously exposed and deplored the inadequate base facilities at Pearl Harbor. His persistent protests, some directly to Roosevelt, that the battlefleet could be held in a higher state of readiness if based on the West Coast finally cost him his job. In hindsight he was right: The battleships became targets rather than deterrents, and after the Japanese attack on Pearl Harbor the survivors were reduced to coastline defense of California, Oregon, and Washington. Ultimately the battleships neither prevented nor won the great sea war of the twentieth century.

===

The reelection of Roosevelt in November 1940 marked the beginning of the final phase of American preparation for a war based on the presidential assumption that the survival of Britain was absolutely essential to American security. As the army's sagacious chief of staff, General George C. Marshall, remarked, "if we lose in the Atlantic we lose everywhere." Germany had become national enemy number one.

The chief of naval operations had reached the same conclusion. Distressed by the president's improvisational naval strategy, Admiral Stark and his staff in early November devised "Plan Dog." This shorthand expression was the naval phonetic for the fourth letter of the alphabet; it signified Stark's fourth and most reasonable strategic option for fighting a two-ocean war. A leading military historian has described it as "perhaps the most important single document in the development of World War II strategy." The admiral showed it to Roosevelt immediately after the election.

Plan Dog advised the president to plan for "an eventual strong offensive in the Atlantic as an ally of the British, and a defensive in the Pacific." When American entry into the European war became unmistakably imminent, the battlefleet would have to be moved from the Pacific to the Atlantic. The navy then must insure the integrity of the Atlantic sea lanes and the preservation of Great Britain. Stark transcended his service bias with a warning to the president that in his opinion, "This purely naval assistance would not . . . *assure* final victory for Great Britain. Victory would probably depend upon her ability ultimately to make a land offensive against the Axis powers." For that war-winning assault, an American expeditionary force would be essential. Roosevelt, Stimson, and Knox read and understood Plan

Dog, but the president's approval had to remain oral and off the record for political reasons.

Stark recognized the political limits of the presidency about as well as anyone in Washington. He sent Plan Dog to the former assistant chief of naval operations, Rear Admiral Robert L. Ghormley, whom Roosevelt had dispatched to London in July as a "Special Naval Observer." This permanent reincarnation of the Sims mission of 1917 was effected by Roosevelt before actual American belligerency so as to short-circuit the delays and Anglo-American misunderstandings that had plagued naval cooperation in the early weeks of Sims's stay in London. The gambit was only partly successful, as the British reaction to Plan Dog would show.

To the cool and deliberative Ghormley, Stark deftly outlined American naval planning and diplomacy for the second and last year of all-out aid to Britain, short of war:

> We may not be able to get the [presidential] directive right now because of the political dynamite in it for the moment, but that should not deter us [naval planners] from going ahead on our own, with the other fellow [Britain] fully understanding that it is on our own, without any backing from the State Department or the White House or anyone else. I should ask the President to let me send you our study . . . but, in line with the *no commitment* idea, it should not appear that the President has seen it.

The Joint Board of the Army and Navy sanctioned Plan Dog as American strategic doctrine and amplified it in the more detailed Rainbow Five Plan of March 1941. The old Orange Plan was out as global strategy, although within the Pacific theater a thrust through the central Pacific remained the navy's operational desideratum throughout World War II. The British also had objections to Plan Dog, because it seemed to write off Singapore, which they continued to hope the Americans would protect with the Pacific Fleet. Ghormley in fact knew that the British considered the great Malay bastion vulnerable to an overland attack, so he could hardly be expected to advocate its defense by the U.S. Navy.

British dissatisfaction with Plan Dog could be inferred from the results of the Anglo-American staff talks held in Washington early in 1941. The "ABC-1" report of March hinted at a limited American naval offensive in the Pacific. The subsequent "ABD"—American, British, Dutch—report of April 1941 similarly opened the door to a finite offensive in the western Pacific, and for that reason both Stark and General Marshall rejected it. But the glimmer of light would later beckon to Admiral Ernest J. King, the service-minded wartime commander who wanted a Pacific war for the navy at any price.

While the American and British naval staffs haggled over details, President Roosevelt spent his political capital shedding the congressional shackles that were blocking aid to Britain. His greatest success came on 11 May 1941 with the passage of the "Lend-Lease Act" permitting him "to sell, transfer title to, exchange, lease, lend, or otherwise dispose of" war matériel to "any country whose defense the President deems vital to the defense of the United States." The door was open to aid Britain directly, without building up the international indebtedness that had crippled England's economic recovery from World War I. Ultimately $31.6 billion of Lend-Lease goods went to Great Britain; $11 billion more went to Soviet Russia following Hitler's June 1941 attack.

By the time Congress passed Lend-Lease, the navy's "neutrality patrols" were becoming what Roosevelt hoped they would be all along: elements of Anglo-American antisubmarine warfare. It began on 1 February 1941 with the formal creation of an Atlantic Fleet commanded by Admiral King. Bases were quickly set up in Argentia, Newfoundland, and Northern Ireland. It intensified in late March when Hitler pushed the operational zone of his U-boats westward to Iceland and the 38th meridian of west longitude. Roosevelt then hesitated. He was tempted to expand the operation, but he feared an isolationist backlash in Congress and worried about what Japan would do now that the Russo-Japanese Nonaggression Pact freed it from the threat of a two-front war. He therefore held back from ordering outright American escorts of British convoys across the Atlantic. Instead, he commanded Admiral King to search for Axis warships anywhere west of 26 degrees west longitude. He advised Prime Minister Churchill, "We will immediately make public to you [the] position [of] aggressor ships or planes when located in our patrol area." In late May he moved about a quarter of the Pacific Fleet to the Atlantic, some "butter" to cover the "big slice of bread" he had given to King.

Roosevelt did not finally decide to order convoy escorts in the western Atlantic until convinced that no amount of diplomatic and economic pressure could budge Japan out of its new lodgement in Indochina. An American war with Japan over Southeast Asia was out of the question, so he might as well go ahead with his undeclared war in the Atlantic. In July he decided to order American convoys for

shipping in the western North Atlantic, but he chose a typically flam-
boyant way to make the annoucement: in a face-to-face meeting with
the British prime minister.

On Sunday, 10 August 1941, in Argentia, Newfoundland, after
much maneuvering on both sides, the two men met in an elaborate
ceremony of divine worship and geopolitical negotiation aboard the
British battleship H. M. S. *Prince of Wales*. On the foredeck Roosevelt,
Churchill, the senior military and naval leaders of both countries, and
the battleship's crew together sang, "Onward, Christian Soldiers."
The president later told his son, "If nothing else had happened, that
would have cemented us. 'Onward Christian Soldiers.' We *are*, and we
will, go on, with God's help." The war in the Atlantic had become an
Anglo-American crusade against the devil in Berlin.

The only tangible naval result of the "Atlantic Charter" conference was Roosevelt's promise to convoy British merchant ships to
Iceland, which the president in July had occupied with marines under the umbrella of hemispheric defense. This unique lesson in geography may have fooled some of the American people, but by the
time the Anglo-American war leaders met aboard *Prince of Wales* no
one in a position of power in Germany, Britain, or the United States
really believed that American naval policy was defensive.

On 1 September, as Roosevelt had promised Churchill, Admiral
King's fleet assumed responsibility for escorting convoys of supply
ships in the western North Atlantic as far east as Iceland. That meant
unrestricted antisubmarine warfare, a dangerous game then as now.
Three days later a U-boat being tracked by the destroyer *Greer* fired
torpedoes at its pursuer, but the salvo missed the mark. Roosevelt
feigned innocence and ordered the navy to "shoot on sight" in self-
defense. The torpedoing of the destroyer *Kearny* and the sinking of the
Reuben James, also an American destroyer, by German submarines in
October forced Congress to modify the Neutrality Act. By the end of
November armed American merchant ships could enter the combat
zone in the eastern Atlantic, and the United States Navy stood watch
over the Denmark Strait to prevent German surface raiders from
breezing past the British, as the battleship *Bismarck* had in May. The
undeclared American war against the German *guerre de course*, surface as well as subsurface, was in full swing. Its nature did not change
after the formal declaration of war with Germany in December 1941.

In the Atlantic war of 1941–1945 the enemy's most lethal weapons system was the submarine or U-boat, which savaged cargo ships

bound for England. The counter-weapon was the Allied antisubmarine (ASW) campaign, in many ways a rerun of World War I.

The naval lessons of World War I had not been well read by the American or European navies. As early as 1919 the submarine was discounted and the capital ship reestablished as the ultimate naval weapon. The Royal Navy concluded that the convoy and a sound-tracking apparatus called ASDIC—and later sonar in the U.S. Navy—had eliminated the submarine as a meaningful threat in future warfare. The Americans agreed, and so apparently did the German naval hierarchy when Hitler began to rebuild the fleet in the mid-1930s. His senior admiral, Erich Raeder, wanted a balanced fleet built around 56,000-ton battleships, roughly the equivalent of the American dream machine, the never built *Montana*.

The prevailing assumption in the mid-1930s was that submarines would not again sink merchant shipping without warning or without providing for the safety of the passengers and crews. In the 1936 Anglo-German Naval Agreement the humane nineteenth-century "cruiser rules" of naval warfare were resurrected, as if the U-boat warfare of Imperial Germany in 1914–1918 had been an aberration rather than a precedent. There were, therefore, very many miscalculations about submarine warfare on both sides of the Atlantic when Europe went to war in 1939.

The one man who correctly read the immediate past was Raeder's top submarine officer, Karl Dönitz. Where other strategists saw the submarine as a fleet escort, Dönitz saw it was "war decisive" if used to starve England into submission. For his indirect war against an entire population Dönitz wanted three hundred U-boats. Allocation of resources to Raeder's balanced fleet limited him to fifty-six at the beginning of the war. As in 1914, Berlin's prewar capital ship construction program had vitiated the German submarine, but Dönitz nonetheless gave his opponents a real run for their money before it was all over.

The allies had a geographic advantage over the U-boat at the onset. Mines laid in the Strait of Dover kept Dönitz's boats out of the English Channel, forcing them to go around Scotland to reach an operational zone in the western approaches to the United Kingdom. But the fall of Norway, the Low Countries, and France in early 1940 gave the German navy sites for submarine bases all along the European coast. The French Atlantic coast submarine pens, soon heavily fortified against air attacks, cut the U-boats' transit time to operating areas by 50 percent. That meant much greater time on station. From his French coastal headquarters in Lorient, Dönitz personally radi-oed commands directing "wolfpacks" of U-boats to close on convoys for the kill. Fair warning was not part of his scenario for contemporary *guerre de course*, and by the autumn of 1940 Britain was losing the Battle of the Atlantic. Some 352,000 tons of shipping went down in October alone.

Several developments made 1941 a much better year for the Anglo-Americans. Implementation of the destroyer-bases deal and Lend-Lease helped; so did Roosevelt's belated September order for the United States Navy to convoy shipping as far east as Iceland. But the British bore the brunt of the U-boat attack in the dark, cold waters between Iceland and the United Kingdom, and it was their strategy that checked Dönitz for the time being.

The British tried something old and something new. From the memory of World War I they reactivated convoy escorts to replace the less effective and very risky antisubmarine patrols by surface warships. Newly developed radar sets were installed on the escorting destroyers, corvettes, and frigates so they could track and even ram surfaced U-boats at night. During daylight, heavy land-based aircraft flew cover from bases in Iceland and Great Britain. The Canadians joined in, permitting unbroken surface escort all the way from Halifax to England beginning in May. From that point on, the escorting of convoys remained the standard operating procedure of antisubmarine warfare in the Atlantic war.

The great breakthrough came in electronic intelligence. The capture of *U-110* on 8 May 1941 yielded an "Enigma" encrypting machine, the analysis of which enabled the British to decipher Dönitz's tactical commands to his U-boat skippers. The British could now steer convoys around wolfpack concentrations, a tactic that changed the course of the war. In August 1941 U-boats sank only 80,000 tons of allied shipping, down from 268,000 tons the previous August. The Battle of the Atlantic was not exactly over when Ger-many declared war on the United States on 11 December 1941, but the blueprint for the Anglo-American defeat of the U-boat had been drawn.

The eventual outcome was not apparent for much of 1942. As soon as hostilities were declared, German U-boats moved into Amer-ican home waters. They took up station off the East Coast and in the Gulf of Mexico, where bright city lights and ships' running lights made tankers and cargo ships easy targets. The American high com-mand was slow to adopt convoys in Gulf and coastal waters, learning

the hard way what the British had learned on the high seas: They
were the only effective means of protecting slow merchantmen. One
specialist estimates that damage to the war effort from the coastal
losses to U-boats in the early spring of 1942, "especially of the oil-
filled tankers, was more severe than that caused by the raid on Pearl
Harbor." By the end of the year, however, blacked-out cities and a
system of interlocking convoys stretching from the mouth of the Mississippi to New Jersey brought an end to Dönitz's "Second Happy
Time."

In the North Atlantic the year 1942 looked grim. For ten months
the British lost the ability to decipher Dönitz's tactical commands.
Worse still, perhaps, the German at last had his three hundred submarines. Hitler had lost faith in the surface navy after the Anglo-
Americans sank his best surface raiders in 1941, and he had finally
allocated substantial industrial resources to U-boat construction. The
United States had not yet had time to expand its shipbuilding capacity
to compensate for lost merchant tonnage and to build escorts numerous enough to provide heavy cover for each convoy. November was
the cruelest month: 700,000 tons went down. Then, in the darkest
hour at sea, technology worked more miracles.

In early 1943 British cryptanalysts again cracked the German
submarine cipher, and convoys could once more be routed around
wolfpacks. The pinpointing of submarines even without decoding became possible through a high-frequency radio direction finder (HF/
DF), which allowed allied sub-hunters to trace submarine radio
transmissions to their source and sink the transmitter. Radar was
improved to the point where the Germans on the surface could not
detect it and therefore did not know they were being "painted" by
allied aircraft or ships. And the ships carried new antisubmarine ordnance, special "ahead thrown" weapons launched to hit submarines in
front of the warships, thus cutting the interception time and increasing the chances of a kill. Those technological advances and the sheer
number of new escorts, including a special light aircraft carrier, accounted for the reversal of fortunes in mid-1943 more than anything
else.

The institution of the Tenth Fleet, Ernest King's personal command over the escorts and submarine hunters of the Central Atlantic,
undoubtedly gave added clout to American antisubmarine warfare.
Using the new technologies for locating submarines, King sent
hunter-killer groups after them. This concept differed from the original patrols, which were hit-and-miss affairs of blind man's bluff, and

they were fruitful supplements to the more passive escorts whose counterattacks were kept within a short range of the convoys being escorted.

=====

Antisubmarine warfare in the Atlantic was tough and crucial to allied victory, but in one way it was simple: ASW was strictly a navy show. Such was not the case with the great amphibious operations in North Africa, Sicily, Italy, and both coasts of France. To stage those vital landings, the navy to some extent had to subordinate itself to army strategy. Moreover, the amphibious navy of troop carriers and landing craft has always been a poor stepchild of the surface fighting fleet. It has not attracted the top officers or abundant appropriations from Congress. But ironically, as a further complication of the picture in 1942 and 1943, amphibious operations drew the direct personal attention of Prime Minister Churchill and President Roosevelt. That in turn meant that the army chief of staff, General Marshall, and the navy's commander-in-chief, Admiral King, were both deeply involved in the planning and execution of the landings.

The most senior Anglo-American leadership was divided over the nature and location of the transatlantic attack on German military forces. Churchill's greatest worry at the December 1941 meeting in Washington was that public opinion would force the United States to abandon its Atlantic-first strategy. Once reassured by Roosevelt that the Pacific theater remained secondary, Churchill and the British chiefs of staff pressed the Americans to plan an attack on German military forces. Marshall and his war plans chief, Dwight D. Eisenhower, consulted the navy and proposed two options: a possible invasion of France in the fall of 1942 to divert German strength westward if Russia's collapse appeared imminent, or a definite landing in France in 1943, followed by a breakout and a war-winning invasion of the industrial heart of Germany. The second option, "Operation Roundup," might have salved the incessant Soviet cry for a "second front" in the west, a demand not really met until June 1944.

The chief of the Imperial General Staff, General Sir Alan Brooke, rejected both options on the grounds that the German army in France was too strong and the risk of being thrown back into the sea too great. A defeated invasion in western France could cost the allies the war. Churchill and his staff officers wanted peripheral action to bleed the Wehrmacht before making ultimate thrusts across France and up the allegedly "soft underbelly" of the Balkans. Much later, it appeared as if Churchill had also been thinking in terms of stopping a westward Soviet march by inserting Anglo-American troops into Eastern Europe before the Red Army arrived, but in 1942 the Soviets were desperately on the defensive, and the Western Allies would be lucky if Russia could hold out until the balance in the west shifted.

In 1942 Churchill's long-range vision focused on preservation of the overseas British Empire much more than on containment of the Soviet Union. The critical maritime axis of the empire was the Mediterranean, as it had been since the Suez Canal was completed in 1869. In early 1942 Gibraltar still ensured limited access from the Atlantic, but much of the North African coast was in hostile German or Vichy French hands. The Afrika Korps of "Desert Fox" Erwin Rommel was besieging El Alamein, 70 miles west of Alexandria, Egypt. If he succeeded, Suez would be Hitler's. The historic lifeline to India, the crown jewel of the empire, would be cut, a political disaster Churchill could not contemplate. The canal had to be saved; the Mediterranean must be the locale for the American army's first encounter with the Axis armies.

George Marshall and Ernest King could dissent, each for different reasons: Marshall to fight first in France, King to shift primary emphasis to the Pacific. But Franklin Roosevelt countermanded his men and sided with Churchill. In July 1942 he sent Marshall and King to London to plan how the U.S. Navy would carry the U.S. Army to North Africa, a place neither service chief wished to attack.

Lieutenant General Dwight D. Eisenhower was tapped for the job of field commander of Operation Torch. He was sent to Gibraltar to plan the North African invasion under the watchful eyes of the overall naval commander, Admiral Sir Andrew B. Cunningham, RN. At Norfolk, Virginia, the Western Naval Task Force was assembled by Rear Admiral H. Kent Hewitt and the army's hottest tank-driver, Major General George S. Patton. "D-day" was set for 8 November 1942. The target was Casablanca, on the Atlantic coast of French Morocco, held by Vichy French troops, who, it was hoped, would not resist the Americans too vigorously.

The allied offensive in the Atlantic began on 24 October 1942, when the amphibians, ferrying 35,000 American soldiers, sortied from Hampton Roads. They were joined at sea by an escort force of three old battleships, the aircraft carrier *Ranger*, and several small antisubmarine "escort" carriers. Evasive maneuvering carried them safely around U-boat concentrations, and in the dark early morning hours of 8 November thousands of Americans struggled ashore at Casablanca from crudely improvised landing craft. The Royal Navy meanwhile ferried Anglo-American contingents from the United Kingdom to landings in Oran and Algiers, inside the Mediterranean on the coast of Vichy French–held Algeria. Once the three main bodies of troops secured beachheads, the navy turned command over to the generals, and the fight against the Afrika Korps became an army job. Eisenhower and Patton pressed eastward; British General Bernard L. Montgomery's Eighth Army broke out at El Alamein and closed the pincers from the east. The armies met in Tunisia while the Anglo-American political-military high commands reconvened in newly captured Casablanca.

The setting was new, the issues old. Once again Marshall insisted on opening a second front in France and the British demanded additional operations in the Mediterranean. To avoid a presidential ukase, the American general yielded one last time. Marshall agreed that the next Axis target would be Sicily, but he would go no farther away from Germany in the Mediterranean. The move after Sicily must be against France, toward the German heartland.

Sicily is a mere 90 miles northeast of Tunisia, an easy hop compared with the transatlantic landings just completed. Strategically, an attack on the Italian island might topple Hitler's mercurial partner, Benito Mussolini, and draw Italy out of the war. At least that was the rationale used to gloss over the serious Anglo-American differences on how to fight the European war.

Other disagreements bedeviling the senior staff officers at Casablanca included army and navy skepticism about General Henry H. Arnold's assertion that strategic bombing could by itself defeat Hitler and British reluctance to approve Admiral King's demand for an immediate, if limited, central Pacific offensive. Both King and Arnold nonetheless won approvals in what had become a process of strategy-making by interservice and interallied compromise. The only area of genuine agreement was that until the U-boat was killed all offensive operations in Europe and the Mediterranean were in some jeopardy. While the Anglo-American naval leadership could not demur, this particular consensus served to place any onus for failure on the navy rather than on another service. From the navy's viewpoint it was coalition warfare at its worst.

"Operation Husky," the invasion of Sicily, was carried out on 9–10 July 1943 by the same team of flag and general officers— Cunningham, Hewitt, Eisenhower, Montgomery, and Patton. The distance was much shorter, and the scale much greater—175,000 men landed this time. The sophistication had improved. Infrared

signal lights guided specially designed transports and landing craft—
the LSTs, LCTs, and LCIs now rolling off the American assembly
lines in quantity. Mistakes were made. The army continued to insist
on night landings for surprise, and darkness caused anxiety if not
confusion among the soldiers. Hewitt lost a destroyer, an LST, and an
ammunition ship. The German army beat the Anglo-Americans in the
race across the island to Messina and escaped to the boot of Italy. But
Mussolini lost face and fell from power. A new Italian government
opened negotiations for peace.

Husky's success did not help Marshall's case for "Roundup."
Another meeting of the top leaders was held, this time in Washington. The outcome was the same as before: a compromise on strategic
objectives. The British wanted Salerno, on the Italian coast south of
Naples. To win American concurrence they at last agreed to a date in
1944 for the cross-Channel invasion of France.

On 9 September 1943 Admiral Hewitt again carried Eisenhower's men ashore, but the Germans had anticipated the landing, and
the resistance was deadly. The Italian armistice saved few allied lives.
Of all the landings in World War II, Salerno came the closest to being
repulsed. Close air support by British land-based aircraft and navy
fliers helped the troops keep the beach, and naval gunfire from battleships, cruisers, and destroyers blocked the final German try at a
breakthrough on 16 September. Lieutenant General Mark Clark's
Fifth Army broke out and occupied Naples, which the navy immediately began converting into an American base. It has been in use
ever since.

Eisenhower headed for London to plan the invasion of Normandy, now named "Overlord." He was lucky to avoid the Churchill-
inspired Anzio landings of January 1944 and the subsequent tactical
stalemate, which found the allied soldiers pinned on the beach for
almost five months. The Germans did not pull back and out of Italy
until a few days before the Normandy landings. The Mediterranean
campaign had lasted about twenty months, and in that time the Soviet
Red Army had held the line from Leningrad to Moscow to Stalingrad.
It now was pushing the Wehrmacht back toward Berlin. The Anglo-
American "operations aimed at the heart of Germany and the destruction of her armed forces" had not yet begun. The utility of the
English peripheral strategy was in doubt.

Churchill nonetheless wanted to continue pressing the Italian
campaign northward, with Vienna the ultimate objective. He would
beat the Red Army into Austria. Eisenhower, backed by Marshall and

Roosevelt, demanded instead a landing on the French Mediterranean coast to coincide with Overlord and draw German troops away from Normandy toward the south of France. The code name was "Dragoon," and the highly experienced Admiral H. Kent Hewitt was placed in charge. At sunrise on 15 August 1944 he executed a textbook-perfect landing embodying everything he had learned at Casablanca, Sicily, and Salerno:

> an extended land-based aerial bombing campaign to knock out enemy airfields and strong points, realistic rehearsals of the landing, a night paratroop drop to seal off the beachhead, an intensive two-hour bombing and bombardment of the beach defenses, rocket firing LCIs preceding the first assault wave to detonate land mines.

A shortage of landing craft, many of which had been shipped to the Pacific for offensive amphibious operations in the Marianas, had delayed Dragoon until mid-August, two months after Overlord. But once launched, the operation permitted Supreme Allied Commander Eisenhower's field generals—Montgomery, Patton, and Omar Bradley—to isolate the German troops in the southwest of France and then to surge toward Paris and Germany on a much broader front. It also opened the large French port of Marseilles to allied shipping, a major logistical asset for the inland armies.

Dragoon was the culmination of the Mediterranean campaign and to some extent justified the British strategy of peripheral envelopment. But in the summer of 1944, and in history books ever since, it was a nearly forgotten sideshow to the operation General Marshall had wanted from the very beginning of the war: the landing in France.

"D-day," the 6th of June 1944, is unique in military and naval annals. The landing on the Normandy coast was the largest, "most complex and most minutely planned military operation in history." Under General Dwight Eisenhower's overall command, 2,700 American and British vessels crossed the English Channel to land five army divisions between Cherbourg and Le Havre. At the two designated American landing beaches, Utah and Omaha, the Western Naval Task Force of Rear Admiral Alan G. Kirk put 55,000 men ashore in one day.

The German resistance at Utah Beach was slight, but Omaha was heavily fortified and resolutely defended by battle-hardened veterans. A short naval bombardment and low tide forced the troops to wade and race through a hailstorm of machine-gun fire. Sheer guts carried the Americans a mile past the beach by nightfall, but they were helped throughout the bloody day by covering fire from twelve destroyers. One of them, the U.S.S. *Frankford,* commanded by Lieutenant Commander James Semmes, ran in to within 400 yards of the beach to blast German fortifications on the bluff above. The *Frankford's* 5-inch guns probably made the first real breach in the German bunkers overlooking Omaha. Once the soldiers had broken through them, Germany was caught between two massive pincers—the Anglo-French-Americans to the west and the Soviets to the east. World War II in the Atlantic was no longer a naval matter. It was at last possible to concentrate exclusively on the navy's war of choice: the fight against Japan in the Pacific.

11

The Navy's War in the Pacific

1941 – 1945

THE Japanese attack on the American battlefleet at Pearl Harbor, Hawaii, on 7 December 1941, had not unduly distressed the sailors of the Atlantic Fleet. Their reaction was one of relief that "the event of war with Japan, long expected by all Navy men, had at last become a reality." As a former engineer of the battleship *West Virginia* recalled, "the news was received in general with a degree of smugness and a firm confidence." Most Atlantic Fleet officers assumed that the damage sustained by the Pacific Fleet would be light, the striking force of Japanese carriers would be quickly hunted down and sunk, and the navy would push across the central Pacific to relieve the Philippines as part of the campaign to sweep the Japanese fleet from the sea and isolate the home islands. After all, this had been the plan for twenty years.

The president, too, had supreme confidence in the invulnerability of the American battlefleet. War might come as a result of his July embargo on American oil exports to Japan, but Roosevelt "did not expect to get hurt" badly in the first exchange. He had relieved the senior Cassandra, Admiral James O. Richardson, after only one year as commander-in-chief of the Pacific Fleet because he did not want to hear dire warnings of exposure and loss risked by stationing the fleet in Hawaii rather than on the continental West Coast. The politically astute army chief of staff, General George C. Marshall, assured him in May 1941 that Hawaii was "the strongest fortress in the world. . . . Enemy carriers, naval escorts and transports will begin to come under air attack at a distance of approximately 750 miles." This forecast assumed Japan might attack Hawaii, an assumption most naval strategists rejected as "utterly stupid," in the words of the assistant war plans officer of the Pacific Fleet. So all the president's men advised him that the Japanese would not attack, and that in any event carrier-based airplanes could not sink battleships. The news of the heavy losses at Pearl Harbor therefore came as a "terrible blow" to Roosevelt and to "his faith in the Navy and its ships." No wonder, then, that when asking Congress for a declaration of war against Japan he called December 7, 1941, "a day that will live in infamy."

Neither naval engineers nor presidential advisers had dreamed that six Japanese aircraft carriers could launch an early Sunday morning strike of about 350 airplanes that would sink the moored battleships *Arizona, Oklahoma, California,* and *West Virginia* and heavily damage four others. The only Pacific Fleet battleship to escape unscathed was the *Colorado,* in drydock on the West Coast, 2,000 miles away. More than two hundred American aircraft were destroyed, most of them on the ground. The dead numbered 2,400, and the wounded 1,300. The potency of Japanese naval aviation had been proved beyond the shadow of a doubt. Gone forever was the cultural arrogance of Captain William D. Puleston, a naval intellectual and admirer of Mahan, who had observed in his 1941 book *The Armed Forces of the Pacific,* "Japan has been energetic in her efforts to create naval aviation, but she is usually a phase behind." Those words were now worth eating.

The carriers *Lexington* and *Enterprise* were safely at sea on 7 December 1941, delivering airplanes to Wake and Midway islands. Their survival, coupled with the now proven efficacy of naval aviation, meant that the aircraft carrier would almost immediately become the main American combatant of the surface war in the Pacific.

The other lucky American break was the Japanese decision to concentrate on the battle wagons and spare the submarine force at Pearl. The Americans now would initiate unrestricted submarine warfare, the very strategy Woodrow Wilson had denounced as immoral in 1914–1917. Their target would be the island empire's crucial lines of communications with resource-rich European colonies in the South Pacific, soon to fall to the rising sun. The United States Navy's fight in the Pacific therefore relied from the outset on two weapons systems—the aircraft carrier and the submarine—disdained in interwar planning as worthy only to screen the battleships that now lay on the coral-and-mud bottom of Pearl Harbor.

For six months navy men reorganized and braced for the worst, unaware that for the United States Navy the worst had already happened. The day after Pearl Harbor Roosevelt and Stark transferred the carrier *Yorktown,* three battleships, and a squadron of new destroyers from the Atlantic to the Pacific. Japan had struck first, and Congress had declared war in response. For a few days the battle of the Atlantic remained unofficial, until Hitler honored the Tripartite Treaty with Japan and Italy and declared war on the United States on 11 December. Now Admiral Stark's Plan Dog could be implemented as national strategy, although for the navy it was not that simple. The dead sailors at Pearl Harbor had to be avenged, and the major Mahanian naval rival had to be crushed decisively.

Ernest J. King was the man in charge. Within a week of Pearl Harbor the president brought the war-seasoned Atlantic Fleet commander to Washington and named him commander-in-chief of the U.S. Fleet—"COMINCH," an acronym better left uninvented. By March 1942 Roosevelt had sacked his old friend, chief of naval operations Harold R. Stark, and had sent him off to London as a high-ranking naval liaison officer. Too deliberative and compassionate for a navy at war, Stark gave way to a man little liked but universally respected for his high intelligence, fiery temperament, and quick decisions. An officer of broad naval experience, King was equally familiar with the elements of surface and aerial warfare. He held the dual titles of chief of naval operations and COMINCH for the duration of the war. His one uniformed peer in Washington was the army chief of staff, General George C. Marshall, a "Europe-first" man by strategic conviction and service loyalty. Genteel in demeanor but iron in will, Marshall was at least a match for King in brilliance.

To provide a forum for playing King off against Marshall, a favorite Roosevelt administrative technique, the president by executive decree reshaped the Joint Board of the Army and Navy into the Joint Chiefs of Staff (JCS). This body became the American counterpart to the British Chiefs of Staff Committee (COS). The chief of the Army Air Forces, General Henry H. "Hap" Arnold, was a member but lacked the independent service base to compete equally with Marshall or King. Overseeing the JCS after July 1942 was the chairman and presidential naval aide, Admiral William D. Leahy, formerly the chief of naval operations and personally known to Roosevelt since

World War I. Since Roosevelt habitually referred to the navy as "us" and the army as "them," the navy was sure to get enough resources to fight a Pacific war regardless of the announced national strategy.

What appeared at first glance to be a tightly organized, unified staff system really had the characteristics of a kingdom in which feudal princes vied for the king's approval and largess. But unless this useful analogy is expanded beyond Washington, D.C., it leaves out two other strong personalities with independent and direct claims to the president's attention. General Douglas MacArthur, a former chief of staff and probably the most charismatic character in the history of the United States Army, was driven from the Philippines in a Japanese attack that coincided with the bombing of Pearl Harbor. He swore he would return to Manila in triumph, took up station in Australia, and carried enough political clout in Washington to win a separate interservice command in the southwest Pacific.

On the other side of the world, in London, Winston Churchill was determined to use Roosevelt to preserve the British Empire as part of the process of defeating Germany and Japan. Joyous that the United States at last was in the war, he and his Combined Chiefs of Staff came to Washington in December 1941 to begin educating the Americans to appreciate the importance of the Mediterranean Sea. This maritime lifeline connected England with India, the British Empire in East Asia, and Australia. Churchill succeeded: The first American amphibious landing in the Atlantic theater came in North Africa, far removed from the coast of France, where George Marshall thought it should be made.

The top strategists' preoccupation with the Mediterranean and Europe gave King a reasonably free hand to call the shots for the Pacific. The first item of business had been to dismiss the Pacific Fleet commander, Admiral Husband E. Kimmel, for failing to prepare a defense against an attack no one had seriously anticipated. Kimmel's attention at Pearl Harbor had been directed against possible sabotage in conjunction with a Japanese attack on the Philippines and in Southeast Asia. He and the senior army commander had parked their aircraft together for easy surveillance by sentries instead of dispersing them. That arrangement greatly increased the damage when the Japanese caught the planes on the ground. It was in fact the extent of the damage to the ships and aircraft of the fleet at Pearl Harbor that bewildered Washington and forced Kimmel's almost immediate dismissal. One of Roosevelt's most intimate advisers, Secretary of the Treasury Henry Morgenthau, noted on 7 December, "It is just unexplainable. . . . They have the whole fleet in one place . . . the whole fleet in this little Pearl Harbor base. They will never be able to explain it." Admiral Kimmel certainly never did explain it, and he became the navy's scapegoat for the inexplicable.

King replaced him with Chester W. Nimitz, the chief of the Bureau of Navigation. The new commander-in-chief of the Pacific Fleet had been waiting cautiously in Washington for the outbreak of war and the inevitable personnel shakedown before risking his own career and reputation in an exposed operational command. His interwar experience had not made him professionally or intellectually audacious. Like others of his generation, he had studied at the Naval War College, where the curriculum consisted principally of endless re-creations of the battles of Trafalgar and Jutland—the fleet actions supposedly most meaningful to a battleship navy—and the refinement of War Plan Orange. By one count, Nimitz's generation of officers practiced for war with enemy Orange—Japan—on charts and board games at least 127 times. Nimitz later said that "the courses were so thorough that nothing that happened in the Pacific War was strange or unexpected." It became a war of self-fulfilling planning fought by a small group of top commanders, about a dozen in all. They had known each other at the Naval Academy between 1901 and 1905 and were professionally and personally dedicated to one another. Nimitz emerged as *primus inter pares* of this elite cadre in 1942.

As Nimitz took up command of the Pacific Fleet, headquartered at Pearl Harbor, the allies were suffering two numbing losses. The Philippine Islands succumbed to the Japanese army after a resistance on Corregidor and Bataan that has entered the folklore of American heroism. Through his shrewd manipulation of press communiqués, General MacArthur became a national hero, even though he was evacuated to safety in Australia in early March, before his troops finally surrendered to the Japanese. The administration in Washington, desperate for symbols of hope in the dark first six months of the war, abetted the enshrinement of MacArthur with the Medal of Honor. This was a safer course than a risky reinforcement of the Philippines through Japanese blockaders. In fact, Washington had abandoned MacArthur's army as early as 3 January on the grounds that a massive relief effort, even if it could be mounted in time, would "constitute an entirely unjustifiable diversion of forces from the principal theater—the Atlantic."

The evacuation and apotheosis of MacArthur had an inevitable strategic consequence: It created the nucleus of a separate command in the southwest Pacific, the leader of which now had such transcendent popular stature that he could demand full partnership in the navy's Pacific war. The central Pacific command of Admiral Nimitz would therefore be diluted as scarce ships were sent south. For a navy addicted to the Mahanian concept of the concentration of force, this was a disturbing and totally unforeseen outcome of twenty years' planning to hold the Philippine Islands as the first step in an orderly naval defeat of Japan.

The second great loss of 1942 was British. Singapore, the Gibraltar of the Malay peninsula, fell to an overland assault of the Japanese army in February. Since 1939 the British had been begging for American help in defending the chokepoint, which controls access to the Pacific from the Indian Ocean, but the United States Navy wanted to base its defense of the Pacific on the purely American California-Hawaii-Philippine axis, not on a long and essentially British supply line running from the East Coast through the Mediterranean, Suez, and the Indian Ocean to Singapore. So Singapore fell on 15 February, giving Tokyo control of the Southeast Asian land mass, rich in foodstuffs and militarily invaluable resources, and placing the Japanese on the threshold of the oil-rich Dutch East Indies and perhaps even Australia itself. By March they were drawing all the high-grade oil they wanted from Borneo, Sumatra, and Java. Their Southern Resources Area stretched from Burma through the East Indies to Wake Island. Looking westward, the entire Indian Ocean, the very heart of the British Empire, lay open to Japanese invasion.

The capitulation of Singapore completed the elimination of Britain as a major factor in the Pacific war, a reduction that had begun with the mortifying loss in Malay waters of the battleship *Prince of Wales* and the battle cruiser *Repulse* to Japanese land-based aircraft on 10 December 1941. This was the first time heavy bombers had successfully attacked and sunk capital ships under way in combat. When juxtaposed with what Japanese carrier-based aircraft accomplished at Pearl Harbor, the sinking of the two heavies marked the end of the useful life of battleships. From the purely British perspective, as the historian John Keegan has concluded, English sea power in the traditional sense of capital ships and strategic chokepoints now ceased to exist between East Africa and the Pacific Ocean. The epoch of Western domination of Asia was closing.

Against that backdrop, the American loss of Wake and Guam in December 1941 appears relatively insignificant, but those two insular way stations on the maritime road to the Philippines were critical to the navy's central Pacific campaign. Eventually Admiral Nimitz would have to retake them, but first he had to help stop the rampaging Japanese advance on all fronts. Defense, never to the American navy's liking, became the order of the day for the first six months of 1942.

The only exceptions to the defensive posture were carrier Admiral William F. Halsey's occasional hit-and-run swipes at Japanese bases in the Marshall Islands and Lieutenant Colonel James H. Doolittle's 18 April raid against Tokyo with army B-25s launched from Halsey's carrier *Hornet*, escorted by *Enterprise*. Those were morale-boosters only, and Nimitz in particular resented the Doolittle sortie as a dangerous diversion of fully half his fleet's carrier force. On the other hand, the B-25s disturbed the Japanese enough to eliminate all staff opposition to the Midway attack of June, an unforeseen consequence that was ultimately beneficial for the U.S. Navy.

The Pacific war's two greatest defensive naval actions were fought within a month of each other. At the Battle of the Coral Sea, 4–8 May 1942, an American carrier fleet turned back a Japanese invasion intended to cut communications between the United States and Australia. Through decrypted radio intercepts Admiral Nimitz had learned that a Japanese strike force would try to capture the small island of Tulagi in the eastern Solomons and Port Moresby on New Guinea, preparatory to moving much farther southeast to New Caledonia, the Fijis, and Samoa. With Halsey's *Enterprise* and *Hornet* diverted north on the Doolittle raid, Nimitz had only the carriers *Lexington* and *Yorktown* for the core of a fleet commanded by Rear Admiral Frank Jack Fletcher.

The Japanese, overconfident and busily planning for the nearly simultaneous raid on Midway, had allocated only three aircraft carriers to cover the landings in the South Pacific. Fletcher's flyers took out one of them, the light carrier *Shoho*, in a sparring match on 7 May. Denied sufficient air cover, the Port Moresby invasion force turned back. The next day, 8 May, both sides mauled each other. *Yorktown* was hit but continued air operations; *Lexington* was torpedoed, her aviation fuel created an inferno, and she was sunk. The Japanese carrier *Shokaku* was heavily damaged and put out of action for weeks; the air group of the *Zuikaku* was decimated, making her temporarily impotent. Neither carrier would be available for Midway.

The Battle of the Coral Sea conforms to the trite generalization:

A tactical victory for one side, a strategic victory for the other. The Americans lost more heavily in percentage of the air power engaged, but a decade of seemingly inexorable Japanese political-military expansion had been checked for the first time. Equally noteworthy, in the words of naval historian Elmer B. Potter, "This was the first battle in history between carrier forces and the first in which the opposing fleets never came within sight of each other." The days of the battleship were numbered.

The most significant carrier battle in history took place on 3–6 June 1942, just northwest of the island of Midway, a gap in Japan's northern defense perimeter and an outpost shielding Hawaii from direct Japanese aggression. Here again electronic intelligence was critical to Nimitz's preparations. Shrewd analysis and a discreet deceptive radio message of his own convinced the Pacific Fleet commander that Japan would soon attack the island. He was right. On 27 May—the anniversary of Tsushima, itself a token of Nelson in the Japanese naval mind—a massive fleet set out from the Inland Sea. The overall commander was Admiral Isoroku Yamamoto, architect of Pearl Harbor, now aboard the 64,000-ton superdreadnought *Yamato*. His carrier strike force commander, Vice Admiral Chuichi Nagumo, had commanded the Pearl Harbor attack of 7 December.

Optimism characterized the Japanese, despite the aerial pinpricks of Halsey and Doolittle and the loss of a small carrier in the Coral Sea. By surprising the Americans the Japanese would overwhelm the defenders of Midway and draw Nimitz's remaining carriers from Pearl Harbor for destruction by Yamamoto's eleven battleships and dozen-plus cruisers. So great were Japanese confidence and aggressiveness that Yamamoto sent some of his ships north to strike and invade Alaska's Aleutian Islands. That diversion and the incapacitation of the *Shokaku* and the downing of the *Zuikaku*'s air group at the Battle of the Coral Sea reduced Nagumo to four carriers. He was in an exposed position. Yamamoto remained 450 miles to the northwest pending contact with the American carriers, at which time he would close for the kill under the cover of Nagumo's fighters. Little matter, for the Japanese believed the Americans had lost two carriers in the Coral Sea.

In reality, *Yorktown* had survived and was patched together in time for the Midway fight. Still, Nimitz's fleet was indeed vastly inferior to Yamamoto's. Frank Jack Fletcher, the tactical commander, controlled only three carriers, *Yorktown*, *Enterprise*, and *Hornet*, plus eight cruisers and fourteen destroyers. The airfield on Midway could be counted as an additional carrier of sorts, but the army air-crews were not schooled in antiship bombing. The odds were very bad.

As the Japanese anticipated, surprise would spell victory. The difference was that the Americans were the ones who achieved the surprise. At dawn on 4 June, within minutes of the time predicted by Nimitz's intelligence officer, Commander Edwin T. Layton, Nagumo launched his strike. He was met by fighters and counterattacking bombers based on Midway, but nothing met him from the American carriers, whose presence to his northeast, well above Midway, he did not suspect. He learned of their whereabouts only when his own aircraft were returning from the strike on Midway. Opting to maximize his firepower, Nagumo ordered his planes rearmed with armor-piercing bombs and torpedoes, and then turned to meet Fletcher's fleet. The Americans launched first, but an entire squadron of low-flying torpedo-bombers from the *Hornet* went down without a hit. Only one aviator survived. The Americans were on the brink of losing the remnants of the Pacific Fleet.

After following false trails away from Nagumo, dive bombers from the *Enterprise* finally found him. At the same moment a squadron of *Yorktown* dive bombers arrived high overhead. The Japanese were scanning the horizon, looking for more low-altitude torpedo planes to gun down. Instead, the sky rained American bombs on decks cluttered with unstored Japanese ordnance just removed from the rearmed airplanes about to launch. It was an inferno. The British historian John Keegan has vividly portrayed the trauma of Nagumo, who at 10:25 A.M. "stood poised on the brink of perhaps the greatest naval victory ever promised an admiral." Five minutes later, as American bombs dropped all over his flagship, the carrier *Akagi*, "he confronted not victory but disaster." With flames licking at the bridge, Nagumo had to be "forcibly transshipped" to a substitute flagship.

The *Yorktown* went down soon after, and Fletcher transferred command to Raymond A. Spruance, aboard a cruiser. That night Spruance evaded Yamamoto's battleships, which were hungry for a gunnery engagement when darkness would blind the American airplanes. When dawn came and the aviators could begin to hunt him down, Yamamoto turned toward Tokyo. The Japanese had lost four fleet carriers at the Battle of Midway, the *Akagi*, *Kaga*, *Hiryu*, and *Soryu*. They also had lost scores of irreplaceable veteran aviators. The Americans lost one carrier, the already badly battered *Yorktown*. *Hornet* and *Enterprise* survived. This was an unambiguous tactical and strategic victory. The war of the Pacific had a long time yet to run, but Japanese expansion had reached its farthest limits. From now on, the Americans were on the offensive, something the navy men liked much better, and to fight the Pacific war they were building a new kind of capital ship.

Less than two weeks after the Battle of Midway, on 14 June 1942, the House Naval Affairs Committee unanimously approved construction of 500,000 tons of aircraft carriers—the figure set for American battleships in the Washington conference of 1921–1922. At almost the same time, the building of the five *Montana*-class "super dreadnoughts" was suspended, never to be resumed. In fact, none of the battleships authorized by the two Vinson bills in June and July of 1940 were ever completed. In December Secretary of the Navy Frank Knox noted that the first six months after Pearl Harbor had demonstrated conclusively "the full part that air power, as a component of sea power, was to play in modern war."

The battle for Guadalcanal, which blanketed the second six months of the Pacific war, sustained the importance of air power in naval warfare but by no means elevated it to the predominance that Pearl Harbor and Midway had foreshadowed. Elated by Midway, Admiral King lobbied the Joint Chiefs of Staff for a limited offensive in the Pacific. Too weak to undertake the long-contemplated Plan Orange offensive in the central Pacific, King conceived a navy drive through the Solomon Islands to check the still-threatened Japanese advance toward the American line of communications with Australia. That much was simple; the rest was disorder and interservice discord.

Midway persuaded General MacArthur that the time was ripe for an offensive in the southwest Pacific, that is, within his area of authority. He proposed a lightning strike against the major Japanese base at Rabaul, on the island of New Britain, to drive the Japanese away from the Solomons. MacArthur lacked troops trained in amphibious operations, and his land-based fighters could not reach Rabaul to cover a landing. His solution was simplicity itself: The Marine Corps, the only American service to perfect the techniques of amphibious warfare in the interwar period, would lend him the specially trained First Marine Division. The navy would provide him with two aircraft carriers, that is, one-half of its Pacific carrier force.

Admiral King hit the roof. He informed Marshall that the navy's Nimitz, not the army's MacArthur, must command in the Solomons. King and the navy would mount an operation "even if no support of army forces in the southwest Pacific is made available." MacArthur retorted that King's obstinacy was part of the navy's historic plan to absorb completely "the national defense function . . . the Army being relegated to merely base, training, garrisoning, and supply purposes." Not likely. King, like MacArthur, simply wanted to create for his service "an active fighting constituency in the Pacific with a rightful call on American resources before the Allies undertook major operations against Germany." Both men would get their way, because in this war strategic decision-making was marked more by compromise at high levels than by dispassionate, rational planning.

The unseemly dispute rocked the Joint Chiefs of Staff in late June 1942. It led to a compromise three-stage plan of operations, code-named "Watchtower." As planning began for the first phase, a navy–marine corps attack on the island of Tulagi, electronic intelligence indicated that the Japanese were building an airfield on Guadalcanal, an island not targeted in the original plan. Watchtower was reshaped accordingly, and the lexicon of classic battles was rewritten.

The issue at Guadalcanal was an airfield. The side that built one would control the air over the Solomons. For Japan, this spelled renewed expansion toward the Australian–American line of communications. For the United States it meant the first step of a painfully slow island-by-island advance to the northwest, ultimately to the Philippines and beyond. For both sides it symbolized offensive rather than defensive warfare.

A Japanese construction unit got to Guadalcanal first, but on 6–8 August marines of the First Division easily drove them into the jungle. The leathernecks seized the nearly completed airfield, renamed it Henderson Field after one of their fliers at Midway, and opened it for business on 17 August. The Marine Corps now had a permanent fixed base for bombers and fighters, an invaluable asset in the ensuing five-month struggle to remain on Guadalcanal in the face of unremitting Japanese attempts to retake it.

The seesaw pattern was established early on. During daylight hours the Japanese fleet was kept out of the area by Marine Corps aviators, sometimes backed by Vice Admiral Frank Jack Fletcher's carrier aircraft or even high-altitude army B-17s flying from Espiritu Santo to the southeast. But at night the Japanese navy owned the "Slot"—a channel along the Solomons. In high-speed runs down the Slot, the nighttime "Tokyo Express" ran reinforcements to Guadalcanal and attacked any American warships unlucky enough to be in the vicinity.

At the Battle of Savo Island on the night of 8–9 August, while the transports were still unloading supplies for the marines a few miles to the south at Guadalcanal, the United States Navy lost four heavy cruisers to night-fighting Japanese cruisers. The Japanese commander fortunately did not stay around to mop up the transports but instead sped to the northwest at about 30 knots. Fletcher had already lost twenty-one fighter aircraft. Knowing that Japan had at least four carriers loose somewhere in the Pacific, he had retired earlier that day to refuel his force. He was not around to chase the Japanese back up the Slot at daybreak on 9 August.

Two weeks later, on 24 August, in the Battle of the Eastern Solomons, Fletcher engaged the *Shokaku* and *Zuikaku* and a light carrier, the *Ryujo*. His bombers knocked out the *Ryujo*, but the *Enterprise* took three hits from Japanese planes. Fletcher again retired, and the marines were left to hold on doggedly to Henderson Field against all challenges from malaria, dysentery, and the Japanese.

Fletcher and the admiral in overall command of Watchtower, Robert L. Ghormley, were too cautious to suit Nimitz and King. They were recalled, and on 18 October the operation was placed under the command of the navy's fire-eating answer to George Patton, Vice Admiral William F. Halsey. Learning that a large enemy fleet of four carriers and four battleships—protected by a screen of fourteen cruisers and forty-four destroyers—was headed south from the Japanese stronghold on Truk, Halsey ordered his two carriers and one battleship—screened by six cruisers and fourteen destroyers—north to "Attack—Repeat—Attack!"

Rear Admiral Thomas C. Kinkaid complied, and at the Battle of the Santa Cruz Islands on 26–27 October the Japanese sank the carrier *Hornet* and heavily damaged the *Enterprise*. Their own carriers *Zuiho* and *Shokaku* were severely damaged. Both forces pulled back in what the Americans stubbornly interpreted as a tactical loss but a strategic victory. If it was, the margin was thin. The navy did not have a single operational carrier in the entire Pacific until *Enterprise* was hurriedly stitched back together. She then rushed to Guadalcanal with repairmen still on board! The challenge now was to repulse a last desperate massive Japanese reinforcement on the island.

Aircraft helped, but the real victor of the 12–13 November "Naval Battle of Guadalcanal" was Rear Admiral Willis A. Lee. He understood how to use the radar of his new battleships, *Washington* and *South Dakota*, in outfighting the Japanese at night. Lee's ships took countless hits, but his radar-guided guns mortally wounded the Japanese battleship *Kirishima*. Abandoned by their fleeing warship-escorts, four Japanese transports beached themselves. At daylight, American fliers from *Enterprise* and Henderson Field found them and bloodied their decks as they disgorged their hapless troops. Secretary of the Navy Frank Knox was exultant: "We can lick them," he told reporters, "I don't qualify that. We'll defeat them." With 35,000 men and two hundred airplanes on Guadalcanal, the marines had won by December 1942.

General MacArthur meanwhile had repulsed a concerted Japanese overland thrust toward Port Moresby on the Papuan peninsula of New Guinea, a thousand miles to the west of Guadalcanal. The cost in Australian and American casualties was very high, but allied morale soared. The distinguished historian of the Pacific war, Ronald Spector, concludes that "the most important results of both Papua and Guadalcanal were psychological. The vaunted Japanese army . . . had been stopped . . . it was the Japanese—not the Allies—who finally gave out."

===

By January 1943 the allies had held fast in the southwest Pacific and had landed in North Africa. It was time to reconsider the strategic options, and for this purpose Franklin Roosevelt and his senior military advisers met with the top English leadership in newly retaken Casablanca in French Morocco. Marshall and King by then had established a cordial personal relationship characterized by mutual respect and empathy. Thus they had been able to agree that while a cross-Channel invasion of France should take the highest priority, some resources ought to be expended in keeping pressure on the Japanese in the southwest Pacific.

At Casablanca the British allowed King to "shoot his line about the Pacific and really get it off his chest." Then they gunned down King and Marshall and insisted on concentrating on operations in the Mediterranean. Spector notes that "the Casablanca talks produced no concrete plan for the defeat of either Germany or Japan—and no ironclad commitment to devote a greater percentage of resources to the Pacific." But the British chiefs of staff did concede that the Americans should somehow retain their hard-won initiative in the Pacific. For King this was a green light, however dim.

Back in Washington, he explained to his Pacific Fleet commander that the American chiefs of staff had won "recognition of the fact that there is a war going on in the Pacific and that it had to be adequately implemented even though the major operation continues in Europe." In a way, however, the "major operation" of the first five

months of 1943 was the American staff struggle over where to hit the
Japanese next in the southwest Pacific and who should command in
the entire Pacific. Representatives from Halsey's and MacArthur's
staffs were called home in February to learn the results of Casablanca
and to help plan the limited offensive in the Pacific. The great sub-
terranean division that had evolved between field commanders and
national military headquarters quickly surfaced. MacArthur's and
Halsey's men wanted far more matériel than an Atlantic-first strategy
could deliver. It took weeks for the JCS just to settle on what it
considered a reasonable plan for southwest Pacific operations, and the
more contentious issue of overall command in the entire Pacific was
deferred indefinitely. In the interim Admiral Nimitz would retain
control of all naval forces, unless they were specifically allocated to
operations within MacArthur's area.

Halsey was assigned to MacArthur by the end of March, an
administratively awkward ad hoc arrangement that worked no harm.
The two grandstanders got along famously when they met in the
general's headquarters in Brisbane, Australia, to plan a shoestring
offensive in the central Solomon Islands. Code-named "Cartwheel,"
the MacArthur–Halsey campaign was one of the navy's two major
Pacific operations in 1943.

Cartwheel consisted of a two-pronged movement to the northwest. Halsey directed the amphibious prong that struck out from
Guadalcanal along the Solomons. MacArthur commanded the more
southwesterly approach to the Admiralty Islands via New Guinea and
New Britain and across the Bismarck Sea. Initially the objective of
both commanders was to bypass and isolate Japanese island strongholds, build new airfields at beachheads along the way to provide
cover for the next landing, and take the 100,000-man bastion of Rabaul. Over MacArthur's objections, the objective was changed in
Washington to the bypassing and isolation of Rabaul itself, an important and wise modification, in the opinion of the historian Samuel
Eliot Morison: "Tarawa, Iwo Jima and Okinawa would have faded to
pale pink in comparison with the blood which would have flowed if
the Allies had attempted an assault on fortress Rabaul."

During Cartwheel, American commanding officers designed
shipboard combat information centers around radar sets to beat the
Japanese in night warfare. The naval construction battalions—the
famous "Seabees"—learned how to clear a jungle area and lay an
airfield of linked steel strips within days of a landing. From fecund
American factories Halsey received the "great preponderance" of new

landing craft—the LSTs, LCIs, LCTs, and LCVPs that made amphibious victory possible for him and for the navy at large in World War
II. Another innovation, the exceptionally light, high-speed, plywood-
hulled "PT" boats, made dashing hit-and-run torpedo raids on ships
of the Tokyo Express. Not to be outdone, Halsey claimed fame for
himself by at least one daringly successful carrier raid against heavy
air concentrations at Rabaul. When it was all over in February 1944,
Rabaul was thoroughly boxed off, and MacArthur began to plan his
famous leaps across island chains of several hundred miles each. He
would stride 1,400 miles in one three-month period of his advance
toward the Philippines, where he landed in October 1944, under the
cover of the Third Fleet.

General MacArthur had wanted to keep Halsey for his own
subordinate Seventh Fleet, popularly dubbed "MacArthur's Navy,"
but King and Nimitz had other plans for their most colorful, risk-
taking carrier admiral. The southwest Pacific was a zone of secondary
interest to the navy. The narrow and treacherous waters of the
Solomons and New Guinea precluded the kind of fleet action King's
navy hungered for. The admiral's heart was in the central Pacific,
where the U.S. Navy could draw out the Japanese for a climactic duel
of Nelsonian proportions. War Plan Orange was not dead after all.
Nor were the interallied and interservice contests for control of strategy.

King initiated the planning for the central Pacific offensive as
early as February 1943. By May the JCS planners had a full-scale
"Strategic Plan for the Defeat of Japan," which King presented to
Churchill and the Combined Chiefs of Staff at the May "Trident"
meetings in Washington. Nimitz would make the primary drive across
the central Pacific toward the Philippines, where he would link up
with MacArthur's simultaneous but subsidiary advance from the
southwest Pacific. After the recapture of the Philippines, China would
be invaded, Hong Kong retaken, and Japan bombed from those mainland bases. Finally, Americans would land on the home islands, and
the Japanese would be compelled to surrender unconditionally, as
Franklin Roosevelt had somewhat precipitously demanded at the Casablanca meeting in January.

Douglas MacArthur objected vehemently to the central Pacific
thrust, ostensibly on highly reasonable grounds. His own movement
north was well-rooted in the vast Australian war base, and it was
supported by heavy land-based bombers at each stage. The proposed
navy push through the central Pacific by contrast involved "hazardous

amphibious frontal attacks against islands of limited value." The supporting carrier-based air cover was lighter than his land-based bombers, and its effectiveness was problematical. That latter objection, of course, cut to the heart of the navy's preference.

By going through the central Pacific, the navy hoped to establish the potency of carrier aviation in combat once and for all. The record in the southwest Pacific had been mixed. The battleships, cruisers, and destroyers of the Tokyo Express had held their own in night warfare. In daylight combat the marine aircraft from Henderson Field and the army's heavy and medium bombers from other hastily built strips proved more decisive than the rarely available carrier wings. The carriers *Lexington, Hornet,* and *Wasp* had been lost; *Enterprise* had been withdrawn repeatedly to repair battle damage. The jury was still out on carrier aviation's utility in a sustained offensive campaign.

By winning Marshall to his concept, King had driven a wedge between the U.S. army's two most senior officers. As the historian Ronald Spector notes, the interservice divisions were shading into disputes between theater commanders and the headquarters staff at Washington. Nimitz and Halsey, in fact, initially opposed the central Pacific thrust as a dangerous diversion from the Solomons campaign, but they were fairly quickly won over by the prospect of a vast, potentially war-winning all-navy campaign grander in scope than anything known in history.

Fast carriers were the keystone of the entire operation. Only two of the older carriers had survived the early battles of the Pacific, but by the fall of 1943 a half-dozen of the new 27,000-ton *Essex*-class attack carriers had reached Pearl Harbor. Accommodating almost a hundred aircraft and bristling with anti-aircraft guns, these maneuverable speedsters bore the brunt of the rest of the war in the Pacific. Backing them in late 1943 was an equal number of swift *Independence*-class light carriers mounting air wings half the size of those on the *Essex* carriers. To knock down the deadly Zero fighter, the specially designed F6F Hellcat was introduced. It could outclimb, outdive, outrace, and outgun the lighter Zero. To screen the strike carriers and transports from enemy attack, the navy had assembled eight escort carriers, twelve battleships, fourteen cruisers, and fifty-six destroyers. While the large-caliber guns of the battleships would be used for offshore bombardment and "softening up" of Japanese emplacements on the islands, it is significant that in cruising formations the battleship now protected the carrier, rather than the other way around, as had been the case in all prewar planning.

In command of the carriers and the ancillary amphibians, collectively designated as the Fifth Fleet, was the victor of Midway, Vice Admiral Raymond Spruance. Like most of the top naval officers in Nimitz's command, Spruance himself was not an aviator. For several months longer the "gun club" of capital ship captains and admirals would dominate the navy, an anomaly breeding great resentment among the aviators, who thought they were winning the war against Japan.

The first major island on the sea road to the Philippines and Japan was a coral-ringed atoll named Tarawa in the Gilbert Islands. Once captured, it could serve as a base for land-based aircraft to cover landings in the Marshall Islands, less than 500 miles to the northwest. Tarawa was heavily defended by the Japanese, and the coral reef posed a hazard unless the tide was high enough to carry the 4-foot-draft LCVPs safely inshore. In December the tide was certain to be sufficient, but the JCS wanted an assault in November, when conditions might be less favorable. Washington's reasoning was purely political, as King told Nimitz. An early offensive in the central Pacific was imperative "so that the British could not back down on their agreements and commitments. We must be so committed in the central Pacific that the British cannot hedge on the recall of ships from the Atlantic."

Spruance had no choice. He bombarded Tarawa with 3,000 tons of shells and waves of carrier bombers, and in the early hours of 20 November 1943 he sent the marines ashore. The tides that morning could not have been much lower. The troop-laden LCVPs grounded on the reef, where they became fixed targets. "One large gun [ashore] was horribly accurate; several times it dropped a shell right on a landing craft just as the ramp came down, spreading a pool of blood around the boat." In three days of fighting, at a cost of one thousand dead and two thousand wounded, the marines captured an island measuring less than 3 square miles. The American public was shocked; the admirals and generals were shocked. But Tarawa had achieved its political purpose.

When Roosevelt and Churchill met for the first Cairo Conference on 22–26 November, Ernest King could cite the commencement of the central Pacific campaign as support for General Marshall's rebuttal of the prime minister's renewed pitch to expand operations in the Mediterranean. The U.S. Army had Overlord; the U.S. Navy had the central Pacific; the British—to paraphrase John Quincy

Adams—must hereafter come as a dinghy in the wake of the American war machine. In the wake of the Red Army, as well. At the Teheran Conference of 28 November–1 December Joseph Stalin made clear his understandable preference for the long-deferred second front in France, provided it took place in 1944, at last.

No one exhibited greater dismay at the loss of life on Tarawa than Douglas MacArthur. He fired off a letter directly to the secretary of war, around the JCS, for the president's eyes. "Give me central direction of the war in the Pacific, and I will be in the Philippines in ten months. . . . Don't let the Navy's pride of position and ignorance continue this great tragedy to our country."

Nimitz was cool. He invited MacArthur's representatives to a strategy session at Pearl Harbor in late January 1944. By then it was too late to cancel the next operation, the attack on the Marshalls, but not too late to stop the one after that, the invasion of the Marianas. MacArthur's delegates and the doubters on Nimitz's own staff persuaded the admiral to endorse the recommendation that the central Pacific push be halted at that point.

Ernest King read Nimitz's "conference notes with much interest, and I must add with indignant dismay." King, of course, had General Marshall's full concurrence for the navy's war, and in early 1944 the central Pacific penetration received new support from an unexpected source: General "Hap" Arnold wanted a base in the Marianas so the very long-range, brand-new B-29 "Superfortresses" could bomb the Japanese home islands directly. MacArthur was a man without a constituency in Washington.

King's determination was not always matched in the fleet. After Tarawa, Nimitz decided to bypass a ring of outer islands and hit directly at the primary target in the Marshalls, Kwajalein Atoll, the Japanese headquarters. Spruance and his seasoned amphibious commander, Richmond Kelly Turner, recoiled. But Nimitz had his orders and simply told his two top tactical admirals they were expendable: "If you don't want to do it, the [Navy] Department will find someone else to do it. Do you want to do it or not?" They decided they did.

Vice Admiral Spruance's Fifth Fleet had grown enormously. Task Force 58 was now composed of twelve carriers and 650 planes screened by eight new battleships and dozens of other escorts. Its commander was the navy's senior aviator in tactical command, Rear Admiral Marc A. Mitscher, "the acknowledged master of the new carrier warfare." The Fifth Amphibious Force under Rear Admiral

Kelly Turner numbered three hundred ships and 84,000 troops. Backed by land-based bombers flying out of Tarawa and Makin in the Gilberts, this massive armada took Kwajalein in six days in early February. The heart of the Marshall Islands was in American hands.

The flag officers involved received an additional star, and Nimitz lost his trepidation about hitting the Marianas next. He did not mind King's searing rebuff to his earlier proposed cancellation of the Marianas invasion, because he himself now wanted to proceed to Saipan, Tinian, and Guam. He understood, as Spector observes, that

> the fighting methods which were to spell the downfall of Japan had come of age in the seas and beaches of the Gilberts and Marshalls. Those methods were the coordinated amphibious assault and fast-carrier warfare. Backed by the awesome industrial output of the United States, they were to prove unstoppable.

The lineup for the Marianas campaign illustrates how truly "unstoppable" the Americans had become by June 1944. Mitscher's Task Force 58 now numbered fifteen carriers, seven battleships, twenty-one cruisers, and sixty-nine destroyers. The defending Japanese "Mobile Fleet" included nine carriers, five battleships, thirteen cruisers, and twenty-eight destroyers. The Japanese were badly outnumbered in every class of ship, but what really counted was the two-to-one American advantage in carrier aircraft: 891 American, 430 Japanese. The hitting power of the Americans was at least twice that of the opposing fleet, a situation very roughly comparable to having twice the weight of broadsides in Nelson's time. And all of this American firepower was merely the cover for the Fifth Amphibious Force of 535 ships and 127,000 troops, two-thirds of them marines.

Kelly Turner landed the Second and Fourth Marine Divisions on Saipan, the most northerly of the three major Marianas Islands, on 15 June. Saipan did not fall easily, nor did Tinian and Guam. Some five thousand young Americans died for those three islands in the summer of 1944, and nearly ten times as many Japanese. The strategic gains were logistics basing for further attacks westward, submarine havens for intensified attacks on the vital shipping in the "Southern Resources Area," and airfields for B-29 raids over Japan.

On 15 June Spruance and Mitscher had taken up station to the southwest, a mighty protective screen blocking the Mobile Fleet from attacking the amphibians. For three days Spruance waited for the Japanese, alerted to their approach by radio intercepts at Pearl Harbor, island coast-watchers, and U.S. submarine pickets. Mitscher wanted to go out after the enemy, but Spruance kept him near the Marianas as a shield.

The prudence of the "quiet warrior" paid off at dawn on 19 June. Task Force 58 radars detected a wave of approaching Japanese naval aircraft; 450 Hellcats were launched and stacked at high altitude to welcome the visitors; bombers from Mitscher's carriers meanwhile pounded the Japanese airfield on Guam to prevent "shuttle-bombing" of the task force. When it was all over, the American fighter pilots called it the "Great Marianas Turkey Shoot." They had downed almost 350 Japanese planes in the greatest eight hours of naval air combat in history.

Convinced that he could now hunt for the enemy fleet without risk of a Japanese end-run toward the Fifth Amphibious Force and the marines ashore on Saipan, Spruance cut loose some of Mitscher's carriers to search and destroy. In the Battle of the Philippine Sea on 19–20 June, they caught and sank the carrier *Hiyo* and two oilers fleeing toward Japan, and damaged two other carriers. A good kill, but not as good as the one scored by the American submarines *Albacore* and *Cavalla* while the Turkey Shoot was raging on the 19th. The two subs slipped into the main body of the Japanese fleet and sank the flagship carrier *Taiho* and the *Shokaku*, a heavy veteran of Pearl Harbor and the Coral Sea.

Mitscher was bitterly unhappy: "The enemy had escaped. . . . His fleet was not sunk." The navy's aviators took up the theme, scoffing at Spruance's caution and ridiculing the idea that the Japanese might have slipped behind Task Force 58 to maul Turner and the marines on the beach of Saipan. But to the end King and Nimitz backed Spruance. He had not unnecessarily risked his own carriers, and he had shielded the landing—the only real strategic objective of the campaign. Most important, by reining in Mitscher before the Turkey Shoot he had positioned Task Force 58 so that its fighters were airborne and waiting to pounce on the incoming Japanese planes on the morning of the 19th. The result was the permanent maiming of Japanese naval aviation. The loss of aircraft hurt the Japanese; the loss of irreplaceable highly trained aviators killed their naval air arm. The Turkey Shoot was a strategic victory as well as a tactical triumph.

The central Pacific thrust had reached a turning point with the capture of the Marianas. Those islands would become the unsinkable aircraft carriers from which General Curtis E. LeMay would launch the 20th Air Force's 1,000-plane B-29 raids against the population of Japan. Momentum and the vestiges of Plan Orange carried the navy westward to the Philippines and the linkup with MacArthur, who was coming from the southwest Pacific. But the China coast remained in Japanese hands, so China had lost its utility as an ally for attacking and invading Japan. A high-level debate began over where to go next. Admiral King thought Luzon, the northernmost major island in the Philippines, might be bypassed in favor of Formosa, 375 miles closer to Japan. MacArthur objected so strongly that a conference including President Roosevelt was held in Honolulu in July. This was a double-header: Washington versus the field commander; navy versus army. A final decision had not been made by the time Roosevelt and Churchill met once more, at Québec in early September. The issue would soon be forced by MacArthur's old comrade-in-arms, William F. Halsey.

After the Marianas, Spruance and his team of senior officers were sent home to rest. The Fifth Fleet was rechristened the Third Fleet and placed under Halsey. This admiral was unusual for having won aviator's wings at the Pensacola, Florida, naval flight training command, as a senior captain. Immediately after certification as a navy pilot in 1935, Halsey had taken command of the carrier *Saratoga*. He continued to command carriers, aviation shore installations, and carrier divisions right into World War II. Aggressive to the point of recklessness, he was widely regarded as a true carrier admiral, a direct contrast in temperament and intellect to Spruance. In September 1944 he was entrusted with the Third Fleet and assigned to cover MacArthur's landing in the central Philippine Islands, the capstone of the old Plan Orange. An aviator finally held the top operational command in the Pacific Fleet.

As soon as his flagship, the battleship *New Jersey*, joined fast-carrier Task Force 38 in the Philippine Sea, Halsey characteristically ordered an air strike on Japanese airfields in the central Philippines. The dramatic results—about two hundred enemy aircraft destroyed—led him to radio a recommendation to abandon the planned invasions of relatively minor islands in the general area and immediately reinforce MacArthur with units from Nimitz's Pacific Fleet. Halsey wanted to accelerate an invasion of Leyte, in the middle of the Philippine archipelago. Nimitz bought the idea, diverted units already under way, and alerted the national high command then meeting with the British at Québec. The upshot was that the timetable for the landing on Leyte was advanced from 20 December to 20 October.

That in turn gave MacArthur an airtight case for following up in Luzon rather than Formosa. But after Leyte, the Philippines would become primarily an army campaign, so on 3 October the JCS ordered Nimitz to plan the invasions of Iwo Jima and Okinawa. The Pacific commander put Spruance in charge of the planning.

Things did not go too well for "Bull" Halsey as commander of the Third Fleet at Leyte Gulf in late October 1944. He was at the eye of a storm of divided counsel and divided authority. His command was not absolute. The invasion force, Vice Admiral Thomas C. Kinkaid's Seventh Fleet, was subordinate to MacArthur; Halsey's boss was Admiral Nimitz. The question of which fleet—Seventh or Third—would block any Japanese attack on the invaders was not fully resolved. Nimitz directed Halsey to "cover and support [the] forces of the Southwest Pacific" but left him a loophole, perhaps out of some staff officer's dissatisfaction with Spruance's refusal to be drawn away from the invaders on Saipan. "In case [an] opportunity for destruction of the enemy fleet offer[s] or can be created," Halsey was advised, "such destruction becomes the primary task."

The Japanese knew their man, if not his orders. They sent major fleets from Borneo and the home islands to charge at the invaders from the South China Sea, entering the Philippines from the west. To draw off Halsey, they sent a decoy force of small or old carriers down from the Inland Sea, approaching the Philippines from the northeast with as much electronic noise as possible. When Halsey learned those carriers were 300 miles to the north, he headed for them with his own heavy carriers and battleships.

In his wake Halsey left Kinkaid's old battleships, some picket submarines, and a few escort carriers—small "flattops" configured for antiaircraft and antisubmarine operations—to face the main Japanese attack from the west. Only extreme determination on the part of the escort carrier commander, Rear Admiral Clifton A. F. Sprague, and heroic suicide runs by American destroyers against enemy battleships held the Japanese at bay. With Kinkaid radioing for help, Nimitz fired a message to Halsey asking where he was and concluding, "the world wonders." The humiliated Halsey reversed the course of his battleships and heavy carriers. He had steamed many miles north and missed the Battle for Leyte Gulf, the last major conventional fleet action of the greatest sea war in history.

Raymond Spruance got the naval war against Japan back on an even keel. Together with Mitscher and Kelly Turner, he masterminded the attacks on Iwo Jima and Okinawa. Midway between the existing B-29 bases in the southern Marianas and Tokyo, Iwo Jima's airfields could support fighter escorts for the B-29s and serve as emergency landing fields for Superfortresses wounded over Japan or short of fuel on the return run. Possession of Okinawa, less than 325 miles south of Kyushu, the southernmost Japanese home island, would permit tightening of the blockade of Japan and intensified bombing of Japanese cities. Most important, Okinawa was the springboard for the invasion of Japan itself, now envisioned by the Americans as the ultimate, but nightmarish, war-winning strike.

The island launching pads did not come at bargain prices. The Japanese by now had abandoned the strategy of resistance at the beaches in favor of deeply entrenched bastions inland. This meant that for both Iwo Jima and Okinawa very heavy casualties were suffered by the marines and soldiers. The navy, meanwhile, lost an unprecedented number of ships and men to the new and fearsome Japanese suicide bombers, the dreaded kamikazes.

Instead of the estimated four days, it took a month to capture Iwo Jima in February and March 1945. Some nineteen thousand Americans were wounded, and seven thousand died. Kamikazes disabled the heavy carrier *Saratoga* and sank the escort carrier *Bismarck Sea*. Okinawa in April, May, and June was worse for the navy, "the most costly naval operation in history," according to the historian Elmer B. Potter. The Fifth Fleet lost thirty-four vessels sunk and 368 damaged, many irreparably. About five thousand sailors died, and almost that number were wounded, many grotesquely burned. Toward the end of May Nimitz relieved Spruance, Mitscher, and Turner, who were stressed almost beyond endurance by remaining continuously on station at the two invasions.

Halsey came back. Fifth Fleet became Third Fleet once again. It began to rove along Japanese waters as soon as Okinawa was "secured" on 21 June. Admiral John S. McCain's carrier Task Force 38 raided Tokyo and other targets along the Japanese coast with impunity. On 17 July Halsey's 105-ship armada hit the large naval base at Yokosuka, outside of Tokyo. The Americans were joined by twenty-eight British warships, politically contrived evidence of the "two-ocean" breadth of the Anglo-American alliance.

Halfway around the world, during a conference with Stalin and Churchill at Potsdam in eastern Germany, the new American president, Harry S Truman, learned that an atomic device had been exploded successfully in a test at Alamogordo, New Mexico. An atomic attack might obviate the need to invade Japan at an estimated cost of

500,000 American casualties. Truman gave the order to bomb Hiroshima.

The atomic age was born on 6 August 1945. The Soviet Union, until then neutral in the Pacific, declared war against Japan on the 8th. The 20th Air Force dropped a second atomic bomb on Nagasaki, Japan, on 9 August. It was all over. Nimitz ordered Halsey to "cease fire" on the 15th. On 2 September 1945 General Douglas MacArthur took the formal Japanese surrender. The ceremony was held aboard Admiral Halsey's flagship, the battleship *Missouri*, at anchor in Tokyo Bay.

————

The Pacific war had ended as it began: with a bang. Most of the dramatic action captured on film and in books took place on the surface, on the beaches, or in the air. But in the Pacific, brave American submariners waged another kind of war in the deep, a war against Japanese transports and oil tankers that led to what the historian Clay Blair called a "silent victory."

Within hours of the attack on Pearl Harbor in December 1941 the chief of naval operations, Admiral Harold R. Stark, ordered the Pacific Fleet to "Execute Unrestricted Air and Submarine Warfare Against Japan." The brunt of that message fell first on the thirty submarines assigned to Admiral Thomas C. Hart, the commander of the Asiatic Fleet. In a 1920 lecture at the Naval War College, then Captain Hart had prophesied, "Any nation that attempts commerce destruction by submarines will tend toward certain of the same practices that the Germans arrived at." In the intervening twenty-one years some naval planners had gradually and reluctantly reached the same conclusion and had incorporated it into the various shadings of Plan Orange. They were well aware that unrestricted submarine warfare contravened an agreement on humane warfare at sea signed by Britain, Japan, and the United States at the London disarmament conference of 1930. But the exigencies of modern warfare had reduced the pious hope of 1930 to a worthless scrap of paper.

A balance sheet drawn for the American submarine force at the opening of the war against Japan would show two major assets: first, a superb, long-range, quiet, maneuverable, and habitable "fleet-class" submarine, the *Tambor* class, and second, elite crews of highly intelligent and fiercely dedicated officers and men. The offsetting liabilities included lack of strategic doctrine, tactical conservatism, and very bad torpedoes. Despite the insights of officers like Hart, the U.S. submariners had not altogether abandoned the basically Mahanian belief that their primary targets should be the enemy's capital ships. Moreover, although they had agreed that under suitable circumstances enemy merchant shipping ought to be targeted, they had not reached a consensus on whether to attack individually or in "wolfpacks." Nor had they established priorities for different classes of merchantmen. For example, until 1944 they did not single out oil tankers en route from the East Indies as the Achilles' heel of Japan's industry and navy.

Tactical conservatism impeded the American submarine campaign in two other ways during the early years of the war. First, the cautious American submariners eschewed periscope-depth attacks in favor of the far less effective "sound" or sonar-guided attacks at deeper submarine depth. Second, the hazards of raiding on the surface at night discouraged them from this mode of attack until the Germans proved that it was indeed a highly effective way to destroy enemy merchant shipping. But the critical chink in the U.S. submarine offensive armament was the torpedo.

The submariner-historian Edward L. Beach and others have explained that the $10,000 steam-driven Mark-14 torpedo often ran at depths so far below the target's steel hull that the magnetic detonator did not activate the explosive warhead. Equally faulty was the alternate detonator, a contact-firing device that jammed when the impact with the target was too direct and severe. Many Japanese ships escaped destruction because of these "duds."

It took almost two years of wartime fleet experience and experimentation to remedy those defects in matériel and in strategic and tactical doctrine. But by the end of 1943 the remedies were in place, and the U.S. submarines began to draw a tight noose around resource-poor, industrial Japan. The Americans now understood that the submarine operates best as a solitary commerce raider, the contemporary counterpart to Raphael Semmes's *Alabama*. Cautious submarine commanders were replaced by men of audacity, unflinching courage, and instinctive tactical judgment. Their historical counterparts were the frigate skippers of the early navy: sublimely self-confident, masterful ship handlers.

By 1944 this generation of tacticians operated from forward bases in New Guinea, the Admiralty Islands, and the Marianas, all acquired in the dual advance of MacArthur and Nimitz. To guide them to the targets of greatest opportunity, the cryptanalysts had broken the Japanese merchant code. Ordnance men had fixed the detonators. The Mark-14 now expoded when aimed true, and a new electric-powered,

wakeless torpedo entered the fleet. The new Mark-18 unfortunately
had the eerie proclivity occasionally to circle around and hit the
submarine that launched it, with fatal consequences to the U.S.S.
Tang in late 1944.

The *Tang*'s loss notwithstanding, in 1944 American submariners
hit their stride in the Pacific. They sank more than six hundred Japanese ships totaling 2.7 million tons, more than the combined totals
for 1941 through 1943. By the end of the year, half of Japan's merchant fleet had gone to the bottom. The oil flow from the East Indies
to Japan was stemmed. The Imperial Japanese Navy was reduced to
refueling with unprocessed crude oil drawn directly from wells in
Borneo, and it could no longer operate from bases in the home islands. The oil shortage was so severe that, in the assessment of the
U.S. Strategic Bombing Survey, it caused "the collapse of the fleet,
the air arm, merchant shipping and all other activities dependent
upon oil fuel." This war-winning result could have been achieved as
early as 1943 if the submarines had "concentrated more effectively in
the areas where tankers were in predominant use after mid-1942."

The American submarine war in the Pacific was primarily a war
against commerce, broadly construed; it was *guerre de course* in
modern garb, not a Mahanian or Nelsonian search for command or
control of the sea. But its impact on the Japanese war machine and on
the Japanese navy's sea-keeping potential was staggering. Of the 8.1
million tons of Japanese merchant marine tonnage sunk in World War
II, American submarines accounted for 4.8 million tons. The strategic
impact of this war against "the logistic support of Japanese military
and naval power" was decisive. After an exhaustive postwar investigation, the United States Strategic Bombing Survey concluded that
"certainly prior to 31 December 1945 . . . Japan would have surrendered even if the atomic bombs had not been dropped, even if Russia
had not entered the [Pacific] war, and even if no invasion had been
planned or contemplated." This feat the American submarines accomplished against daunting odds: They began the war committed to
fighting warships rather than tankers or cargo ships; they fought for
two years with faulty torpedoes; and they "were never available in
sufficient numbers to enforce a blockade."

The strategy of Raphael Semmes and the *Alabama* was vindicated by twentieth-century submarine technology, and it was the
judgment of the authors of the Strategic Bombing Survey that it could
also have been confirmed by American carrier warfare in the Pacific,

had not the navy been wedded to a strategy of Mahanian fleet engagements and War Plan Orange:

> Carrier-borne air attacks, when directed against large concentrations of merchant shipping, were by far the most devastating attacks of all. They were, however, sporadic and not part of a continuing program to neutralize enemy shipping lanes. . . . Even the raid on Truk [in early 1944] was designed more to seek out and destroy naval units than to sink merchantmen.

As a result, in tonnage of Japanese shipping sunk during World War II, carrier-based aircraft came in a distant second to the submarines, with a score of 1.3 million tons.

While concentrating on what they did best, the American U-boats did not spare warships. The historian Ronald Spector succinctly sums up the devastating picture:

> The U.S. submarine offensive against Japan was one of the decisive elements in ensuring the empire's defeat. A force comprising less than 2 percent of U.S. Navy personnel had accounted for 55 percent of Japan's losses at sea. U.S. submarines sank over 1,300 Japanese ships including a battleship, eight aircraft carriers, and eleven cruisers in the course of the war.

Spector's accounting does not include the dozens of Japanese destroyers knocked out or, on the humane side, the five hundred downed airmen rescued by American submarines. One of them, Lieutenant (junior grade) George H. W. Bush, survived to become president of the United States in 1989.

Many of the submariners were less fortunate. A plaque on the sea wall at the U.S. Naval Academy memorializes the fifty-two submarines "still on patrol." Lost forever are the 374 officers and 3,131 brave men who with their sacrifice proved that *guerre de course* could be decisive in the twentieth century, regardless of what the Mahanians thought.

———

To the extent that the Pacific war vindicated the concept of great battlefleets fighting for command of the sea, the contest was something of a self-fulfilling prophecy. War Plan Orange, the document embodying the strategic doctrine, simply was not allowed to die.

Since the presidency of Theodore Roosevelt the United States Navy had planned to fight Japan. In the years before World War I and at the beginning of the war in Europe in September 1939, the navy had seriously considered only one war: one fought at sea by great fleets against the Japanese navy. For the commander-in-chief of the navy during the war, Admiral Ernest King, the Atlantic war was regrettable. From the outset, he moved mountains to get on with the war against Japan. He succeeded because the industrial capacity of the United States was sufficient to sustain what Samuel Eliot Morison called a "Two-Ocean War." It all worked out pretty much as Admiral Harold Stark had predicted to the Japanese ambassador, Admiral Kichisaburo Nomura, on the eve of Pearl Harbor:

> If you attack us we will break your empire before we are through with you. While you may have initial success due to timing and surprise, the time will come when you too will have your losses, but there will be this great difference. You will not only be unable to make up your losses but will grow weaker as time goes on; while on the other hand we will not only make up our losses but will grow stronger as time goes on. It is inevitable that we shall crush you before we are through with you.

So, from the very broadest viewpoint, there were no surprises. But from one particular and highly significant viewpoint there was a major unforeseen development: the replacement of the battleship by the aircraft carrier as the core of the battlefleet. All of the great surface engagements of the Pacific in World War II were won by carrier and amphibious task forces. In his annual report for 1945, Secretary of the Navy James V. Forrestal, who had flown navy airplanes in World War I, engraved this lesson for posterity: "The carrier is today the spearhead of the modern fleet just as the battleship was twenty-five years ago."

Thus by 1945 naval aviators had won two wars: one against the Japanese and the other against their own "gun club" of senior capital-ship officers. The United States never constructed another battleship, but forty-five years after World War II it continued to build its entire fleet around carriers. The ubiquitous *Essex*-class carrier indeed was the harbinger of the future.

12

In Search of a Mission

1945 – 1962

THE United States Navy's mastery of the seas at the close of World War II was without historical precedent. Any parallel between the American navy in 1945 and the Royal Navy at the time of Trafalgar is specious. In 1805 insular England's grand opponent, Napoleonic France, could no longer challenge the Royal Navy to a fleet engagement, but French frigates and smaller ships remained active as commerce raiders in the Mediterranean, Atlantic, and West Indies. Moreover, Napoleon's armies continued to fight Britain and its allies on the continent for another decade. In 1945 the continent of Europe was hideously disfigured but technically at peace. The United States Army and the Soviet Red Army waxed supreme in the West and the East. In the air, the United States Army Air Forces held a global monopoly on the ultimate weapon of mass destruction, the atomic bomb. And the United States Navy faced no challenge in any class of vessel by any power in any ocean or sea. The descent from this pinnacle began immediately.

In 1945 the United States fleet was built around battle groups of *Essex*-class carriers, which had proved their worth in the Pacific campaign, and various designs of light and escort carriers used in the antisubmarine battle for the Atlantic. In all, the number of carriers exceeded one hundred. Then the navy was subjected to the same budgetary contraction that afflicted all the services. The war was over, and the "boys" must be brought home. Their implements of war were discarded or, in the case of hundreds of navy ships, put into "mothballs," a system of preservation and storage conceptually not unlike "ordinary" in the nineteenth century.

A few ships launched before the termination of hostilities did manage to enter the active ranks. Most significantly, two aircraft carriers of a new heavier class, the 45,000-ton *Midway* and the *Franklin D. Roosevelt*, were commissioned in September and October 1945. The third and last of the class, the *Coral Sea*, joined the fleet in October 1947. But those three additions to the battlefleet were exceptional. Most of the postwar carriers were the *Essex*-class veterans of the Pacific war, eight in all. Nine other light or escort carriers remained in commission. The first modern "supercarrier" was not commissioned until 1955. The decade in between was a tough time for the U.S. Navy.

James V. Forrestal presided over the navy's adjustment to peace. A naval aviator in World War I, Forrestal was a phenomenally successful investment banker whose liberal political views had enabled him to enter the Roosevelt administration as the first under secretary of the navy in August 1940. In effect he served as the navy's chief procurement officer and thus knew the physical structure of the service as well as anyone in Washington. When Secretary Frank Knox died in April 1944, Forrestal was the logical successor. He immediately began visits to the fighting fleets, including one to Saipan with Richmond Kelly Turner just before the amphibious asault on Iwo Jima. Convinced of the need for a stable postwar Japan, Forrestal opposed Franklin Roosevelt's doctrine of unconditional surrender and favored retention of the emperor.

Forrestal distrusted the Soviet Union from early on. In September 1944 he denounced Americans who ignored legitimate United States security interests overseas but did not question Soviet ambitions for "the Baltic Provinces, half of Poland, all of Bessarabia and access to the Mediterranean." He espoused a strong defense establishment as a deterrent to "any international ruffian who attempts to impose his will on the world by force." His was one of the early voices to cite appeasement as a negative lesson for American policymakers: "If Hitler and Mussolini had known that this country was prepared to fight, I do not believe [either] would have acted as he did." Speaking before a commencement audience at Princeton, his undergraduate alma mater, Forrestal in June 1944 urged the new graduates: "Remember that America can never isolate itself from European or world wars."

A cold warrior from the beginning, Forrestal also was a navy man through and through. While an economy-minded Congress was cutting his proposed budget for fiscal 1947 from $5.1 to $4.1 billion, he was arguing his case for the navy as the cornerstone of a strong defense and a nonisolationist foreign policy in the era of the American monopoly of the atomic bomb. In appearances before Carl Vinson's House Committee on Naval Affairs, Forrestal didactically restated the classic twentieth-century purpose of the United States Navy:

> In the future, as in the past, the key to victory and to the freedom of this country will be in the control of the seas and of the skies above them. Attacks upon us or attacks by us must cross on, over, or under the sea. That fact is an accident of geography which you can confirm by any map. No enemy can reach us without coming across the sea. We cannot reach or defeat an aggressor without crossing the sea. Therefore, control of the ocean and of the air over it is the key to our own security. . . . The control of the sea and the air above it is the mission of the United States Navy. . . .

The atomic bomb had not changed that mission.

Forrestal stated this proposition as a question: "Does the atomic bomb immediately destroy the usefulness of all navies now in existence? It does not. In the first place, the atomic bomb, although immensely destructive, is still a bomb, requiring land- or carrier-based planes to deliver it." Carl Vinson agreed. In October 1945 he remarked on the floor of the House, "[T]he atomic bomb may change the type of ships in our Navy, but it does not affect the mission of the Navy to control the sea and the air above the sea." But matters were not quite that simple.

To the secretary of the navy the nation appeared to be endangered by the Soviet Union. To the navy as a whole the imminent danger seemed to be coming from a budget-cutting Congress. To the naval aviators who credited themselves with winning the war in the Pacific, the real threat came from the proponents of strategic air power who thought the decisive American contribution to World War II was strategic saturation bombing of enemy industrial and urban strongholds. In the opinion of the strategic air power men, the army air forces had won the last war, and atomic bombs would win the next. An irrelevancy in the nuclear age, naval aviation was an expensive luxury the nation could not afford in the aftermath of demobilization.

To survive the appalling onslaught from recent comrades-in-arms, the uniformed leadership of the navy began planning to reconfigure the fleet. In December 1945 Rear Admiral Harold B. Sallada, chief of the navy's Bureau of Aeronautics, proposed for "serious consideration" the development of an "additional type" of carrier that would support fourteen aircraft with a combat radius of 2,000 miles, each plane weighing 100,000 pounds. Sallada's proposal received the crucial backing of Admiral Marc Mitscher, deputy chief of naval operations for air. Mitscher had first called for carriers able to launch very long-range strikes during the Pacific island campaigns of World War II. In July 1946 Under Secretary of the Navy John L. Sullivan took the navy's case directly to President Truman. Sullivan wrote, "In order to enable Carrier Task Forces to deliver atomic bombs, it will be essential to modify the carrier aircraft and alter aircraft carriers. . . . This will require advanced peacetime preparations." Sullivan, Mitscher, and Sallada had correctly identified the technical problem facing the navy: Atomic bombs were too large for carrier-borne planes.

In 1946 atomic bombs still resembled the 10,000-pound monsters dropped on Japan. Designing a new class of aircraft carrier and miniaturizing "the bomb" would take years, so the navy adopted some short-term expedients. It pressed North American Aviation to build the AJ1 Savage. With a planned weight of 45,000 pounds, including a 10,000-pound bomb, this hybrid prop-jet aircraft would be deployed on the three *Midway*-class carriers. The limits of the *Midway, Franklin D. Roosevelt,* and *Coral Sea* would be pushed to the maximum, and the *Essex*-class carriers were altogether excluded from an atomic mission because of their smaller size.

At the same time the design of a new class of carrier was pressed, the end result of which was the huge ships whose function is both sea control in the Mahanian sense and strategic in the sense of being able to deliver atomic weapons to targets in the Soviet Union. Daniel Gallery, a brash antisubmarine-carrier admiral in the recent Atlantic war, took the offensive against proponents of land-based air power in December 1947:

> The carrier can transport the bomber across the ocean and launch it 1,000 miles from the target. Instead of building the trans-oceanic range into the bomber, and thereby penalizing its performance over enemy territory, we build a trans-oceanic range into the carrier. We design the airplane for maximum performance on a comparatively short flight.

Gallery concluded by proposing that the primary mission of the atomic navy should be to deliver atomic weapons "on the capital and industrial centers of the enemy." Control of the sea became the navy's "secondary mission." The admiral magnanimously allocated to the newly autonomous U.S. Air Force the primary mission of defending the continental United States against air attack. Gallery's broadside was part of a desperate navywide effort to maintain the credibility of naval aviation in the face of the growing popularity of the air force and to perpetuate the surface navy's traditional status.

———

The United States Navy of 1947 had by no means abandoned its own twentieth-century strategic mission of command of the sea. In fact, the postwar decline of the Royal Navy made that mission seem more vital than ever before. At a news conference on 28 February 1947 Secretary of the Navy Forrestal explained the "rising duties" of the American navy: "For years the United States never even had to think of security of the sea. The British Navy took care of that. Now our fleet is doing it."

Forrestal was referring to a hidden facet of the historically ambivalent Anglo-American naval relationship. Since the presidency of James Monroe, American statesmen understood that for security from aggression by a continental European power the United States depended at least in part on the Royal Navy. That had been a major consideration in the decision to fight alongside Britain in the two world wars. In the mid-1940s the Soviet Union had supplanted Germany—which itself had supplanted France at the turn of the century—as the dominant continental power menacing the Anglo-Americans. Britain had declined precipitously as an industrial and naval power and was experiencing great difficulty retaining its overseas empire in Asia and Africa, an ultimately futile effort.

With the Royal Navy weakened, the United States Navy signaled its intention to expand its role geographically in the defensive partnership against the major power on the continent of Europe. In April 1946 the battleship *Missouri*, a symbol of the victory over Japan, called at Istanbul. In August the new heavy carrier *Franklin D. Roosevelt* visited Athens. Two months later the navy established a new command, U.S. Naval Forces, Mediterranean, destined ultimately to become the mighty Sixth Fleet. The new presence in the eastern Mediterranean of the navy's only atomic-capable carriers anticipated by only a few months London's announcement of Britain's inability to continue supporting Greece and Turkey in their wars against Communist-led insurgents.

President Truman reacted with the "Truman Doctrine." On 12 March 1947, in a speech before a joint session of Congress, he dramatized, simplified, and universalized the situation in Greece and Turkey. "I believe that it must be the policy of the United States to support free peoples who are resisting attempted subjugation by armed minorities or by outside pressures." The State Department came closer to geopolitical reality in a report describing Turkey as "the stopper in the neck of the bottle through which Soviet political and military influence could most effectively flow into the eastern Mediterranean and Middle East." Alfred Thayer Mahan would not have expressed it differently.

The issue was historic: confinement of Russia to the Black Sea, above the Turkish-controlled Bosporus and Dardanelles, true chokepoints in the Mahanian sense. England and France had fought the Crimean War in part for that goal; the United States now adopted it as American national policy. America's most influential diplomat, George F. Kennan, labeled it "containment." Soviet Premier Joseph Stalin raised the obvious question, "What would Great Britain do if Spain or Egypt were given this [Turkish] right to close the Suez Canal, or what would the United States Government say if some South American Republic had the right to close the Panama Canal?" He could not comprehend that in the Anglo-American mind Panama, Gibraltar, and Suez were pieces of real estate qualitatively different from the Bosporus and Dardanelles.

Secretary of the Navy Forrestal understood the difference and wholeheartedly approved of containment. He had raised the specter of Soviet intrusion into the Mediterranean as early as 1944. He had read Kennan's thesis in the form of a very long telegram from the American embassy in Moscow in 1946 and helped publicize it in the July 1947 issue of the influential journal *Foreign Affairs*.

The quasi-official exposition of the containment doctrine coincided with a host of midsummer changes in the national defense posture. In a June commencement speech at Harvard University the new secretary of state, General George C. Marshall, proposed what became known as the "Marshall Plan" for European economic recovery. The funds generated ultimately restored war-ravaged Western Europe to industrial health and established a firm political base for an anti-Soviet alliance. At the same time Congress, although unwilling to increase the defense budget much above the annual average of about $15 billion, did prove willing to enact a relatively inexpensive reformation of the defense establishment.

The National Security Act of 27 July 1947 created the Department of Defense as a cabinet-level agency, lowered the army and navy to subcabinet posts, added the air force to the roster as a fully autonomous service equal to the army and navy, gave statutory basis to the Joint Chiefs of Staff (JCS), and created the Central Intelligence Agency. For the navy, the upshot of the reorganization was the reappearance of an old rival in thicker armor. The United States Air Force spent the next three years trying to absorb naval aviation, by now the core of the surface navy. It failed to do so in large measure because Forrestal moved up to become the first secretary of defense, and because the new secretary of the navy, John L. Sullivan, was a tough fighter backed by admirals willing to lay their careers on the line for the survival of the service as they conceived it.

Forrestal's appointment as secretary of defense in September 1947 was ironic and tragic. In a two-year struggle over unification of the services he had opposed the idea, because there was "no human being capable, in my judgment, of sitting on top of all that and assuring that you have the fine integration and efficiency which is presumed would result from that consolidation." He correctly feared that the civilian secretary would be dependent on the military chiefs for the expertise on which to base sound policy decisions. He deeply believed in civilian control of the military and had vigilantly guarded the navy secretary's powers in frequent wartime clashes with Admiral Ernest King, whose hunger for power knew no limits.

Forrestal had reshaped the office of the chief of naval operations after the war so as to diffuse the CNO's power and keep him definitely subordinate to the secretary of the navy. Instead of consolidation, Forrestal maintained, the defense establishment needed greater decentralization and more small, autonomous agencies whose heads knew their outfits inside out. Whether or not he had it in mind, that is the way a navy task force ideally operated in World War II. Every skipper was the technical, as well as operational and administrative, master of his ship. The massed combination of those autonomous units gave the admiral in tactical command massed power that was reliable and flexible in application. Not a bad model for a huge governmental organization.

Because he was a team player, Forrestal accepted the new post. He probably also hoped to establish precedents that would check the military men in future administrations. He certainly intended to resolve once and for all the contest between the air force and the navy over air power. In March 1948, at his behest, the Joint Chiefs of Staff met at Key West, Florida, to hammer out a compromise. Forrestal incorporated their conclusions in an executive order declaring that "strategic air warfare has been assigned as a primary function of the Air Force, and the Navy is assigned as a primary function the conduct of air operations necessary for the accomplishment of objectives in a naval campaign." This was a thin reed on which to hang a radically new ship and a specially configured air wing, but that did not stop the navy from laying the keel of the U.S.S. *United States*.

The *United States* was the world's first supercarrier. Designed to the specifications of Admirals Gallery and Mitscher, she would displace 65,000 tons. Her elevators could handle 100,000 pounds of aircraft and equipment. She would mount four powerful catapults, and she was designed with particular attention to the placement of atomic bomb magazines and bomb elevators. She would carry an air wing of eighty fighters and eighteen bombers. Estimates of her construction cost varied from $189 million to $500 million. Either figure was a very large sum at a time when the total defense budget was limited to about $15 billion per year. The navy promised to build her by cutting other programs rather than seek an increase in the naval budget. She was never completed.

On 1 March 1949 President Truman asked for Forrestal's resignation as secretary of defense. He was replaced by Louis Johnson, a political fundraiser in Truman's recent campaign and a longtime supporter of the air force's intercontinental nuclear bomber, the B-36. Within days Johnson canceled construction of the *United States*, whose keel had just been laid. The New York *Times* interpreted the cancellation as a naval defeat in interservice warfare: "The action represents, in effect, a full victory of the Air Force over the Navy in the interdepartmental battle of strategies that broke out when the Air Force was created as a separate service. It resolves in favor of the Air Force the question whether the national defense program should be secured to the long-range land-based bomber, such as the B-36, or the seagoing aircraft carrier and accompanying naval bombers." That was certainly the navy's interpretation. Secretary of the Navy John Sullivan resigned in protest, and Chief of Naval Operations Admiral Louis E. Denfeld led a celebrated "revolt of the admirals" that cost him his job.

Forrestal also paid dearly. He had once joked that as secretary of defense he would need the "combined attention of [Monsignor] Fulton Sheen and the entire psychiatric profession by the end of another year!" But those were not enough. The intensification of the Cold War in 1948, the refusal of the president and Congress to raise the defense budget despite the globalism of containment, the interminable interservice bickering, and the burden of caring for a bedridden alcoholic wife cost him his life as surely as if he had been a sailor in combat. Shortly after his resignation, Forrestal entered the Bethesda Naval Hospital for psychiatric care and on 22 May plunged to his death from his seventh-floor suite. He had served the navy since 1940, with a dedication far "above and beyond the call of duty."

With Forrestal dead and the Navy Department purged of its most determined air power enthusiasts, it seemed as if naval aviation was doomed to second-class status as an umbrella for amphibious operations. But the Korean War saved the day for the supercarrier and allowed the navy to build a force structure to last until the end of the twentieth century.

On 25 June 1950 North Korea, a Soviet satrapy, invaded South Korea. The American army, which had been occupying South Korea since the end of World War II, reeled back toward the harbor of Pusan on the southeast tip of the Korean peninsula. President Truman at once ordered the army to stand in defense of the American client state. He sent Seventh Fleet cruisers to shield the retreating Americans with gunfire while an American and a British carrier, the *Valley Forge* and the *Triumph*, moved in to fly close air support missions over the troops. At the president's direction, the Seventh Fleet blockaded the Korean coast to prevent the movement of enemy men and matériel by sea.

From the United Nations Security Council, which the Soviets were boycotting, Truman extracted a resolution empowering him to act under U.N. auspices. The Korean War became the Cold War's first test case of the willingness of the West to resist what it perceived as Soviet-inspired acts of aggression. The trick was to localize the conflict.

Truman feared that the People's Republic of China and the Nationalist Chinese on Taiwan might attack each other and ensnare the United States in a broader regional war, which in turn could escalate into a direct Soviet–American confrontation. He therefore sent part of the Seventh Fleet to patrol the straits between the mainland and

Taiwan. That picket duty became a permanent feature of Seventh Fleet operations, and it seemed to confine the war to the Korean peninsula.

The nation's first "limited war" was primarily a foot soldier's slogging campaign. As the historian Dean C. Allard has observed, for the navy the "pattern of logistical support, gunfire and carrier air cover of the Allied ground troops, interdiction of enemy supply lines, and blockade of the enemy coast" was established early and continued throughout the war.

The two highlights of naval activity were amphibious. The first occurred at Inchon, a port city tucked behind a narrow channel and mud flats on the west coast of South Korea. The inspiration to stage an amphibious landing in that most unlikely location, where the tidal range exceeds 30 feet, came from the fertile imagination of General Douglas MacArthur, the United Nations commander. As had often been the case in World War II, Washington doubted the wisdom of the field commander, but MacArthur's eloquence won over the army chief of staff and the chief of naval operations, Admiral Forrest P. Sherman, in a conference held at the general's Tokyo headquarters on 23 August 1950.

The "American Caesar's" luck held one last time. At dawn on 15 September 1950, from the command ship *Mount McKinley*, he watched the navy land a heterogeneous amphibious group of marines, army soldiers, and Koreans. The tides were right, and the landing caught the North Korean occupiers off guard. Within ten days MacArthur's men took Kimpo airfield, the largest in Korea, and Seoul, the South Korean capital. The North Koreans surrounding the Americans at the Pusan perimeter were now cut off and had to fight their way back north with heavy losses. MacArthur seemed to have been divinely inspired. Washington could do nothing but approve his battle cry to move across the 38th parallel into North Korea. He promised to have the "boys" home for Christmas.

Inchon went to the heads of the American political leadership and caused Truman to alter the goal of the war from containment and the defense of South Korea to the liberation of North Korea. As MacArthur's soldiers approached the Yalu River, the demarcation between Korea and China, the People's Republic of China gave warning, but MacArthur discounted its threats to intervene even when confirmed in the detailed reports of his own intelligence officers. On 25 November 1950 a force estimated at 180,000 Chinese troops, who had crossed the Yalu undetected, hit two divided and overextended

American armies advancing toward the river along the east and west coasts of the Korean peninsula. The stunned Americans began a painful, costly retreat back to the 38th parallel. Once again, the navy's ability to move troops along a coastline paid off handsomely. In December 1950 the Seventh Fleet pulled out about 105,000 soldiers and marines who had retreated to the port of Hungnam in the face of the overpowering numbers of Chinese troops. The evacuation was covered by the air wings of six light carriers and the gunfire of a surface force including two heavy cruisers and the battleship *Missouri*. The historian Jack Sweetman describes it as "an exemplary amphibious operation in reverse."

By early 1951 the war had deteriorated into a stalemate, with the two sides in confrontation roughly along the 38th parallel. Vice Admiral Charles Turner Joy, who had initially commanded the naval forces, became the senior United Nations negotiator at interminable armistice talks that dragged on until the election of Dwight D. Eisenhower as president of the United States.

As a direct result of the prolonged war, the American defense budget expanded exponentially. The navy's annual budget quadrupled from $4 billion in fiscal 1950 to $16 billion in fiscal 1952; the navy alone now had a budget equal to the 1949 total for all the services. The greatest impact of the fiscal revolution fell on naval aviation.

From the beginning of the Korean War in June 1950, the navy flew close air support and logistical interdiction missions from Pacific Fleet *Essex*-class carriers. The three *Midways* were kept on the U.S. East Coast and in the Mediterranean in anticipation of a major Soviet move. They were the navy's only "strategic" or nuclear-capable carriers. Desperate for a role in nuclear warfare, the navy had modified some P-2V Neptune long-range antisubmarine patrol aircraft to carry atomic weapons in one-time launches off the *Midway*-class carriers. The Neptunes, too big for storage in the hangar decks, had to be "pre-positioned" on the flight decks. Once launched, they could not be recovered on board, so after dropping their weapons the aircrews were supposed to ditch at sea for rescue by submarines. In 1948—the year of the "fall" of Czechoslovakia and the Berlin Airlift—the navy actually deployed Neptunes in this configuration for a time during the Mediterranean cruises of the *Midway* and her sister ship, the *Franklin D. Roosevelt*.

While the *Midways* patrolled the Mediterranean, the *Essex*-class carriers off the Korean peninsula demonstrated anew their unquestioned ability to respond quickly in a changing operational environment. They proved themselves as ideal tactical weapons systems and reinforced the appreciation for the carrier as a support system for ground warfare conducted within aerial range of the fleet. But the navy drew a somewhat different lesson in a fiscal and geopolitical climate transformed by the war.

President Truman's approval of a National Security Council memorandum, "NSC 68," in the spring of 1950 pointed the way to the kind of aircraft carrier the navy would have to acquire once the Korean War was over. Described by one historian as "the American blueprint for the next decade," NSC 68 proclaimed that "every consideration of devotion to our fundamental values and to our national security demands that we achieve our objectives by the strategy of the cold war, building up our military strength in order that it may not have to be used." The supercarrier therefore would need to combine the classical Mahanian sea control role of battleships with the modern atomic or "strategic" function of deterrence.

The marriage of old and new functions manifested itself in the congressional debate of late 1950 and early 1951 leading to authorization of the first completed supercarrier, the U.S.S. *Forrestal*. On 12 January 1951 the House Armed Services Committee drew the desired lesson from World War II. The proposed supercarrier was "not a revolutionary weapon. It is an improved conventional carrier into which the lessons of World War II and thereafter will be built." Representative Dewey Short of Missouri concurred: "The function of carriers is to gain and retain complete control of the seas." Representative Carl Vinson took the next step in his ever ready defense of the supercarrier: "It may be possible . . . that the airplanes that fly off . . . this type of carrier will carry . . . the atomic bomb. Now, that is not an encroachment on the function of the Air Department. It is simply an addition to and augmenting of the striking force of the Air Force." The sharp-eyed Senate Committee on Armed Services recognized an old idea in fresh dress and "took notice of the fact that this carrier replaced the much disputed 'super' carrier which was canceled by the former Secretary of Defense." True enough, but with the Cold War growing hot, Congress was ready to vote for the surface navy's only nuclear weapons delivery system.

Displacing 60,000 tons, topped by a flight deck nearly 1,000-feet long, and nesting an air wing of almost a hundred aircraft, the *Forrestal* was launched in 1954. She was, as anticipated by the House Armed Services Committeee in 1951, "a prototype" supercarrier and was followed down the ways by sister ships at the rate of one per year for most of the rest of the decade. *Forrestal's* specially designed all-jet, 70,000-pound A-3D Skywarriors could carry atomic bombs to an enemy far beyond the water's edge. The only significant modification to subsequent supercarriers was the incorporation of nuclear-powered propulsion plants in nine of them. The navy at last had the perfect weapon for the modern age. Or so it appeared.

With the supercarrier the United States Navy could claim a role in the strategic or nuclear bombing of the Soviet Union in the event of total war, something that seemed likely at the time of the Korean War. But the bombing of targets several hundred miles inland was not in any sense a derivative of any historic mission of the navy. The big guns of battleships, which the bombers of aircraft carriers had replaced because of their greater range and versatility, had been designed to sink enemy ships. In the Pacific war the sinking of Japanese carriers at Midway and the elimination of the enemy's carrier-based striking power in the Marianas Turkey Shoot symbolized the essence of American naval aviation at work. The Halsey–Doolittle raid on Tokyo was dismissed as a morale-booster, just as the atomic bombing of Hiroshima and Nagasaki were unpleasant indices of the demonstratively much greater potential of land-based bombers. With this, however, there was a problem: What to do about the submarine and its revival of the ancient strategy of raiding an enemy's freighters and transports rather than attacking his battlefleet?

The submarine did not fit easily into the strategic scheme of the postwar United States Navy. The power of the carrier admirals, who had displaced the "gun club" captains and admirals of the interwar years; the challenge from the air force; and the Cold War itself all combined to focus attention and funding on the aircraft carrier as a weapon for fighting the Soviet Union. But the identification of the Soviet Union as the navy's new primary enemy led to awkward consequences, because geographically the Soviet Union differs fundamentally from Japan, the type of power the navy was currently configured to fight.

In simplest terms, Russia is a massive continental power to whom sea power in the Mahanian or any other sense is at best a tertiary concern. Unlike the Royal Navy or the Imperial Japanese Navy, the twentieth-century Soviet navy became and remained what its Russian antecedent always was: an adjunct of the army whose purpose was coastal defense and, when possible, the interdiction of enemy naval and commercial vessels. It is not stretching analogies too far to say that the Soviet navy sprang from the same geopolitical bedrock that lay beneath the nineteenth-century American navy. Both Russia and the United States are essentially continental powers.

Soviet Russia followed its national historical imperatives after World War II. In the period between the Japanese surrender on the *Missouri* and the beginning of the Korean War in June 1950, the Soviet Union put to sea the world's largest fleet of submarines—about 350, or more than twice the U.S. inventory. Continental Russia was putting its faith in the ultimate modern weapon for a strategy of coastal defense and *guerre de course*.

This growing force seriously threatened the American resupply of England and Europe, the planning premise behind the North Atlantic Treaty Organization since 1949. It also gradually came to menace the Sixth Fleet in the Mediterranean, that is, the nuclear heart of the Cold War navy as well as the "southern flank" of NATO and the locus of the Anglo-American naval containment of the Soviet Union. The U.S. Navy's response was construction of an antisubmarine line of defense stretching from Greenland through Iceland to the United Kingdom—the so-called Greenland-Iceland-UK gap. That purely defensive array relied on high technology: elaborate submerged and airborne sonar sensors to detect passing Soviet submarines, which in time of war would be attacked by mines, depth charges, and torpedoes from airplanes, ships and allied submarines— if, that is, the allies had modern submarines with which to "hunt and kill" the Soviet U-boats.

The early development of a modern American submarine force coincided with the winding down of the Pacific war. In May 1945 Secretary Forrestal established the Office of Research and Invention to investigate how new technologies could be applied to undersea warfare. In February 1946 Admiral Nimitz, King's successor as chief of naval operations, speculated that a properly designed submarine should be the "most successful vehicle for carrying atomic weapons to within short distances of coastal targets." That summer the United States started detonating atomic weapons at Bikini Atoll in the south Pacific. Secretary Forrestal witnessed the tests, one purpose of which was to determine whether capital ships could survive a nuclear attack. As with the Billy Mitchell bombings of the 1920s, the navy refused to reach a negative conclusion. But Alvin M. Weinberg, a scientist associated with the Manhattan Project, which had produced the atomic bomb, starkly predicted that the "navy of the future, if there is any such, will consist of submarines which will travel a thousand feet below the ocean" surface.

Weinberg may have understood atomic power, but he grossly underestimated the intricacies of navy politics and the tenacity of the surface-ship admirals. They were not about to scrap the battlefleet, regardless of the destructive force of new weapons. And Nimitz's interesting speculation was far ahead of weapons delivery technology. It would take a decade of engineering research for the concept of a submarine-launched atomic-warhead missile to reach the drawing boards. During that decade submarine development took a radically different tack, yet it was one that ultimately led back to a submarine-launched ballistic missile, the Polaris.

Atomic power came first to the American submarine force not as a weapon of destruction but as a means of propulsion for the "attack" submarine, that is, the submarine whose purpose is to destroy enemy ships and submarines. One man was largely—but not solely—responsible for that turn of events.

Hyman G. Rickover was never popular in the United States Navy. Brilliant, outspoken, and caustic, he exacerbated the anti-Semitic instincts of his classmates at the Naval Academy. After graduation in 1922, he specialized in engineering assignments and earned a master's degree in electrical engineering at Columbia University in 1929. As head of an electrical design section of the Bureau of Ships during World War II, his "severely practical approach, his tireless energy, and his refusal to compromise on technical excellence paid off handsomely." In 1946 the deputy bureau chief, Rear Admiral Earle W. Mills, selected Captain Rickover to head the small navy team sent to the atomic plant at Oak Ridge, Tennessee, to learn about the state of the nuclear art in the United States. When he returned, Rickover was the navy's premier nuclear expert and the leader of a small coterie of subordinate naval officers that he would fashion into a team to develop "a nuclear-powered navy second to none."

The obstacles Rickover faced were daunting. There was no navy-wide consensus on what to do with nuclear energy; the unsolved engineering problems were innumerable and highly complex; and funds were scarce. Two historians of the nuclear navy, Richard G. Hewlett and Francis Duncan, give a fair and wise summary of the situation in the Bureau of Ships in 1946 and 1947. Nuclear power was

only one of the many possibilities for improving the performance of ships to be built for the postwar fleet. Following the balanced fleet concept, the bureau was designing a variety of new ships, including submarines, heavily armored aircraft carriers, submarine-killer ships, and destroyers. Of all these the submarine seemed to offer the greatest challenge. What the Navy needed was a new propulsion plant and a new hull design capable of high speed at substantial depth. In the spring of 1946 the Bureau of Ships was not at all certain how it should use its limited funds. . . . Nuclear power offered enormous advantages, but development would be long and difficult.

Rickover cut through the impediments with his technical brilliance and political skills. Quite simply, he knew more about atomic energy than anyone else in the navy, and he knew more about the navy than anyone on the governing Atomic Energy Commission, to which he was assigned as the navy's representative. He also knew more about both the navy and atomic energy than any of the congressmen on the Joint Committee on Atomic Energy, before which he testified on behalf of the navy and the Atomic Energy Commission. From that unique position he spearheaded design, construction, and testing of a nuclear reactor light and powerful enough to generate steam for driving the turbines of United States attack submarines.

It would be grossly mistaken to conclude that Rickover worked in isolation from the top strategists in the navy. In 1948, while Rickover was building a prototype nuclear engine for the navy, Admiral Nimitz's staff elevated the question of nuclear power to the national strategic level. Basing his findings on a study by Captain Arleigh A. Burke, a first-rate tactician in World War II and a future chief of naval operations, Nimitz in April 1948 warned the Joint Chiefs of Staff that the "seriousness of the Russian submarine menace is emphasized by the fact that they now have over five times the number of undersea craft that Germany had at the outbreak of World War II."

The numbers were frightening enough, but the quality was even more alarming. Postwar Soviet submarine technology was built upon captured German U-boats and technicians, and Soviet shipyards were spewing out improved versions of the formidable German Type XXI attack boat. In February 1948 the highly respected Admiral Raymond A. Spruance, Nimitz's successor as the Pacific Fleet commander, said that the "high submerged speed and great underwater endurance" of the Soviet submarines was "probably the greatest threat that exists today to the safe use of the sea." Spruance alluded obliquely to American troops stationed abroad and warned that a solution must be "reached to the problem of how to destroy this submarine" before the United States could safely "operate our armed forces overseas." At the same time, the "Operational Development Force" noted ominously in a report to the General Board that "the tactical characteristics of the medium speed, deep diving snorkel equipped [Soviet] submarine have virtually nullified the effectiveness of most of our World War II ASW procedures, tactics, and doctrines."

The navy therefore had identified the threat by the time the Korean War loosened the congressional purse strings for defense spending, and Rickover by then was ready with the plans for a nuclear-powered submarine. In 1952 the keel of the U.S.S. *Nautilus* was laid, and on 17 January 1955 she signaled, "under way on nuclear power." From that revolutionary beginning the United States Navy in the next thirty-five years constructed a fleet of ninety-eight fast, deep-diving attack submarines armed with nuclear-tipped torpedoes. Those were to be the Soviet navy's deadliest enemy in the last third of the twentieth century.

Rickover's nuclear power plants were first used in attack submarines for several very good reasons. Most fundamental was a perception that the greatest strategic maritime threat lay with the huge Soviet fleet of submarines. On the premise that the deadliest submarine-killer is another submarine, the U.S. Navy concentrated on attack submarines of its own, once *Nautilus* had unequivocally demonstrated the feasibility of powering submarines with nuclear engines.

In the critical early years of reactor design, roughly from 1947 to 1950, stringent budget ceilings precluded large-scale simultaneous funding of another unproven weapons technology, a missile launched from under water. The Polaris missile, as it would come to be known, was almost as visionary as a nuclear-driven submarine. To be effective as a weapon it would require a specially designed nuclear warhead much lighter than any in existence in the early 1950s. For safety and ease of handling, it should be propelled by solid fuel, not the liquid fuels then used in American ballistic missiles. Moreover, Polaris intermediate-range ballistic missiles made sense as deterrents to Soviet–American war only if mounted in nuclear-powered submarines able to remain submerged for indefinite periods, a dubious proposition before the completion of *Nautilus*.

The indifference if not outright opposition of submariners also impeded the advent of ballistic missile submarines. As the submariner-historians Edward L. Beach and Paul R. Schratz have demonstrated, the attack submariner—especially the diesel-boat skipper of World War II—was an aggressive loner hungry for *guerre de course* adventure. Such men loathed the prospect of sitting quietly beneath the ocean for tedious weeks on end, tending their missiles and waiting for the call to total war that everyone hoped would never be sounded. For all these reasons, therefore, the navy did not begin full-scale development of the Polaris and its submarine-launcher until 1956, well into the first administration of President Dwight D. Eisenhower.

The retired five-star general had entered the presidency in 1953 pledging to end the Korean War, which he did almost immediately through negotiations and a bit of nuclear blackmail directed at the People's Republic of China. From Harry Truman he had inherited an expanding strategic—that is, nuclear—arsenal and vehicles for delivering atomic weapons on targets in the Soviet Union. However, all the delivery systems except the intercontinental B-36 bomber had operating radiuses of only 1,500 miles. That factor alone compelled Eisenhower to seek military bases overseas, and thus was created a ring of American alliances surrounding the Soviet Union. Eisenhower's confidence in nuclear weapons also enabled him to limit severely the size of the American army. He preferred to arm the soldiers of allies rather than support a huge and expensive peacetime American army, to which he was philosophically opposed.

In its totality, the Eisenhower strategy bore a striking resemblance to the historic British naval and military posture. England traditionally relied on ships of the line to shield the British Isles from invasion and European allies with large standing armies to defeat combinations of hostile continental powers. Eisenhower sought the same contribution from America's allies in the North Atlantic Treaty Organization and the other multilateral and bilateral alliances he sponsored. The "strategic" or nuclear forces, including the supercarriers and the new ballistic-missile-carrying submarines, would defend the American homeland through deterrence. Furthermore, for Eisenhower there existed one major European continental enemy, the Soviet Union, just as for Britain there historically had been a single major, threatening continental European foe, either France or Germany.

Beyond Europe, there was an informal empire to police, and here again the parallel with Great Britain at its zenith is instructive. Under Eisenhower the United States Navy practiced "gunboat diplomacy," the finite application of force to effect discrete political ends in distant places. For the Royal Navy in the age of sail—and for the nineteenth-century American navy as well—the ship of choice for this mission was the frigate. For Eisenhower it became the aircraft carrier, in combination with the Marine Corps.

That Eisenhower should pattern his strategy after Britain's is not surprising. He was carefully tutored by the British beginning with his leadership in the North African campaign of World War II. Harold Macmillan, a future prime minister, had been assigned to Eisenhower's immediate staff in part for that purpose. Much of Eisenhower's subsequent wartime service was in England, where he imbibed the British way of war from Churchill, Macmillan, and Admiral Louis Lord Mountbatten. Whether his apprenticeship in British global thinking was appropriate for a future American president is another matter.

Under Eisenhower the Cold War reached a nadir. The death of Joseph Stalin in 1953 initiated a destabilizing three-year struggle for power within the Soviet Union. In January 1954 Secretary of State John Foster Dulles, a doomsday diplomat preoccupied with the Communist "monolith," threatened the Soviets with "massive retaliation" if they pressed expansionist schemes anywhere in the world. He and the president considered using nuclear weapons to forestall the Communist conquest of French Indochina (Vietnam) but in the end they let the French fall. In 1956 the Suez Canal crisis unhinged the Anglo-French-American alliance while the West was watching helplessly as Soviet tanks crushed the popular uprising in Hungary. In the fall of 1957 the Soviets orbited a satellite around the earth. *Sputnik* hit the Americans where they lived: in their pride of world leadership in technology.

Those somber events actually helped the chief of naval operations, Admiral Arleigh Burke, to win presidential and congressional endorsement for the Polaris system. Eisenhower gave him the opening in a National Security Council meeting on 2 December 1955. The president swore he would have a reliable ballistic missile system quickly, even if he had to chair the project himself. Burke ran with the ball. Pledging the "Special Projects Office" of Rear Admiral William F. Raborn to absolute secrecy, Burke personally ordered it to propose ways to solve the problems of warhead weight and missile propellant. Raborn also was to come up with the design specifications of the missile-carrying submarine. Only then would Rickover be cut in. Burke's fear was that Rickover would take over the whole program if alerted too early.

The deceptive tasking paid off handsomely. In the summer of 1956 the nuclear physicist Edward Teller suggested the possibility of a high-yield 600-pound warhead. By the end of the year Raborn was confident he could come up with a solid-fuel propellant. In April 1957

Rickover received a description of the submarine that the Special Projects Office wanted. Measuring 350 feet in length and displacing 6,500 tons, the huge vessel would carry sixteen ballistic missiles with a range of 1,200 miles. On 17 June 1957 Admiral Burke approved the ship's characteristics. The historians Hewlett and Duncan conclude, "The Polaris submarine now had the highest priority of any project in the Navy."

It was a phenomenal start to what has become a mainstay of American nuclear deterrence. As the historians of the "nuclear navy" incisively observe, "The Navy was in a strong position with Polaris. Burke's realization of the importance of missiles, Raborn's ingenuity in getting the project in motion, and Rickover's accomplishments in providing a suitable platform for the missile system all gave the Navy a head start in meeting the demands which the Russian accomplishments would produce." The cooperative miracle Burke had worked was best illustrated by the career of the nuclear-powered attack submarine *Scorpion*. Laid down at Groton, Connecticut, in November 1957, she was cut in half early the next year so that a 130-foot ballistic missile compartment could be inserted in her midsection. Renamed the *George Washington* and commissioned in December 1959, she made the first underwater Polaris launch in July 1960.

The *George Washington* departed from Charleston, South Carolina, on her first operational deployment that November, almost exactly five years after President Eisenhower galvanized Burke into action. By August 1962 Congress had authorized forty-one ballistic-missile-launching submarines. The final one, the U.S.S. *Will Rogers,* was commissioned on 1 April 1967. Floyd D. Kennedy, Jr., a historian of the "Cold War navy," concludes, "The Polaris program must rank . . . as one of history's most successful advanced-technology endeavors." It in turn led directly to the more advanced Poseidon and Trident submarine-launched ballistic missile systems with which the navy would close out the twentieth century.

In a government where strategy is made by compromise, there was a price for the navy to pay. Admiral Burke audaciously gave the unproven Polaris his highest priority, but he also believed in a balanced fleet. To him that meant an expanding fleet of nuclear-driven attack submarines and nuclear-powered surface vessels, including aircraft carriers. He simply could not extract from Eisenhower or the Congress all that he wanted.

Eisenhower was especially dubious about the wisdom of building nuclear-propelled aircraft carriers, which like any surface ship were vulnerable to attack by enemy aircraft and submarines. The first one, the *Enterprise*, was included in the 1958 shipbuilding program at an estimated 50 percent increase in cost over an oil-fueled super-carrier. Burke wanted a second nuclear-powered carrier, but he also wanted nuclear-driven cruisers and frigates. He made shrewd trade-offs with the other services and concessions to the president's de-mands for a cost-conscious weapons procurement policy. The Polaris program was accelerated, construction of nuclear-powered attack sub-marines was maintained, the second nuclear-propelled carrier was postponed, and the development of reactors for smaller surface ships was continued. But the sheer expense of reactor-powered ships doomed the navy's dream of an all-nuclear fleet from the outset.

The navy of the 1950s also incurred high operating expenses from its continuation of "gunboat diplomacy." Historically, in the nineteenth century, the navy had intervened overseas with frigates and sloops, rarely with ships of the line. Theodore Roosevelt had made a global show of force with battleships in the cruise of the Great White Fleet, but his decisive 1903 intervention in Panama was ac-complished with lesser vessels. In the interwar years the navy placed heavy reliance on riverine gunboats for keeping order in China. After World War II, as the United States became the policeman of the "free world" in the late Truman and Eisenhower years, the navy gradually began to use aircraft carriers as an overseas "presence" with the threat of overflight by navy bombers as an inducement to better behavior on the part of small or "third world" nations. Often accom-panying the carrier task group in this new mission was a contingent of amphibious ships and embarked marines prepared to go ashore as a last resort.

All of this was done with "conventional" weapons but under the "nuclear umbrella," which discouraged an excessive Soviet reaction to the American policing of its informal global empire. But it caused a permanent confusion about precisely what was the purpose of an aircraft carrier, and that in turn led to the design of even larger platforms whose air group had two incompatible sets of ordnance: nuclear bombs for deterrence or massive retaliation, and nonnuclear weapons for use in crises involving small nations, perhaps in close air support of the marines heading inland. It can be argued that this nonnuclear facet of naval operations was the real justification for con-tinuing to maintain a surface navy in the age of missiles and atomic weapons. It is certainly true that the Eisenhower administration prac-ticed "gunboat diplomacy"in this way.

In July 1958 the Christian-party president of Lebanon, Camille Chamoun, appealed for an American show of force to bolster himself against Syrian-backed Moslems, whose insurgency promised to gain momentum following an anti-Western coup in nearby Iraq. The pro-Soviet overtones of the Iraqi coup gave Eisenhower a perfect opportunity to implement the so-called Eisenhower Doctrine, which pledged "to use armed forces to assist any nation or group of nations requesting assistance against aggression from any country controlled by international communism." Eisenhower telephoned Admiral Burke, and within hours of Chamoun's request the Sixth Fleet was on its way.

Aircraft from the old attack carrier *Essex* flew cover as a marine amphibious force crossed the beaches of Lebanon. The unopposed marines were greeted by vacationers in bathing suits as they headed for Beirut's international airport. A total of five thousand leathernecks landed in two days, the *Essex* took up station off the coast, and an antisubmarine carrier, the *Wasp,* came up to search for hostile Soviet or Soviet-supplied Egyptian submarines. The navy went on global alert, doubling the watch on chokepoints where Soviet submarines exit from home waters. Nothing happened, and by 1 October the marines were back aboard their ships. The landing had provided excellent public relations for the navy, but it was no indication of the dangers that intervention in Lebanon could entail if there had been serious opposition. That tragic lesson had to be learned a generation later, during the administration of President Ronald Reagan.

Soon after the landing in Lebanon, the Eisenhower administration ordered the *Essex* east through Suez, to add firepower to the Seventh Fleet during a showdown between "Nationalist China" and the People's Republic of China over possession of the Quemoy islands at the mouth of Amoy harbor on the mainland shore of the Straits of Formosa (Taiwan). The Chinese Nationalist Army kept Quemoy heavily garrisoned, blocking the port of Amoy to all but neutral shipping. In August 1958 the mainland Chinese began artillery bombardment of the islands from the surrounding shores. Some 130 miles to the northeast similar pressure was being brought against the tiny Nationalist-held Matsu island group, which blocked the other main Chinese port on the Taiwan Strait. Eisenhower concluded that an invasion was in the offing and instructed Secretary of State Dulles to warn Peking (Beijing) publicly that the United States would not tolerate the fall of Quemoy or Matsu.

The navy added punch to Dulles's prose. In addition to the

27,000-ton *Essex*, the nuclear-capable heavy carrier *Midway* was ordered out from Pearl Harbor. The Seventh Fleet swiftly assembled a potent armada in the waters between Taiwan and Quemoy: five attack carriers, an antisubmarine carrier, two heavy cruisers, numerous destroyers, and several amphibious ships. *Midway* was the only carrier large enough to operate nuclear-armed bombers efficiently, but the others packed some nuclear payload. In addition, the Far East Air Forces moved significant land-based tactical aircraft into the troubled area, and the Strategic Air Command placed its 2,800 bomber and tanker force on heightened alert. The United States also was reported to have nuclear-capable missiles emplaced on Taiwan. The major cities of China were therefore directly threatened, and a queer modus vivendi was soon reached whereby the mainland bombarded Quemoy every other day, and both the Nationalists and the Communists resupplied their garrisons on the day in between. By the end of October the crisis had passed.

Eisenhower had achieved his announced purposes in the western Pacific at the same time that he was employing "gunboat diplomacy" with restraint and effectiveness in the eastern Mediterranean. The two military postures together were greater than the sum of their parts. Without firing a shot in anger, the president and Admiral Burke had shown the flag to both the Soviet Union and the People's Republic of China. The United States had successfully pursued discrete political goals on behalf of client states halfway around the world.

After the Lebanon and Quemoy–Matsu episodes ended, the two operational fleets—the Sixth and the Seventh—resumed their normal patrols as part of the nuclear deterrent. But another six months elapsed before the first supercarrier, the U.S.S. *Ranger*, arrived in the western Pacific in 1959. Only then did the Seventh Fleet acquire the credible atomic punch long enjoyed by the more prestigious Sixth Fleet in the Mediterranean. About the same time, target intelligence planners from the air force and navy discovered that uncoordinated war plans had programmed pilots of one service to fly into nuclear fireballs detonated over "designated ground zeroes" by aircraft of the other service. To remedy that condition—dubbed "fratricide"—the combined staffs devised the "Single Integrated Operations Plan" (SIOP) for coordinated "laydown" of nuclear weapons, a highly classified remedy to chaotic nuclear planning.

By the late 1950s there was a great deal of anxiety in the United States about the state of the nation's nuclear arsenal. Capitalizing on this, the 1960 Democratic presidential candidate, John F. Kennedy, chose to campaign on a platform accusing Eisenhower of tolerating a "missile gap" between the United States and the Soviet Union. Democrats alleged that by 1962 the Soviets would enjoy a 3-to-1 advantage over the United States in intercontinental ballistic missiles (ICBMs). In addition to the real and projected Soviet edge in this decisive category of nuclear delivery systems, the United States superiority in bombers had lost much of its credibility after Russia shot down a U-2 reconnaissance aircraft. High-altitude bombers could no longer penetrate Soviet airspace without falling victim to their missile defenses. As Kennedy confirmed when he entered office in 1961, nuclear weapons could deter Soviet leaders only if they were convinced of two things: that United States retaliation to any atomic strike was capable of causing unacceptable destruction within Russia, and that the American leadership had the will to use that capability. Each of those prerequisites was suffering from erosion. To address both problems, the president and his hawkish cold warriors systematically modernized their nuclear missile arsenal with improved submarine-launched missiles and with a fleet of hardened and dispersed ICBMs. They discarded the Eisenhower–Dulles single-option strategy of massive retaliation. They fashioned a doctrine called "flexible response," meaning that the United States could wage a variety of wars simultaneously and could, at will, "escalate" conflicts from guerrilla engagements to incremental nuclear encounters.

At the lower end of the spectrum, Kennedy and Secretary of Defense Robert Strange McNamara created the "Special Forces," or "Green Berets," to fight communist insurgencies in the Third World. At the high end, the nuclear punch of the air force and navy was increased several times. Between 1961 and 1963 the number of air force ICBMs increased from 63 to 631—nearly four hundred of which were solid-fuel, silo-launched second-strike missiles. The Minuteman total would soon reach a thousand. The navy commissioned the first nuclear-powered supercarrier, the *Enterprise*, in November 1961, tested the expanded-range Polaris A-3 missile in August 1962, and commissioned the U.S.S. *Lafayette*, the first of a refined class of ballistic-missile launching submarines, in April 1963.

Throughout his tragically short presidency, John Fitzgerald Kennedy spoke eloquently of the American resolve to "pay any price, bear any burden, meet any hardship . . . oppose any foe to assure the survival and the success of liberty." But when confronted with definitive resistance from Soviet client states or the Soviet Union itself, he backed down. In April 1961, four months after taking office, the new president allowed a poorly conceived CIA-sponsored refugee invasion to proceed against Fidel Castro's Cuba, then withheld promised U.S. air support that might have allowed the invaders either to get ashore or to withdraw. As a result, in the "Bay of Pigs" humiliation the invaders were killed or captured as they landed on the beaches.

In July Kennedy proclaimed Berlin "the great testing place of Western courage and will." But he did nothing when the Soviets retaliated by erecting the wall that pierced the city for twenty-eight years. The president and the "action intellectuals" who surrounded him began to chafe at this pattern of verbal assertiveness and physical inhibition, and in October 1962 they helped precipitate the Cuban missile crisis, which one of them described as a "reprise on the Bay of Pigs business and this time there will be no charges that somebody weakened at the crucial moment."

On 16 October the president learned from his intelligence advisers that the Soviet Union had built forty-two launching pads for intermediate-range ballistic missiles in Cuba. With a striking radius in excess of 1,000 miles, these nuclear-tipped vehicles could hit targets in the Eastern United States with virtually no warning. The appearance of American invulnerability had been shattered, although the nascent "second strike" capability of the Strategic Air Command and the navy's submarine-launched ballistic missiles guaranteed the devastation of Soviet Russia if the Kremlin were foolish enough to permit the launching of the Cuban-based missiles.

Secretary of State Dean Rusk and some of the civilian members of the specially contrived Executive Committee favored a "surgical air strike," but the Joint Chiefs of Staff could not guarantee total destruction of the missiles. The JCS instead advised an invasion to remove the missiles and Castro at one stroke. The president's brother, Robert, warned him away from a surprise attack that would recall the Japanese bombing of Pearl Harbor and might in addition invite a Soviet countermove against Berlin. He settled on a naval "quarantine" of Soviet arms shipments to Cuba and a televised demand for the removal of the missiles. This dual approach would capitalize on two undeniable American assets: the proximity of United States forces to Cuba and John Kennedy's charismatic television personality.

The president announced his "quarantine" over national television on 22 October, and for the next six days the world tottered on the brink of nuclear holocaust. A solution was reached because each side scared the other into accepting some responsibility for causing the faceoff. Thus, Soviet Premier Nikita S. Khrushchev offered to deactivate his missile sites if the United States would withdraw its own intermediate-range missiles from Turkey, a geopolitical American analog to Soviet-influenced Cuba. President Kennedy publicly denounced such a deal as unacceptable, but privately Robert Kennedy assured the Soviets that the American missiles would come out of Turkey as soon as the Cuban crisis evaporated. By the end of October the crisis was effectively over, although Kennedy did not publicly lift the "quarantine" until 20 November.

Declassified documents reveal that the "quarantine" was really a "blockade" in the minds of the participants, but the term was not used in public because a "blockade" is an act of war. In any event, the United States Navy was the principal agent of Kennedy's interdictory measures, the detailed planning for which began well before the intelligence briefing of the president on 16 October, allegedly the incipient point of American intervention.

On 1 October Secretary of Defense McNamara and the Joint Chiefs of Staff had alerted the commander-in-chief of the Atlantic Fleet, Admiral Robert L. Dennison, "to be prepared to institute a blockade of Cuba." At Admiral Dennison's suggestion, the navy's "widespread preparations" were masked as an exercise named PHIB-RIGLEX 62, and on 6 October "further specific orders for the highest state of readiness were issued." On 17 October, the day after Kennedy was briefed, Chief of Naval Operations George W. Anderson alerted all American fleet commanders "to be prepared to order as many ships as possible to sea on a 24-hour notice." The next day Admiral Dennison received a new title: "Commander, Blockade Force." On the 20th McNamara directed the chief of naval operations "to prepare the position and policy papers, scenario, and implementing instructions for the limited blockade." The summary of the crisis later compiled for McNamara concludes, "Admiral Anderson's scenario was followed closely in implementing the quarantine."

That "scenario" was disseminated among the Joint Chiefs of Staff, which under Secretary McNamara's guidance "positively decided" on Sunday, 21 October, "that our first objective would be to block further shipments of offensive military equipment to Cuba, and that our aim was also to see that offensive weapons were removed from Cuba." With the goal defined, the operating plan promulgated, and the ships on the move, Kennedy took his case to the television viewers of the world the next day. The establishment of the "surface quarantine line" at a radius of 500 miles from Cuba was set for 10:00 A.M. Wednesday morning.

The instructions to the American destroyers on station echoed the orders issued to blockading ships since the dawn of the age of sail. The destroyers were to intercept Soviet-bloc cargo vessels approaching the ring around Cuba and contact them with "all available communications, including . . . flag hoists, blinking lights, radio, loud speakers, etc." If a ship did not stop, "warning shots were to be fired across the bow." If it resisted, it would be destroyed, but only as a last resort and with a minimum loss of life. Ideally, the merchant skipper would permit the American destroyer to send over a boarding party. "Visit and search were to include examination of the manifest and inspection of the cargo." Depending on the results of that inspection, the boarding party might serve as a prize crew and take "control of the ship's operation." It then would be brought to an American port under the escort of a destroyer.

Those were orders that any nineteenth-century American naval officer would have understood instinctively. It is a sad commentary on the dissipation of valuable tradition that during the Cuban crisis of 1962 the high command in Washington found it necessary to assign U.S. Coast Guard officers, "who were expert in search-and-visit procedures," to Admiral Dennison's flagship.

Blockade procedures in any case became largely a moot issue prior to their implementation. Early in the morning of Wednesday, 24 October—the first day of the blockade—all of "those Soviet ships en route to Cuba which were capable of carrying questionable cargoes . . . reversed their courses." Only one Soviet-registered ship, a solitary tanker, the *Bucharest,* continued toward Cuba. Intercepted by the destroyer *Gearing* and the carrier *Essex* before dawn on 25 October, she was allowed to continue without boarding, because her configuration precluded her from carrying "contraband." The next day a party from the destroyers *Joseph P. Kennedy, Jr.* and *John R. Pierce* boarded a Lebanese freighter under Soviet charter. No contraband was found, and the *Marcula* was permitted to proceed to Cuba. She was the only ship "stopped and boarded during the entire Quarantine Operation."

In other words, although the blockade was maintained until 20 November, the navy did not once intercept a Soviet or Soviet-chartered cargo vessel inbound to Cuba with missiles or bombers. The Soviets had recalled any such ships prior to the actual establishment of the forbidden zone. The destroyer navy therefore was largely restricted to harassing the handful of conventionally powered Soviet submarines in the vicinity, in one case maintaining "35 hours of continuous contact" before forcing the boat to surface. After 7 November the fleet also inspected Soviet vessels leaving Cuba with missiles. It sighted and photographed a total of 42 missiles aboard exiting ships, but because the "ships did not . . . sail a single transit route . . . there was some difficulty in finding all of them."

The record of ships at sea and hours logged by naval aircraft was impressive: Ninety ships directly involved in the blockade steamed a total of 780,000 miles; ninety-three others had been operating in indirect support during the period from 24 October to 20 November. Sixty-eight aircraft squadrons flew nine thousand sorties totaling 30,000 hours aloft, but many of those missions were flown by "shore-based" aircraft, that is, from air bases in Florida and not from aircraft carriers. Those nonetheless remain large numbers, and interpreting their exact meaning is necessarily a subjective exercise.

The quarantine force, designated Task Force 136, consisted primarily of two cruisers and several squadrons of destroyers. It is suggestive that the only carrier assigned to the blockading force, the old *Essex*, was classed as a "support carrier," that is, one dedicated to antisubmarine warfare. The heavies, the "attack carriers," were kept elsewhere. Specifically, the nuclear carrier *Enterprise* and the large conventionally powered *Independence* were assigned to a separate task force charged with defense of the American base at Guantánamo Bay on Cuba, should it come under attack from Castro's forces. The other large carriers in service remained on station with the Sixth or Seventh Fleet in the Mediterranean and the western Pacific. This means that the Cuban missile crisis was not a strategic encounter for the navy in the sense of a direct confrontation between major elements of the Soviet and American fleets.

For the U.S. Navy the crisis therefore was "conventional" in a historic sense: A large number of relatively small ships established a blockade to interdict trespassers and identify the nature of their cargos before either seizing them or allowing them to pass unmolested. There could be no engagement of capital ships—battleships or aircraft carriers—because neither side committed such warriors to the contest. The Soviets could not commit them because they had never built any; the Americans did not commit them because there was no worthy foe, that is, there was no opposing fleet of major surface combatants. In other words, in the Cold War episode during which the Soviet Union and the United States came closest to nuclear war, the United States Navy found its greatest relevance in a large number of relatively small and inexpensive ships performing commerce-interdiction functions and practicing techniques of antisubmarine warfare. The hugely expensive nuclear-equipped carrier force so painstakingly constructed since World War II had been relegated to a reserve or contingency status in the dangerous autumn of 1962. Its utility would remain the fundamental question of American naval policy and strategy in the age of limited war and "gunboat diplomacy" that opened in 1963.

13

Toward a Six-Hundred-Ship Navy

1963 – 1990

AFTER the resolution of the Cuban missile crisis in the fall of 1962, the navy was free to continue construction of supercarriers and to perfect the submarine-launched ballistic missile force. In April 1963, the U.S.S. *Lafayette* (SSBN 616), the first of a new class of ballistic-missile-launching submarines, was launched. In October the navy fired an expanded-range Polaris missile from a submerged submarine for the first time.

These high-technology strategic weapons systems seemed like the sensible way to wage a Cold War that was in an ugly phase. Soviet Premier Nikita S. Khrushchev had thrown up the Berlin Wall and had taunted the young American president with promises to "bury" the United States. John Fitzgerald Kennedy replied with harsh rhetoric of his own, but after the Cuban faceoff he apparently was seeking less provocative policies in the gray areas of the Third World, where postcolonial regimes were battling insurgencies labeled "communist-inspired" in the United States. One of those civil wars soon diverted the navy from its calculated policy of developing its strategic forces as part of the nuclear deterrent.

Since the Geneva Conference of 1954 the United States had kept a protective arm around the part of the former French colony of Indochina known as South Vietnam. President Dwight D. Eisenhower had sent a few military advisers to encourage the South Vietnamese government to fight insurgents backed by the communist North Vietnamese regime in Hanoi, but the American commitment to South Vietnam was still quite limited when John Kennedy became president in 1961. The growing unpopularity of South Vietnam's premier, Ngo Dinh Diem, and the probability of a coup attempt by dissatisfied officers in Diem's army soon forced Kennedy to send special investigatory missions to Vietnam. Some members of the commissions recommended an increased American military involvement to stabilize the government—or to ensure that the architects of any successful coup were pro-American—and then get on with the feeble war against the Viet Cong insurgents.

An incongruous combination of high- and low-technology military systems mesmerized the interventionists in the Kennedy administration. Walt Whitman Rostow, an economics professor on the president's staff, was fascinated by two "unexploited counterguerrilla assets," helicopter gunships and the army's "Green Beret" special forces. Rostow advised the president that it was "somehow wrong to be developing these capabilities but not applying them in a crucial theater." John Kenneth Galbraith, the American ambassador to India and another former economics professor, objected that in the space age no "real estate" in Southeast Asia was strategically crucial to the United States. Kennedy went with the hawks. In 1961 there were about nine hundred American military "advisers" in South Vietnam; at the time of Kennedy's assassination in November 1963 there were 16,700. Ten years after the end of the Korean War the ground was laid for another "limited war." The "nuclear navy" soon would have to scramble to find itself a mission in this war or risk being eclipsed by the army and air force in the annual contest for appropriations.

President Lyndon Baines Johnson inherited Kennedy's advisers and their goals in South Vietnam. They saw Vietnam much as Truman and his men had seen Korea: Failure to fight Communism in these marginal countries would lead to disaster in Europe. As Secretary of State Dean Rusk told the French ambassador in July 1964, if the United States did not resist in Vietnam, "our guarantees with regard to Berlin would lose their credibility." But Johnson understood the political risks of vastly expanding the American military commitment in the year he hoped to win election to the presidency in his own right. So he temporized as long as he could. He soothingly assured the "generals in Saigon that Lyndon Johnson intends to stand by our word," and he raised the level of American military "advisers" in South Vietnam to 23,300. He also rejected proposals by the Joint

Chiefs of Staff to initiate major ground and air attacks against North Vietnam.

By midsummer 1964 opinion at the top echelon of the White House staff was shifting toward applying direct pressure against North Vietnam to compensate for the failure to induce reforms in the south and to preclude large-scale intervention by Hanoi. The "scenario" called for congressional approval of air strikes against North Vietnam. In August the navy unexpectedly provided the perfect justification for a congressional resolution.

Early in the morning on 1 August, while engaged in electronic surveillance in the Gulf of Tonkin off the coast of North Vietnam, the American destroyer *Maddox* was attacked by three North Vietnamese torpedo boats. The attackers were repulsed with the help of aircraft from the U.S.S. *Ticonderoga*. The night before, South Vietnamese gunboats implementing the U.S.-approved "OPLAN 34A" had bombarded a nearby island, and the North Vietnamese apparently concluded that the *Maddox* was covering them. The navy ordered the *Maddox* to continue operating in the Gulf of Tonkin and then sent the destroyer *Turner Joy* to escort her. An additional carrier, the *Constellation*, was rushed down from Hong Kong. The freedom of the seas was at issue, but this forward deployment of the two destroyers was certainly provocative.

On the night of 4 August, in heavy weather some 60 miles off the North Vietnamese coast, the *Maddox* and *Turner Joy* reported that they were under attack by North Vietnamese gunboats. Washington was fully ready this time. Secretary of Defense McNamara expressed the consensus that "we cannot sit still as a nation and let them attack us on the high seas." The secretary disregarded follow-on messages from the captain of the *Maddox* cautioning that "freak weather effects" and "overeager" sonar operators made his earlier reports of an attack unreliable. At McNamara's recommendation, President Johnson late in the afternoon of 4 August (local Washington time) authorized retaliatory air raids against North Vietnamese torpedo boat bases and fuel dumps.

Shortly after noon on 5 August, the carriers *Ticonderoga* and *Constellation* launched sixty-four strike aircraft against what the president publicly described as "gun boats and certain supporting facilities in North Vietnam." Extensive damage was inflicted, but not without cost. One navy pilot was shot down and killed. Another, Lieutenant (j.g.) Everett Alvarez, Jr., became Hanoi's first American captive, and he remained a prisoner of war for seven years. The pattern of the war as it pertained to carrier aviation was set with this first mission.

Saying nothing about OPLAN 34A or the *Maddox*'s electronic mission off North Vietnam, the president on 7 August elicited from a pliant Congress the "Gulf of Tonkin Resolution" authorizing him to take "all necessary measures to repel any armed attacks against the forces of the United States and to prevent further aggression." The overwhelming vote in Congress (416–0 in the House; 82–2 in the Senate) and the air raids of 5 August substantially enhanced Johnson's stature with the populace during a tense presidential campaign against the hawkish Republican Senator Barry M. Goldwater. For the remainder of 1964 Johnson left the two carriers of Task Force 77 in the Gulf of Tonkin "standing by for retaliatory strikes over North Vietnam with various bomb loads and missiles." The only missions they actually flew were over South Vietnam. Johnson had assumed a masterful presidential stance that could intimidate foreign enemies and domestic political foes with equal effectiveness.

Within days of his inauguration on 20 January 1965 Johnson used the congressional blank check to escalate the reprisals against North Vietnam into what became "America's longest war." On 7 February 1965 eight American soldiers died in a Viet Cong attack on an army barracks in Pleiku and a nearby helicopter base. Four days later the Viet Cong hit an American enlisted men's compound. Three navy carriers, the *Ranger, Coral Sea,* and *Hancock,* sent their bombers north in an operation named "FLAMING DART." They flew in the "fog, rain, and low visibility characteristic of the northeast monsoon" and encountered deadly accurate anti-aircraft fire. A quasi-official historian of the naval air war in Vietnam concluded that it was already evident at this very early date that "with tactical operational decisions made at long distance for political purpose" the "tit-for-tat response was not likely to deter the Communists from further attacks inside South Vietnam."

Task Force 77 soon grew to include four or five aircraft carriers sent to the western Pacific—"WESTPAC"—from the Pacific and Atlantic fleets. They operated from two points in the South China Sea: "Yankee Station" in the Gulf of Tonkin off the coast of North Vietnam, and "Dixie Station" well to the south off the coast of South Vietnam. Dixie Station carriers provided close air—or fighter—cover for ground troops engaging the Viet Cong insurgents. The carriers in

Yankee Station had the infinitely more difficult and dangerous mission of bombing targets in North Vietnam under the code name "ROLLING THUNDER."

On 29 March 1965 a ROLLING THUNDER attack from the carriers *Coral Sea* and *Hancock* forecast the shape of things to come. The two ships launched a total of seventy aircraft, which headed for a radar and communications installation on a small island in the Gulf of Tonkin. A low cloud cover forced the pilots to drop down into anti-aircraft battery range. Three of the first six aircraft over the target were piloted by air squadron commanders. They were hit and went down. That was just the beginning of the tragedy. A year later, in March 1966, Task Force 77 carrier planes flew 6,500 sorties and lost eleven aircraft with ten air crewmen. Twenty-one planes and fifteen men went down the next month.

The most maddening obstacle facing the avaitors of Yankee Station was the direct operational control exerted by officials in Washington over every mission, a factor that precluded a flexible response to changing tactical and meteorological conditions. In addition to severely limiting the airmen's choice of targets, Washington often selected the route and altitude of approach to a target, a life-threatening compulsion. North Vietnam threw up deadly obstacles of its own: anti-aircraft battery fire, surface-to-air missiles (SAMs) fired from mobile sites that were very hard to find and destroy, and high-performance Russian-built MiG fighters armed with air-to-air missiles.

The high cost of inflicting relatively slight punishment on North Vietnam was fully understood by Admiral U. S. Grant Sharp, the senior Pacific commander, who took his case to the Joint Chiefs of Staff at the end of 1965. "It was obvious," he concluded

> that our air operations in 1965 had not achieved their goal. . . . We had not forced Hanoi to the peace table. We had not scared Hanoi out of the war. We had not caused any diminution whatsoever of his carrying the war into South Vietnam. In fact, the reverse was true.

Admiral Sharp wanted "a properly oriented bombing effort" to break the North's will and avoid "a long and costly war."

The admiral was not destined to see a loosening of operational control by Washington. The Johnson administration continued to hope that tightly regulated use of force would permit an American withdrawal from Vietnam without defeat or intervention by China or the Soviet Union.

The year 1967 marked the high—and low—point of the naval air war in Vietnam. Eleven aircraft carriers at one time or another launched strikes as part of Task Force 77. Forty-six North Vietnamese MiG jet fighters were knocked out, but at the cost of 133 navy planes, a 9 percent increase in losses over the previous year. One senior official in the administration finally began to appreciate "the limits of air power" as employed in Vietnam. On 10 October Secretary of Defense McNamara expressed his disillusionment: "I do not think [the bombing] has in any significant way affected their war making capability." He had concluded that "the North Vietnamese still retain the capability to support activities in South Vietnam . . . at present or increased combat levels." An outspoken naval aviator cogently noted the demoralizing impact of McNamara's confession: "To the pilots who were risking their lives daily under the restrictive targeting system and flight rules imposed by Secretary McNamara, who were not allowed to destroy the supplies where they could be seen, it was a disheartening judgment."

But the navy continued to bomb North Vietnam and to lose aircraft and men. In Johnson's thirty-seven-month bombing campaign between 1965 and 1968, 421 navy planes were shot down and 450 aviators were lost. Later, 130 more airplanes went down in President Richard M. Nixon's limited bombing campaign of 1969–1971. Not all the lost airmen were killed; many became prisoners of war and, in the opinion of naval strategist Frank Uhlig, Jr., "a weapon for the enemy to use against us. When the people of the United States realized the savage conditions under which the prisoners existed year after year, their release became a principal U.S. war aim." The avaitors of the Vietnam War had become hostages, and their plight exposed a hitherto unappreciated liability of aviation in the dawning era of proliferating low-cost anti-air missiles.

To the question, "What had it accomplished?" there is no satisfying answer. Very early on, Rear Admiral John D. Hayes, a respected naval commentator, concluded that "used as it was in Vietnam, the naval power of the United States did not succeed either in improving the military and political situation there or in reducing the cost of the war." Another sympathetic observer, Vice Admiral Malcolm W. Cagle, concluded from his comprehensive review of the navy's air war that at best the bombing slowed North Vietnam's resupply of its own troops and of the Viet Cong insurgents in the South, but it had not forced Hanoi "to make peace."

Admiral Cagle's more general conclusions about the use of air-

craft carriers in Vietnam—and in Korea two decades earlier—bear
directly on the nature of American sea power at the end of the twentieth century. He noted that in those two limited wars the "carriers
had been employed as floating airfields—tied to a geographic station
less than a 100 miles from the enemy's coast, sending aircraft against
targets deep in the enemy's land." This stationary positioning of the
carriers "made no use of a prime advantage of carriers—their mobility." It also made them sitting ducks. In the words of Admiral Roy L.
Johnson, at one time the commander-in-chief of the Pacific Fleet,
"we might have gotten in serious trouble by operating near a fixed
point" if there had been "a serious air threat or submarine threat in
the Gulf of Tonkin." Therefore, Cagle concluded, the prolonged operation of carriers from nearly fixed points "should not become a
practice." Vietnam—and Korea—thus represented an inappropriate
operational deployment of aircraft carriers, and yet those wars comprised the principal operational use of the great carrier armada America built after World War II.

The two limited wars also allegedly caused, "in the minds of
many," an incorrect understanding of the aircraft carrier's true function. From Vietnam and Korea, according to Admiral Cagle, the false
conclusion was drawn that "the primary purpose" of carriers was
"sea-based tactical air augmenting . . . land-based tactical air." Not
so, said the admiral. He offered a corrective: The "main mission for
attack aircraft carriers is to assist in carrying out the Navy's prime
mission, control of the seas." The carrier, in other words, was
Mahan's modern tool. The goal remained command of the seas; the
strategic line back to Trafalgar ran straight and clear; the real purpose
of the carrier was to destroy an enemy's fleet as Nelson destroyed
Villeneuve's in 1805. But a dilemma existed: There had been no
formidable enemy fleet since the defeat of Japan in 1945.

=====

The air war was not the U.S. Navy's only war in Vietnam. American sailors also waged a "brown-water" fight reminiscent of the Mexican and Civil wars. This nineteenth-century-style war featured small
combatants, relatively junior officers, and seasoned enlisted men. It
began in the administration of President Kennedy, himself a veteran
of "unconventional" naval warfare—the Pacific "PT" torpedo-boat
campaign of World War II. On 29 April 1961 Kennedy approved
American naval training for Vietnamese "Junk Force" crews in order
to strengthen South Vietnam's coastal patrols. From that point until
early 1965, in the words of Kennedy's successor Lyndon B. Johnson,

"We increased assistance to the Vietnamese Navy to enable it to protect the coast against infiltration from the North and to patrol the inland waterways used extensively by the Viet Cong."

Three combat groups were created: the Sea Force, the River Force, and the Junk Force. To get those "forces" to fight aggressively in the American manner, naval advisers were attached "at the unit level." In May 1965 there were 235 advisers working under the supervision of the "Naval Advisory Group," a section of the supreme American headquarters in Vietnam, the "Military Assistance Command Vietnam" (MACV), headed by Army General William C. Westmoreland. By then, in the opinion of Thomas J. Cutler, the closest student of the topic, the "die was cast: the American Navy had begun its coastal and riverine involvement in Vietnam."

The problem was that unlike the air war, where ships, aircraft, and tactical doctrine existed to organize a sustained bombing campaign, the United States Navy itself lacked suitable vessels, trained men, or an ongoing tradition and doctrine with which to advise the South Vietnamese Navy on how to fight in rivers and along the coast. After every previous brown-water experience—from the gunboats of Thomas Jefferson through the Civil War monitors to the Yangtze River (Chang Jiang) patrols of the twentieth century—the navy had largely dismissed its shallow-draft experience as irrelevant to its true purpose—blue-water operations.

In the opening stages of the surface sailors' war in Vietnam improvisation was the name of the game. The navy contracted with South Vietnamese shipbuilders for diesel-driven junks, but they were built carelessly of green wood. Worms bored out their leaky hulls, and the Vietnamese crews lacked the mechanical aptitude for preventative maintenance of the engines. More reliable were the World War II–vintage British and American landing craft that U.S. advisers converted into armed riverine and coastal patrol vessels. Old LCMs (Landing Craft, Mechanized) were loaded with machine guns and used for heavy fire-support missions. On a platform such as this a navy lieutenant and one or two chief petty officers would risk their lives alongside Vietnamese "counterparts" in an unending attempt to stem the flow of food and supplies from North Vietnam to soldiers and Viet Cong in the south.

The first American naval officer to fall was Lieutenant Harold Dale Meyerkord of St. Louis, Missouri. He was hit with small arms fire from a jungle-lined river bank while sitting on the raised deckhouse of a converted LCM in the aftermath of what the navy officially described as "an amphibious assault and destroy operation" on 16 March 1965. In trying to pull his mortally wounded boss below decks, Meyerkord's chief petty officer, Eugene Barney, was severely wounded. The chief survived to receive the Bronze Star; the lieutenant had a ship named after him, the destroyer escort *Meyerkord*. The brown-water war beginning in Vietnam was a long, long way from the high-technology war the modern American navy had been built to fight.

About the time of Lieutenant Meyerkord's death the navy was forced to reappraise its largely "advisory" role in the war in the south. On 3 March 1965 an army helicopter discovered a North Vietnamese trawler literally disguised as an island making its way from the South China Sea to South Vietnam. It took the South Vietnamese, prodded by the Americans, five days to capture the vessel, which was found to carry North Vietnamese army regulars as well as a storehouse of arms and ammunition manufactured in Eastern Europe. The Americans were outraged by both the discovery and the slow pace of the capture. The so-called Vung Ro Incident led immediately to an upgrading of the U.S. Navy's participation in the offshore interdiction of suspicious vessels moving along South Vietnam's coast on the South China Sea. The operational code name was "MARKET TIME."

It soon became apparent that the relatively deep draft of U.S. destroyers kept them too far offshore for maximum effectiveness in surveillance of the hundreds of small vessels plodding along the coast. There was nothing suitable for inshore patrols in the navy's inventory, so the Johnson administration turned to the Coast Guard for a flotilla of 82-foot-long, 5.5-foot-draft patrol boats (WPBs). Modified to carry a mortar and heavier machine guns, and put under the command of two officers and nine enlisted men, they were rushed to Vietnam. When the navy discovered that oil drillers in the Gulf of Mexico used very shallow-draft aluminum boats to ferry crews to offshore rigs, it ordered a naval version from the manufacturer. In less than six weeks, the first "Swift boats"—or more formally, PCFs (Patrol Craft, Fast)— were ready to join the WPBs as part of Task Force 115, the Coastal Surveillance Force. By May 1965 the U.S. Navy was ready to "stop, search, and seize vessels not clearly engaged in innocent passage" along the South Vietnamese coast, regardless of the distance out from the shore line.

Behind the WPBs and PCFs lurked the destroyers and the radar-picket destroyer escorts. Above all of them flew land-based navy patrol craft from bases as far away as the Philippines. The aviators could "go home at night," but for the men on the surface vessels the blockade duty of Task Force 115 was not unlike that of Union blockaders along the Confederate coast during the Civil War. It was hot, humid, and tedious work performed aboard improvised vessels, and when the enervating tedium gave way suddenly to quick movement and sudden danger, the change of pace was welcome.

Between June 1966 and June 1968 MARKET TIME sailors boarded more than 400,000 suspicious itinerant vessels, an average of 16,000 per month. The percentage of supplies intended for the enemy in the south intercepted in this manner cannot be estimated with any precision, but evaluations by several groups within and without the navy have uniformly praised MARKET TIME for significantly reducing the flow. Even the normally skeptical Elmo R. Zumwalt, Jr., the commander of U.S. Naval Forces Vietnam from September 1968 to May 1970, concluded, "By the time I arrived on the scene, the interdiction mission had pretty much been accomplished as far as the coast [was] concerned."

The navy also tried to interdict the movement of men and supplies by the Viet Cong in the sprawling Mekong Delta. Constituting about one-fourth of the area of South Vietnam, the rice-rich alluvial plain is cut by four large branches of the major river, called the Mekong by Westerners. The best that could be hoped for was to keep the main channel feeding Saigon open and to inconvenience the Viet Cong by going up the innumerable canals and river branches in search of sampans loaded with men and war matériel. For this limited purpose the navy in December 1965 authorized "Operation GAME WARDEN" and in February 1966 put it into effect under the organizational designation Task Force 116.

Once again, the navy's proud blue-water tradition offered no guidance in devising weapons platforms and tactical doctrine. The former were not so hard to acquire, because the flourishing and competitive American pleasure-boat industry had imaginative naval architects who knew how to modify designs to suit special purposes. Within a few weeks of the navy's call for proposals, shipbuilders were making final bids for contracts on a 31-foot fiberglass boat drawing only inches and driven by water-jet pumps. A yard in Bellingham, Washington, landed the contract for 120 boats costing $75,000 each. Delivery was set for 1 April 1966, and training began on California's Sacramento River, where the sloughs bear some resemblance to the marshy waterways of the Mekong Delta.

An approximate tactical doctrine could be devised from war gaming in central California, but by and large it had to evolve in actual combat. The basic idea was to operate the new riverine fighters, called PBRs (Patrol Boat, River) in pairs, with the trailing boat providing cover for the lead boat while it investigated the cargo of a suspect Vietnamese water craft. The Viet Cong proved ingenious at setting traps for the PBRs, which could be hurt badly by heavy fire pouring out of impenetrable mangrove forests lining the rivers and tributaries. Gradually, therefore, a force of modified army "Huey" helicopter gunships—called "Seawolves" by the navy—was assembled to provide air support to the PBRs.

A typical PBR mission lasted twelve hours, and the Seawolf had an on-station loiter time of only about 1.5 hours. That left the PBRs on their own too much of the time, so in late 1968 the navy decided to cover them more regularly with fixed-wing aircraft. The platform chosen was the OV-10A "Bronco" of the new Light Attack Squadron Four, commissioned at Naval Air Station North Island, California, on 3 January 1969. The "Black Ponies," as the squadron's airmen called their propeller-driven twin engine aircraft, carried machine guns, 20-mm cannon and supersonic "Zuni" rockets as well as illuminating flares for night operations. One historian describes this load as "a phenomenal amount of firepower." The Black Ponies arrived in Vietnam in April 1969 and quickly became a favorite of the PBR sailors. They had three attributes that enabled them to save many PBRs from destruction: "quick response time, heavy firepower, and long staying time."

It is impossible to assess with precision the exact impact of GAME WARDEN on the movement of enemy men and matériel through the waterways of the Mekong Delta, but it is indisputable that the PBRs boarded and searched a staggering number of watercraft, an average of 100,000 a month according to one report. Equally indicative that GAME WARDEN was serious business is the estimate of Rear Admiral Sayre A. Swarztrauber that by 1970 more than a hundred sailors in the force had been killed by enemy fire. "Yet, in spite of this high risk," Lieutenant Commander Thomas J. Cutler asserted, "the Navy never had difficulty filling its GAME WARDEN billets."

Beginning in December 1966 a second major American contingent operated in the Mekong Delta. The Mobile Riverine Force was jointly commanded by a navy captain and an army colonel. Its mission was to drive at least some of the Viet Cong from parts of the Delta. The idea of a shared army–navy operational command was consciously drawn from the Civil War experience on the Mississippi River. The Civil War also at least marginally inspired the Mobile Riverine Force's heaviest armed assault vessels, the so-called monitors, which replicated the configuration and silhouette of the double-turreted Union monitors. The use of the Civil War as a point of reference for naval warfare suggests how irrelevant the navy's twentieth-century bluewater experience had become by the mid-1960s.

The 2d Brigade of the specially reactivated Ninth Infantry Division—General Westmoreland's World War II division—was assigned to the Mobile Riverine Force to carry the fight to the Viet Cong in the delta. The soldiers were embarked in platoon-size units aboard converted amphibious landing craft nested alongside three or four larger headquarters ships of Task Force 117. From this mobile base the troops were ferried to spots along the rivers and canals of the delta where Viet Cong strongholds were believed to exist. The army men would land, and the armored carriers and the escorting monitors would back offshore and position themselves to provide covering fire and cut off the fleeing enemy. At the end of two or three days, the soldiers climbed back aboard the landing craft and rode down river to the headquarters and barracks ships. The entire operation was coordinated by a battalion commander orbiting overhead in a helicopter.

Neat and tidy in theory, it was bloody awful in practice. The Viet Cong soon perfected their marine ambush techniques in waterways so narrow that the monitors and assault craft of Task Force 117, caught in heavy fire, often could not turn around. By the middle of 1967 the Viet Cong had a rocket with a 500-yard range capable of penetrating a foot of armor. A four-hour battle on 11 September illustrated the carnage that now could be inflicted on the sailors of the Mobile Riverine Force. In a carefully prepared Viet Cong ambush along a thin 2-mile stretch of river, eighteen American boats were damaged, five navy men were killed, and seventy-seven were wounded. The monthly historical supplement published by the commander, U.S. Naval Forces Vietnam, made the hollow claim that it was all worthwhile because the Viet Cong suffered many more casualties than the Americans.

The best justification for the Mobile Riverine Force came during the Communist "Tet Offensive" of February 1968, the turning point in the war. While the claimed number of Viet Cong killed cannot be validated, the high mobility of the force did permit it to help save the major cities of the delta. "Had the force not been created and introduced into the delta a year earlier," Thomas Cutler concluded, "the

Tet Offensive would more than likely have had a much different outcome in this southern 'rice bowl' region of South Vietnam."

That rationalization did not satisfy Vice Admiral Elmo R. Zumwalt, Jr., who took command of all American naval forces in Vietnam on 29 September 1968. A briefing by the navy boss of the Mobile Riverine Force, Captain Robert S. Salzer, convinced the admiral that Cambodia was shipping large quantities of supplies across its border along the waterways of the Mekong Delta. Worried that the slackened pace of operations was demoralizing his sailors, Zumwalt planned a restructuring and a new aggressive strategy. He designated it with the acronym "SEA LORDS," for South-East Asia Lake, Ocean, River, and Delta Strategy. As explained by Lieutenant Commander Cutler, the new strategy would "form an interdiction barrier across the upper reaches of the Mekong Delta. . . . This barrier would be intensive and would close off, or at least seriously hamper, the flow of supplies from Cambodia."

Zumwalt cleared the concept with General Creighton W. Abrams, Westmoreland's replacement as the senior commander of all U.S. forces in Vietnam. On 5 November 1968 the admiral issued Operation Plan 111-69 putting SEA LORDS into effect under the organizational designation Task Force 194. For almost two years, until it was disbanded as part of President Richard M. Nixon's "Vietnamization" process, this special task force set up naval barriers along rivers and canals roughly paralleling the Cambodian border.

SEA LORDS's success, like that of all the navy's "in-country" operations, is questionable. On the one hand, the riverine boundaries created a "front" of sorts in an otherwise very fluid and irregular war. A geographic line with friendly forces on one side and the enemy on the other was the kind of reference point American soldiers and sailors could understand and appreciate. Admiral Zumwalt records his own optimistic appraisal in a characteristically personal tone: "By the spring of 1969, the Navy was blockading the entire river-and-canal system along the Cambodian border and as a result, General Adams told me, Viet Cong activity in the delta was much reduced and overall U.S. casualties were considerably reduced."

On the other hand, after the Tet Offensive of 1968 popular support for the war was fast eroding in the United States. Sailors now came to Vietnam questioning their own presence and mission. They were more anxious to survive their tour than to distinguish themselves by gallant dedication to duty. Admiral Zumwalt's flag secretary later recalled visits from "young lieutenants" who came to COMNAVFORV headquarters to discuss the problems of conscience "they had in executing . . . orders" that might involve killing innocent Vietnamese. To compound the uncertainty, the casualty rate for navy men in SEA LORDS was the highest for the surface navy in Vietnam. The official ratio was thirty enemy killed for every dead American SEA LORDS sailor, but that was scant recompense in a time of profound national doubt about the moral justification for the Vietnam War.

On 2 November 1968 Vice Admiral Zumwalt briefed General Abrams, who had just returned from Washington with instructions from President Johnson "to turn the war over to the Vietnamese." In contrast to the other briefers, who were still predicting an American victory in 1976 or somewhere down the road, Zumwalt presented a plan for rapidly giving the South Vietnamese navy full responsibility for the naval war. Zumwalt coined another acronym, "ACTOV," for Accelerated Turnover to the Vietnamese, and said the U.S. Navy could be relieved of all operational missions by mid-1970. He was in step with developments in Washington. In a speech a year later, on 31 December 1969, President Nixon proclaimed "Vietnamization" the official policy of the United States. The wheel had come full circle: Americans assumed advisory roles as they prepared to withdraw, just as they had when first moving into Vietnam a decade earlier.

During the 1960s the material condition of the U.S. Navy had declined visibly. Funds normally allocated to new ship construction, maintenance, and overhaul went instead to fighting the war in Vietnam. Meanwhile, the Soviet navy under Admiral Sergei G. Gorshkov was building a very substantial oceangoing surface fleet. As the analyst Michael T. Corgan has shown, in the late 1970s internal Soviet politics would check this historical deviation and the Russians would return to their tradition of maintaining a navy as a coastal adjunct to the army's continental defense. But at the time, the Soviet blue-water challenge to American naval supremacy appeared quite menacing.

It became Zumwalt's chore to rebuild the U.S. Navy to meet the apparent Soviet threat. On 1 July 1970, at age forty-nine, he became the youngest chief of naval operations in history. He was selected because he had strong bipartisan support. Prior to going to Vietnam he had served as executive assistant to one of Washington's most influential figures, Paul Nitze. A co-author of the critical post–World War II United States Strategic Bombing Survey, Nitze also had written NSC 68 for the Truman administration. As Lyndon Johnson's

secretary of the navy, he expressed his disillusionment with the endless bombing of North Vietnam, a view he transmitted to Melvin R.
Laird, Richard Nixon's incoming secretary of defense. Thus primed,
Laird was receptive when Nitze's protégé, Admiral Zumwalt, ex-
trolled the virtues of ACTOV during a familiarization tour of Vietnam
in February 1969. Zumwalt's selection as the next CNO followed
naturally.

In his first interview with Nixon's Secretary of the Navy John H.
Chafee, Zumwalt emphasized his deep concern about "the accelerating obsolescence of the U.S. Navy . . . as opposed to the impressive
growth and modernization of the Soviet Navy." In other words, he
was safely and conventionally hawkish toward the Soviet Union. He
also was a "surface line officer" and not an aviator. The previous three
chiefs of naval operations had been pilots and had reserved the choic-
est seagoing flag commands—the Mediterranean Sixth and the Pacific
Seventh Fleets—for fellow aviators. That demoralizing monopoly of
high command by one group of officers at the expense of those who
traced their institutional lineage back to John Paul Jones was intol-
erable to Chafee. Zumwalt seemed like the man to redress the balance.

Zumwalt's vision of the proper configuration of the navy for the
1970s and 1980s reflected an astute political intelligence at work. He
adopted the standard premise that the Soviet navy was the principal
antagonist of the U.S. Navy. He expressed appreciation for the vital
role in national defense played by the navy's "strategic" or nuclear-
delivery units—the ballistic-missile-launching submarines and the big
aircraft carriers. He made a Mahanian distinction between the dif-
fering geopolitical bases of the Soviet Union, "a land Power," and the
United States, a "world island." These Cold War premises led him to
a conventional exposition of "the double mission of the U.S. Navy: to
keep the seas open for commercial and military traffic of all kinds,
which we call 'sea control,' and to make it possible to apply military
power overseas, which we call 'projection.' "

Zumwalt's conceptual break with post-1945 American naval
strategy came with his visionary prescription of the right navy for the
"double mission." He noted that during Vietnam, and in Korea before it, too many of the navy's "sea-control forces—anti-submarine
planes and their carriers and ships suitable for patrol and escort
duty—were allowed to obsolesce and, finally, retire without replacement." Worse still, development of "new types of ships from which
planes or helicopters could operate, new techniques for combating

submarines, new vessels to escort convoys, new kinds of weapons with which to fight on the surface was postponed for many years." Zumwalt identified what he called the "high" type of vessels, which had not suffered fiscal attrition: heavy carriers and attack and ballistic-missile submarines. The "air CNOs" had preserved funding for the former; Admiral Hyman Rickover had induced Congress to continue building the latter.

As the chief of naval operations, Zumwalt proposed to build a fleet of what he called "low" vessels for the "sea control" mission. By that he meant many relatively inexpensive ships in place of a few very expensive ones. Zumwalt explained that "in most cases seven or five or even three ships of moderate capability would contribute far more to the success of this mission than one supership." This "high–low mix" became Zumwalt's byword. It was a fiscally responsible and strategically sound way to meet the U.S. Navy's global commitments in conditions other than nuclear war between the two superpowers. But it was heresy to the navy's carrier admirals, and it quickly ran afoul of Admiral Rickover.

Rickover's domination of the navy's nuclear power program had troubled Zumwalt for a long time. In 1959, when under consideration for command of a new nuclear-powered frigate, Zumwalt had been subjected to one of Rickover's candidate-screening interviews. Those degrading experiences were legendary in the navy, but usually they were inflicted on graduating midshipmen or very junior officers. The "Rickover treatment" was especially humiliating for a senior officer who was at the time an aide to the assistant secretary of the navy. He passed muster but was nonetheless assigned command of an oil-driven frigate. Personally scarred, Zumwalt correctly regarded Rickover "as an independent baron within the Navy."

Upon becoming chief of naval operations, Zumwalt resolved to accommodate Rickover's expensive submarine and surface nuclear building program as much as he could without gutting his own preference for a large number of inexpensive ships. He decided that it was vain to try to block the biennial continuation of Rickover on active duty. The old curmudgeon, legally retired from the navy, remained in harness only by virtue of special acts of Congress, the seat of his real power and influence. Rickover was so firmly entrenched that twice Zumwalt brushed aside suggestions by National Security Adviser Henry A. Kissinger that he be forcibly retired once and for all. But conciliation was of no avail, and Zumwalt finally convinced himself that the "management system" of Admiral Rickover had become so "un-American and autocratic" that he had "to tangle" with him during the congressional appropriations hearings for the fiscal 1974 budget.

The ostensible issue was the future of Admiral Zumwalt's "Sea Control Ship," but the real issue was which man would shape the navy of the future. Zumwalt described the Sea Control Ship (SCS) as "an extremely austere carrier" costing approximately $100 million, or one-eighth what a large nuclear-powered carrier cost in 1973 dollars. Displacing a mere 17,000 tons—20,000 less than the famed *Essex* carriers of World War II—the SCS would have a top speed of 25 knots and a range of 7,500 nautical miles. She would carry fourteen helicopters and three "Harrier" AV-8 vertical takeoff and landing (V/STOL) fighter planes. The helicopters would combat submarines with sonobuoys, depth charges, and torpedoes. The Harriers would form a defensive envelope over the ship. The SCS would have no catapults or arresting cables, the technological marvels that permit American aircraft carriers to launch and recover supersonic jet aircraft.

In peacetime, Zumwalt's SCS would "show the flag in dangerous waters, especially the Mediterranean and the western Pacific, where the Sixth and Seventh Fleets operate." The big carriers would withdraw to the broad oceans, "out of reach of an enemy [that is, Soviet] first strike." The survivability achieved by repositioning the large carriers would reestablish their credibility as a deterrent to nuclear war.

In wartime, Zumwalt proposed to transpose "the positions of the two kinds of carriers . . . the big, powerful ones would fight their way into the most dangerous waters, destroying [the] opposition . . . with their planes, and the Sea Control Ships would serve in mid-ocean." The "chief wartime mission" of the SCS would be to convoy "merchantmen, troop transports, and naval auxiliaries in need of air protection from the time they left the reach of land-based air until they entered areas where the deployed [large] carriers were operating."

For Zumwalt the great firepower of the large carriers assured them of critical roles in any "major war." Since he made no real distinction between nuclear and nonnuclear wars, Vietnam presumably fell into the category of a "major" nonnuclear war. The deployment of the heavy carriers on Yankee Station therefore had been an appropriate use of their great "offensive capability." North Vietnam posed no threat on the high seas—it could not wage *guerre de course*—and therefore convoys were superfluous. But the absence of any kind of "sea control" ship in the American inventory would have been disastrous to the resupply of the ground forces in Vietnam if the enemy had possessed a submarine capability of any magnitude whatsoever. The Vietnam War, by these definitions, could not have been fought. The SCS therefore was essential to the nation's ability to wage war in the future.

Without fully realizing it, Admiral Zumwalt was proposing a naval strategy perfectly consonant with the historic American naval strategy of *guerre de course* and the classic mission of the United States sailing frigates. While publicly committed to the Mahanian notion of the United States as a "world island," Zumwalt was propounding a non-Mahanian continentalist naval doctrine. His envious observation in 1976 that the Soviet Navy had two small carrier sea control ships "in operation" and had begun construction of a third— the *Kiev, Minsk,* and *Novorossiysk*—is revealing. The Russian naval tradition is preeminently one of coastal defense and *guerre de course* and by Zumwalt's own admission, "the Soviet Union is a land power in both an economic and a political-military sense."

To prescribe a continentalist navy strategy for the United States Navy in the age of Mahanian "sea power" was to court disaster, and that precisely was what befell Zumwalt's SCS in December 1973. Funding for the ship was deleted from the fiscal 1974 budget at the last minute by Congressman George H. Mahon, chairman of the House Appropriations Committee and a longtime opponent of naval aviation. Zumwalt blamed Rickover's persistent opposition and insidious influence on Mahon for this congressional destruction of the core "low" component of his strategy. He noted the irony that in the middle of the bitter fight he had the duty of ceremonially promoting Rickover from vice to full admiral, an advancement ordained by Congress.

This convenient fixation on Rickover obscured other factors that contributed to the collapse of the most imaginative naval strategy proposed by any chief of naval operations since the office was created. As the nation withdrew from Vietnam in 1973–1974, the navy was experiencing one of the traditional and cyclical budget retrenchments characteristic of postwar periods in American history. In a tight fiscal climate, many powerful interest groups within the navy and Congress still favored nuclear propulsion for all large ships, especially the three nuclear-powered aircraft carriers then in design or under construction, the *Nimitz, Dwight D. Eisenhower,* and *Carl Vinson.* Those ships individually cost approximately $2.5 billion, and each one mounted an air wing of one hundred aircraft. Zumwalt, in other words, was contending against a combination of shipbuilding, aircraft, and electronics industries epitomizing the American "military-industrial complex." It is no wonder that he lost.

The Watergate scandal (1973–1974) compounded his frustration at the end of his four-year term as chief of naval operations. Zumwalt was convinced that after the debacle Richard Nixon was a "wrecked President" served badly by "an unprincipled Secretary of State." The navy's top admiral saw great issues as extensions of individual personalities and sought as his own successor someone who would continue his reforms in personnel policy, a man who

> believed in the "high–low" mix and had the stamina and the wisdom to protect it from the stratagems of Admiral Rickover and to sell it on Capitol Hill. Above all, I wanted a successor with the integrity and strength of character to keep the Navy from being suffocated in the political miasma that was enveloping ever more closely the . . . White House.

He chose Admiral James L. Holloway III, who came "from a family of admirals."

When Holloway became the chief of naval operations on 1 July 1974 he immediately articulated a naval strategy built around the twin concepts of "sea control" and "projection of power" but dropped all references to the sea control ship. Holloway's navy would control or command substantial segments of the world's oceans with battle groups centered on large aircraft carriers, preferably nuclear-powered ones. From "secure areas" in the ocean the navy could "project" force ashore, that is, it could hammer targets and enemies on land with a variety of weapons: aircraft, missiles, amphibious forces, and even the 16-inch guns of the four mothballed *Iowa*-class battleships. Commissioned during World War II, the *Iowa*, *New Jersey*, *Missouri*, and *Wisconsin* had been taken out of service early in the Cold War. The *New Jersey* was temporarily brought back to serve as a bombardment platform off the Vietnam coast in 1968, and all four again reentered the fleet between 1982 and 1989.

Holloway's strategy was a classic Cold War proposal modified to provide for massive overhaul of the aging oil-driven large carriers—the "Service Life Extension Program" (SLEP). It also incorporated funding requests for more *Nimitz*-class nuclear-powered carriers.

Given the danger to carrier-based battle groups posed by the increasing accuracy of airborne antiship missiles, the Holloway navy of necessity pressed for development of a nuclear-powered cruiser mounting the state-of-the-art electronic "Aegis area air defense system."

In the dying days of the Nixon administration any searching debate about naval policy was impossible, and in his brief tenure as president Gerald Ford had to concentrate on rebuilding the people's confidence in their political system and on winning the office in his own right in the 1976 election. Therefore, as the analysts James A. Nathan and James K. Oliver observed, "for the most part the Ford administration did not fundamentally challenge the Navy's concept of sea control and projection as the basis for force structure planning and expansion in the late twentieth century." It certainly did not resurrect the high-low mix or the sea control ship.

In 1976 Ford was defeated by Jimmy Carter, a Georgia Democrat who had graduated from the U.S. Naval Academy and had served as a junior officer on Rickover's nuclear submarines. The new president's naval background seemed to augur well for the gradual nuclearization of the surface navy with little change in underlying strategic assumptions, but it did not turn out that way. The civilian hierarchy of the Carter administration was composed mostly of men drawn from outside the Washington bureaucratic and governing elite. They were determined to reduce the defense budget even if it meant challenging the navy's favorite weapons system, the large aircraft carrier. Admiral Holloway bespoke the navy's alarm and reluctance to eliminate even one of the fourteen carrier battle groups: "Without carriers we feel that we would have to revert to a Coast Guard type of Navy."

Carter's men nonetheless moved quickly to cut naval appropriations. They rejected a proposed 90,000-ton nuclear-driven replacement for the old carrier *Midway*, which had been commissioned in September 1945. At the same time the early Carter budgets deleted requests for a nuclear-powered strike cruiser, the "CSGN," touted by the navy as a versatile platform for cruise missiles, Aegis, V/STOL vertical or short takeoff and landing aircraft, and helicopters. Congress resisted both cuts and refused to allocate funds for the modest oil-fueled 60,000-ton carrier proposed by the administration. With Congress on the navy's side, a political stalemate ensued. The naval reduction that analysts like Nathan and Oliver saw as an inevitable result of fiscal and budgetary imperatives was postponed for more than a decade, and in fact a dramatic reconstruction and expansion of the navy took place in the 1980s.

Elected by a resounding electoral margin in 1980, Republican Ronald Reagan was committed to expanding the defense budget to meet the perceived global threats of Moscow's "Evil Empire." As much of an outsider to Washington as Carter had been, Reagan selected as his first secretary of the navy an insider who had long advised the navy, John F. Lehman, Jr.

Born in Philadelphia on 14 September 1942, John Lehman came from a distinguished American Irish Catholic family with roots reaching back to the 1600s. A self-proclaimed warrior-statesman, Lehman admired those qualities in Theodore Roosevelt, whose influence on the battleship navy matched Lehman's impact on the carrier navy. Broadly educated in the humanities, Lehman replicated Roosevelt in erudition, belief in geopolitical "realism," and military-naval romanticism. In his memoirs he recalls a boyhood spent in suburban Philadelphia, under the glide path of navy aircraft returning to Willow Grove Naval Air Station. Listening to the approach of these "romantic gladiators," he dreamed of becoming a navy pilot. "There was never any doubt in my mind," he wrote as former secretary of the navy, "that this was the zenith of all human accomplishments." From earliest childhood he bonded himself to naval aviation, "and I always have felt more at home with naval aviators than with any other peer group."

Before he could reinforce the large carrier as the navy's centerpiece, Lehman had to dethrone Admiral Rickover, whom he regarded as the "high priest and prophet" of the nuclear-power community and therefore a dangerous rival. Conceding that Rickover's circuitous route through the old Atomic Energy Commission and Congress had probably been necessary to build the nuclear-powered submarine force in the 1950s, Lehman believed that by the 1970s Rickover's institutional autonomy and resistance to automation in submarines had made him an impediment to the future evolution of the American nuclear submarine force. Specifically, Lehman cited Rickover's refusal to consider proposals to investigate the potential of new nonnuclear propulsion technologies submitted by Dr. Harold Agnew, a former director of the Los Alamos Nuclear Laboratory in New Mexico, and the admiral's rejection of automated control systems in nuclear-powered submarines. The net result was a steady and inordinate increase in the size and cost of American fleet submarines.

Beyond those significant concerns, the secretary objected to

Rickover's manipulation of the navy's officer personnel policies, one feature of which was the elevation of technical education and expertise at the expense of the humanities. The secretary accused the admiral of an Orwellian plan for the "creation of a kind of new socialist man for the nuclear program." Lehman knew that it took great technical expertise to operate nuclear-powered vessels, but he also recognized that technical knowledge may not make an officer a fine tactician, a superior strategist, or an inspiring leader.

Lehman spent a year laying the groundwork with congressional "satraps" and then partially solved "the Rickover problem" in a vituperative meeting with President Ronald Reagan on 8 January 1982. When the showdown ended Lehman had won, and Rickover was forced at last to retire. But in Lehman's opinion, the Rickover-trained nuclear power admirals who remained in high places throughout the Reagan presidency continued to exert a baneful influence on many aspects of naval policy. He found them to be especially vengeful toward any senior surface line or aviation officer who challenged promotion practices skewed in favor of nuclear-power officers. In the final months of his tenure as secretary, he charged that "the nukes mutinied and succeeded in achieving a measure of revenge for my retiring their prophet, Rickover." Whether or not Lehman's accusations were valid, it was true that from 1986 to 1990 the chief of naval operations, Carlisle A. H. Trost, was a nuclear-power officer whom Lehman had not recommended for the post because the admiral allegedly "had made a career as a Pentagon staff officer."

From his first days in office, at the same time that he was maneuvering against Rickover, Secretary of the Navy Lehman began to revamp American naval strategy so as to highlight the large aircraft carrier's role in modern warfare. Convinced that the power of his own office "had atrophied from the lack of exercise" and that American naval power vis-à-vis the Soviet Union had shrunk dangerously under President Carter, Lehman killed two birds with one stone. He chaired daily meetings of a departmental "Naval Policy Board" to articulate a strategic rationale for the 600-ship navy to which the 1980 Republican Party platform had committed the administration.

Secretary Lehman built his 600-ship command-of-the-seas navy around the modern capital ship, the large aircraft carrier. Echoing the standard quasi-official contention that the United States was somehow a "continental island," obligated to resupply allies in Western Europe during a conflict with the Soviet Union, Lehman decided that the way to protect transatlantic shipping was to carry the sea battle north to the Soviet maritime heartland. In his "maritime strategy," which remained naval doctrine after he left office in 1987, the navy was "tasked to ensure that . . . the fight will be pressed to Soviet territory and targets with a primary objective of the systematic destruction of Soviet forces and their military infrastructure." This meant that in the event of a Soviet–American war Lehman would send carrier task groups to "the North Sea and the Baltic throat" and up into the Norwegian Sea to attack the Soviet navy in its home ports and bases. The previously accepted defensive posture, which kept attacking Soviet submarines above a line running from Greenland through Iceland to the United Kingdom, struck Lehman as "a childish concept of creating a watery Maginot Line."

Lehman's aggressiveness elicited criticism from analysts who pointed out that the carrier battle groups could encounter deadly weather and severe resistance. Some of the carriers would probably be lost. The cost in men and matériel would be too great and the strategic gain too marginal to justify the strategy. But in 1988 Lehman responded that his strategy had already been vindicated. Soviet naval operations had "switched dramatically to their home waters. The net strategic result appears to us to be a Soviet fleet positioning and training to counter our new maritime strategy." Perhaps so, but it is far more likely that the retrenchment of the Soviet navy was an early symptom of the "Gorbachev revolution" that by late 1989 was leading to the dissolution of the "Evil Empire" in Eastern Europe. As the Soviet Union receded, the historic Russian norm of a coastal defense navy was reestablishing itself, and the rationale for Secretary Lehman's massive buildup was being dissipated.

If the large aircraft carrier was central to John Lehman's strategy for fighting a nuclear war against the Soviets, it also was his weapons system of choice for limited wars or exercises in "gunboat diplomacy." His insistence on certain kinds of aircraft and tactics for the air wings on the carriers demonstrated clearly that Lehman had borrowed a leaf from Theodore Roosevelt's book on interventionism. From the outset of his tenure as navy secretary Lehman criticized the service for concentrating on "light attack" aircraft, that is, the A-4 Skyhawk, a single-seat jet bomber that had flown thousands of daylight raids over North Vietnam. Lehman instead favored a larger, electronically sophisticated, two-man night-flying bomber, the A-6 Intruder. He insisted that the carrier battle groups regularly plan for night bombing raids, a dangerous tactic pilots understandably avoided as much as possible. To reward his gladiators, he devised a new command structure whereby the air wing commander on each large carrier would assume operational command of the battle group during air strikes, thereby earning recognition as a senior combat commander and eligibility for promotion to rear admiral. Lehman used a series of aerial attacks—the modern equivalent of a nineteenth-century frigate's "gunboat diplomacy"—to perfect his doctrine.

On 23 October 1983 a terrorist attack on the U.S. Marine Corps garrison in Beirut, Lebanon, killed 241 marines and wounded one hundred. When subsequent aerial reconnaissance flights by naval aircraft were fired on by Syrian-supplied surface-to-air missiles, the president ordered a retaliatory attack against Syria. That occurred on 4 December, and the navy lost two carrier-based bombers. One aviator died and one was held prisoner for a month. John Lehman had no role in the raid, because the operational military chain of command bypasses the service secretaries, but he found great fault with the operation. Denouncing it as an obsolete, Vietnam-style daylight raid "against useless targets," he intensified his reform of naval doctrine, strategy, and command.

The test of Lehman's tactics came when the administration authorized a punitive raid against Libya in retaliation for numerous acts of terrorism in Europe and the Mediterranean. After months of painstaking interservice planning, about 1:00 A.M. on the morning of 15 April 1986, navy and air force aircraft struck the Libyan capital of Tripoli and a military complex at Benghazi 450 miles to the east. The air defenses around the two centers were "among the most sophisticated and thickest in the world," but in Lehman's judgment they were defeated "utterly," and the carefully choreographed raids went off without a single navy plane being hit.

Lehman interpreted the attack as a highly successful vindication for the changes in tactical doctrine he had initiated following the aircraft losses in Lebanon. Central among those was a simplified chain of command, operational autonomy for the Sixth Fleet commander, and a raid at night rather than in daytime. More broadly, he read the air raids as ample justification for a large-carrier navy: "Here at last was the payoff from the six-hundred-ship navy and the Reagan buildup." Conceding that there was "a real role for the small-ship navy so beloved of congressional reformers," he sarcastically hoped to see "many more" small ships "in the Libyan navy and the Soviet navy" but not in his own navy.

===

In April 1987 John Lehman resigned as secretary of the navy, just a month before the navy had to face the consequences of trying to protect oil tankers traversing the Persian Gulf during the very ugly war between Iran and Iraq. The navy's protracted indifference to modernizing and expanding its small surface combatants exacted a tragic price on 17 May 1987, when with very little warning the frigate *Stark* was struck by a missile from an Iraqi aircraft. Thirty-seven American sailors died. The United States intensified its patrols, directing them mainly against Iran, Iraq's opponent in a seemingly endless war.

For over a year the United States and Iran bloodied each other. On 14 April 1988 the frigate *Samuel B. Roberts*, a sister ship of the *Stark*, was hit by a moored mine in the Gulf. Her crewmen escaped serious injury, but her keel snapped and she had to be carried home to Charleston, South Carolina. Four days after the incident, on 18 April, A-6 aircraft from the nuclear supercarrier *Enterprise*, stationed several hundred miles out at sea, sped into the Gulf and sank an Iranian frigate. Hurting for ships and desirous of getting some kind of control over the narrow Gulf waters, the navy sent in an Aegis-cruiser, a class of warship built to "command the air" above battle groups far at sea, not a ship designed for operations in restricted waters over which civilian airliners regularly flew. The result was disaster. On 3 July 1988, the Aegis-cruiser *Vincennes* "fired in error" on an Iran Air jetliner, killing 290 passengers.

Former Secretary of the Navy Lehman's interpretation of the *Vincennes* tragedy was in keeping with his penchant for the carrier as panacea. "If the *Vincennes* had . . . air cover [from carriers] in 1988, the F-14s on fighter CAP [combat air patrol] station would have visually identified the airbus before firing." And yet the *Vincennes* carried the Aegis system, the most sophisticated electronics and missile anti-aircraft array in the United States Navy, one that presumably could distinguish between friend and foe overhead. The implication of the tragedy therefore was profoundly disturbing: The high-technology weapons systems designed for blue-water warfare were inappropriate for finite naval interventions and patrols in restricted waters, especially since twenty-four-hour-a-day carrier air cover over the gunboat diplomats exceeded the capacity of a globally deployed navy.

===

John Lehman was the most forceful evangelist for the doctrine of preparation for a nuclear naval war against the Soviet Union to emerge in the generation between the Cuban crisis and the unraveling of the Soviet empire in 1989–1990. His concept of a "maritime strategy" carried aggressiveness to a new level of risk at the very moment when internal factors within the Soviet Union were shaping Mikhail Gorbachev's revolution and promising to end the Cold War without an Armageddon. His perception was fundamentally archaic.

The truly visionary naval leader of the generation spanning Vietnam and the Gorbachev revolution was Admiral Elmo R. Zumwalt, Jr. His tactical innovations as the senior naval officer in Vietnam showed an adaptability and practicality that were rare in a navy whose hierarchy had been taught to think in terms of rigid war-fighting doctrines conceived to defeat major powers. Tapped at an early age to become the navy's senior officer, Admiral Zumwalt brought his fresh insights to Washington. For four years he fought to restructure the navy around new kinds of ships designed from the beginning to fight "conventional" and limited wars or to intervene effectively in episodes of modern "gunboat diplomacy." In the end he was defeated by a pragmatic alliance formed between key congressmen and the navy's two leading interest groups, the aviators and the Rickover-led nuclear-power officers. Still, when the Soviet empire in Eastern Europe began to crumble in 1989 and the American defense budget in 1990 came under its closest congressional scrutiny since the beginning of the Cold War, it began to appear that the harbinger of the American navy of the future was not John Lehman but Elmo Zumwalt.

The 1991 war in the Middle East did not vitiate Zumwalt's criticism. As "Desert Shield" unfolded in late 1990, the carrier admirals were hesitant to enter the restricted waters of the Persian Gulf, where their thin-hulled ships might prove highly vulnerable to missile attacks by small vessels operating from coastal havens. They cautiously sent in the *Midway* and *Ranger*, both earmarked for retirement and thus the most expendable carriers in the fleet. Later, at the height of "Desert Storm," as many as four carriers did operate in the Gulf at one time, but this large commitment came only as a result of the direct insistence of the chairman of the Joint Chiefs of Staff, army General Colin L. Powell. Whether the navy of the future would willingly risk its blue-water behemoths in the coastal waters of an enemy armed with deadly antiship missiles remained to be seen.

Epilogue

Two centuries ago, in the first decade of American constitutional government, the U.S. Congress shaped a navy to suit the national purpose. Intended to keep open the trade routes of the Mediterranean in the face of North African piracy and to counter French incursions on the United States maritime trade in the West Indies, the navy was small, fast, and bold. Its audacious skippers and brave crews struck the enemy at will, attacking warships when the chances of glory and victory seemed high and seizing merchantmen when the opportunity for profitable prize money beckoned. This navy of frigates, sloops, and brigs that sailed independently across international waterways became the American hallmark and the instrument of "gunboat diplomacy" for almost one hundred years.

At times a counterpoint was sounded. In the Mexican and Civil wars the navy of the United States established blockades, sought complete command of the seas, and launched amphibious campaigns, just as the Royal Navy of Great Britain traditionally did in England's wars against nearby rivals. Still, this was a minor theme played out only occasionally. The dominant motif was not the destruction of enemy navies; it was coastal defense, commerce raiding, and commerce protection in an era of exuberant commercial and continental expansion.

At the end of the nineteenth century, in the interval between the Anglo-German-American crisis over Samoa and the opening of the Spanish–American War, the Congress reshaped the navy to meet new national goals. Having rounded out its continental borders, the United States now was seeking an overseas political and territorial empire and a place of equality with the greatest navies of Europe. The frigates gave way to massive battleships with thick steel belts of impenetrable armor and large-caliber guns that could sling heavy projectiles for miles, obliterating targets ashore and destroying any smaller ship unfortunate enough to get caught within the trajectory.

The new American navy found an easy victory in the war with Spain, and it established itself as the premier capital ship navy in the two world wars of the twentieth century. By 1945 the U.S. Navy commanded every sea on the globe, but again a subsidiary and contrapuntal theme was sounded. The rapid advances in submarine technology meant that the old way of war—*guerre de course,* or the raiding of the enemy's transport fleets and the protection of one's own sea lanes of communication—remained a vital ingredient of victory and a deadly threat to transatlantic alliances.

For almost a half-century following World War II the Congress elected to stay with the capital ship navy as embodied in battle groups of aircraft carriers, but as the last decade of the twentieth century opened it seemed that another end-of-the-century reshaping of the American navy was inevitable. The putative enemy, the Soviet Union, was in political and economic disarray; its empire in Eastern Europe was collapsing, to be replaced by traditional national groupings and a reunited Germany. In the Pacific, the Philippines were no longer entirely friendly or submissive, and the possibility of having to evacuate bases acquired almost one hundred years ago became a distinct possibility. The "American century" in the Pacific was closing, and a new era of collaborative sharing and hopeful partnership with dynamic Japan was opening.

At home, in the summer of 1992, the mood was rapidly shifting from one of internationalism and fiscal generosity to one of military and fiscal retrenchment. The navy would be reshaped, as it had been at the end of each of the two previous centuries. This time the adjustment might prove more painful. It seemed starkly inevitable that the navy of the twenty-first century would be smaller in every respect than the capital ship fleet of Alfred T. Mahan, the two Roosevelts, and John F. Lehman.

But the past may be prologue after all. If so, this people's navy may well become what it was in the glorious age of John Adams, Thomas Jefferson, Edward Preble, and Stephen Decatur: a modest but proud expression of the democratic will at work.

Bibliographical Essay

Introduction

THIS bibliographical essay is limited to secondary works, mostly books, many of which are available at major university libraries across the country. For primary sources, the reader must consult the printed congressional debates and documents and the archival records of the U.S. Navy. Some of the latter are available on microfilm, but most must be viewed at the National Archives or the Division of Naval History in the Washington Navy Yard. For the student or scholar able to make the trip, two libraries in the Washington, D.C. area house almost every secondary source in print: the library of the Division of Naval History at the Washington Navy Yard and the Nimitz Library of the U.S. Naval Academy in Annapolis.

The following essay is simply organized. It begins with a list of the most useful general bibliographies and then mentions some of the more valuable secondary works transcending chronological boundaries. The remainder, the bulk of the essay, is organized by chronological periods, with subdivisions by topic. These chronological sections correspond closely to the chronological limits of the chapters of the book, but they are not exact duplicates. In three cases, periods covered by more than one chapter are combined into one bibliographical discourse. In every case, the reader should browse through the essay dealing with preceding and subsequent chapters to unearth books useful in the chapter under primary scrutiny.

Bibliographies

Myron J. Smith, Jr., is without question the premier American naval bibliographer. See Myron J. Smith, Jr., comp., *American Naval Bibliography*, 5 vols. (Metuchen, N.J.: Scarecrow Press, 1972–1974); *World War II at Sea: A Bibliography of Sources in English*, 3 vols. (Metuchen, N.J.:

Scarecrow Press, 1976); and his *The United States Navy and Coast Guard, 1946–1983* (Jefferson, N.C.: McFarland, 1984).

Other useful general bibliographies are Paolo E. Coletta, comp., *A Bibliography of American Naval History* (Annapolis, Md.: Naval Institute Press, 1981), and *idem*, comp., *A Selected and Annotated Bibliography of American Naval History* (Lanham, Md.: University Press of America, 1988); Robin Higham, ed., *A Guide to the Sources of United States Military History* (Hamden, Conn.: Archon Books, 1975); Robin Higham and Donald J. Mrozek, eds., *A Guide to the Sources of United States Military History: Supplement I* and *Supplement II* (Hamden, Conn.: Archon Books, 1981, 1986).

A more specialized bibliography of obvious significance is John B. Hattendorf and Lynn C. Hattendorf, comps., *A Bibliography of the Works of Alfred Thayer Mahan* (Newport, R.I.: Naval War College Press, 1986).

General Histories

The most frequently cited general American naval histories published in the twentieth century are Robert G. Albion, *Makers of Naval Policy, 1798–1947*, ed. Rowena Reed (Annapolis, Md.: Naval Institute Press, 1980); Robert G. Albion and Jennie B. Pope, *Sea Lanes in Wartime: The American Experience, 1775–1945*, 2d ed. (Hamden, Conn.: Archon Books, 1968); Edward L. Beach, *The United States Navy: 200 Years* (New York: Holt, 1986); Bernard Brodie, *Sea Power in the Machine Age* (Princeton, N.J.: Princeton University Press, 1943); Kenneth J. Hagan, ed., *In Peace and War: Interpretations of American Naval History, 1775–1984*, 2d ed., rev. (Westport, Conn.: Greenwood Press, 1984); Edwin B. Hooper, *United States Naval Power in a Changing World* (New York: Praeger, 1988); Dudley W. Knox, *A History of the United States Navy*, rev. ed. (New York: G. P. Putnam's Sons, 1948); Nathan Miller, *The U.S. Navy: An Illustrated History* (Annapolis, Md.: Naval Institute Press, 1977); Charles O. Paullin, *Paullin's History of Naval Administration, 1775–1911: A Collection of Articles from the U.S. Naval Institute Proceedings* (Annapolis, Md.: Naval Institute Press, 1968); Elmer B. Potter, ed., *Sea Power: A Naval History*, 2d ed. (Annapolis, Md.: Naval Institute Press, 1981); Harold Sprout and Margaret Sprout, *The Rise of American Naval Power, 1776–1918* (Princeton, N.J.: Princeton University Press, 1939; repr. Naval Institute Press, 1990); and Jack Sweetman, *American Naval History: An Illustrated Chronology of the U.S. Navy and Marine Corps, 1775–Present* (Annapolis, Md.: Naval Institute Press, 1984).

Chronologically and Regionally Broad Histories

Some accounts are too restricted to class as general naval histories and too broad to fit into tight chronological or topical confines. The most important of them are Clayton R. Barrow, comp. and ed., *America Spreads Her*

Sails: U.S. Seapower in the Nineteenth Century (Annapolis, Md.: Naval Institute Press, 1973); Thomas A. Bryson, *Tars, Turks, and Tankers: The Role of the United States Navy in the Middle East, 1800–1979* (Metuchen, N.J.: Scarecrow Press, 1980); James A. Field, Jr., *America and the Mediterranean World, 1776–1882* (Princeton, N.J.: Princeton University Press, 1969); Curtis T. Henson, *Commissioners and Commodores: The East India Squadron and American Diplomacy in China* (University: University of Alabama Press, 1982); Robert E. Johnson, *The Far China Station: The U.S. Navy in Asian Waters, 1800–1898* (Annapolis, Md.: Naval Institute Press, 1979); Robert E. Johnson, *Thence Round Cape Horn: The Story of United States Naval Forces on Pacific Station, 1818–1923* (Annapolis, Md.: Naval Institute Press, 1963); David F. Long, *Gold Braid and Foreign Relations: Diplomatic Activities of U.S. Naval Officers, 1798–1883* (Annapolis, Md.: Naval Institute Press, 1988); Vincent Ponko, *Ships, Seas, and Scientists: U.S. Naval Exploration and Discovery in the Nineteenth Century* (Annapolis, Md.: Naval Institute Press, 1974); and William N. Still, Jr., *American Sea Power in the Old World: The United States Navy in European and Near Eastern Waters, 1865–1917* (Westport, Conn.: Greenwood Press, 1980).

Social Histories

The three most valuable recent social histories of the navy are Frederick S. Harrod, *Manning the New Navy: The Development of a Modern Naval Enlisted Force, 1899–1940* (Westport, Conn.: Greenwood Press, 1978); Harold D. Langley, *Social Reform in the United States Navy, 1798–1862* (Urbana: University of Illinois Press, 1967); and Peter Karsten, *The Naval Aristocracy: The Golden Age of Annapolis and the Emergence of Modern American Navalism* (New York: Free Press, 1972).

Collective Biographies

The most successful recent collective biographies are William B. Cogar, *Dictionary of Admirals of the U.S. Navy*, vol. 1, *1862–1900* (Annapolis, Md.: Naval Institute Press, 1989); Paolo E. Coletta, ed., *American Secretaries of the Navy*, 2 vols. (Annapolis, Md.: Naval Institute Press, 1980); and Robert Love, ed., *The Chiefs of Naval Operations* (Annapolis, Md.: Naval Institute Press, 1980).

Chronological Periods

1775–1783

The contextual backdrop to the naval history of the Revolution is discussed in R. Ernest Dupuy, Gay Hammerman, and Grace P. Hayes, *The American Revolution: A Global War* (New York: David McKay, 1976); Geoffrey Symcox, comp., *War, Diplomacy, and Imperialism, 1618–1763* (New York: Harper, 1973). The statecraft behind the naval policies can be traced in Samuel Flagg Bemis, *The Diplomacy of the American Revolution* (New York: Appleton-Century, 1935; repr. Indiana University Press, 1957); Jonathan R. Dull, *A Diplomatic History of the American Revolution* (New Haven: Yale University Press, 1985); William Stinchcombe, *The American Revolution and the French Alliance* (Syracuse, N.Y.: Syracuse University Press, 1969); and, most pointedly, Barbara W. Tuchman, *The First Salute* (New York: Alfred A. Knopf, 1988).

General naval histories of the Revolution are Gardner W. Allen, *The Naval History of the American Revolution*, 2 vols. (Boston: Houghton Mifflin, 1913; repr. Corner House Publishers, 1970); William M. Fowler, *Rebels Under Sail* (New York: Scribner's, 1976); Nathan Miller, *Sea of Glory: The Continental Navy Fights for Independence* (New York: David McKay, 1974); and Charles O. Paullin, *The Navy of the American Revolution* (Chicago: Burrows Bros., 1906; repr. Haskell House, 1971).

Representative histories of states' navies are John W. Jackson, *The Pennsylvania Navy, 1775–1781* (New Brunswick, N.J.: Rutgers University Press, 1974); Louis F. Middlebrook, *History of Maritime Connecticut During the American Revolution, 1775–1783* (Salem, Mass.: The Essex Institute, 1925); Robert L. Scheina, "A Matter of Definition: A New Jersey Navy, 1777–1783," *American Neptune*, vol. 39, no. 3 (July 1979); and Robert A. Stewart, *The History of Virginia's Navy of the Revolution* (Richmond, Va.: Mitchell & Hotchkiss, 1934).

For the navies of ally and enemy, see Jonathan R. Dull, *The French Navy and American Independence* (Princeton, N.J.: Princeton University Press, 1975), and William M. James, *The British Navy in Adversity: A Study of the War of American Independence* (New York: Longmans, Green, 1926).

The Mahanian view of the Revolution at sea was tendered by the master himself, Alfred T. Mahan, *The Major Operations of the Navies in the War of American Independence* (London: S. Low, Marston, 1913; repr. Greenwood Press, 1969). For correctives in favor of *guerre de course*, see William B. Clark, *Ben Franklin's Privateers* (Baton Rouge: Louisiana State University Press, 1956); William J. Morgan, "American Privateering in America's War for Independence, 1775–1783," *American Neptune*, vol. 36, no. 2 (April 1976); and David Syrett, *Shipping and the American War, 1775–1783* (London: Athlone Press, 1970).

It is impossible to understand the debate over strategy and policy without some grasp of ship types. The classic study is Howard I. Chapelle, *The History of the American Sailing Navy* (New York: Norton, 1949), but see also Jack Coggins, *Ships and Seamen of the American Revolution* (Harrisburg, Pa.: Stackpole Books, 1969), and especially William Gilkerson, *The Ships of John Paul Jones* (Annapolis, Md.: Naval Institute Press, 1987).

Pertinent biographies of American naval officers include William B. Clark, *Gallant John Barry, 1745–1803* (New York: Macmillan, 1938), and the same author's *Lambert Wickes: Sea Raider and Diplomat* (New Haven: Yale University Press, 1932); Charles L. Lewis, *Admiral de Grasse and American Independence* (Annapolis, Md.: Naval Institute Press, 1945); William J. Morgan, *Captains to the Northward: The New England Captains in the Continental Navy* (Barre, Mass.: Barre Gazette, 1959); Samuel Eliot Morison, *John Paul Jones: A Sailor's Biography* (Boston: Little, Brown, 1959); and Ralph Paine, *Joshua Barney: A Forgotten Hero of Blue Water* (New York: Century, 1924).

1783–1800

The diplomatic background to naval policy in these formative years is covered in Albert H. Bowman, *The Struggle for Neutrality: Franco-American Diplomacy During the Federalist Era* (Knoxville: University of Tennessee Press, 1974); Samuel Flagg Bemis, *Jay's Treaty: A Study in Commerce and Diplomacy* (New York: Macmillan, 1923), and *idem, Pinckney's Treaty* (New Haven: Yale University Press, 1960); Alexander DeConde, *Entangling Alliance* (Durham, N.C.: Duke University Press, 1958), and *idem, The Quasi-War* (New York: Scribner's, 1966); and Lawrence Kaplan, *"Entangling Alliances with None"* (Kent, Ohio: Kent State University Press, 1987).

The events leading to the construction of the first post–Revolutionary War frigates are discussed in Donald B. Chidsey, *The Wars in Barbary: Arab Piracy and the Birth of the United States Navy* (New York: Crown, 1971), and Ray W. Irwin, *The Diplomatic Relations of the United States with the Barbary Powers, 1776–1816* (Chapel Hill: University of North Carolina Press, 1931; repr. Russell & Russell, 1970).

The broadest naval brush is wielded in Alfred Thayer Mahan, *The Influence of Sea Power upon the French Revolution and Empire, 1793–1812,* 2 vols. (Boston: Little, Brown, 1892). The particulars surrounding the creation of the United States Navy are covered in Marshall Smelser, *The Congress Founds the Navy, 1787–1798* (Notre Dame, Ind.: University of Notre Dame Press, 1959), and Craig L. Symonds, *Navalists and Antinavalists: The Naval Policy Debate in the United States, 1785–1827* (Newark: University of Delaware Press, 1980). The two earliest undeclared naval wars are treated in Howard P. Nash, *The Forgotten Wars: The Role of the U.S. Navy in the Quasi-War with France and the Barbary Wars, 1798–1805* (South Brunswick, N.J.: A. S. Barnes, 1968). The general story of the navy in this era is William M. Fowler, *Jack Tars and Commodores: The American Navy, 1783–1815* (Boston: Houghton Mifflin, 1984).

The most useful naval biographies for this somewhat undertreated period are Eugene S. Ferguson, *Truxtun of the Constellation* (Baltimore: Johns

Hopkins Press, 1956; repr. Naval Institute Press, 1982), and James C. Bradford, ed., *Command Under Sail: Makers of the American Naval Tradition, 1775–1850* (Annapolis, Md.: Naval Institute Press, 1985).

1801–1815

Biography provides the best backdrop for these years of naval-commercial expansion and defense of neutral rights. Three classics bracket the leading American statesmen: Dumas Malone, *Jefferson the President*, 2 vols. (Boston: Little, Brown, 1970, 1974); Irving Brant, *James Madison*, 6 vols. (Indianapolis: Bobbs-Merrill, 1941–1961); and Samuel Flagg Bemis, *John Quincy Adams and the Foundations of American Foreign Policy* (New York: Knopf, 1949).

The perennial problem of North Africa is treated in Gardner Allen, *Our Navy and the Barbary Corsairs* (Boston: Houghton Mifflin, 1905; repr. Archon Books, 1965); Charles F. Gallagher, *The United States and North Africa* (Cambridge: Harvard University Press, 1963); and Charles L. Lewis, *The Romantic Decatur* (Philadelphia: University of Pennsylvania Press, 1937; repr. Books for Libraries Press, 1971).

The relations of the United States with the two principal European antagonists are treated in Clifford L. Egan, *Neither Peace nor War. Franco-American Relations, 1803–1812* (Baton Rouge: Louisiana State University Press, 1983); Bradford Perkins, *The First Rapprochement* (Philadelphia: University of Pennsylvania Press, 1955); and *idem, Prologue to War* (Berkeley: University of California Press, 1961).

The military-naval contest that established the national identity of the United States is the topic of Reginald Horsman, *The War of 1812* (New York: Knopf, 1969); John K. Mahon, *The War of 1812* (Gainesville: University of Florida Press, 1972); Julius W. Pratt, *Expanionists of 1812* (New York: Macmillan, 1925); and Bradford Perkins, *Castlereagh and Adams: England and the United States, 1812–1823* (Berkeley: University of California Press, 1964).

For the causal issues of trade and neutral rights, see Herbert W. Briggs, *The Doctrine of Continuous Voyage* (Baltimore: Johns Hopkins Press, 1926); Anna C. Clauder, *American Commerce as Affected by the Wars of the French Revolution and Napoleon, 1793–1812* (Clifton, N.J.: A. M. Kelley, 1972; orig. c. 1932); Louis M. Sears, *Jefferson and the Embargo* (Durham, N.C.: Duke University Press, 1927; repr. Octagon Books, 1966); and James F. Zimmerman, *Impressment of American Seamen* (Port Washington, N.Y.: Kennikat Press, 1966; orig. c. 1925).

The navy during the war can be viewed in William S. Dudley, ed., *The Naval War of 1812: A Documentary History* (Washington: Government Printing Office, 1985); Edward K. Eckert, *The Navy Department in the War of 1812* (Gainesville: University of Florida Press, 1973); Cecil S. Forester, *The Age of Fighting Sail: The Story of the Naval War of 1812* (Garden City,

N.Y.: Doubleday, 1956); John E. Jennings, *Tattered Ensign: The Story of America's Most Famous Fighting Frigate, U.S.S.* Constitution (New York: Crowell, 1966); Dean R. Mayhew, "Jeffersonian Gunboats in the War of 1812," *American Neptune,* vol. 42, no. 2 (April 1982); Kenneth Poolman, *Guns Off Cape Ann: The Story of the* Shannon *and the* Chesapeake (Chicago: Rand McNally, 1962); and Hugh F. Pullen, *The* Shannon *and the* Chesapeake (Toronto: McClelland & Stewart, 1970).

America's two classic navalists have offered their interpretations of the war in Alfred T. Mahan, *Sea Power in Its Relations to the War of 1812,* 2 vols. (Boston: Little, Brown, 1905; repr. Greenwood Press, 1968), and Theodore Roosevelt, *The Naval War of 1812* (New York: Putnam, 1882, repr. Haskell, 1968).

Robert Fulton and the Jeffersonians were looking into the future of new technologies, as is explained in Wallace Hutcheon, *Robert Fulton: Pioneer of Undersea Warfare* (Annapolis, Md.: Naval Institute Press, 1981), and Alex Roland, *Underwater Warfare in the Age of Sail* (Bloomington: Indiana University Press, 1978).

Regardless of the visionaries, this was the classic period of the sailing frigate, and an epitome of the type can now be seen in Portia Takakjian, *The Frigate* Essex (Annapolis, Md.: Naval Institute Press, 1990).

This is probably the richest period for American naval biography. See Leonard F. Guttridge and Jay D. Smith, *The Commodores* (New York: Harper & Row, 1969; repr. Naval Institute Press, 1984); Edwin P. Hoyt, *The Tragic Commodore: The Story of Oliver Hazard Perry* (New York: Abelard-Schuman, 1966); David F. Long, *Nothing Too Daring: A Biography of Commodore David Porter, 1780–1843* (Annapolis, Md.: Naval Institute Press, 1970), and *idem, Ready to Hazard: A Biography of Commodore William Bainbridge* (Hanover, N.H.: University Press of New England, 1981); Linda M. Maloney, *Captain from Connecticut: The Life and Times of Isaac Hull* (Boston: Northeastern University Press, 1986); Christopher McKee, *Edward Preble: A Naval Biography, 1761–1807* (Annapolis, Md.: Naval Institute Press, 1972); Charles O. Paullin, *Commodore John Rodgers* (Cleveland: Clark, 1910); and Paul B. Watson, *The Tragic Career of Commodore James Barron, U.S. Navy* (New York: Coward-McCann, 1942).

1815–1860

The artificiality of a bibliographical split of the period 1815–1860 has led to a combined listing for the two chapters treating those years.

This very active era of "gunboat diplomacy" is carefully detailed in John H. Schroeder, *Shaping a Maritime Empire: The Commercial and Diplomatic Role of the American Navy, 1829–1861* (Westport, Conn.: Greenwood Press, 1985). A related facet of naval activity was the numerous limited wars described in Gardner Allen, *Our Navy and the West Indian Pirates* (Salem, Mass.: Essex Institute, 1929); Francis B. Bradlee, *Piracy in the West Indies and Its Suppression* (Salem, Mass.: Essex Institute, 1923; repr. Library Editions, 1970); George E. Buker, *Swamp Sailors: Riverine Warfare in the Everglades, 1835–1842* (Gainesville: University of Florida Press, 1975); Raymond L. Shoemaker, *Diplomacy from the Quarterdeck: The United States Navy in the Caribbean, 1815–1830* (Bloomington: Indiana University Press, 1976); and Richard Wheeler, *In Pirate Waters* (New York: Crowell, 1969).

The most famous case of threatening to use force to achieve diplomatic goals was Matthew C. Perry's expedition to Japan, which is lovingly described in Samuel E. Morison, *"Old Bruin": Commodore Matthew C. Perry, 1794–1858* (Boston: Little, Brown, 1967).

Science, exploration, and commercial expansion went hand in hand, as is shown in Hildegarde Hawthorne, *Matthew Fontaine Maury: Trail Maker of the Seas* (New York: Longmans, Green, 1943); Daniel Henderson, *The Hidden Coasts: A Biography of Admiral Charles Wilkes* (New York: Sloane, 1953; repr. Greenwood Press, 1971); Charles L. Lewis, *Matthew Fontaine Maury: The Pathfinder of the Seas* (Annapolis, Md.: Naval Institute Press, 1927; repr. AMS Press, 1969); William J. Morgan and others, eds., *Autobiography of Rear Admiral Charles Wilkes, U.S. Navy, 1798–1877* (Washington: Government Printing Office, 1978); William Stanton, *The Great United States Exploring Expedition of 1838–1842* (Berkeley: University of California Press, 1975); David B. Tyler, *The Wilkes Expedition: The First United States Exploring Expedition 1838–1842* (Philadelphia: American Philosophical Society, 1968); and Frances L. Williams, *Matthew Fontaine Maury: Scientist of the Sea* (New Brunswick, N.J.: Rutgers University Press, 1963).

Representative biographies of the gunboat diplomats include Carroll S. Alden, *Lawrence Kearny, Sailor Diplomat* (Princeton, N.J.: Princeton University Press, 1936); James C. Bradford, ed., *Captains of the Old Steam Navy: Makers of the American Naval Tradition, 1840–1880* (Annapolis, Md.: Naval Institute Press, 1986); David F. Long, *Sailor-Diplomat: A Biography of Commodore James Biddle, 1783–1848* (Boston: Northeastern University Press, 1983), and Robert E. Johnson, *Rear Admiral John Rodgers, 1812–1882* (Annapolis, Md.: Naval Institute Press, 1967).

The Mexican War stemmed in part from naval expansionism, as can be seen in K. Jack Bauer, *Surfboats and Horse Marines: U.S. Naval Operations in the Mexican War, 1846–1848* (Annapolis, Md.: Naval Institute Press, 1969); Joseph T. Downey, *The Cruise of the* Portsmouth, *1845–1847: A Sailor's View of the Naval Conquest of California*, ed. Howard Lamar (New Haven: Yale University Press, 1958), and Glenn W. Price, *Origins of the War with Mexico: The Polk–Stockton Intrigue* (Austin: University of Texas Press, 1967).

The ships remained wooden-hulled and the guns remained smoothbores, but steam was entering the fleet. Four books tell this story of stasis and change: James P. Baxter, *The Introduction of the Ironclad Warship* (Cambridge: Harvard University Press, 1933; repr. Archon Books, 1968); Donald L. Canney, *The Old Steam Navy*, vol. 1, *Frigates, Sloops, and Gunboats, 1815–1885* (Annapolis, Md.: Naval Institute Press, 1990); Spencer Tucker, *Arming the Fleet: U.S. Navy Ordnance in the Muzzle-Loading Era* (Annapolis, Md.: Naval Institute Press, 1989); and Virginia S. Wood, *Live Oaking: Southern Timber for Tall Ships* (Boston: Northeastern University Press, 1981).

The educational and social structures of the navy underwent great change in this period, as is shown in Russel B. Nye, *George Bancroft: Brahmin Rebel* (New York: Knopf, 1944); Jack Sweetman, *The U.S. Naval Academy: An Illustrated History* (Annapolis, Md.: Naval Institute Press, 1979); and James E. Valle, *Rocks and Shoals: Order and Discipline in the Old Navy, 1800–1861* (Annapolis, Md.: Naval Institute Press, 1980).

One great naval-maritime issue continued to trouble Anglo-American relations following the War of 1812, and the classic study is Hugh G. Soulsby, *The Right of Search and the Slave Trade in Anglo-American Relations, 1814–1862* (Baltimore: Johns Hopkins Press, 1933).

1861–1890

The naval operations of the Civil War attracted an early audience leading to books by three naval experts, Daniel Ammen, *The Atlantic Coast* (New York: Scribner's, 1883); Alfred T. Mahan, *The Gulf and Inland Waters* (New York: Scribner's, 1883); and James R. Soley, *The Blockade and the Cruisers* (New York: Scribner's, 1883). A similar study is Charles B. Boynton, *The History of the Navy During the Rebellion*, 2 vols. (New York: Appleton, 1867–1968; repr. University Microfilms International, 1976). A modern multivolume treatment is Virgil C. Jones, *The Civil War at Sea*, 3 vols. (New York: Holt, Rinehart & Winston, 1960–1962). Somewhat more modest syntheses are Bern Anderson, *By Sea and by River: The Naval History of the Civil War* (New York: Knopf, 1962; repr. Greenwood Press, 1977); James M. Merrill, *The Rebel Shore: The Story of Union Sea Power in the Civil War* (Boston, Mass.: Little, Brown, 1957); and Richard S. West, *Mr. Lincoln's Navy* (New York: Longmans, 1957; repr. Greenwood Press, 1976).

Three useful biographies of the Union navy's top leadership are Charles L. Lewis, *David Glasgow Farragut* (Annapolis, Md.: Naval Institute Press, 1941–1943; repr. Arno Press, 1980); Alfred T. Mahan, *Admiral Farragut* (New York: Appleton, 1892); and John Niven, *Gideon Welles: Lincoln's Secretary of the Navy* (New York: Oxford University Press, 1973).

The most famous naval battle of the war is the topic of William C. Davis, *Duel Between the First Ironclads* (Garden City, N.Y.: Doubleday, 1975), and Adolph A. Hoehling, *Thunder at Hampton Roads* (Englewood Cliffs, N.J.: Prentice-Hall, 1976). The less glamorous story of trying to strangle the South is told in Robert Carse, *Blockade: The Civil War at Sea* (New York: Rinehart, 1958).

The Civil War was very much a brown-water war, as the following books attest: Samuel Carter, *The Final Fortress: The Campaign for Vicksburg, 1862–1863* (New York: St. Martin's Press, 1980); Harpur A. Gosnell, *Guns on the Western Waters: The Story of the River Gunboats in the Civil War* (Baton Rouge: Louisiana State University Press, 1949); Ludwell H. Johnson, *Red River Campaign: Politics and Cotton in the Civil War* (Baltimore: Johns Hopkins Press, 1958); James M. Merrill, *Battle Flags South: The Story of the Civil War Navies on Western Waters* (Rutherford, N.J.: Fairleigh Dickinson University Press, 1970); John D. Milligan, *Gunboats down the Mississippi* (Annapolis, Md.: Naval Institute Press, 1965; repr. Arno Press 1980); and, somewhat more broadly, Rowena Reed, *Combined Operations in the Civil War* (Annapolis, Md.: Naval Institute Press, 1978).

An overall understanding of the navy of the Confederate States can be gleaned from John T. Scharf, *History of the Confederate States Navy from Its Organization to the Surrender of Its Last Vessel* (New York: Rogers & Sherwood, 1887; repr. Books for Libraries Press, 1969); Joseph T. Durkin, *Stephen R. Mallory: Confederate Navy Chief* (Chapel Hill: University of North Carolina Press, 1954; repr. University of South Carolina Press, 1987); William N. Still, Jr., *Confederate Shipbuilding* (Athens: University of Georgia Press, 1969; repr. University of South Carolina Press, 1987); and Tom H. Wells, *The Confederate Navy: A Study in Organization* (University: University of Alabama Press, 1971).

The great story of the Confederate navy concerns the raiders, for which see James D. Bulloch, *The Secret Service of the Confederate States in Europe: Or, How the Confederate Cruisers Were Equipped* (New York: G. P. Putnam's Sons, 1884; repr. Burt Franklin, 1972); Stanley F. Horn, *Gallant Rebel: The Fabulous Cruise of the C.S.S.* Shenandoah (New Brunswick, N.J.: Rutgers University Press, 1947); Frank L. Owsley, *The C.S.S. Florida: Her Building and Operations* (Philadelphia: University of Pennsylvania Press, 1965); and Raphael Semmes, *The Confederate Raider* Alabama (Gloucester, Mass.: Peter Smith, 1969). For the Confederacy's more traditional kind of raiders, see William M. Robinson, Jr., *The Confederate Privateers* (Columbia: University of South Carolina Press, 1990). The lasting impact of Confederate *guerre de course* is the topic of George W. Dalzell, *The Flight from the Flag: The Continuing Effect of the Civil War upon the American Carrying Trade* (Chapel Hill: University of North Carolina Press, 1940).

Steam and iron were fighting their way into both navies, as can be seen in Robert MacBride, *Civil War Ironclads: The Dawn of Naval Armor* (Philadelphia: Chilton Books, 1962); Maurice Melton, *The Conferderate Ironclads* (South Brunswick, N.J.: T. Yoseloff, 1968); and William N. Still, Jr., *Iron Afloat: The Story of the Confederate Armorclads* (Nashville: Vanderbilt University Press, 1971; repr. University of South Carolina Press, 1985).

Both sides encountered critical diplomatic problems with the two major

European powers, Great Britain and France. These issues are covered in Stuart L. Bernath, *Squall Across the Atlantic: American Civil War Prize Cases and Diplomacy* (Berkeley: University of California Press, 1970); John Bigelow, *France and the Confederate Navy, 1862–1868* (New York: Harper, 1888; repr. Bergman, 1968); Lynn M. Case and Warren F. Spencer, *The United States and France: Civil War Diplomacy* (Philadelphia: University of Pennsylvania Press, 1970); Regis A. Courtemanche, *No Need of Glory: The British Navy in American Waters, 1860–1864* (Annapolis, Md.: Naval Institute Press, 1977); Norman Ferris, *The Trent Affair: A Diplomatic Crisis* (Knoxville: University of Tennessee Press, 1977); Frank J. Merli, *Great Britain and the Confederate Navy, 1861–1865* (Bloomington: Indiana University Press, 1970); and Frank E. Vandiver, *Confederate Blockade Running Through Bermuda, 1861–1865* (Austin: University of Texas Press, 1947; repr. Kraus, 1970).

The background for the postwar navy is found in Charles S. Campbell, *The Transformation of American Foreign Relations* (New York: Harper & Row, 1976); Walter LaFeber, *The New Empire: An Interpretation of American Expansion, 1860–1898* (Ithaca, N.Y.: Cornell University Press, 1967); and Milton Plesur, *America's Outward Thrust: Approaches to Foreign Affairs* (DeKalb: Northern Illinois University Press, 1971).

The 1873 episode which exposed the navy's frailty is discussed in Richard H. Bradford, *The* Virginius *Affair* (Boulder: Colorado Associated University Press, 1980). The operations of the transitional navy of the 1880s are the subject of Kenneth J. Hagan, *American Gunboat Diplomacy and the Old Navy, 1877–1889* (Westport, Conn.: Greenwood Press, 1973), but the generation's most dynamic officer is best studied in Frederick C. Drake, *The Empire of the Seas: A Biography of Rear Admiral Robert Wilson Shufeldt, U.S.N.* (Honolulu: University of Hawaii Press, 1984).

Facets of the "new navy" are dealt with in Lawrence C. Allin, *United States Naval Institute: Intellectual Forum of the New Navy, 1873–1889* (Orono: University of Maine Press, 1976); Jeffery M. Dorwart, *The Office of Naval Intelligence: The Birth of America's First Intelligence Agency, 1865–1918* (Annapolis, Md.: Naval Institute Press, 1979); and Ronald Spector, *Professors of War: The Naval War College and the Modern American Navy* (Newport, R.I.: Naval War College Press, 1977).

Three of the architects of the "new navy" are portrayed in Mark D. Hirsch, *William C. Whitney* (New York: Dodd, Mead, 1948); Leon B. Richardson, *William E. Chandler* (New York: Dodd, Mead, 1940); and Robert Seager II, *Alfred Thayer Mahan* (Annapolis, Md.: Naval Institute Press, 1977).

The technological aspects of the final transition from sail to steam are now well covered in John D. Alden, *The American Steel Navy* (Annapolis, Md.: Naval Institute Press, 1972); Frank M. Bennett, *The Steam Navy of the United States* (Pittsburgh: Warren & Co., 1896; repr. Greenwood Press,

1972); Edward W. Sloan, *Benjamin Franklin Isherwood, Naval Engineer* (Annapolis, Md.: Naval Institute Press, 1965); and Leonard A. Swann, *John Roach, Maritime Entrepreneur: The Years as Naval Contractor, 1862–1886* (Annapolis, Md.: Naval Institute Press, 1965). For the dawn of the ultimate new technology, see Richard K. Morris, *John P. Holland, 1841–1914: Inventor of the Modern Submarine* (Annapolis, Md.: Naval Institute Press, 1966).

1890–1898

The break at 1890 is easier to justify thematically than bibliographically, and much of the literature listed in the previous and succeeding sections pertains equally well to the 1890s. The following listing is therefore brief.

For the transformation to battleships, see especially Benjamin F. Cooling, *Benjamin Franklin Tracy: Father of the Modern American Fighting Navy* (Hamden, Conn.: Archon Books, 1973), and Walter R. Herrick, *The American Naval Revolution* (Baton Rouge: Louisiana State University Press, 1966).

Two crises that helped legitimize battleships are described in Joyce S. Goldberg, *The "Baltimore" Affair* (Lincoln: University of Nebraska Press, 1986), and Paul M. Kennedy, *The Samoan Tangle* (New York: Barnes & Noble, 1974).

Prominent officers of the decade are the subjects of James C. Bradford, ed., *Admirals of the New Steel Navy: Makers of the American Naval Tradition, 1880–1930* (Annapolis, Md.: Naval Institute Press, 1990); Paolo E. Coletta, *French Ensor Chadwick: Scholarly Warrior* (Lanham, Md.: University Press of America, 1980); and Richard S. West, *Admirals of American Empire* (Indianapolis: Bobbs-Merrill, 1948). The central naval figure of the Spanish–American War has been carefully dissected in Ronald Spector, *Admiral of the New Empire: The Life and Career of George Dewey* (Baton Rouge: Louisiana State University Press, 1974; repr. University of South Carolina Press, 1988).

Many of the decade's officers themselves wrote provocative memoirs, including George Dewey, *Autobiography of George Dewey, Admiral of the Navy* (New York: Scribner, 1913; repr. Naval Institute Press, 1987); Robley D. Evans, *A Sailor's Log* (New York: Appleton, 1901); Caspar F. Goodrich, *Rope Yarns from the Old Navy* (New York: The Naval History Society, 1931); and Winfield S. Schley, *Forty-Five Years Under the Flag* (New York: Appleton, 1904).

The two most useful analyses of the Spanish–American War by officers are French E. Chadwick, *The Relations of the United States and Spain*, 2 vols. (New York: Scribner's, 1909–1911; repr. Russell & Russell, 1968), and Alfred T. Mahan, *Lessons of the War with Spain* (Boston: Little, Brown, 1899; repr. Books for Libraries Press, 1970).

A scholarly account of the war with an emphasis on the military-naval aspects is David F. Trask, *The War with Spain in 1898* (New York: Macmillan, 1981), and a specialized analysis of one of the causes is Hyman G. Rickover, *How the Battleship* Maine *was Destroyed* (Washington: Government Printing Office, 1976).

1898–1918

General treatments of the period include Lester H. Brune, *The Origins of American National Security Policy: Sea Power, Air Power, and Foreign Policy, 1900–1941* (Manhattan, Kans.: MA/AH Publishing, 1981); Richard D. Challener, *Admirals, Generals and American Foreign Policy: 1898–1914* (Princeton, N.J.: Princeton University Press, 1973); George T. Davis, *A Navy Second to None* (New York: Harcourt, Brace, 1940; repr. Greenwood Press, 1971); John A. S. Grenville and George B. Young, *Politics, Strategy and American Diplomacy: Studies in Foreign Policy, 1873–1917* (New Haven: Yale University Press, 1966); and Seward W. Livermore, "The American Navy as a Factor in World Politics, 1903–1913," *American Historical Review*, vol. 63, no. 4 (July 1958).

The dynamic relationship between naval and foreign policy in Latin America, the West Indies, and the Caribbean can be traced in David Healy, *Gunboat Diplomacy in the Wilson Era: The U.S. Navy in Haiti, 1915–1916* (Madison: University of Wisconsin Press, 1976); Warren G. Kneer, *Great Britain and the Caribbean, 1901–1913* (East Lansing: Michigan State University Press, 1975); Walter LaFeber, *The Panama Canal* (New York: Oxford University Press, 1978, 1989); David McCullough, *The Path Between the Seas: The Creation of the Panama Canal, 1870–1914* (New York: Simon & Schuster, 1977); Allan R. Millett, *The Politics of Intervention: The Military Occupation of Cuba, 1906–1909* (Columbus: Ohio State University Press, 1968); Dana Munro, *Intervention and Dollar Diplomacy in the Caribbean, 1900–1921* (Princeton, N.J.: Princeton University Press, 1964); Robert E. Quirk, *An Affair of Honor: Woodrow Wilson and the Occupation of Veracruz* (Lexington: University of Kentucky Press, 1962; repr. Norton, 1967); Ronald Spector, "Roosevelt, the Navy, and the Venezuela Controversy: 1902–1903," *American Neptune*, vol. 32, no. 4 (October 1972); Jack Sweetman, *The Landing at Veracruz: 1914* (Annapolis, Md.: Naval Institute Press, 1968); and Richard W. Turk, "The United States Navy and the 'Taking' of Panama, 1901–1903," *Military Affairs*, vol. 38, no. 3 (October 1974).

The definitive two-volume study of naval policy and diplomacy in the Far East is William R. Braisted, *The United States Navy in the Pacific, 1897–1909* and *1909–1922* (Austin: University of Texas Press, 1958, 1971). Selected aspects of America's Pacific naval policy are covered in Robert A. Hart, *The Great White Fleet: Its Voyage Around the World, 1907–1909* (Boston: Little, Brown, 1965); Seward W. Livermore, "American Naval-Base Policy in the Far East, 1850–1914," *The Pacific Historical Review*, vol. 13, no. 2 (June 1944); James R. Reckner, *Teddy Roosevelt's Great White*

Fleet (Annapolis, Md.: Naval Institute Press, 1988); and Michael Vlahos, "The Naval War College and the Origins of War-Planning Against Japan," *Naval War College Review*, vo. 33, no. 4 (July–August 1980).

The European aspects of American naval policy for the entire period are the subjects of Dean C. Allard, "Anglo-American Naval Differences During World War I," *Military Affairs*, vol. 44, no. 2 (April 1980); Holger H. Herwig, *Politics of Frustration: The United States in German Naval Planning, 1889–1941* (Boston: Little, Brown, 1976); William N. Still, Jr., *American Sea Power in the Old World: The United States Navy in European and Near Eastern Waters, 1865–1917* (Westport, Conn.: Greenwood Press, 1980); and Seth P. Tillman, *Anglo-American Relations at the Paris Peace Conference of 1919* (Princeton, N.J.: Princeton University Press, 1961).

This period of American naval history was replete with exeptionally talented civilian and uniformed leaders. The civilians' legacy of biography, autobiography, and edited papers includes Howard K. Beale, *Theodore Roosevelt and the Rise of America to World Power* (Baltimore: Johns Hopkins Press, 1956); John M. Cooper, Jr., *The Warrior and the Priest: Woodrow Wilson and Theodore Roosevelt* (Cambridge: Belknap Press, 1983); E. David Cronon, ed., *The Cabinet Diaries of Josephus Daniels, 1913–1921* (Lincoln: University of Nebraska Press, 1963); Josephus Daniels, *The Wilson Era*, 2 vols. (Chapel Hill: University of North Carolina Press, 1944, 1946); Raymond A. Esthus, *Theodore Roosevelt and Japan* (Seattle: University of Washington Press, 1966); Robert H. Ferrell, *Woodrow Wilson and World War I* (New York: Harper & Row, 1985); Mark A. De Wolfe Howe, *George von Lengerke Meyer: His Life and Public Services* (New York: Dodd, Mead, 1919); Arthur S. Link, *Wilson the Diplomatist: A Look at His Major Foreign Policies* (Baltimore: Johns Hopkins Press, 1957); John D. Long, *The New American Navy*, 2 vols. (New York: Outlook, 1903); Frederick W. Marks, *Velvet on Iron: The Diplomacy of Theodore Roosevelt* (Lincoln: University of Nebraska Press, 1979); and Nathan Miller, *FDR: An Intimate History* (Garden City, N.Y.: Doubleday, 1983).

The officers' stories are represented in Paolo E. Coletta, *Admiral Bradley A. Fiske and the American Navy* (Lawrence: Regents Press of Kansas, 1979); Robley D. Evans, *A Sailor's Log* (New York: Appleton, 1901); Edwin A. Falk, *Fighting Bob Evans* (New York: Cape & Smith, 1931); Mary Klachko with David F. Trask, *Admiral William Shepherd Benson, First Chief of Naval Operations* (Annapolis, Md.: Naval Institute Press, 1987); Elting E. Morison, *Admiral Sims and the Modern American Navy* (Boston: Houghton Mifflin, 1942; repr. Russell & Russell, 1968); Ronald Spector, *Admiral of the New Empire: The Life and Career of George Dewey* (Baton Rouge: Louisiana State University Press, 1974; repr. University of South Carolina Press, 1988); and Yates Stirling, *Sea Duty: The Memoirs of a Fighting Admiral* (New York: Putnam's, 1939).

The question of maritime neutrality in the age of the U-boat is covered in Thomas A. Bailey and Paul B. Ryan, *The Lusitania Disaster: An Episode in Modern Warfare and Diplomacy* (New York: Free Press, 1975); Ross Gregory, *The Origins of American Intervention in the First World War* (New York: Norton, 1971); Ernest R. May, *The World War and American Isolation, 1914–1917* (Cambridge: Harvard University Press, 1959); Jeffrey J. Safford, *Wilsonian Maritime Diplomacy, 1913–1921* (New Brunswick, N.J.: Rutgers University Press, 1978); and Charles C. Tansill, *America Goes to War* (Boston: Little, Brown, 1938; repr. Peter Smith, 1963).

The naval strategy of World War I is the subject of Dean C. Allard, "Admiral William S. Sims and the United States Naval Policy in World War I," *American Neptune*, vol. 35, no. 2 (April 1975); Charles R. Brown, "The Development of Fleet Aviation During the World War," *U.S. Naval Institute Proceedings*, vol. 64, no. 9 (September 1938); Paolo E. Coletta, *Sea Power in the Atlantic and Mediterranean in World War I* (Lanham, Md.: University Press of America, 1989); J. A. English, "The Trafalgar Syndrome: Jutland and the Indecisiveness of Modern Naval Warfare," *Naval War College Review*, vol. 32, no. 3 (May–June 1979); Adolph A. Hoehling, *The Great War at Sea: A History of Naval Action, 1914–1918* (New York: Crowell, 1965); Irving B. Holley, Jr., *Ideas and Weapons: Exploitation of the Aerial Weapon by the United States During World War I* (New Haven: Yale University Press, 1953; repr. Government Printing Office, 1983); Richard A. Hough, *The Great War at Sea, 1914–1918* (New York: Oxford University Press, 1983); William S. Sims, *The Victory at Sea* (London: J. Murray, 1920; repr. Naval Institute Press, 1984); Philip Lundeberg, "Undersea Warfare and Allied Naval Strategy in World War I, Part I: to 1916," *Smithsonian Journal of History*, vol. 1, no. 3 (1966); Alexander W. Moffat, *Maverick Navy* (Middletown, Conn.: Wesleyan University Press, 1976); and David F. Trask, *Captains & Cabinets: Anglo-American Naval Relations, 1917–1918* (Columbia: University of Missouri Press, 1972).

The Anglo-German-American naval dénouement at Paris is told best by William R. Braisted, *The United States Navy in the Pacific, 1909–1922* (Austin: University of Texas Press, 1971).

1919–1933

The broad national policies of the Republican era are treated in Warren I. Cohen, *Empire Without Tears: America's Foreign Relations, 1921–1933* (Philadelphia: Temple University Press, 1987); L. Ethan Ellis, *Republican Foreign Policy, 1921–1933* (New Brunswick, N.J.: Rutgers University Press, 1968); Robert H. Ferrell, *American Diplomacy in the Great Depression: Hoover–Stimson Foreign Policy, 1929–1933* (New Haven: Yale University Press, 1957); Arnold A. Offner, *The Origins of the Second World War: American Foreign Policy and World Politics, 1917–1941* (New York: Praeger, 1975); and Joan Hoff Wilson, *Herbert Hoover* (Boston: Little, Brown, 1975).

Two divergent interpretations of the navy in this period appear in Charles A. Beard, *The Navy: Defense or Portent?* (New York: Harper, 1932), and Harold Sprout and Margaret Sprout, *Toward a New Order of Sea Power, 1918–1922* (Princeton, N.J.: Princeton University Press, 1940; repr. Greenwood Press, 1969). See also Edward M. Earle, "The Navy's Influence on Our Foreign Relations," *Current History*, vol. 23, no. 5 (February 1926).

The Washington conference, a pivotal episode in twentieth-century American naval history, is covered in William R. Braisted, *The United States Navy in the Pacific, 1909–1922* (Austin: University of Texas Press, 1971); Thomas H. Buckley, *The United States and the Washington Conference, 1921–1922* (Knoxville: University of Tennessee Press, 1970); Thomas C. Hone, "The Effectiveness of the 'Washington Treaty' Navy," *Naval War College Review*, vol. 32, no. 6 (November–December 1979); and Robert H. Van Meter, "The Washington Conference of 1921–1922: A New Look," *Pacific Historical Review*, vol. 46, no. 4 (November 1977).

The other conferences on naval limitations are treated in Meredith W. Berg, "Admiral William H. Standley and the Second London Naval Treaty 1934–1936," *Historian*, vol. 33, no. 2 (February 1971); William F. Trimble, "Admiral Hilary P. Jones and the 1927 Geneva Naval Conference," *Military Affairs*, vol. 43, no. 1 (February 1979); and Raymond G. O'Connor, *Perilous Equilibrium: The United States Navy and the London Naval Conference of 1930* (Lawrence: University of Kansas Press, 1962; repr. Greenwood Press, 1969).

For the navy and its two main protagonists, see Roger Dingman, *Power in the Pacific: The Origins of Naval Arms Limitation, 1914–1922* (Chicago: University of Chicago Press, 1976); Norman Gibbs, "The Naval Conferences of the Interwar Years: A Study in Anglo-American Relations," *Naval War College Review*, vol. 30 (Summer 1977); Ira Klein, "Whitehall, Washington, and the Anglo-Japanese Alliance 1919–1921," *Pacific Historical Review*, vol. 41, no. 4 (November 1972); Stephen W. Roskill, *Naval Policy Between the Wars*, vol. 1, *The Period of Anglo-American Antagonism, 1919–1929* (New York: Walker, 1968); Thaddeus V. Tuleja, *Statesmen and Admirals: Quest for a Far Eastern Naval Policy* (New York: Norton, 1963); and Gerald E. Wheeler, *Prelude to Pearl Harbor: The United States Navy and the Far East, 1921–1931* (Columbia: University of Missouri Press, 1963).

The impact of technological change on naval policy, planning, and strategy is the subject of Ernest Andrade, Jr., "Submarine Policy in the United States Navy, 1919–1941," *Military Affairs*, vol. 35, no. 2 (April 1971); Richard D. Burns, "Regulating Submarine Warfare, 1921–1941: A Case Study in Arms Control and Limited War," *Military Affairs*, vol. 35, no. 2 (April 1971); Charles M. Melhorn, *Two-Block Fox: The Rise of the Aircraft Carrier, 1911–1929* (Annapolis, Md.: Naval Institute Press, 1974); Clark G. Reynolds, *The Fast Carriers: The Forging of an Air Navy* (New York: McGraw-Hill, 1968; repr. Krieger, 1978); Richard K. Smith, *The Airships*

Akron and Macon: Flying Aircraft Carriers of the United States Navy (Annapolis, Md.: Naval Institute Press, 1965); and Archibald D. Turnbull and Clifford L. Lord, *History of United States Naval Aviation* (New Haven: Yale University Press, 1949).

A valuable biography of an officer who shaped the period is Gerald E. Wheeler, *Admiral William Veazie Pratt, U.S. Navy: A Sailor's Life* (Washington: Government Printing Office, 1974).

1933–1945

The policies of the central American figure of this twelve-year epoch, Franklin D. Roosevelt, are covered in James M. Burns, *Roosevelt: The Lion and the Fox* (New York: Harcourt, Brace, 1956); Robert Dallek, *Franklin D. Roosevelt and American Foreign Policy, 1933–1945* (New York: Oxford University Press, 1979); Robert A. Divine, *The Illusion of Neutrality* (Chicago: University of Chicago Press, 1962), and the same author's *Roosevelt and World War II* (Baltimore: Johns Hopkins Press, 1969); Frederick W. Marks, *Wind over Sand: The Diplomacy of Franklin Roosevelt* (Athens: University of Georgia Press, 1988); Arnold A. Offner, *The Origins of the Second World War* (New York: Praeger, 1975); David Reynolds, *The Creation of the Anglo-American Alliance, 1937–41* (Chapel Hill: University of North Carolina Press, 1982); Gaddis Smith, *American Diplomacy During the Second World War, 1941–1945* (New York: Wiley, 1985); and Theodore A. Wilson, *The First Summit: Roosevelt and Churchill at Placentia Bay, 1941* (Boston: Houghton Mifflin, 1969).

For Roosevelt's naval policy prior to the formal declaration of war against Germany in December 1941, see Patrick Abbazia, *Mr. Roosevelt's Navy: The Private War of the U.S. Atlantic Fleet, 1939–1942* (Annapolis, Md.: Naval Institute Press, 1975), and Thomas A. Bailey and Paul B. Ryan, *Hitler vs. Roosevelt: The Undeclared Naval War* (New York: The Free Press, 1979). A British perspective is Harald Busch, *U-boats at War* (London: Putnam, 1955), and the German side is told in Holger Herwig, "Prelude to *Weltblitzkrieg:* Germany's Naval Policy Toward the United States of America, 1939–1941," *Journal of Modern History,* vol. 43, no. 4 (December 1971).

The critical question of Anglo-American naval relations prior to the formal American declaration of war is well covered in James R. Leutze, *Bargaining for Supremacy: Anglo-American Naval Collaboration, 1937–1941* (Chapel Hill: University of North Carolina Press, 1977); and Stephen W. Roskill, *Naval Policy Between the Wars,* vol. 2, *The Period of Reluctant Rearmament, 1930–1939* (Annapolis, Md.: Naval Institute Press, 1976).

There is no synthesis of the U.S. Navy in the Atlantic war to compare with Ronald Spector's masterful account of the Pacific campaign. Until one appears, it is necessary to sample John Creswell, *Sea Warfare, 1939–1945: A Short History* (New York: Longmans, 1950); Trevor N. Dupuy, *The Mil-*

itary History of World War II, 19 vols. (New York: Watts, 1962–1965), especially vol. 4, *The Naval War in the West: The Raiders*, and vol. 5, *The Naval War in the West: The Wolf Packs;* Robert H. Freeman, ed., *Sunk in Action: The United States Navy in World War II* (Ventnor, N.J.: Shellback Press, 1986); Samuel E. Morison, *The Two Ocean War: A Short History of the United States Navy in the Second World War* (Boston: Little, Brown, 1963), a distillation of his quasi-official *History of United States Naval Operations in World War II*, 15 vols. (Boston: Little, Brown, 1947–1963); Stephen W. Roskill, *The War at Sea, 1939–1945*, 3 vols. (London: Her Majesty's Stationery Office, 1954–1961); and Stanley E. Smith, ed., *The United States Navy in World War II* (New York: Morrow, 1966).

For the American navy's top strategists, see Ernest J. King, *U.S. Navy at War, 1941–1945: Official Reports to the Secretary of the Navy* (Washington: Navy Department, 1946); Ernest J. King and Walter M. Whitehill, *Fleet Admiral King: A Naval Record* (New York: Norton, 1952); and B. Mitchell Simpson, *Admiral Harold R. Stark: Architect of Victory, 1939–1945* (Columbia: University of South Carolina Press, 1989).

Electronics intelligence was the crucial technology in the successful campaign against the German U-boats. See, for example, Patrick Beesly, *Very Special Intelligence: The Story of the Admiralty's Operational Intelligence Centre, 1939–1945* (Garden City, N.Y.: Doubleday, 1978), and Ronald Lewin, *Ultra Goes to War* (New York: McGraw-Hill, 1978).

For other aspects of the fight against the German submarines, see John E. Broome, *Convoy Is To Scatter* (Totowa, N.J.: Rowman & Littlefield, 1972); Peter Elliott, *Allied Escort Ships in World War II* (London: Macdonald & Jane's, 1977), and *idem, American Destroyer Escorts of World War II* (London: Almark, 1974); Ladislas Farago, *The Tenth Fleet* (New York: Oblensky, 1962); Charles D. Gibson, *The Ordeal of Convoy NY 119* (New York: South Street Seaport Museum, 1973); Peter Gretton, *Crisis Convoy: The Story of HX231* (Annapolis, Md.: Naval Institute Press, 1974); Edwin P. Hoyt, *U-boats Offshore: When Hitler Struck America* (New York: Stein & Day, 1978); Martin Middlebrook, *Convoy* (New York: Morrow, 1977); Jürgen Rohwer, *The Critical Convoy Battles of March 1943* (Annapolis, Md.: Naval Institute Press, 1977); Theodore Rosco, *United States Destroyer Operations in World War II* (Annapolis, Md.: Naval Institute Press, 1953); and Jak P. M. Showell, *U-Boats Under the Swastika: An Introduction to German Submarines, 1935–1945* (London: Ian Allan, 1973).

One German surface raider was especially terrifying to the Allies, and it is the subject of Ludovic Kennedy, *Pursuit: The Chase and Sinking of the* Bismarck (New York: Viking, 1974). That any battleship even existed when World War II began is analyzed in Richard A. Hough, *Death of the Battleship* (New York: Macmillan, 1963).

The least glamorous but fundamentally vital features of the war in the Atlantic are covered in Duncan S. Ballantine, *U.S. Naval Logistics in the*

Second World War (Princeton, N.J.: Princeton University Press, 1947); John G. Bunker, *Liberty Ships: The Ugly Ducklings of World War II* (Annapolis, Md.: Naval Institute Press, 1972); Robert Carse, *The Long Haul: The United States Merchant Service in World War II* (New York: Norton, 1965); Robert H. Connery, *The Navy and the Industrial Mobilization in World War II* (Princeton, N.J.: Princeton University Press, 1951); Irving Crump, *Our Tanker Fleet* (New York: Dodd, Mead, 1952); and Frederick C. Lane, *Ships for Victory: A History of Shipbuilding Under the U.S. Maritime Commission in World War II* (Baltimore: Johns Hopkins Press, 1951).

Equally vital to the Atlantic war's outcome were amphibious operations, which can be appreciated from David A. Howarth, *D-Day: The Sixth of June, 1944* (New York: McGraw-Hill, 1959); Jacques Robichon, *The Second D-Day* (New York: Walker, 1962); Raymond de Belot, *The Struggle for the Mediterranean, 1939–1945* (Princeton, N.J.: Princeton University Press, 1951); Martin Blumenson, *Anzio: The Gamble that Failed* (Philadelphia: Lippincott, 1963); and Hugh Pond, *Salerno* (Boston: Little, Brown, 1961).

The monumental study by Ronald Spector, *Eagle Against the Sun: The American War with Japan* (New York: Free Press, 1985), is complete topically and bibliographically, and it would be superfluous to duplicate Spector's work here.

1945–1990

Like one or two earlier periods, the era since World War II does not divide bibliographically into neat chronological units. Moreover, since the war the United States Navy has lost its autonomy and become a part of the much larger Department of Defense bureaucratic apparatus. One feature of this new structure has been an inordinate preoccupation with weapons technology and classified documents. For all of these reasons, the literature on the navy is less satisfying, rich, and humane than for the nearly two centuries preceding the defeat of Japan in 1945.

In this period the navy became perhaps more political than ever before, and this phenomenon is examined in Vincent Davis, *The Admirals Lobby* (Chapel Hill: University of North Carolina Press, 1967), and *idem, The Politics of Innovation: Patterns in Navy Cases* (Denver: University of Denver, 1967).

For 1945–1950, see Paolo E. Coletta, *The United States Navy and Defense Unification, 1947–1953* (Newark: University of Delaware Press, 1981), and Wilbur H. Morrison, *Wings over the Seven Seas: The Story of Naval Aviation's Fight for Survival* (South Brunswick, N.J.: A. S. Barnes, 1975).

The Korean War receives uneven treatment in Malcolm W. Cagle, *The Sea War in Korea* (Annapolis, Md.: Naval Institute Press, 1957); James A. Field, *History of United States Naval Operations: Korea* (Washington: Government Printing Office, 1962); Richard Hallion, *The Naval Air War in Korea* (Baltimore: Nautical & Aviation Publishing Co. of America, 1986);

Robert D. Heinl, *Victory at High Tide: The Inchon-Seoul Campaign* (Philadelphia: Lippincott, 1968, repr. Nautical & Aviation, 1979); and from a peculiar vantage point, C. Turner Joy, *How Communists Negotiate* (New York: Macmillan, 1955).

The monumental naval story of the late 1940s and 1950s was the development of nuclear-powered attack submarines and ballistic-missile-launching submarines. This tale is told in William R. Anderson and Clay Blair, Jr., *Nautilus 90° North* (Cleveland: World, 1959); Edward L. Beach, *Around the World Submerged: The Voyage of the* Triton (New York: Holt, Rinehart and Winston, 1962); John Bentley, *The* Thresher *Disaster: The Most Tragic Dive in Submarine History* (Garden City, N.Y.: Doubleday, 1975); Clay Blair, *The Atomic Submarine and Admiral Rickover* (New York: Holt, 1954); James F. Calvert, *Surface at the Pole: The Extraordinary Voyages of the USS* Skate (New York: McGraw-Hill, 1960); Francis Duncan, *Rickover and the Nuclear Navy* (Annapolis, Md.: Naval Institute Press, 1990); Richard G. Hewlett and Francis Duncan, *Nuclear Navy, 1946–1962* (Chicago: University of Chicago Press, 1974); Norman Polmar, *Atomic Submarines* (Princeton, N.J.: Van Nostrand, 1963); *idem, Death of the* Thresher (Philadelphia: Chilton, 1964); Norman Polmar and Thomas B. Allen, *Rickover* (New York: Simon & Schuster, 1981); and Harvey M. Sapolsky, *The Polaris System Development* (Cambridge: Harvard University Press, 1972).

The overarching story of the 1960s and 1970s is the Vietnam War, which is fitfully discussed in Thomas J. Cutler, *Brown Water, Black Berets: Coastal and Riverine Warfare in Vietnam* (Annapolis, Md.: Naval Institute Press, 1988); Edwin B. Hooper, *Mobility, Support, Endurance: A Story of Naval Operational Logistics in the Vietnam War, 1965–1968* (Washington: Government Printing Office, 1972); Edwin B. Hooper, Dean C. Allard, and Oscar P. Fitzgerald, *The United States Navy and the Vietnam Conflict* (Washington: Government Printing Office, 1976); Edward J. Marolda and G. Wesley Pryce III, *A Short History of the United States Navy and the Southeast Asian Conflict, 1950–1975* (Washington: Naval Historical Center, 1984); Peter B. Mersky and Norman Polmar, *The Naval Air War in Vietnam* (Annapolis, Md.: Nautical & Aviation Publishing Co., 1981, 1986); Ulysses S. Grant Sharp, *Strategy for Defeat: Vietnam in Retrospect* (San Rafael, Calif.: Presidio Press, 1978); and Frank Uhlig, Jr., ed., *Vietnam: The Naval Story* (Annapolis, Md.: Naval Institute Press, 1986).

The only real attempt to assess the naval policy of the only president who was a Naval Academy graduate, Jimmy Carter, is James A. Nathan and James K. Oliver, *The Future of United States Naval Power* (Bloomington: Indiana University Press, 1979). The most recent period receives sympathetic treatment in Frederick H. Hartmann, *Naval Renaissance: The U.S. Navy in the 1980s* (Annapolis, Md.: Naval Institute Press, 1990), and the most glamorous ship type of the decade is depicted in Robert F. Sumrall

Iowa Class Battleships: Their Design: Weapons, and Equipment (Annapolis, Md.: Naval Institute Press, 1988).

The thin list of biographies for Cold War naval figures includes Elmer B. Potter, *Admiral Arleigh Burke* (Annapolis, Md.: Naval Institute Press, 1990); Robert G. Albion and Robert H. Connery, *Forrestal and the Navy* (New York: Columbia University Press, 1962); and Arnold A. Rogow, *James Forrestal: A Study of Personality, Politics, and Policy* (New York: Macmillan, 1963). The best autobiographical offerings are John F. Lehman, Jr., *Command of the Seas* (New York: Scribner's, 1988); Paul R. Schratz, *Submarine Commander: A Story of World War II and Korea* (Lexington: University Press of Kentucky, 1988); and Elmo R. Zumwalt, Jr., *On Watch: A Memoir* (New York: Quadrangle, 1976).

Index

412